How to Get Published in the Best Management Journals

Second Edition

Edited by

Mike Wright

Professor of Entrepreneurship and Director, Centre for Management Buyout Research, Imperial College Business School, London, UK

David J. Ketchen, Jr.

Harbert Eminent Scholar and Professor of Management, Raymond J. Harbert College of Business, Auburn University, USA

Timothy Clark

Provost and Professor, Singapore Management University, Singapore

Edward Elgar
PUBLISHING

Cheltenham, UK • Northampton, MA, USA

© The Editors and Contributors Severally 2020

All rights reserved. No part of this publication may be reproduced, stored in a retrieval system or transmitted in any form or by any means, electronic, mechanical or photocopying, recording, or otherwise without the prior permission of the publisher.

Published by
Edward Elgar Publishing Limited
The Lypiatts
15 Lansdown Road
Cheltenham
Glos GL50 2JA
UK

Edward Elgar Publishing, Inc.
William Pratt House
9 Dewey Court
Northampton
Massachusetts 01060
USA

Paperback edition 2020

A catalogue record for this book
is available from the British Library

Library of Congress Control Number: 2019951890

This book is available electronically in the Elgaronline
Business subject collection
DOI 10.4337/9781789902822

ISBN 978 1 78990 281 5 (cased)
ISBN 978 1 78990 282 2 (eBook)
ISBN 978 1 83910 989 8 (paperback)

Typeset by Columns Design XML Ltd, Reading
Printed and bound in Great Britain by TJ International Ltd, Padstow

Contents

List of figures, tables and boxes   ix
List of contributors   xi
Preface   xix

1. Publishing in management: exhilaration, bafflement and frustration   1
   Mike Wright, David J. Ketchen, Jr. and Timothy Clark

PART I   THE PUBLISHING PROCESS

2. The publishing process: a case study   13
   Petra Andries and Mike Wright

3. Getting published: a view from a journal editor and journal ranker   25
   Geoffrey Wood and Pawan Budhwar

4. Ethics and integrity in publishing   33
   Ben R. Martin

5. Sustaining a publications career   57
   Mike Wright

6. Why publish in Asian management journals?   83
   Daphne W. Yiu

7. Squeezing lemons to make fresh lemonade: how to extract useful value from peer reviews   94
   William H. Starbuck

8. Managing a research pipeline   114
   Brian L. Connelly

9. Everything you always wanted to know about research impact   127
   Anne-Wil Harzing

10. Positioning papers for publication   142
    Jay B. Barney

PART II   RESOLVING PRACTICAL KEY ISSUES

Section II.I   Becoming a Scholar

11 Rules of the game redux 2.0   155
    Denny Gioia

12 Learning by walking through the snow   161
    R. Duane Ireland

13 It's all about contribution! Using the discussion to define
    and develop your paper's contributions   164
    Donald D. Bergh

14 'You miss 100% of the shots you don't take'   168
    Annette L. Ranft and Anne D. Smith

15 Why I don't want to co-author with you and what you can
    do about it   172
    David J. Ketchen, Jr.

Section II.II   Getting Your Methods Right

16 Are your results really robust?   178
    Bruce T. Lamont and Gonzalo Molina Sieiro

17 The reviewers don't like my sample! What can I do?   184
    Brian K. Boyd

18 When being normal is not enough: a few thoughts about
    data, analyses and (the storm of) re-analyses   192
    Philip L. Roth and Wayne H. Stewart, Jr.

Section II.III   Navigating the Review Process

19 Selling your soul to the devil? Mistakes authors make when
    responding to reviewers   196
    Pamela L. Perrewé

20 Respond to me – please!   201
    James G. Combs

21 Challenging the gods: circumstances justifying the protest
    of a journal rejection decision   205
    Gerald R. Ferris

22	Beginner's muck: maximizing your paper's chances of success with a novice editor *Kevin G. Corley and Beth S. Schinoff*	209

Section II.IV   Understanding the Journals

23	Publishing in the top journals: the secrets for success *Michael A. Hitt*	215
24	Hitting your preferred target: positioning papers for different types of journals *Yehuda Baruch*	220
25	Targeting journals: a personal journey *Franz W. Kellermanns*	233
26	'Read the damn article', or the appropriate place of journal lists in organizational science scholarship *M. Ronald Buckley and John E. Baur*	240
27	Publishing in special issues *Timothy Clark*	246
28	Open access and open conversations: the role of digital technologies in promoting and extending published work *Aija Leiponen and Will Mitchell*	252
29	Should you publish in an open access journal? *Charles C. Snow*	261

PART III   PUBLISHING ACROSS DISCIPLINARY BOUNDARIES

30	Publishing in finance versus entrepreneurship/management journals *Douglas Cumming*	268
31	Publishing in management journals: how is it different from economics journals? *Saul Estrin and Sumon Kumar Bhaumik*	282
32	Publishing in management journals as a social psychologist *Rolf van Dick*	296
33	Publishing historical papers in management journals and in business history journals *Steven Toms*	304

34 Publishing human resource management research in different
   kinds of journals 312
   Bill Harley

35 Publishing in top international business and management
   journals 321
   Stephen Tallman and Torben Pedersen

36 Publishing at the interfaces of psychology and strategic
   management 334
   Gerard P. Hodgkinson

Index 347

Figures, tables and boxes

FIGURES

5.1	Developing a sustainable publications career	70
5.2	Thirty-eight years of management buyouts and private equity research	71
7.1	Simulated evaluations of 1000 papers by pairs of reviewers	98
8.1	Management scholars with multiple top-tier publications	115
8.2	The research pipeline	116
9.1	Average h-index per academic for five different disciplines in three different databases, July 2015	137
9.2	Average hIa per academic for five different disciplines in three different databases, July 2015	137
31.1	Theory and hypotheses development for management journals: an example	291

TABLES

2.1	Summary of insights from the review process	21
5.1	An illustration of sustaining publication output	59
5.2	Emerging economies research	74
7.1	Reviewers' recommendations to editors	98
8.1	Summary of recommendations for moving projects from one stage to the next	125
9.1	Research metrics across data sources, February 2019	134
9.2	Level of appointment (full professor/associate professor) and academic age of the top ten academics ranked by h-index and hIa-index	136
17.1	Checklist for sample design preparation	185
24.1	Take-aways	229
31.1	Structures of standard empirical papers in economics and management	283
31.2	Empirical analysis for economics journals: an example	289

BOX

35.1 Abstracts from web pages of editorial policies for *JIBS*, *JWB* and *GSJ*   322

Contributors

Petra Andries is Professor of Entrepreneurship and Strategy at Ghent University. She conducts research in the field of entrepreneurship and innovation. Petra has published in international journals (for example, *Strategic Entrepreneurship Journal*, *Journal of Business Venturing*, *Research Policy* and *Journal of Product Innovation Management*) on topics including entrepreneurial strategies, business model development, entrepreneurial teams and collaborative innovation. She has also provided companies and policy-makers with advice in these domains.

Jay B. Barney, Presidential Professor of Strategic Management, holds the Pierre Lassonde Chair in Social Entrepreneurship at the David Eccles School of Business at The University of Utah. As President of the Strategy Division of the Academy, he was elected a Fellow of the Academy of Management (AOM) and a Fellow of the Strategic Management Society, and received the Irwin Outstanding Educator Award for the Business Policy and Strategy Division of AOM. He currently serves as the Editor-in-Chief of the *Academy of Management Review*.

Yehuda Baruch is Professor of Management at the Southampton Business School, University of Southampton. His research focuses on careers and global human resource management (HRM). He has written 150 refereed papers and 50 books and book chapters. He was an Associate Editor of *Human Resource Management* (US) and Editor of *Group & Organization Management* and *Career Development International*.

John E. Baur in an Assistant Professor at the University of Nevada, Las Vegas. He took his PhD from the University of Oklahoma and holds the distinction of being trained by M. Ronald Buckley. He publishes his research primarily in the areas of organizational leadership, workplace deviance and team dynamics.

Donald D. Bergh is the Louis D. Beaumont Chair of Business Administration and Professor of Management at the University of Denver. He has served as Associate Editor of the *Academy of Management Journal*, *Organizational Research Methods*, *Journal of Management Studies* and, most recently, as Chair of the Scientific Integrity and Rigor Task Force of the *Journal of Management*.

Sumon Kumar Bhaumik is a Professor of Finance at the Management School of the University of Sheffield and a Research Fellow at IZA – Institute of Labor Economics, Bonn. He has published in leading journals in economics, management/international business and finance, and is a member of the editorial board of the *Journal of World Business*.

Brian K. Boyd is Chair Professor of Management at the City University of Hong Kong School of Business. He has served multiple terms as associate and guest editor at several journals, and has also received awards for outstanding service to the editorial boards of the *Academy of Management Journal* and the *Strategic Management Journal*.

M. Ronald Buckley is the J.C. Penney Company Chair of Business Leadership and a Professor of Management and a Professor of Psychology in the Michael F. Price College of Business at the University of Oklahoma. He took his PhD at Auburn University, mentored by many wonderful, caring and thoughtful professors who are mentioned in his chapter. To them he owes a great debt! War Damn Eagle!

Pawan Budhwar is the 50th Anniversary Professor of International HRM at Aston Business School and an Associate Pro-Vice Chancellor International, Aston University. He is the Co-Editor-in-Chief of *British Journal of Management*. Pawan's research interests are in the field of strategic HRM, international HRM and emerging markets with a specific focus on India. Pawan is the co-founder and first President of the Indian Academy of Management, an affiliate of the Academy of Management. He is a Fellow of the Higher Education Academy, British Academy of Management, the Academy of Social Sciences and the Indian Academy of Management.

Timothy Clark is Provost and Professor at Singapore Management University. He is a former Associate Editor of *Human Relations* and former General Editor of the *Journal of Management Studies*. He has served, and continues to serve, on numerous editorial boards and has been Chair of the Publications Committee of the British Academy of Management.

James G. Combs (PhD, Louisiana State University) is the Della Phillips Martha Schenck Chair of American Private Enterprise at the University of Central Florida and Visiting Professor at the University of Ottawa. His research interests include family business, franchising, research synthesis and corporate governance.

Contributors xiii

Brian L. Connelly is Professor and Luck Eminent Scholar at Auburn University's Harbert College of Business. He conducts research on corporate governance, competitive dynamics and negative organizational events. Brian recently completed a term as Associate Editor for the *Academy of Management Journal* and is Editor-Elect for the *Journal of Management*. He has published in these and other journals, such as the *Strategic Management Journal* and *Organization Science*.

Kevin G. Corley is Chair of the Management & Entrepreneurship department at the W.P. Carey School of Business at Arizona State University. His research largely springs from the question, 'Why do people in organizations experience change the way they do?' Answering this question has led him to do field research focused on foundational concepts such as identity, image, identification, culture and learning. His research has appeared in the *Academy of Management Journal*, the *Academy of Management Review*, *Administrative Science Quarterly*, *Organization Science* and the *Academy of Management Annals*. He recently served as an Associate Editor at the *Academy of Management Journal* focused on qualitative methods, helped co-edit a special issue on mixed-methods research at *Organizational Research Methods* and serves as an expert of qualitative methods on the *Journal of Management*'s new Methods Task Force.

Douglas Cumming, JD, PhD, CFA, is the DeSantis Distinguished Professor of Finance and Entrepreneurship at the College of Business, Florida Atlantic University, and a Visiting Professor of Finance at Birmingham Business School, University of Birmingham. Douglas has published over a dozen books and 175 articles in journals such as the *Academy of Management Journal*, the *Journal of Financial Economics* and the *Review of Financial Studies*, and is a 2019 Silver Award recipient for publications in the *Journal of International Business Studies*.

Saul Estrin is a Professor of Managerial Economics and Strategy and the founding Head of the Department of Management at the London School of Economics. He works on international business and entrepreneurship. He is an Associate Editor of *Small Business Economics* and was on the editorial boards of the *International Journal of Industrial Organization*, *Journal of Comparative Economics*, *Journal of Business Venturing* and the *Journal of World Business*.

Gerald R. Ferris is the Francis Eppes Professor of Management, Professor of Psychology and Professor of Sport Management at Florida State University. He received a PhD in Business Administration from the University of Illinois at Urbana-Champaign. Ferris has research interests in the areas of social influence and effectiveness processes in organizations.

Denny Gioia is the Robert and Judith Auritt Klein Professor of Management in the Smeal College of Business at Penn State. Previously he worked for Boeing Aerospace at Cape Kennedy during the Apollo programme and for Ford as corporate recall coordinator. Current theory/research focuses on the ways in which identity and image relate to sensemaking, sensegiving and organizational change.

Bill Harley is Professor of Management at the University of Melbourne. His research has been published in journals including the *Journal of Management Studies*, the *British Journal of Industrial Relations* and *Work, Employment and Society*. From 2010 to 2015, Bill was Associate Editor/General Editor of the *Journal of Management Studies*.

Anne-Wil Harzing is Professor of International Management at Middlesex University, London, a Fellow of the Academy of International Business and a 2019 Silver Award recipient for publications in the *Journal of International Business Studies*. She has published more than 120 journal articles and book chapters in international management and bibliometrics and has been listed on the Web of Knowledge Essential Science Indicators top 1 per cent most cited academics in economics and business worldwide since 2007.

Michael A. Hitt is a University Distinguished Professor Emeritus at Texas A&M University and a Distinguished Research Fellow at Texas Christian University. He is a former Editor of the *Academy of Management Journal* and the *Strategic Entrepreneurship Journal*. He is a former President of the Academy of Management and Strategic Management Society and a Fellow in both organizations, as well as a Fellow in the Academy of International Business.

Gerard P. Hodgkinson is Professor of Strategic Management and Behavioural Science (Alliance Manchester Business School) and Vice-Dean for Research (Faculty of Humanities) at the University of Manchester, UK. From 1999 to 2006 he was the Editor-in-Chief of the *British Journal of Management*, and from 2005 to 2016 he co-edited the *International Review of Industrial and Organizational Psychology* (now incorporated as the Annual Review issue in the *Journal of Organizational Behavior*). He is currently an Associate Editor of the *Journal of Management* and serves on the editorial boards of the *Academy of Management Review* and the *Strategic Management Journal*.

R. Duane Ireland is a University Distinguished Professor, holds the Benton Cocanougher Chair in Business at Texas A&M University and serves as the executive associate dean in Mays Business School. He is a former Editor of the *Academy of Management Journal*, a former President of the Academy of Management and a Fellow of the Academy of Management and of the Strategic Management Society.

Franz W. Kellermanns is the Addison H. & Gertrude C. Reese Endowed Chair and Professor of Management in the Belk College of Business at the University of North Carolina – Charlotte. He holds a joint appointment with the Center for Family Business at the WHU–Otto Beisheim School of Management (Germany).

David J. Ketchen, Jr. currently serves as Harbert Eminent Scholar and Professor of Management in the Raymond J. Harbert College of Business at Auburn University. He has served as an Associate Editor for seven scholarly journals and has served as an editorial board member for 14 journals. In 2018, Auburn awarded him its highest honour for research and its highest honour for all-around faculty performance.

Bruce T. Lamont (PhD, University of North Carolina) is the Jim Moran Eminent Scholar of Business Administration in the College of Business at Florida State University. His current research addresses the effective management of acquisition integration processes, knowledge investments and novel applications of theory to the African context.

Aija Leiponen is a Professor with the Dyson School of Applied Economics and Management at Cornell University and has held appointments at Imperial College London (UK) and Aalto University (Finland). Her research in the field of strategy focuses on the impact of inter-organizational cooperation on innovation in digital industries and has been published in the *Strategic Management Journal*, *Management Science*, *Organization Science*, *Research Policy* and several applied economics journals. She was the inaugural Co-Editor for media innovations of the Strategic Management Society.

Ben R. Martin is Professor of Science and Technology Policy Studies at the Science Policy Research Unit (SPRU), University of Sussex, where he was formerly Director. He has carried out research for 40 years on science policy, establishing techniques for evaluating scientific research and pioneering 'technology foresight'. Since 2004, he has been Editor of *Research Policy*.

Will Mitchell is the Anthony S. Fell Chair in New Technologies and Commercialization at the Rotman School of Management of the University of Toronto. He publishes actively in the strategy field, with an emphasis on business dynamics in developed and emerging markets, and teaches courses on related strategy topics in degree and executive programmes. He is a Consulting Editor for the *Strategic Management Journal*.

Gonzalo Molina Sieiro is a doctoral student at Florida State University, with interests in strategic management.

Torben Pedersen is a Professor at Bocconi University, Italy. His research interests are mainly on globalization, organizational design, offshoring/outsourcing, knowledge management and subsidiary strategies. He has published more than 100 journal articles and books on these topics and is Co-Editor of the *Global Strategy Journal*.

Pamela L. Perrewé is the Robert O. Lawton Distinguished Professor, the Haywood and Betty Taylor Eminent Scholar of Business Administration and Distinguished Research Professor at Florida State University. She has focused her research interests in the areas of job stress, coping, organizational politics, emotion and personality.

Annette L. Ranft (BS, Appalachian State University; MS, Georgia Tech; PhD, UNC-Chapel Hill) is the Dean and Wells Fargo Professor at the Harbert College of Business, Auburn University. She has served as an Associate Editor of the *Journal of Management* and on numerous editorial boards of top journals.

Philip L. Roth is a Professor of Management at Clemson University (PhD, University of Houston). Phil's interests involve employee selection and meta-analysis. He is a Fellow of the Society for Industrial and Organizational Psychology (SIOP). He served as Chair of the Research Methods Division and representative for the Human Resources Division of the Academy of Management.

Beth S. Schinoff is an Assistant Professor of Management and Organization at the Carroll School of Management at Boston College. She is particularly interested in how people relate to each other in organizations. Her research has been published in top management journals such as the *Academy of Management Review*, the *Academy of Management Perspectives* and the *Annual Review of Organizational Psychology and Organizational Behavior*.

Anne D. Smith (BS, McIntire School of Commerce, University of Virginia; MBA, PhD, UNC-Chapel Hill) is the Department Head, Professor of Management and King & Judy Rogers Professor in Business at the Haslam College of Business, University of Tennessee, Knoxville. She serves on the *Organizational Research Methods* editorial board.

Charles C. Snow is Professor Emeritus of Strategy and Organization at The Pennsylvania State University. He is a Fellow of the Academy of Management, a founding member of the Organizational Design Community, and the founding Co-Editor of the *Journal of Organization Design*.

William H. Starbuck is a Courtesy Professor at University of Oregon and Professor Emeritus at New York University. He edited the *Administrative Science Quarterly*, chaired the screening committee for Fulbright awards in business management and was President of the Academy of Management. His research interests include research methodology, innovation and societal trends.

Wayne H. Stewart, Jr. is Professor of Management at Clemson University (PhD, University of North Texas). His research interests entail themes of uncertainty and change, including individual and team issues in entrepreneurship, and managing flexibility and adaptability for organizational rejuvenation, particularly in transition contexts.

Stephen Tallman is the E. Claiborne Robins Distinguished Professor of Business at the University of Richmond in the USA. He is the founder and past co-editor of the *Global Strategy Journal*. His research interests include global strategies, international alliances and joint ventures, industry clusters and knowledge management in the multinational firm.

Steven Toms is Professor of Accounting at Leeds University Business School. His research interests cover accounting, accountability, performance measurement and corporate governance from a historical perspective. He specializes in cotton and textile history from the Industrial Revolution to the present day. He was editor of *Business History*, 2007–13.

Rolf van Dick studied psychology at Philipps-University Marburg and earned his PhD at the interfaces of social, organizational and health psychology in 1999. He was Professor of Social Psychology and Organizational Behavior at Aston University, Birmingham, and since 2006 he has been Professor of Social Psychology and serves as Vice President at Goethe University. He was visiting professor in Tuscaloosa (USA, 2001), Rhodos (2002), Katmandu (2009), Rovereto (2016), Bejing and Shanghai

(2016) and at the Work Research Institute, Oslo (2016–18). Rolf van Dick published more than 200 papers and books, and he served as (Associate) Editor of the *European Journal of Work and Organizational Psychology*, the *British Journal of Management*, the *Journal of Personnel Psychology* and *Leadership Quarterly*.

Geoffrey Wood is Dean and Professor of International Business at Essex Business School. He has authored, co-authored or edited 12 books and over 120 articles in peer-reviewed journals. He is Editor in Chief of the *British Journal of Management* and serves on the British Academy of Management (BAM) Council. He is also Editor of the 'ABS Journal Ranking List'.

Mike Wright was Professor of Entrepreneurship and Director of the Centre for Management Buyout Research at Imperial College Business School, London at the time of his passing. He was Chair of the Society for the Advancement of Management Studies and was a Fellow of the British Academy, of the Strategic Management Society and of the British Academy of Management. He served as a Co-Editor of the *Journal of Management Studies*, the *Strategic Entrepreneurship Journal*, *Academy of Management Perspectives* and the *Journal of Technology Transfer*. He edited numerous special issues of leading journals in management, entrepreneurship and finance.

Daphne W. Yiu is Professor of Management at the Chinese University of Hong Kong. She received her PhD in Management from the University of Oklahoma. Her research interests lie in corporate and international strategy, strategies in emerging markets and Asia, business groups, corporate governance and international entrepreneurship. Professor Yiu has published in leading management journals. She was elected President and Fellow of the Asia Academy of Management, and Representative-at-Large at the Global Strategy Interest Group of the Strategic Management Society. She is currently a Senior Editor at the *Journal of World Business* and the *Asia Pacific Journal of Management*, Editor at *Corporate Governance: An International Review* and incoming Associate Editor at the *Academy of Management Journal*.

Preface

Advancing knowledge by publishing in leading journals is at the heart of the academic enterprise. Promotion systems for academics in management in universities around the world stress the significance of an individual scholar's contribution based on his or her published work, primarily in refereed journals. Thus, career advancement, scholarly reputation and pay are intimately tied to being able to publish in journals. Yet publishing research is a tough and competitive business, with acceptance rates in good journals being very low.

All three of us have extensive editing and publishing experience, and have been involved in numerous workshops and conference sessions designed to help colleagues publish their work. At the time we created the first edition of this book, it seemed to us that available support was at best uneven and that colleagues might find benefit from some codified guidance from those who have been successful in navigating the publishing process. Our aim in the first edition of this book, therefore, was to offer a series of chapters to help demystify the journal publishing process. The chapters were designed to provide practical advice on a wide range of important topics. We were fortunate to attract quite a few contributors who are thought leaders within the management discipline.

For this second edition, to reflect both omissions in the first edition and emerging challenges in publishing, the authors of existing chapters have added new material and we have introduced several new chapters. In particular, we have added new, longer chapters on 'Managing a research pipeline' (Brian L. Connelly, Chapter 8) and 'Positioning papers for publication' (Jay B. Barney, Chapter 10). This adds a lot of 'star power' to the book – the former has been named the next Editor of the *Journal of Management* and the latter currently edits the *Academy of Management Review*. As there is growing emphasis not just on getting published, but also on ensuring that research is read and acted upon, we have also introduced material on research impact relating to impact among academics (Anne-Wil Harzing, Chapter 9), among practitioners and policy-makers (Chapter 1), and more widely through the use of digital technologies (Aija Leiponen and Will Mitchell, Chapter 28). We have also added new material relating to working with inexperienced editors; an increasingly pervasive situation (Kevin G. Corley and Beth S. Schinoff, Chapter 22).

As before, we are extremely grateful to these very busy and experienced contributing authors for taking the time to share their thoughts on the publication process. Thanks are also due to Fran O'Sullivan for her encouragement and support for this endeavour.

Mike Wright
David J. Ketchen, Jr.
Timothy Clark

1. Publishing in management: exhilaration, bafflement and frustration

Mike Wright, David J. Ketchen, Jr. and Timothy Clark

Scholars find the journal publishing process exhilarating, baffling and frustrating in equal measure. The professional joy and excitement of receiving an acceptance letter following a long drawn-out process in which you have diligently responded to successive rounds of reviewers' comments is probably only matched by a letter awarding a research grant. Contrast this to the sense of dejection and distress that accompanies a rejection letter. This is further exacerbated if the reviewers' comments and decision appear to be harsh and if they make little sense. It is even more disappointing if the paper appears to have been progressing through different rounds of reviewing only to be rejected late in the process. Therefore, we have to start all over again. We may not realize it but academics are not dissimilar to actors in that they constantly have to audition their work in journals or to research funders. Learning to live with rejection is a key part of the role. We cannot be successful with every submission.

THE PUBLISHING LANDSCAPE

The chances of acceptance are well below 10 per cent at most prestigious journals and they tend to be lower the 'better' the journal. Indeed, there is a familiar adage that if you are not being rejected, you are not aiming high enough. There is increasing pressure on academics to publish in journals, and in what are considered to be the 'right' journals in particular. While individual departments and schools have had internal 'private' journals lists for many years to aid colleagues' decisions when submitting work and to aid assessments of quality at the point of recruitment or promotion, a number of 'public' national and international journals lists have gained prominence in recent years. These have increasingly replaced the business and management journal rankings produced by services such as the Web of Science™.

In the United Kingdom, the Chartered Association of Business Schools created the 'Academic Journal Guide' in 2015 building on the 'ABS Guide 2010'. This ranked journals from across the spectrum of business and management subject areas under five categories ranging from 4* ('journals of distinction', JODs) to 1 (journals of 'modest standard') based on a combination of metrics and consultation with expert peers and scholarly associations. A revised version was published in 2018 to include new journals and to ensure consistency in ranking JODs, which meant in some cases identifying JODs in subject areas where they were previously absent. Reflecting the evolving nature of journal quality, a full review of the guide is scheduled for 2021.

Since 2007, the Australian Business Deans Council has produced successive iterations of its Journal Quality List. The latest version encompassed 2767 journals and rated them A* to C. In France, Centre National de la Recherche Scientifique (CNRS) has produced a 'Journal Ranking in Economics and Management' since 2004. This ranks journals from 1 ('distinguished') to 4 ('low selectivity'). In 2008, the European Science Foundation developed an 'initial' journal list for humanities – the European Reference Index for Humanities (ERIH). Now run by the Norwegian Social Science Data Services (NSD), this was relaunched 2014 as ERIH Plus and has been extended to include the social sciences. Although not an evaluative ranking service, journals are included in accordance with published criteria. The main aims of this initiative are to 'enhance the global visibility of high-quality research in the humanities and social sciences across Europe, and to facilitate access to research journals published in all European languages' (ERIH Plus 2019). Finally, several trade publishers have produced journal lists as part of the intellectual capital or research scores in their Master of Business Administration (MBA) rankings. The most prominent are the lists used by *Bloomberg Business Week* and the *Financial Times*.

Given that several of these lists contribute to the rankings of business schools, they have a significant influence on the perceptions of reputations of schools and therefore impact on the scholars whose published work in these journals undergirds their rankings. As two of the editors of this volume noted in an editorial for the *Journal of Management Studies* (Clark and Wright 2007, p. 613):

> Whereas the ranking of journals in which people publish has always had implications for personal reputation, peer recognition and career advancement, increasingly it is impacting much more directly on institutional reputations and department rankings and in turn on access to resources and potential recruitment of staff and students. Individual publication choices and success are therefore assuming ever greater institutional significance.

To manage institutional reputations, individual business schools are increasingly abandoning their own lists and adopting those mentioned above. As a consequence, scholars in different business schools are being encouraged to submit only to those journals that are more highly ranked on these lists. It comes as no surprise that submission rates, desk rejection rates (that is, rejection by the editors prior to seeking reviewer comments) and overall rejection rates in 'top tier' journals have increased (Judge et al. 2007, p. 501; Monastersky 2005). Indeed, we have experienced such trends during our tenures as editors of different journals, with submission rates increasing significantly, desk rejection rates creeping to over 50 per cent and general acceptance rates dropping to well below 10 per cent (see, for example, Clark and Wright 2007).

Although we lack the hard data needed to draw a firm conclusion, our observation when acting as journal editors over the past two decades is that landing reviewers who are bona fide experts on a journal submission's topic has become increasingly difficult over time. Leading journals are attracting increasing numbers of submissions every year while the pool of available expert reviewers appears to be increasing only slightly if at all. This has created a basic supply–demand imbalance that does not work in authors' favour. A potential result is that any given submission may not be receiving the same calibre of expert vetting as it would have in years past. Relative to 10 or 20 years ago, a paper that you submit today may be assigned to reviewers who are much less experienced and who know far less about your specific topic.

Beyond this systemic macro trend, a quick immersion into the voluminous literature on the peer-review process indicates that there are a number of failings that either individually or in combination may prevent or forestall innovative material from being published in highly regarded journals. In a seminal study on peer review, Peters and Ceci (1982) resubmitted 12 articles to the psychology journals in which they had already been refereed and published 18 to 32 months earlier. To disguise the papers, a number of 'cosmetic' alterations were made to the titles, abstracts and opening paragraphs in the introduction, but their meaning was not changed. In addition, fictitious names for authors and institutional affiliations were used. Nine of the manuscripts were sent out for review (three were rejected). Only two of the 18 reviewers recommended that the papers be accepted. Hence, only one article was accepted, with the consequence that one journal made an identical evaluation over the two periods of time. This article generated a voluminous response (over 70 commentaries in the same issue) and provoked heated discussion across different disciplines as to the ability of the review process to determine the level of quality, interestingness, contribution and likely impact of an article under consideration (see, for example, Bedeian 2003; Campanario 1998; Miller 2006; Osterloh and Frey 2015; Starbuck 2003, 2005). Given the critical weaknesses in the review process, it has been questioned by a range of commentators whether superior quality work is published in journals as a consequence of reviewers' comments and, therefore, whether the most able scholars are being hired and promoted on the basis of such published work. This literature highlights three general flaws in the journal review process.

First, reviewers are often accused of being overly harsh in their judgements. They approach manuscripts assiduously looking to expose weaknesses rather than balancing these with an equivalent appreciation of the merits. In a system where the work of others is evaluated anonymously, the incentives to be constructive and polite may lessen. People may communicate more bluntly than they would face to face.

Furthermore, reviews are solicited from people who are invariably busy and have simply added a further task to their already over-committed diaries. In these circumstances, reviewers may adopt a shorthand approach in which they prioritize the finding of faults and weaknesses rather than engaging positively with the ideas, arguments and evidence in the paper from the author's point of view. In addition, as Starbuck (2003) suggests, this approach may in part arise from reviewers seeing themselves as superior to the authors (in their role as reviewers). He comments: 'Occasionally reviewers seem arrogant, disrespectful, even nasty' (Starbuck 2003, p. 344). They believe they know better than the authors and could write a better article. They therefore often see their role as telling the author to write the paper they would write. This can lead to a situation where authors feel their ideas are unappreciated, undervalued and ignored.

Managing reviewers is a key task that falls to editors. In our experience, there are three basic approaches that editors take to this task. 'Posties' (or, in US terminology, mail carriers) simply collect the reviews, add little independent thought or synthesis of reviewers' ideas, pass along reviews to the authors and accept a paper only if the reviewers say to do so. Editors abdicating their authority in this way can be very harmful to authors. For example, authors may feel that they are being forced to write the paper the reviewers want them to write or respond to points that are superficial, misguided or just wrong. In these circumstances, reviewers may become uninvited ghost writers and/or veto wielders.

In one baffling case, a revision of a conceptual paper was rejected without all of the reviews being received. One reviewer recommended acceptance with no further revisions, a second reviewer vehemently opposed the paper and the third reviewer was not sent the revision owing to an administrative glitch. The action editor based his decision on the fact that the negative reviewer 'was extremely forceful' in his or her comments. After it became known that the third reviewer was not given the opportunity to participate, the action editor refused the authors' request to collect the third review and then revisit his decision. Worse, in the first round of review, the decision letter had been written based on the first two reviews and the third review was sent to the authors about a week later with no effort to reconcile important discrepancies between it and the other reviews. Sure enough, some of the very negative reviewer's key concerns about the revision revolved around material that was added to the paper in order to respond to the third reviewer. Although most 'postie editors' are not as callow and impotent as this, the anecdote illustrates the danger of allowing reviewers to dominate decision-making in the review process.

A much different approach is adopted by 'emperors'. These editors downplay or even disregard the reviews; only their opinions matter, even if they know little about the subject matter. Luckily these people are few and far between. Similar to the emperor in Hans Christian Andersen's legendary fable, however, they resist being told that they have no clothes.

Finally, 'judges' live by the mantra that reviewers review and editors decide. They gather relevant evidence by reading the paper and studying the reviews, analyse the evidence and make informed decisions. This is important because just making decisions by tallying up the reviewers' recommendations regarding revise or reject can be highly misleading as some reviewers may recommend reject yet make many comments that can be addressed, while other reviewers may be extremely negative in their comments yet recommend revision. When revision opportunities are granted, judges synthesize reviewers' input in their decision letters in order to give authors the best opportunity to succeed. Importantly, judges are not afraid to contradict a reviewer in an effort to advance the state of research knowledge. Some editors of this type emphasize that reviewers must 'step into the framework of the authors when evaluating a paper, rather than imposing their preferred framework or perspective on those authors (and thereby asking the authors to write the reviewer's preferred paper)' (Miller and Van de Ven 2015, p. 118, see also Clair 2015).

Second,[1] as Peters and Ceci (1982) suggest, a number of factors have been found to bias reviewer judgements (for a full review, see Campanario 1998). Where authors' identities are known, their institutional affiliations and social networks may influence judgements. However, these factors are reduced when a blind review process is used, although not eradicated because with the Internet and electronic dissemination of manuscripts an author's identity is very difficult to hide (see Hillman and Rynes 2007). Here issues such as the apparent complexity of language, use of citations, appropriate jargon, sophisticated statistical procedures, and presentation of positive and significant results that do not merely replicate previous findings have all been found to influence or bias decisions.

Third, and perhaps the area which has received greatest empirical attention, studies in a range of disciplines have consistently reported low overall inter-referee agreement (see Cicchetti 1980, 1991; Gottfredson 1978; Hendrick 1977; Scar and Weber 1978; Scott 1974). Evidence within management studies is more scant. Starbuck (2003) reports a study he undertook while editor of *Administrative Science Quarterly*. An examination of 500 pairs of reviews revealed a correlation of 0.12. He concluded that 'It was so low that knowing what one reviewer had said about a manuscript would tell me almost nothing about what a second reviewer had said or would say' (Starbuck 2003, p. 346).

TOWARD RIGOR *AND* RELEVANCE

Concerns about journal lists and the nature of the review process have contributed to a heated debate about the journal publishing and academic evaluation system (see, for example, the exchange between Harley 2019 and Phillips 2019; see also Tourish 2019). A further dimension of the debate relates to concerns that pressure to publish in top journals is taking management research away from relevance for practice and policy. The two are not necessarily mutually exclusive. Indeed, addressing relevance to practice and policy can create a virtuous circle of identifying more interesting research questions that can help with getting into top journals.

A brief anecdote offers an illustration of a virtuous circle. One of this volume's co-editors was approached by a former MBA student about helping his employer win a defence contract that was currently held by an industry leader. The MBA alumnus believed that academic concepts and frameworks could be the differentiator that would lead his company to victory in the open-bid process. With the help of a six-doctorate (PhD) consulting team, the MBA alumnus's company won the 10-year, $11.2 billion contract. However, the story does not end there. Insights obtained via the consulting project fuelled articles that appeared in *Journal of Operations Management* (that is, Ketchen and Hult 2007), *Strategic Entrepreneurship Journal* (Ketchen et al. 2007) and *Business Horizons* (Ketchen et al. 2008). In the last of these, two professors, the MBA alumnus and a co-worker at the company collaborated as co-authors. Success via this type of author team might be the ultimate expression of the virtuous circle between theory and practice.

Influencing billion-dollar contracts is rare, but other opportunities for real-world impact abound. There appears to be growing momentum from journal editors, others from various parts of the management discipline (Wiklund et al. 2019) and in neighbouring fields (Craighead et al. 2019) to encourage rigorous submissions that are impactful for practice and policy. Once an article is published, disseminating the knowledge it generates to practitioners and policy-makers via leading business press outlets such at the *Financial Times* and the *Wall Street Journal* is a powerful way to complete a virtuous cycle. A dilemma arises here, however, in that the public relations staff at many colleges and universities seem to lack the contacts and skills to place researchers' work in that calibre of outlet. Our experience has been that editors at business press outlets welcome contact from faculty and are willing to work with academics to craft a message that will resonate with their readers. In part, this often involves replacing words such as 'disseminating' and 'resonate' with simpler alternatives.

Looking to the future, real-world impact is likely to increase in importance for faculty. Some evaluation systems, such as the UK's Research Excellence Framework (REF) exercise, now include assessment of impact cases that need to show how international-level research has had an impact on policy and practice (Pidd and Broadbent 2015). For example, one of the co-editors of this volume demonstrated that evidence from their systematic studies of employment and employee relations showed that the impact of private equity investment was more positive than had been portrayed in unrepresentative cases used in media and policy debates (Amess and Wright 2007; Bacon et al. 2010). This evidence influenced the European Parliament to modify its proposals for the regulation of the private equity industry which would otherwise have disadvantaged private equity acquirers compared with corporate acquirers. Details on this and other examples of impact cases can be found in REF (2014).

Whether we like it or not, the nature of academic publishing is that it is a winner-takes-all system; there are no benefits for not publishing, and someone who may be only marginally better receives a disproportionate amount of the benefits available (Phillips 2019). In this context, authors need to take every step they can within the confines of professionalism and ethics to maximize their submission's chance of success. Accordingly, this book's chapters are intended to provide actionable advice that authors can leverage. In case our thoughts in this brief introduction are taken as overly pessimistic, we want to stress that we have found the research process to be personally and professionally fulfilling, as have the authors who have contributed to this book. Our hope is that each reader will find one or more tips in the chapters that follow that resonate, will act on these tips and will be better able to place research papers in our discipline's leading journals.

CONTENTS OF THE SECOND EDITION

We have structured the book in three parts. The book can be read in its entirety, but many readers may prefer to dip into various topics to suit their particular needs. Part I contains general contributions on important aspects of the publishing process. We start in Chapter 2 with an in-depth case study of a paper travelling through the review process which includes the perspectives of the authors, the editor and the reviewers. This chapter sets the scene for the remainder of the book and is followed by a chapter that examines the range of issues arising at different stages in the journal submission and review processes (Chapter 3). Ethics and integrity in academic research has always been important, but it has taken on particular significance in recent years. Accordingly, we devote Chapter 4 specifically to this topic. Since academic careers are not just about getting that first job and then achieving tenure but are also about sustaining publications in the long run, Chapter 5 outlines some strategies for achieving this. Increasingly the focus of attention is on publishing in leading international journals, which are often US based. However, as Chapter 6 shows, using the example of Asia, other contexts can provide opportunities to publish quality research. This chapter discusses the similarities and differences in publishing Asian research in Asian management journals compared with those in North America. Chapter 7 presents insights into the deficiencies of the review process and how authors should consider and approach feedback from reviewers. The three chapters new to this second edition in Part I deal first, in Chapter 8, with the important issues relating to managing your research pipeline to ensure that publishing momentum is maintained, then Chapter 9 addresses issues relating to how to maximize your academic impact, with

Chapter 10, tackling how to position a paper for publication, providing a bridge to the more specific topics in the subsequent parts of the book.

Part II contains short contributions on specific topics essential to resolving practical key issues in undertaking good research and the preparation of publishable manuscripts. We have organized this part into four sections relating to 'Becoming a Scholar' (Chapters 11–15), 'Getting Your Methods Right' (Chapters 16–18), 'Navigating the Review Process' (Chapters 19–22) and 'Understanding the Journals' (Chapters 23–29). In soliciting these chapters, we encouraged authors to draw on their considerable experience as authors, editors and reviewers to share candid confidences that readers might not obtain elsewhere. The contributors fully embraced this charge and we have found some great 'behind the curtain' tips while editing their chapters.

Part III (Chapters 30–36) contains contributions that address publishing across disciplinary boundaries. This part delves into the challenges of publishing in journals for scholars from other related disciplines, including business history, economics, finance, human resource management, international business and psychology, and for management scholars seeking to publish their work in journals in these areas. Each author presents insights into key issues of difference in the positioning of papers, use and development of theory, data and methods, analysis and discussion of findings and contribution. The authors also identify differences in the review process between management journals and these other areas, and provide specific examples from their own experience.

NOTE

1. This and the next paragraph are replicated with permission from Clark and Wright (2007).

REFERENCES

Amess, K. and M. Wright (2007), 'The wage and employment effects of leveraged buyouts in the UK', *International Journal of the Economics of Business*, **14** (2), 179–95.

Bacon, N., M. Wright, L. Scholes and M. Meuleman (2010), 'Assessing the impact of private equity on industrial relations in Europe', *Human Relations*, **63** (9), 1343–70.

Bedeian, A.C. (2003), 'The manuscript review process: the proper role of authors, referees, and editors', *Journal of Management Inquiry*, **12** (4), 331–8.

Campanario, J. (1998), 'Peer review for journals as it stands today – part 1', *Science Communication*, **19** (3), 181–211.

Cicchetti, D. (1980), 'Reliability of reviews for the American Psychologist', *American Psychologist*, **35** (3), 300–303.

Cicchetti, D. (1991), 'The reliability of peer review for manuscript and grant submission: a cross-disciplinary investigation', *Behavioral and Brain Sciences*, **14** (1), 119–86.

Clair, J.A. (2015), 'Toward a Bill of Rights for manuscript submitters', *Academy of Management Learning & Education*, **14** (1), 111–31.

Clark, T. and M. Wright (2007), 'Reviewing journal rankings and revisiting peer reviews: editorial perspectives', *Journal of Management Studies*, **44** (4), 612–21.

Craighead, C.W., D.J. Ketchen and J.L. Darby (2019), 'Taking AIM at theoretical and pragmatic impact: a call for actionable, insightful, and measurable research', *Journal of Business Logistics*, online, 17 June, doi:10.1111/jbl.12214.

European Reference Index for the Humanities and the Social Sciences (ERIH Plus) (2019), 'Background', accessed 8 August 2019 at https://dbh.nsd.uib.no/publiseringskanaler/erihplus/about/index.

Gottfredson, S. (1978), 'Evaluating psychological research reports: dimensions, reliability and correlates of quality judgements', *American Psychologist*, **33** (10), 920–34.

Harley, B. (2019), 'Confronting the crisis of confidence in management studies: why senior scholars need to stop setting a bad example', *Academy of Management Learning and Education*, **18** (2), 286–97.

Hendrick, C. (1977), 'Editorial comment', *Personality and Social Psychology Bulletin*, **3** (1), 1–2.

Hillman, A. and S. Rynes (2007), 'The future of double-blind review in management', *Journal of Management Studies*, **44** (4), 622–7.

Judge, T.A., D.M. Cable, A.E Colbert and S.L. Rynes (2007), 'What causes a management article to be cited: article, author, or journal?', *Academy of Management Journal*, **50** (3), 491–506.

Ketchen, D.J. and G.T. Hult (2007), 'Bridging organization theory and supply chain management: the case of best value supply chains', *Journal of Operations Management*, **25** (2), 573–80.

Ketchen, D.J., R.D. Ireland and C. Snow (2007), 'Strategic entrepreneurship, collaborative innovation, and wealth creation', *Strategic Entrepreneurship Journal*, **1** (3–4), 371–85.

Ketchen, D.J., W. Rebarick, G.T. Hult and D. Meyer (2008), 'Best value supply chains: a key competitive weapon for the 21st century', *Business Horizons*, **51** (3), 235–43.

Miller, C.C. (2006), 'Peer review in the organizational and management sciences: prevalence and effects of reviewer hostility, bias and dissensus', *Academy of Management Journal*, **49** (3), 425–31.

Miller, C.C. and A.H. Van de Ven (2015), 'Peer review, root canals, and other amazing life events', *Academy of Management Discoveries*, **1** (2), 117–23.

Monastersky, R. (2005), 'The number that's devouring science', *The Chronicle of Higher Education*, **52** (8), A12, accessed 2 December 2015 at http://chronicle.com/free/v52/i08/08a01201.htm.

Osterloh, M. and B.S. Frey (2015), 'Ranking games', *Evaluation Review*, **39** (1), 102–29.

Peters, D. and S. Ceci (1982), 'Peer-review practices of psychological journals: the fate of published articles, submitted again', *Behavioral and Brain Sciences*, **5** (2), 187–255.

Phillips, N. (2019), 'What is academic success anyway? A rejoinder to "confronting the crisis of confidence in management studies"', *Academy of Management Learning and Education*, **18** (2), 306–9.

Pidd, M. and J. Broadbent (2015), 'Business and management studies in the 2014 Research Excellence Framework', *British Journal of Management*, **26** (4), 569–81.

Research Excellence Framework (REF) (2014), 'Impact case studies', accessed 12 August 2019 at http://impact.ref.ac.uk/CaseStudies/Results.aspx?val=business+and+management.

Scar, S. and B. Weber (1978), 'The reliability of reviews for the *American Psychologist*', *American Psychologist*, **33**, 935.

Scott, W. (1974), 'Interreferee agreement on some characteristics of manuscripts submitted to the *Journal of Personality and Social Psychology*', *American Psychologist*, **29** (9), 698–792.

Starbuck, W.H. (2003), 'Turning lemons into lemonade: where is the value in peer review?', *Journal of Management Inquiry*, **12** (4), 344–51.

Starbuck, W.H. (2005), 'How much better are the most prestigious journals? The statistics of academic publication', *Organization Science*, **16** (2), 180–200.

Tourish, D. (2019), *Management Studies in Crisis: Fraud, Deception and Meaningless Research*, Cambridge: Cambridge University Press.

Wiklund, J., M. Wright and S. Zahra (2019), 'Conquering relevance: entrepreneurship research's grand challenge', *Entrepreneurship Theory and Practice*, **43** (3), 419–36.

PART I

The Publishing Process

2. The publishing process: a case study
Petra Andries and Mike Wright

INTRODUCTION

The review process can be lengthy and involve major changes to all aspects of a paper. As authors, reviewers or editor on a paper we tend to see only our side of the process, or at best have a partial view of the other parties' perspectives through decision letters and authors' responses. In this chapter we use a case study of a paper passing through the review process to interweave these different perspectives. One of us, Petra, was lead author on the paper, while the other, Mike, was the action editor. We present the process in the form of a first-person dialogue between us, interspersed with comments from the reviewers. We conclude with some general reflections for the publishing process.

BACKGROUND TO THE PAPER

Petra: As a new doctoral student, I interviewed several founders of technology-based ventures. I asked them what decisions were keeping them awake at night. Besides the questions whether and when to go global, another important issue emerged. The majority of these entrepreneurs were not sure how to develop their technologies into viable business models. They were faced with not only significant levels of technological uncertainty, but also major market uncertainties. Overall, they stated they did not have any insights or guidelines on how to create, deliver and capture value from their technologies. Studying the literature, I found that two possible approaches to business model development under such uncertainty were advanced, namely, focused commitment and sequential experimentation, but that little empirical evidence was available on how to implement these approaches or on their usefulness. Given this gap in the literature, and the clear need of practitioners for more insights, I decided to dedicate my doctorate to the topic of business model development in highly uncertain contexts.

THE INITIAL SUBMISSION

Petra: In December 2009, together with co-authors Koenraad Debackere and Bart Van Looy, I submitted the paper to *Strategic Entrepreneurship Journal* (*SEJ*). Although the journal was fairly new, it had the aspiration and potential to become a top journal in the field of entrepreneurship, and we believed that both content-wise and methodologically our paper could fit in this outlet. The paper, which was at that point in time titled 'Simultaneous experimentation as an entrepreneurial strategy for emergent markets: transcending the trade-off between flexibility and funding?', started from the observation that defining a viable business model in emerging, uncertain industries is difficult and that the approaches advanced in the available literature have their limitations. On the one hand, a dedicated focus on one specific business model allows for attracting resources and realizing first-mover advantages, but hinders flexibility. On the other hand, sequential experimentation financed through bootstrapping allows for flexible business model adaptation, but imposes resource constraints. As new ventures would benefit from both resources and flexibility, the main purpose of the paper was to investigate whether and how ventures in emerging industries characterized by uncertainty could balance the attainment of financial resources with flexibility when developing their business models.

The paper combined two different methods in order to research this issue. In the first part of the paper, we used six in-depth case studies, identifying two approaches to business model development, and mapping the rationale and consequences of both approaches in terms of flexibility and resource acquisitions. The main contribution of the initial submission was in the identification of 'simultaneous experimentation' as an approach to business model development (see also the abstract of the initial paper in the appendix to this chapter). This approach had not been identified previously in the literature and had the potential to enable both resource acquisition and flexibility. The second part of the paper consisted of an analytical model comparing the expected profits of different approaches, suggesting that in emerging industries characterized by uncertainty, simultaneous experimentation is more appropriate than focused commitment.

Mike: At the time I was an associate editor of the *SEJ*. When I was assigned the paper from the co-editors to be the action editor, I realized that I needed reviewers who could evaluate both the qualitative and the analytical part of the paper. The *SEJ*'s policy is to have two reviewers. I decided to contact one case study expert, as well as one expert in analytical modelling who had at the same time an open mind to alternative research methods. I selected the particular reviewers based on my tacit knowledge built up over time both as an editor and researcher of who was active in these areas and likely to provide a good review.

ROUND ONE

Mike: When the reviews came back in March 2010, I immediately noticed that the reviewers differed in their appreciation of and commenting on the paper. Reviewer 1 was encouraging about the paper's potential in terms of topic and qualitative approach, but questioned if the authors could deliver. A first main concern regarded the coding of the business model changes, where the reviewer indicated a disconnection between the conceptual framework used and the actual coding. Secondly, he/she truly disliked the analytical part of the paper, arguing that this type of modelling is in general uninteresting and lacks managerial relevance.

> **Reviewer 1:** I don't mean to be impertinent, but such an approach epitomizes what's wrong with management research. No manager would ever take this seriously – there is no face validity to the analysis, nor is there relevance to the framework. These attempts – and yours is just the one in front of me – reflect a physics envy that has led to the irrelevance of management science anywhere outside our little academy.

Mike: Reviewer 2 on the other hand found the mixed methods interesting, but thought the analytical model was flawed and needed better justification.

> **Reviewer 2:** The manuscript is well written. The topic is interesting. I especially appreciate the use of a multi-method approach. My main concern is regarding the limitations of the analytical framework (and hence its contributions and implications).

Mike: Despite the criticisms, the reviewer was very constructive in his/her feedback, providing several suggestions for improvement of the analytical model. In his/her review of the analytical model, the reviewer also questioned the logic of the paper, and more precisely the relevance of the 'resource acquisition' concept for the development of the paper as a whole:

> **Reviewer 2:** The front end of the paper offers the notion of 'acquiring financial resources' (and related concepts of flexibility and commitment towards investors) when arguing about the type of business model approach

(focused versus unfocused). However, the analytical development appears disconnected from the acquisition of financial resources. ... Again, the discussion on funding acquisition seems to be a distraction. As far as I can tell, this work is about two types of business model development, and that is it.

Mike: Authors perhaps do not realize, but reviewers frequently disagree in their comments on papers. The reviewers on this paper had particularly notable differing views on some aspects. In particular, as the reviewers took different positions with respect to the analytical model, I provided guidance in my correspondence with the authors. I supported the suggestion of reviewer 1 to drop the analytical model from the paper. My reasoning here was based on the disconnection between the analytical model and the front end of the paper, as identified by reviewer 2. It seemed to me that to pursue the development of the model along the lines of reviewer 2 would take the paper in a different direction, away from the novelty of the fieldwork.

Petra: That the editor clearly took a position was of great help to us as we were confronted with two opposing reviews. We decided to drop the analytical model completely, and explained in our reply to reviewer 2 that this decision was following suggestions by reviewer 1 and by the editor. However, two important issues remained. First, we decided to completely redo the coding of the business model changes, following closely the conceptual framework used in the paper. The analyses based on this new coding did not lead to different results. Second, a decision had to be made regarding the notion of 'resource acquisition', and, as a consequence, also regarding the notion of 'flexibility'. A first option was to abstain from discussing these notions in the introduction section and to no longer use them for demonstrating the disadvantages of focused commitment and sequential experimentation. The main research question would then simply be what kind of approaches to business model development existed. Afraid that this would significantly reduce the contribution of the paper, we instead decided to rewrite the introduction section explaining in greater detail that the resource acquisition problem related to experimentation called for further research. It took us several months to implement these changes, and we resubmitted the paper in July 2010.

ROUND TWO

Mike: I sent the revised paper back to the same reviewers. When I received their reports, I was confronted with even more diverging reviews, which were emphasized in their confidential comments to me. Reviewer 1 was very positive while reviewer 2 was disappointed with the turn the paper had taken.

> **Reviewer 1:** The paper has potential to be outstanding with some editing. They are very close. ... I would be willing to let this go without seeing it again. ... So few longitudinal papers of this magnitude ever make it through the review process, and this one holds important insights into entrepreneurial organizing and methods.

> **Reviewer 2:** In the first version I especially appreciated the use of a multi-method approach. Now that it is no longer the case (i.e., the analytical model has been removed), the work is not as rigorous.

Mike: In comments to the authors, reviewer 2 repeated that he/she still saw a disconnection between the external financing discussions and the approaches to business model development, and raised doubts about the appropriateness of one specific case study. My view was that the authors were making progress and that the authors should be encouraged in the direction they were taking. It did not seem to me that reintroducing the analytical model would add novelty to the paper's contribution. Reviewer 1 raised a number of smaller issues that were easy to deal with, and that pertained mostly to the way the literature section was organized, and to the presentation of the results in figures and tables. In addition to these comments, in my decision letter giving the authors the opportunity for a further major revise and resubmit, I asked them to bring out their contribution more clearly, stating:

> **Editor:** From my own reading of the paper, I think you need to do the following to bring this out. First, you need to strengthen the research gap and your contribution to addressing it in the Introduction. For example, a short paragraph in the Introduction would help to sharpen this. Second, it would help to encapsulate your theoretical contribution if you were to develop some testable propositions. At present, it is a bit too general. Third, in the Concluding section, you should again stress your contribution.

Petra: In our reaction to this second round of reviews, which we received in October 2010, we made several changes to the paper. First, we made another attempt at better explaining the research gap and contribution by expanding the introduction section. Second, we again added more information on the case study selection and on the period documented for each case. Third, we provided much more textual information and tables on different steps of the analyses. All these changes significantly increased the length of the paper. Finally, we debated among ourselves on the development of testable propositions. We found it difficult to develop testable propositions that logically resulted from the qualitative analysis and, as a support for one of the five propositions we developed, we reintroduced the analytical model in an appendix, and resubmitted the paper in June 2011.

ROUND THREE

Mike: I again sent the paper back to the same reviewers. When the reviewers read this second revision of the paper, they reacted very differently. Reviewer 1 expressed his/her appreciation of the work that had been put into the revisions, and wrote in the confidential comments to me that he/she 'loved' the paper and would accept it without any further changes. Reviewer 2, however, was still very negative about the paper, but admitted at the same time that he/she was not an expert in qualitative research:

> **Reviewer 2:** I am afraid I cannot upgrade from the previous two rounds of reviews. Please note, however, that I am not an expert on case study analysis, which I now view as this manuscript's main research approach (the formal model has become a distraction that can be removed).

Mike: At this point, it was clear to me that, if I gave the authors another chance, there was no use in going back to the reviewers given these comments. I prioritized reviewer 1's assessment over reviewer 2's. The paper was now more squarely in reviewer 1's domain of expertise, while this was not the case for reviewer 2. Instead, I would have to guide the authors myself. Based on my own reading, I therefore communicated to the authors my own main concerns about the paper. First, I asked for additional clarification on the study cases selection:

> **Editor:** You also need to say more about … why you only looked at emergent industries and not a 'control' group of non-emergent industries/firms, why six was an appropriate number of firms – while you go for maximum variation, why is this more appropriate for the approach you are adopting than looking for 'extreme cases' (Eisenhardt)? You say very little about your interviews – with whom? When? How many? How long? How many times? Etc.

I also again urged the authors to drop the analytical model, and to rephrase the propositions so they could be tested empirically. I also requested they demonstrate more clearly how the propositions were derived from the case study evidence and how they fit together. This is a very important issue in helping making a coherent conceptual contribution in qualitative papers; at this point the propositions were rather ad hoc. I stressed that a clear conceptual framework could help in this respect, and would also allow the contribution of the paper to be brought out. I suggested that the effectuation literature could be an option. Finally, I asked for more information on the coding of business model changes. Whereas the paper at that time coded business model changes, the coding did not distinguish between tweaks to the initial business model or the development of a completely new one.

Petra: This new round of reviews was quite a disappointment for us as authors. It was September 2011, we had now been in the review process for almost two years, and had in this period recoded all the data and rewritten practically every part of the paper. Nevertheless, the same comments kept coming back. As a result, the momentum was a bit lost at this point, resulting in fruitless discussions among us as authors on how to revise the paper.

As I had no more ideas left on how to deal with the comments that had been raised before, I decided to tackle the one new issue that the editor had raised, namely, the distinction between incremental and radical business model changes. I added an additional layer of coding to the cases, which resulted in new and very interesting insights. It turned out that the ventures using simultaneous experimentation developed a portfolio of experiments in which each experiment was closely related to another experiment in the portfolio. However, by developing a portfolio of such related experiments, they actually generated a highly diverse set of business model experiments. This finding was novel and conceptually important, since it went against the common assumptions in the organizational learning literature that only distant search (that is, experimentation with unrelated business models) would generate variety. This was a key turning point in the development of the paper. Not only did it solve the editor's practical concern about the coding, it also made it clear to us that the right way forward was to position the paper in the organizational learning literature rather than the effectuation literature that the editor had initially suggested. The funny thing was that the organizational learning literature stream had a central role in my doctoral dissertation, but we had failed to see its relevance for this particular paper. It was as if all the pieces were finally falling into place.

By adding this additional layer of analysis, the paper made a much larger contribution. Also, from the analyses, it became much easier to develop interesting and testable propositions. The use of organizational learning theory as a conceptual framework suddenly made writing it all up and bringing out the contribution more simple. We did not need the resource acquisition notion anymore, and neither did we need the analytical model. The case study analyses, with this new layer, findings and conceptual framework, could stand on its own. We resubmitted the new version in March 2012.

ROUNDS FOUR AND FIVE TO THE FINISHING LINE

Petra: Once we had made the above turn, we had little difficulty encompassing the remaining comments that followed in the final two review rounds, and that related mainly to the presentation of the data and analyses and to the drastic shortening of the paper. In line with the editor's suggestion, the propositions were once more rephrased in a more symmetric way, with comparable propositions formulated for both identified approaches to business model development.

Mike: Although the authors had introduced the propositions, I felt that I needed to push them a bit more in these last rounds to polish the elegance of the propositions so that the novelty of the conceptual contribution would be much clearer and more coherent. This can take more than one iteration to achieve, but it is worth doing as the paper is more likely to get cited. The other issue, again very common as a paper goes through multiple rounds, is the need to reduce its length. This could be, and was, achieved without loss of content by dropping superfluous references, tables and figures, as well as wordsmithing the paper.

The paper was accepted in July 2012, 31 months after submission, and was eventually published as Petra Andries, Koenraad Debackere and Bart van Looy (2013), 'Simultaneous experimentation as a learning strategy: business model development under uncertainty', *Strategic Entrepreneurship Journal*, **7** (4), 288–310. The abstract of the final paper can be found in the appendix to this chapter.

LOOKING BACK: REFLECTIONS FOR THE PUBLISHING PROCESS

Some summary reflections on the insights we gained from the review process are shown in Table 2.1.

Table 2.1 Summary insights from the review process

	Editor's perspective	Author's perspective
For authors	Persistence and tenacity are important.	Don't be afraid to write the paper as it really evolved. If some concepts emerged from the analyses, then it is fine to show that.
	Need to let go of cherished material.	Think thoroughly about case study selection. It is a crucial decision that is difficult to change afterwards.
	Spend time pre-submission on focusing and framing the paper.	Need to manage author tensions on how to revise the paper. Undertake concrete actions to move forward instead of having fruitless discussions.
	Take especial care in addressing both Reviewers when they are split, and to avoid losing the more positive one in dealing with negative ones.	Take each Reviewer comment seriously. Acknowledge the shortcomings of the paper.
	There is a need to show significant improvements across review rounds.	Follow editors' and Reviewers' suggestions for improvement, unless you are convinced that there are better ways of solving the problem.
For editors	As there are not many great papers out there, editors need to be aware of diamonds in the rough and work with authors.	Pointing out the flaws in a paper is important, but providing constructive suggestions for improving it is even more valuable.
	Editors need to provide clear guidance to authors in cases of split Reviewers. This guidance may well go beyond Reviewer comments.	Try to work with Reviewers that remain polite. Even authors of lower quality papers have most probably gone through a great deal of effort to develop them and deserve a minimal level of courtesy and respect.

Mike: Looking back on this lengthy submission and review process, it seemed to me that the paper was a diamond in the rough that took some time to bring out. In my view, it is not unusual for it to take some time to demonstrate convincingly how novel propositions arise from the data. Despite the reviewers' comments it seemed to take some time for the authors to drop their model and the quantitative material. This may have been because of their search for the way forward, but usually I'd expect authors to follow a recommendation and let go. The material on the case selection also took a little time to polish, and I would suggest that it is important for qualitative researchers to pay particular attention to this issue at the outset. The good thing, and the reason why I continued through so many revision rounds, is that the authors showed significant progress in every round. As an editor, I really like to work with authors and help them move their paper forward.

Petra: I've learned a lot from this review process. First, I think we made the process unnecessarily difficult for ourselves by explicitly positioning the paper with respect to resource constraints and flexibility. We were afraid that simply asking what kinds of approaches to business model development existed would be insufficient for capturing the reader's interest. Therefore, we had added the discussion on resource acquisition and flexibility to the front end of the paper, although these concepts actually emerged from the case study analyses. I learned that it is not necessary to write up a qualitative paper as if all the central constructs were known beforehand. It is fine to show how the insights really emerged, with some constructs coming from the literature and others emerging from the case study analyses. Also, the multiple comments and questions on the cases we selected has made me much more aware of the importance of a well-thought-out approach to case study selection.

As for working with co-authors, this lengthy revision process taught me that, in times of tension on how to revise the paper, it is better to focus on concrete actions, such as additional analyses requested by the reviewers. Tackling the practical issues first can provide new insights that allow you to move forward with other comments, without getting stuck in fruitless discussion between co-authors.

Furthermore, I have learned a lot about the willingness of some reviewers and editors to help anonymous colleagues in improving their work. In review processes of other papers, I was at times shocked by the impoliteness and negativity of certain reviewers. In the case of this particular paper, however, I was truly impressed with the two reviewers' and the editor's constructive critiques and suggestions for improvement, without which the paper would not have made the contribution it does now. Seeing how much effort these colleagues devoted to the reviews was a real inspiration, and I try to be equally constructive when serving as a reviewer myself.

Finally, this review process is a good illustration of how – as an author – you can accommodate the comments of the editor and the reviewers while staying loyal to what you think is the core message and strength of the paper. While it is important to acknowledge the shortcomings of your paper as pointed out by the editor and the reviewers, it is not always necessary to exactly follow their proposals on how to resolve these issues. Since, as an author, you are well aware of the field and of your data, it is possible to come up with different, but even better solutions.

POSTSCRIPT

Petra: Six years after publication, the article has received 163 citations according to Google Scholar and has been awarded the Strategic Entrepreneurship Journal 2019 Best Paper Prize. This attention of other scholars in the field has led to new contacts, new collaborations and a new job at a different research institute. The review process itself, and in particular the guidance and engagement of the editor, Mike Wright, re-ignited my enthusiasm for academic research, and have led to my personal decision to abandon, at the age of 39, my permanent job as manager of a policy research centre and take up a tenure track position at my new institute, Ghent University, where I'm now a tenured associate professor.

Over the past years, the lessons learnt during the review process of this article, and in particular aspects related to the positioning of a paper and the development of a theoretical contribution, have been extremely valuable when working on other studies. On the one hand, these insights have allowed me to make a clear theoretical contribution in journals that value this (for example, *Strategic Entrepreneurship Journal*, *Research Policy* and *Journal of Business Venturing*). On the other hand, they have enabled me to better judge whether a specific study would fit a specific type of journal. I have, for example, developed a very interesting case study of a for-profit social enterprise that successfully internationalized through business model experimentation. The study made no substantial contribution to theory, but was very relevant for social entrepreneurs, and found its way to a journal that emphasizes practical relevance. I try to pass these insights on to my PhD students and to other authors when reviewing their papers.

Importantly, the review process also taught me the value of constructive feedback, and I keep this in mind whenever I review a paper for a journal. Criticizing someone's work is easy; providing constructive feedback and guidance usually takes substantially more time and effort. Nevertheless, as we all want to be able to improve our papers, it is a part of my job that I take very seriously.

APPENDIX

Abstract of the Initial Submission

The unpredictable nature of emergent markets implies that ventures entering such markets are confronted with technological and commercial uncertainty. Defining a viable business model under such circumstances is a complex and precarious endeavour. Previous research has either advanced the idea of focus – in order to attract resources and realize first mover advantages – or sequential experimentation financed through bootstrapping, implying limited resources during initial phases of the venture. As such, a trade-off between flexibility and resource acquisition has been introduced. Within this contribution we explore how ventures starting up in emergent industries can balance the attainment of financial resources with flexibility and business model adaptation. Based on a sequence analysis of six case studies, we identify two distinctive approaches to business development in emergent industries: focused commitment versus simultaneous experimentation. Our findings reveal that focused commitment is instrumental for acquiring resources but at the same time impedes flexibility, while simultaneous experimentation allows to attract resources while maintaining manoeuvring space for business model adaptation. An analytical comparison of both approaches suggests that simultaneous experimentation is indeed a more viable strategy when entering emergent industries.

Abstract of the Published Paper

Ventures operating under uncertainty face challenges defining a sustainable value proposition. Six longitudinal case studies reveal two approaches to business model development: focused commitment and simultaneous experimentation. While focused commitment positively affects initial growth, this commitment and lack of variety jeopardize long-term survival. Simultaneous experimentation implies lower initial growth levels, but facilitates long-term survival by enacting variety in a resource-effective manner. This paper enriches organizational learning theory by demonstrating that not only distant search but also simultaneous experimentation results in variety. Moreover, simultaneous experimentation implies effectual behavior and reconciles the apparent juxtaposition between 'action' and 'planning'.

3. Getting published: a view from a journal editor and journal ranker

Geoffrey Wood and Pawan Budhwar

INTRODUCTION

The opportunity to share your ideas with a wider audience is one of the most rewarding parts of being an academic. Finding your work side by side with leading scholars in the field, and being part of a wider debate, is very much part of this. However, while getting published is considerably easier than coming up with genuinely new ideas, the task brings with it its own challenges; some, but not all, are due to the expansion of the business school ecosystem, with increasing numbers of schools raising their requirements as to where and how much scholars should publish. Most quality journals reject the overwhelming majority of submissions. Hence, publishing in leading journals has become increasingly competitive. This short review seeks to provide some insights to maximize your chances of success.

HOW TO CHOOSE A JOURNAL, AND HOW DO JOURNAL RANKINGS FIT IN?

Level of Work

The journal ecosystem is diverse and rich, and there is a huge range of journals to choose from. In the case of the UK, many universities require staff to produce work of at least 3* level[1] (in some instances, higher) on the Chartered Association of Business School (CABS) List to be included in the Research Excellence Framework (an exercise carried out every five or six years to assess and rank the research quality of higher education institutions in the UK); if you are subject to this logic, then the list of options immediately becomes much narrower. Three key issues are worth considering here. The first is that you have to be realistic; some work, owing to limitations in data, method or theoretical underpinnings, will never get published in a journal that is highly respectable (for example, ranked 3* or 4* using the 'Chartered ABS Guide' system). Getting such work published in lower-ranked journals means your ideas might not initially reach as wide an audience as would otherwise be the case.

It could be argued that too many articles published in modestly ranked journals may create the impression of excessive 'noise' on your curriculum vitae (CV) unless there is a clear upward trajectory. However, a note of caution is due here. Most top journals started off from modest beginnings, and some articles in modestly ranked journals have ended up being widely cited. It is also worth considering that more modestly ranked journals are often more open to very innovative and unusual work; some (but not all) of the most highly ranked journals are more conservative in terms of what they take. Again, a well-run journal with a relatively modest ranking (say, Chartered ABS 2), but which carries some interesting work, may attract a wide readership. Once a paper starts attracting significant numbers of citations, it is likely to that it will continue to do so, regardless of the outlet. However, the best regarded journals are likely to find it a great deal easier to find reviewers, and this means that the paper is likely (but not always) to get better reviews quicker. Finally, top journals are able to insist that paper submissions are well polished, with high standards of technical presentation; aspiring to such journals means that you have to raise your own game in this is regard, which is desirable in its own right.

Right Fit

Most journals clearly highlight the kinds of areas (for example, general management, organization studies, work psychology) and nature (for example, empirical versus review or academic versus practitioner orientated) of manuscripts they will publish. In order to ensure the right fit exists between a given manuscript ready for submission and the chosen journal it would be sensible to do a thorough analysis of the type of manuscripts the journal has been publishing. It would be helpful if you could find some related debates and discussions taking place in the journal related to your own research and the contents of your manuscript. It is also worth scrutinizing editorials, as they often summarize what the editors are looking for. If you are not citing anything from the journal, this may indicate a poor fit. Referees are likely to be drawn from the ranks of those who have published in the journal in the past, and telling them that their work is so trivial as to not even be worth mentioning is not a good place to start.

Avoiding Desk Rejection

Most top journals desk reject a high number of papers (typically 50 per cent or more of submissions). There are four things to consider here. First, you need to ensure the basic fundamentals of the research on which the manuscript is based are in place (that is, the 'why', 'what' and 'how' questions are adequately addressed). This will include clear and timely aims/research questions, an up-to-date literature analysis (highlighting gaps worth filling), appropriate theoretical underpinning for the research (less valid for practitioner journals), relevant and robust methodology, suitable data analysis in the case of empirical papers, useful discussion highlighting the rationale for main findings and the implications/contributions of the research. Depending on the nature of the research investigation and analysis, other elements, such as theoretically driven hypotheses and proposed linkages between independent and dependent variables, and recommendations for future research should also be included.

It is also important to ensure the writing in the manuscript is of good quality (for example, error free, jargon free, reader friendly and in accordance with the submission guidelines of the journal). This can be challenging for inexperienced authors, and (in the case of anglophone journals) those whose first language is not English and who are not proficient in it. Steps should be taken to ensure this (for example, via peer reviews or with the help of a professional copy editor). Also take the necessary care in preparing the submission, such as making sure it adheres to the journal's style (not that of the journal's closest rival, as it might appear to a critical reader that the paper has already been rejected at least once), and make reference to previous work published in the journal (checking carefully that you are not in effect duplicating work already published, but equally important, where possible, link your work with the published work in the journal).

The second is to look closely at your data; does it really bring new information to the table? For example, there are vast bodies of work based on student studies, for the simple reason that it is easy. However, no matter what you call them ('future business leaders', 'emerging entrepreneurs'), they are your students, with the inevitable power imbalances with faculty. Third, as noted previously, you should make sure the literature review is up to date and at least indicates some awareness of the target journal; a lack of attention to this is a sure sign of the zombie paper that has been subject to multiple rejections, but simply will not go away. Zombies can certainly be safely interred somewhere, but it is harder if everybody can see what they are.

Finally, be cautious of using esoteric statistical tests (as opposed to novel approaches that may take a field forward) that nobody knows much about; this is sometimes a sign that an author has run wild with one of the many commercial software statistical analysis and modelling packages but does not really know what he or she is doing. There is then a need to understand what the given journal considers appropriate statistical tests and levels of analysis. A recent trend has been to expect good descriptives prior to launching into the multiple regressions, as this helps reassure the reader that there is genuinely something of value in the findings, rather than evidencing skill in p-hacking (also known as data dredging).

The success rate of publishing in leading journals has become a great deal tougher as a large number of scholars from emerging markets have raised their skills and aspirations to publish in these journals, and the journals are increasingly overloaded. Again, better PhD training has made recent graduates very much aware of journal hierarchies and ways of enhancing one's success in getting published. Also, if you are reading this chapter, there are many others also reading it and taking its lessons to heart!

Editors of established journals cannot carry more than a limited number of submissions, and tend to look for obvious faults; do not make it easy for them! Positive features that editors look for are clarity (that is, can you tell what the paper is about by reading it), balanced structure (devoting appropriate space to each part of the paper, from introduction to conclusion), an interesting and timely research problem, convincing theoretical underpinning of the same (for academic-orientated journals), novelty (without being freaky; in reality, this is a difficult balance), being interesting (that is, giving readers good reasons to carry on reading and citing the paper) and clear implications.

DEALING WITH REVIEWERS

How are Reviewers Selected?

There are four broad ways in which reviewers are selected. The first is that they are chosen from among the editor's list of personal contacts. The second is that they are thrown up by a keyword search of the journal's electronic database of existing reviewers and those who have submitted papers. The third is that they are nominated by the author him or herself. Fourth, some editors look at the references used in the manuscript to identify potential reviewers.

The first group are likely to be experienced reviewers (as the editor will probably have used them before), but may not be very narrow subject experts with highly specialized expertise on the topic of the paper. This is not a bad thing, as they are likely to mirror the typical reader, and if you cannot clearly explain what you are doing, it is highly likely that you are writing rubbish. As they are personal contacts of the editor, they may reflect his or her interests.

The second are likely to know a great deal about the topic, but may not always be that experienced (depending on how the database is compiled; for example, some include authors of unsuccessful papers). The third are the most dangerous; our experience is that often-nominated reviewers will either reject the paper or refuse to review it at all. Regrettably, in business and management studies, 'friends' are not always 'friends' under the cloak of anonymity. The fourth should be able to do a good review job as they are aware of research developments in the field.

Dealing with Reviewer Comments

There are a number of different grades of revise and resubmit. A minor changes verdict (unusual on the first round) normally means that, as long as you faithfully take on board the reviewers' comments, you are likely to get published. If you think a reviewer is wrong, it is not wise to engage in trench warfare, but instead attempt to promote a compromise revision that will satisfy him or her, while tactfully pointing out what may not be accomplished.

A major revise and resubmit (often with the high risk proviso added) is a very much less secure business. Here it is wise not only to seek to incorporate the changes, but also to invest a great deal of time in the response to the reviewer, and get the opinions of friendly experts as to whether or not you have done enough. Most people do not like bad news; many authors will try and bluff themselves that the reviewers are wrong, and try to wear them down with obfuscation and half measures, inevitably leading to a reject.

A reject and resubmit normally follows a limited review by the editor; he or she clearly believes the paper has merits but is unlikely to survive the review process unless some obvious faults are carefully attended to. Cynics have suggested that this is a way of relieving the difficulties of finding reviewers and of scaring away authors when the journal is overloaded, as invariably some authors will be so disheartened that they leave empty-handed.

Resubmission and Responding

Upon receiving a revise and resubmit decision, it is critical to do a thorough revision job, but how you respond to the reviewers' comments, both in the revised manuscript and in your response letter, is equally important. Meeting the given time target to resubmit is also important and practical, not only for your manuscript but also for the original reviewers to remember your manuscript.

All the points raised by the reviewers must be systematically addressed and a convincing response provided in the response letter. If you disagree with some of the reviewers' points, then you should raise them in your response letter to the editor with a solid rationale and evidence for each point. A good response letter will not only address every point raised by both the action editor and the reviewers, but will also provide an acknowledgement of the useful comments of the reviewers and a clear logic for all the responses and details of the amendments carried out (where, why and how). Thanking the reviewers for their insights is always welcome as long as authors do not go over the top with it. Any document submitted should be error free. This is often a challenge for non-native speakers of English, who should seek relevant help to ensure this.

Yourself as a Reviewer

It may seem perfectly rational to deluge journals with your own work, while refusing to review other authors' papers, as this will free up time to whack out yet more papers. This is clearly unethical. However, selfish scholars who are undeterred by appeals to their conscience need to carefully consider two points. The first is that reviewing lots of papers gives you a much clearer idea of the quality of competing work, what types of papers are sent out to review (compared with desk rejected) by a particular journal and what is the current state of the literature. The second is that most journals and publishers keep electronic records of reviewers, including how many papers they have refused and the quality of their reports. If you repeatedly refuse to review papers or give poor quality reviews, this greatly reduces your chances of ever being invited onto an editorial board or to guest edit a journal special issue. Also, if a paper is a close call and the author has consistently refused to review, the close call might turn into a rejection. If you are community minded, you probably need to write two reviews for every paper you submit.

Changes in the Journal Ecosystem

In many countries, there have been moves to promote open access publishing, in part as a reaction to the high cost of journal subscriptions (in addition to the free or low-cost academic time provided to publishers for article writing, reviewing and journal editing). While undeniably well-intentioned, these moves seem to have backfired in that the political influence of the publishers has been hugely discounted; in many national contexts, this has simply translated into proposals or policies for publishers to be paid additional sums in return for 'gold' open access to articles by scholars from a particular institution or even a particular country.

This development has meant that many publishers are now keen on expanded page counts for journals, as this means that there is more content for which 'gold' open access can be sold (especially as the dominant mode of distribution is now electronic, thereby saving on printing and postage costs); the term 'gold' being truly apposite. This may mean, and in some instances already has meant, that some journals will carry many more articles. This sounds like good news for scholars, but it will depress citation counts, unless journals – as is the case in the sciences – draw a distinction between full-length articles and other types of papers (communications, letters, provocations and so on). The latter do not count as articles in the article count for journals, but individual outputs do count for citation purposes. That is, citations to them constitute part of the numerator, but the articles do not count as part of the denominator in calculating citations; which explains why natural science journals have such high citation scores. This may mean there are many more opportunities to get published in top journals; however, this is unlikely to be greater than the increase in scholars seeking to get into them. Chapter 29 in this volume discusses open access publishing in more detail.

CONCLUSION

By avoiding some obvious mistakes, and taking care to understand the journal and what its reviewers might expect, you have a very much greater chance of not being desk rejected. While revise and resubmits can themselves be daunting, this verdict indicates interest from the journal in your work and that there is indeed some merit in your paper.

NOTE

1. 4* = meaning that they publish 'most original and best executed research'; 3* = meaning that they publish 'original and well executed research'.

4. Ethics and integrity in publishing*
Ben R. Martin

INTRODUCTION

Academic researchers operate in an increasingly competitive environment. They compete for research funds (with success rates for grant applications now often 20 per cent or lower), tenure and promotion. Their institutions compete in research assessment exercises or in international university rankings. Academics are subject to ever more intrusive forms of evaluation, often heavily dependent on performance indicators linked to success in publishing – in particular, numbers of publications, numbers of citations, numbers of highly cited papers or articles in top journals (frequently linked with journal impact factors), and your personal h-index.[1]

For most of its history, the academic community has operated within relatively loose norms and conventions with regard to what constitutes 'research integrity' and the ethics of publishing (Schminke 2009, p. 586). That was sufficient until recently. Academics constituted a 'Republic of Science', in which a combination of the values instilled in young researchers and 'self-policing' through peer review ensured that the great majority did indeed carry out their research with integrity (Anderson et al. 2013, pp. 220–22; Martin 2013, p. 1005). Research misconduct was infrequent and generally low level, with the penalties for transgressing (loss of reputation, funding or position) strong enough to deter all but a few (Martin 2012, p. 97).

However, over the past 25–35 years, evaluations and performance indicators have become more pervasive, and the level of competition (both individual and institutional) much more intense. Freeman et al. (2001, p. 2293) liken the current situation to a 'tournament' which offers 'players' a chance of a major prize (tenure, a chair, a scientific medal or an honour), but which 'fosters intense competition by amplifying small differences in productivity into large differences in recognition and reward. ... Because the differences in rewards exceed the differences in output, there is a disproportionate incentive to "win"'. Hence, it is perhaps not surprising that more researchers are being tempted to 'cut corners' (Anderson et al. 2013, p. 237–8; see also Bedeian et al. 2010, pp. 720–21; Edwards and Roy 2017; Walsh et al. 2019). As Mumford et al. (2007, p. 362) note in their study of environmental influences on ethical decision-making by PhD students: 'excessive competitive pressure may lead to the acquisition of beliefs likely to engender the potential for unethical decisions throughout an individual's career'.[2] Similarly, Necker (2014, p. 1747) found that 'perceived pressure is ... positively related to the admission of being involved in several unaccepted research practices ... consistent with the notion that the "publish or perish" culture motivates researchers to violate research norms'.

Unethical behaviour may take various forms – borrowing ideas or material from others without acknowledgement, slicing research results into ever thinner 'salami' papers, recycling already published material without bringing this to the reader's attention, p-hacking[3] or tidying up data to increase the apparent statistical significance of the findings (thus enhancing the chances of publication). Often the boundary between acceptable and unacceptable research behaviour is ill defined, with little by way of universally accepted rules (Hall and Martin 2019). Inevitably, some have sought to take advantage of this, trying to unilaterally shift the boundary between what constitutes acceptable and unacceptable research behaviour in their favour.

The aim of this chapter is to set out as clearly as possible the rules of the game, and to explain how these are interpreted by academic gatekeepers such as journal editors. This includes offering advice on how to avoid ending up in a situation where your integrity as a researcher might be called into question.[4]

The structure of the remainder of the chapter is as follows: in the next section, we consider the nature and extent of the problem. This is followed by sections on research misconduct and on inappropriate or questionable research conduct. The penultimate section discusses misbehaviour by editors. The chapter ends with a summary of the main conclusions.

NATURE AND EXTENT OF THE PROBLEM

First, we need to consider what is meant by integrity in respect of research. The primary aim of scientific research is to produce 'reliable knowledge' (Ziman 1978). As Anderson et al. (2013, p. 218) state:

integrity is a matter of trustworthiness ... Research findings have integrity if they can be trusted ... The integrity of research findings is, in turn, dependent on the integrity of the research process that produced them, including data, methods of analysis, and presentation and interpretation in publications. Here, integrity is a matter of careful and precise work that meets the standards of the scientific method and best practice in the relevant field(s), as well as transparency in the presentation of all results and appropriately justified interpretations of all findings.

Over the past 15–20 years, problems with research integrity have escalated rapidly. To take one measure, the number of retractions by journals of articles found to be flawed has risen more than tenfold in just ten years (Karabag and Berggren 2016, p. 1; van Noorden 2011, p. 26). This is just for the most serious cases where a full retraction of the paper is deemed necessary; for each of these there are many others that are subject to some form of 'corrigendum', 'erratum' or an editor's 'expression of concern' (van Noorden 2011, p. 26).

While problems with research integrity initially centred mainly on biomedical research, they are now widespread throughout research.[5] In management studies, Honig and Bedi (2012) found that 13 per cent of papers selected (after peer review) for presentation at the Academy of Management contained significant plagiarism (that is, more than 5 per cent of plagiarized text) while a further 12 per cent contained at least some amount of plagiarism. As we shall see later, plagiarism is universally regarded as a serious form of research misconduct, but there are various, less serious misdemeanours which are far more common. In a survey of economists, Necker (2014, p. 1747) found that no less than 'Ninety-four percent report having engaged in at least one unaccepted research practice'.

Journal editors are faced with a growing number and range of cases not just of research misconduct, but also other forms of inappropriate or questionable behaviour (Schminke and Ambrose 2011, p. 399). They are struggling to keep such problems in check, to which numerous editorials lay testimony.[6] The wider support of the academic community is essential if the problems are not to escalate further.

RESEARCH MISCONDUCT

Research misconduct is conventionally defined as 'fabrication, falsification, or plagiarism in proposing, performing, or reviewing research, or in reporting research results'.[7] This is the definition adopted by the US National Institutes of Health (the world's largest research-funding agency) and widely used by others. The American Psychological Association, for instance, uses a similar definition.[8]

In social sciences, a number of cases of data fabrication (defined as 'Making up data or results and recording or reporting them'[9]) have come to light. For example, the social psychologist, Diederik Stapel, 'perpetrated an audacious academic fraud by making up studies that told the world what it wanted to hear about human nature' (Bhattacharjee 2013).[10] While the number of detected cases of data fabrication is low, the real incidence is undoubtedly much higher. For example, a survey of business school faculty by Bedeian et al. (2010) revealed that 'one out of four respondents (26.8%) reported knowledge of instances where faculty have fabricated results'. Moreover, this only covers cases known to colleagues, so the real incidence may be considerably higher.

Rather more common are instances of data falsification, which is defined as 'Manipulating research materials, equipment, or processes, or changing or omitting data or results such that the research is not accurately represented in the research record'.[11] A recent example of this concerns Brian Wansink, a world-leading expert on eating behaviour and the author of hundreds of highly cited papers. He has been found to be engaging in various research practices that are highly questionable and widely criticized, and, at the time of writing (February 2019), 17 of his papers had been retracted.[12] There is growing evidence of researchers engaging in similar dubious practices to inflate the apparent statistical significance of their empirical findings, in particular to generate exaggerated p-values ('p-hacking', see Head et al. 2015; Simonsohn et al. 2015). Such practices include manipulating the data to obtain findings significant at the 1 per cent or 5 per cent level, continuing to collect data until such significant findings are obtained and then stopping, and trying numerous hypotheses or models until finding one that gives a 'significant' result at the 1 per cent or 5 per cent level.

As social scientists have developed more sophisticated statistical techniques, so these sharp practices may not always be immediately apparent to referees or editors. Concern over the inflation of statistical significance first emerged in the biomedical area, with Ioannidis (2005) concluding that most discovered true associations are inflated. However, the resulting 'reproducibility crisis' is certainly not confined to biomedical research (Baker 2016). For example, Bakker and Wicherts (2011, p. 666) found that 'around 18% of statistical results in the psychological literature are incorrectly reported'. An analysis of three leading accountancy journals by Basu and Park (2014, p. 1) showed that 'the frequencies of *p*-values just below conventional significance levels are higher than frequencies just above these levels',[13] a finding that 'likely derive[s] from selective reporting of statistically significant results or searching across research designs for *p*-values for Test variables below conventional significance levels' (Basu and Park 2014, p. 1). Doubts have also been raised about the reproducibility of findings in management (Bergh et al. 2017) and economics (Camerer et al. 2016). (We return later to the issue of retrospectively fitting hypotheses to data in order to arrive at supposedly significant findings.)

Bedeian et al. (2010) focused specifically on misconduct in the field of management research. In a survey of faculty at over 100 leading US business schools, they found that 'Close to 80% of survey respondents reported knowledge of faculty who either have "withheld methodological details or results" or "have selected only those data that support a hypothesis and withheld the rest" (i.e., "cooking" data)' (Bedeian et al. 2010, p. 718). In addition, 'some 60% of respondents reported knowledge of faculty who have "dropped observations or data points from analyses based on a gut feeling that they were inaccurate," what many would consider an example of "data trimming"' (Bedeian et al. 2010, p. 719).[14] The latter is a particularly grey area, since Winsorization (the assigning of lesser weight to what appears to be a spurious outlier or modifying its value so it is closer to other sample values) is a fairly common statistical technique (see, for example, Ruppert 2006 [2014]). The boundary between acceptable Winsorization (that is, modifying outliers) and unacceptable data-trimming (that is, completely dropping outliers) is a fine one, and therefore the onus is very much on authors to be completely open with their readers so that the latter can make their own judgement as to whether the specific methodology employed is acceptable in the circumstances, or not.

Plagiarism, the third main form of research misconduct, can be defined as 'The appropriation of another person's ideas, processes, results, or words without giving appropriate credit'.[15] This also now seems to be widespread. In their survey of business schools, Bedeian et al. (2010, p. 718) found that 'Over 70% percent [of faculty] reported being aware of colleagues who have engaged in plagiarism, or stated more formally, have "used another's ideas without permission or giving due credit"'.

There are a number of instances of blatant plagiarism where whole sections or even entire papers are lifted from other sources and presented as the author's 'own' work. A prominent example is Tony Antoniou, formerly Dean of Durham University's Business School, who lost his job after it was revealed that a journal article and large parts of his PhD thesis had been based on plagiarism (Tahir 2008). Another example is Hans Werner Gottinger, who on a dozen or more occasions was caught misappropriating the work of others and presenting it as his own (Abbott

2007; Martin and other editors of *Research Policy* 2007; Martin 2012). Journal editors occasionally come across such cases. Fortunately, they often involve 'authors blessed with a singular degree of stupidity or laziness, who are either unaware that merely substituting their name at the top of an existing paper is unlikely to fool anyone, or unwilling to put in the effort needed to camouflage their plagiarism in a more sophisticated manner' (Martin 2013, p. 1007).

Much more common, however, are papers where there are repeated instances of a few sentences being lifted from other sources without this being apparent to the reader. The rules on plagiarism make it clear that an author has just two choices: either to place such material in quotation marks (or indent it for longer quotations), or to paraphrase it, that is, to rewrite it entirely in the author's own words. There is no third way. Many authors assume that citing the source at the end of the lifted material is somehow sufficient to avoid a charge of plagiarism. However, the rules here are clear; this, too, is a form of plagiarism. The instructions given to students by universities on plagiarism and how to avoid it are typically very explicit on such matters.[16] If your paper falls foul of your own university's rules for students on plagiarism, then an editor is unlikely to believe your claim you were unaware that failure either to place lifted material in quotation marks or to paraphrase it constitutes plagiarism.

INAPPROPRIATE AND QUESTIONABLE RESEARCH CONDUCT

Besides research misconduct, there are certain forms of behaviour that are widely judged to be inappropriate, while other activities are less clear-cut and are often grouped together under a heading such as 'questionable' research conduct (for example, Banks et al. 2016; Butler et al. 2017; Fanelli 2009; Hall and Martin 2019; John et al. 2012).[17] The former category covers activities where there are some conventions or guidelines but perhaps not universal consensus on what constitutes the rules of the game.[18] The latter includes activities that, while not necessarily explicitly ruled out, nevertheless would be considered by most reasonable researchers as antithetical to the spirit of the research enterprise.[19] Let us consider some common examples.

Salami Publishing, Redundant Publication and Self-Plagiarism[20]

In recent years, there have been growing numbers of cases involving self-plagiarism and the related phenomena of salami publishing and

Ethics and integrity in publishing 39

redundant publication. Of these, salami publishing is perhaps the least serious and the one where the rules are least clear. It can be defined as:

> the deliberate attempt by an author or team of authors to inappropriately inflate the total of publications yielded by a particular research study ... through a process of subdividing the published output into a number of thin 'slices' or 'least publishable units', thereby either generating a greater number of separate publications than is merited by the overall contribution to knowledge offered by that study, or creating a situation where the research community would instead be better served by the results being combined in a single or a smaller number of publications. (Martin 2013, p. 1008)

Salami publishing can often result in redundant (or duplicate) publication, which may be defined as 'a paper where the existence of one or more prior (or contemporaneous) papers by the same author(s) means that the new paper offers insufficient of an original contribution to knowledge to merit publication in its own right' (Martin 2013, p. 1008).[21] In some cases, redundant publication can involve the more serious offence of self-plagiarism.[22]

> 'Self-plagiarism' can be defined as the practice by an author (or co-authors) of reproducing text, ideas, data, findings or other material from one or more earlier (or contemporaneous) papers by the same author(s) *without explicitly citing or otherwise acknowledging those other papers*, thereby misleading the reader (and in particular referees and editors) as to the level of originality of that paper. Such an attempt to present one's own previously published work as though it were original is a form of deception (in contrast to plagiarism, which is a form of theft). (Martin 2013, p. 1008, emphasis added)

A prominent case of self-plagiarism in management studies came to light in 2012. In just six years, the individual concerned had gone from PhD student to full professor at a leading German university, publishing more than 60 journal articles, including over 12 in top journals. When suspicions were aroused, many were found to be very closely related, with most being based on just two studies. Not only had the author failed to cite other closely related papers (thereby misleading editors about the originality of his work), he had also camouflaged the similarities by giving the same variable different names in different papers. A couple of years earlier, the individual had been feted as 'the undisputed shooting star of business science in Germany'.[23] In terms of journal publications, he came top in the 'under 40' age-group category of the *Handelsblatt* research ranking of German-speaking business school faculty, and second overall. However, once the offences came to light,[24] 16 of his articles were retracted by journals, and he was subsequently forced to resign from his chair.[25]

In cases of alleged self-plagiarism, the debate frequently hinges on what constitutes prior publication. In the pre-digital age, editors were often more relaxed about this. Authors would sometimes contend that they were free to publish in effect the same study in different journals if those journals were aimed at different audiences. That argument may have had some merit in former times, when researchers had to go to libraries to access publications and could only keep up with a few selected journals in their field. Now in the digital age, however, most journals are accessible through university libraries and a simple keyword search is likely to find any relevant article, whatever journal it was published in.[26] Consequently, many editors now take a tougher line. A recent casualty was Bruno Frey, who with colleagues published papers in four journals on the same study (about who survived the sinking of the *Titanic*). Each article failed to cite the others, thus deceiving readers about the level of that paper's originality. On learning of the deception, the editor of one journal wrote a public letter to Frey and colleagues, stating that their 'publication of this substantive material in multiple journals simultaneously' represented 'a violation of the spirit of the editorial agreement' that they signed when submitting the paper and claiming it was 'original work' (Autor 2011, p. 239).

By convention, there are still a few, specific exemptions with regard to what constitutes prior publication. In particular, doctoral theses do not count.[27] Likewise, working papers and conference presentations have traditionally been seen as pre-prints rather than publications. In the past, the difference was easier to spot since the former frequently took the form of typescript mimeos. However, in the electronic age, with papers typeset so that they resemble the format of published articles, and with those papers widely circulated in digital form, the boundary between a pre-print and a publication is much more blurred. Electronic working papers may be widely circulated for some period of time, during which they may earn numerous citations.[28] Conference papers, which in the past might be circulated only to conference attendees on a CD-ROM, are now often made publicly available through the conference website and therefore might be considered a form of publication. As a result of this blurring of the boundaries, editors may take different views as to where you draw the line between pre-publication and publication.[29]

My own view (shared by many journal editors but certainly not all) is that working papers and conference papers are circulated to elicit critical feedback and are thus a necessary part of the quality control and improvement process essential in research. A particular problem can arise, however, when conference papers are published as part of the conference proceedings. If a fairly full version of a paper appears in such proceedings, for many editors that constitutes prior publication.[30] If, however, only a short version (for example, a quarter the length) is what appears in the proceedings, an editor may take the view that the full paper still exhibits sufficient originality to merit publication in a journal. Where an author is in any doubt as to what constitutes prior publication, the rule is simple: inform the editor of the full facts and ask for a ruling. Editors much prefer to be told in advance about such complications rather than finding out later at third hand. When thus approached by an author, editors are likely to be sympathetic and offer a way round the potential problem, for example, by suitably differentiating the new paper from the earlier version.[31]

Retrofitting Hypotheses to Empirical Results (or HARKing)

As the use of increasingly sophisticated statistical methods has grown, and as journals have come to place a premium on methodological rigour, so the temptation has grown among researchers to engage in a process of retrofitting hypotheses to empirical results in order to increase the apparent statistical significance of the findings. This phenomenon has been termed HARKing (Hypothesizing After the Results are Known) by Kerr (1998), who identified various forms as well as the driving forces. As Leung (2011, p. 471) notes: 'The pure form of this practice is likely to breach research ethics and impede theoretical development by suppressing the falsification process.' In particular, 'when such hypotheses are data driven, they are inherently susceptible to capitalization on chance and are nothing more than a disguised form of data dredging' (Bedeian 2004, p. 207).

Evidence of how widespread this research behaviour now is comes from a survey by Bedeian et al. (2010, p. 719) of US business school faculty, over 90 per cent of whom reported knowledge of such practices. This very high incidence may partly reflect that HARKing is not always easy to detect, especially if the authors have been adept in covering their tracks (for example, by revising the literature review and retrospectively modifying the paper's motivation). However, probably a more important reason is that these practices are often explicitly encouraged by referees, who may call for certain hypotheses to be recast or dropped, particularly those yielding null results, and for new ones to be added (Anon. 2015; Bedeian 2004, p. 207). Further evidence that the practice is now very common comes from O'Boyle et al. (2017), who compared the empirical findings from PhD theses with those from subsequent journal articles based on the same doctoral studies. They found that 'from dissertation to journal article, the ratio of supported to unsupported hypotheses more than doubled ... The rise in predictive accuracy resulted from the dropping of statistically non-significant hypotheses, the addition of statistically significant hypotheses, the reversing of predicted direction of hypotheses, and alterations to data' (O'Boyle et al. 2017, p. 376). They describe this form of publication bias[32] in which 'ugly initial results metamorphosize into beautiful articles' as 'the Chrysalis Effect' (O'Boyle et al. 2017, p. 376). While some researchers may take a different view, arguing perhaps that they were encouraged down this route by reviewers, many editors would nevertheless see this as inappropriate research behaviour. Although difficult to spot, once an author has been caught, editors and others may subsequently treat all his or her papers as suspect, since the charge is equally hard to disprove. The author's reputation in the research community will therefore suffer accordingly. Once more, the rule is to be open with the reader about whether a hypothesis has been revised or added, for instance, at the prompting of a referee (Anon. 2015; Hollenbeck and Wright 2017).

Gift Authorship

Being listed as one of the authors of a paper means taking full responsibility for the content and not just accepting credit for the contribution. However, as the pressures to publish have grown, there has been a tendency for authors to be added who have made no substantial contribution, perhaps in return for a reciprocal favour with another paper. In their survey of business school faculty, Bedeian et al. (2010, p. 720) found that 'Nearly eight of ten (78.9%) respondents reported knowledge of instances where faculty have "inappropriately accepted or assigned authorship credit"'. The effect is to artificially inflate the reputation of the 'honorary' authors. The rules of the Academy of Management Code of Ethics are clear: authorship should be 'based on the scientific or professional contributions of the individuals involved' and researchers should take authorship credit 'only for work they have actually performed or to which they have contributed'.[33]

Some Specific Examples of Inappropriate or Questionable Research Conduct

To guide the reader through these rules and conventions and help them see exactly where the boundary lies, let us consider some common examples of inappropriate or questionable research conduct.[34] The first involves repeated instances of phrases or sentences lifted from other sources, especially in the literature review section. As noted above, either the author must place the lifted text in quotation marks, or they must rewrite it entirely in their own words. Listing the source is not sufficient, although omitting it makes the offence worse, since it suggests a premeditated intention to deceive the reader. Editors may be prepared to overlook one or two cases of this in a paper as an honest error, but not if persistently repeated.

Similar comments refer to the case of an author who makes use of an idea, concept, methodological approach or whatever from another source without proper attribution. Scientific knowledge is the product of a collective endeavour, where each generation 'stands on the shoulders' of those who have gone before, giving them full and explicit credit for each of the intellectual building blocks used in the author's study. An occasional oversight may perhaps be forgivable but repeated failure to adhere to this convention again risks being interpreted as a deliberate attempt to exaggerate the originality of the author's own research by downplaying the contributions of others. Such 'carelessness' is likely to be spotted by referees. Moreover, once an individual acquires a reputation for such intellectual self-aggrandizement, it takes years to overcome.

The next example of inappropriate behaviour focuses not so much on prior publication but on what might be termed parallel publication. When a paper is submitted to a journal, it is judged primarily on whether it represents a substantial original contribution to knowledge. Most journals require the submitting author to confirm the paper has not been published previously in whole or part. Many authors duly tick this box but often fail to divulge that one or more closely related papers have been submitted, or are about to be submitted, to other journals.[35] Only after the paper in question has been accepted does the editor find out that a significant part of its supposed contribution has also been made in one or more parallel papers. If the existence of those parallel papers had been disclosed at the start so that the editor was able to check its specific contribution compared with the parallel papers, then that paper may have been rejected. To this extent, editors are likely to feel that they have been deliberately misled and may as a result reject or retract the paper in question.

This problem has become increasingly common in recent years following a shift in the nature of many PhD theses from a monograph to a thesis based on journal articles, this often being the preferred choice for young researchers concerned about developing their curriculum vitae and enhancing their career prospects. In business schools, such theses typically consist of three, or so, closely related papers that inevitably overlap to a certain extent in terms of topic, data, methods and/or theory. This poses a problem for editors of the journals to which such papers are submitted, and who, with the aid of referees, are required to make a judgement as to the originality of the submitted paper, something that is clearly related to the nature and extent of the overlap with the other papers making up that student's thesis. Again, the rule is simple: when submitting a paper to a journal, explain to the editor about the related papers, setting out not only the differences between them but also how and where they overlap, and offer to make those other papers available to the editor so that they can make a judgement as to the overlap and differences, and hence the degree of originality of the paper being submitted to their journal. Such transparency is likely to elicit the support and help of the editor.[36]

The failure to acknowledge the existence of one or more parallel papers is common and becoming more so as pressure mounts on researchers to publish more articles. Authors challenged about this come up with various excuses. The first excuse is that the journals are aimed at different audiences so they are justified in preparing two articles with overlapping contributions. As noted above, this explanation might have had some validity in the pre-digital age, but much less so now. Furthermore, the explicit consent of the editors of both journals involved must be obtained by the author beforehand.

A second excuse that authors come up with is that they failed to disclose the existence of the parallel paper(s) in order to ensure a double-blind review process. This is disingenuous because journals often require both a full and a blinded version of the paper, with the former (seen only by the editor) citing all relevant sources. Even when this is not the case, it is perfectly straightforward to anonymize any identifying references (for example, with a phrase such as 'identifying reference temporarily suppressed') while informing the editor as to the exact references so that they can check the degree of overlap in contribution and hence judge the level of originality of the paper under consideration.

A third and even more specious 'explanation' is that 'My supervisor told me not to include self-citations in my papers'. This is simply incorrect; authors are expected to cite all material that pertains to the claimed originality of the paper in question. If a reference is not appropriate, then a mention in the acknowledgements section regarding the parallel paper(s) is another option. Failing that, the existence of any parallel papers (whatever stage of preparation they are at) should be declared in the covering letter to the journal editor at the time of submission so the editor can form a judgement about the submitted paper's originality.

Finally, some authors, when challenged about their failure to divulge other parallel papers, try to hide behind the letter of the law, saying that they were asked only to confirm that the submitted paper had not been published previously in whole or in part. Such a response suggests premeditated intent to hide from the editor related papers that, if declared, would lead to the editor taking a different view on the submitted paper's originality. The rule here, as elsewhere, is simple: if in any doubt, tell the editor at the start about the circumstances. Editors thus approached tend to be more sympathetic and work with the author to find an acceptable way forward.[37]

UNSCRUPULOUS EDITORS, JIF-BOOSTING RUSES AND COERCIVE CITATIONS

In case this chapter is seen as implying that only authors and relatively junior researchers are guilty of misconduct, let me stress that senior academics,[38] including editors, sometimes overstep the mark.[39] Editors, too, are under pressure from growing competition between journals and the ill-considered use of performance indicators. Journals are increasingly judged by a single metric – the journal impact factor (JIF). When first introduced, this may have been a reasonable indicator of journal standing, although much less so for social sciences where the two-year citation window is far too short. However, over recent years, this indicator has been subject to a growing range of game-playing activities, some perhaps just within the rules, others certainly not. At the more 'innocent' end of the spectrum is the publication of various forms of non-research articles (for example, editorials and discussion papers) which, because of the idiosyncratic way in which JIF is calculated, can add to a journal's citation total without counting in the denominator of the equation used to calculate the average number of citations per paper on which the JIF figure is based. More egregious is the publication of apparently helpful editorials advising prospective authors what type of papers the journal accepts, which then go on to list all articles published over the previous two years (that is, the period used to calculate the JIF). One editorial of this type can single-handedly raise a journal's JIF by 50 per cent or more.[40]

An ingenious ruse employed by some journals (often high-ranking, at least in terms of JIF) is to make numerous articles available online but to delay publishing them for one or two years, or even longer. During that wait, online papers accrue citations for the journal while not counting in the denominator of the JIF calculation. Thus, if the number of papers waiting in the online queue is similar to the number of articles published every two years, the number of papers earning citations can double without affecting the denominator and hence potentially double a journal's JIF.[41] Then, when a paper that has waited in the online queue is finally published in a journal issue, it gets a further two years to contribute to that journal's JIF (that is, a form of double-dipping). However, that is only the first of several benefits for the journal's JIF. A second benefit derives because, by that stage, papers that have already existed in online form for one or two years are likely to be accruing citations at a far faster rate (perhaps up to double) than in their first two years, further inflating the JIF. The JIF benefits do not stop there. A third benefit can be derived if an astute editor cherry-picks from among the online papers those now earning the most citations and ensures these are published next,[42] while uncited papers are left to continue languishing in the online queue, thereby preventing them from diluting the JIF. All very ingenious! Also, since no rules have apparently been broken, this is unlikely to be viewed as research misconduct. However, this type of disingenuous manipulation of the JIF figure by editors would surely be seen by most as questionable behaviour,[43] not least by the hundreds of frustrated authors of papers held in the online queue for a couple of years who run the risk of their papers being scooped (Martin 2016).

Another troubling aspect of JIF-related behaviour is the pressure imposed by editors on authors to cite more articles published in the journal to which a paper has been submitted. There are concerns that some journals will no longer consider papers that contain fewer than a given number of citations to articles in that journal. My own view as editor of a leading journal is that this is inappropriate. Work on a particular topic is inevitably published in a range of related journals, and no single journal can pretend that it has a monopoly position with regard to previous relevant research. However, editors can reasonably expect authors to relate their paper to literature that the journal's readers are familiar with, some of which may have been published in the journal but much of which will almost certainly have been published in similar journals.

Where editors do understandably get irritated is when a paper has been rejected by another journal, and then submitted to their journal without the authors having made any effort to reorient the topic to the interests of readers of that new journal. (This is often apparent from an unnaturally high percentage of references to one particular journal.) Failure to do even the most basic work in reorienting the paper before resubmission to the second journal is likely to irritate the receiving editor and increase the risk of desk rejection.

The most insidious form of misconduct by editors involves coercive citation. At a particular point in the editorial process, the journal editor asks (or advises) the author to include more citations from the journal. Often this occurs towards the end of the process, with a message to the effect that the paper is close to being accepted, subject to the author adding some (unspecified) references to articles published in the journal over the past two years. This emphasis on recent articles is a clue to the game being played, namely, trying to inflate the journal's JIF. That this often occurs towards the end of the editing process is deliberate, since authors are then at their most vulnerable to such pressure. It constitutes a blatant abuse of power by editors, particularly over junior researchers (who are more likely to accede).

The phenomenon of coercive citation was exposed in a survey of several thousand social scientists conducted by Wilhite and Fong (2012). They showed that this misconduct was not confined to lesser journals (as one might have expected); top journals, leading publishers and the most eminent professional associations were all involved.[44] My advice to authors confronted with such editorial pressure is simple: stand firm and resist. If the editor repeats the threat, indicate that you intend to take the matter up with members of the advisory board for the journal or the publisher, or with the international and widely respected Committee for Publication Ethics (COPE).

CONCLUSIONS

This chapter has considered not only outright misconduct but also various forms of inappropriate or questionable conduct. All of these seem to be on the increase, not least because of ever more pervasive pressures associated with evaluation and performance indicators. You, as an individual researcher, will certainly be subject to those pressures, and may even on occasion be tempted to cut corners. However, you should bear in mind that reputation is all important to your future and your career prospects. Once damaged, that reputation can never be fully regained.[45] Moreover, your collaborators may also suffer collateral damage to their reputations (Hussinger and Pellens 2019), as may your institution (Tahir 2008).

For research misconduct, the rules on data fabrication or falsification and on plagiarism are clear and universally agreed. They are set out by professional associations such as the Academy of Management (summarized in Schminke 2009) and by journals and publishers. In addition, further guidance on the rules can be obtained from Armstrong and Green (2017) and from COPE's website.[46]

The rules are often less clear with regard to inappropriate research behaviour, while for questionable research practices there may be no explicit rules. However, this should not be interpreted to mean 'All that is not forbidden is allowed'. There are a number of simple guidelines or questions you should address when deciding whether a particular research practice is acceptable or not. These include:

1. If this were a piece of work by one of my students, would it meet the university rules (for example, with regard to plagiarism)?
2. Is there something in (or about) this paper which, if the full facts became known to my colleagues, would result in me being embarrassed?
3. Would I object if the journal editor revealed to the wider research community exactly what I had done in this study or paper, and named me as the author?

If the answer to any of these is 'yes' or even 'perhaps', that should give pause for thought. If in doubt about something, raise it with the editor[47] for advice on how best to proceed. Honesty and transparency will generally bring sympathy and help with how best to overcome the potential problem. Failure to disclose, in contrast, runs the risk of being construed as a deliberate premeditated attempt to deceive.

Let me end with a plea. With the growing prevalence of research misconduct or inappropriate behaviour, the problem cannot be left to editors alone to sort out. If you spot clear evidence of misconduct or of inappropriate or questionable behaviour (whether by a colleague or the author of a paper you are reviewing, or by an editor or whoever), report it to the appropriate authority. Do not 'cross to the other side of the road', leaving the problem to someone else to deal with. This merely makes the situation worse for everyone, resulting over time in a 'tragedy of the commons' (Martin 2009, p. 66; see also Hardin 1968). In some respects, unethical behaviour is contagious in that misconduct by some can negatively affect the behaviour of others (Gino et al. 2009; Tourish and Craig 2018). Conversely, in a community where it is widely known that not only do most practitioners abide by the rules, but they also cooperate in seeing the rules are adhered to and enforced, fewer will be tempted to transgress. As Anderson et al. (2013, p. 253) conclude, 'There is simply no better protection for the integrity of science than the careful and watchful commitment of researchers as they go about their everyday work ... This is the responsibility of all researchers as the guardians of research integrity'.

NOTES

* This is a revised and updated version of the chapter published in 2016 in the first edition of this book. The author acknowledges the support of SPRU and the University of Sussex Business School, and help from *Research Policy* editors who, together with numerous referees, have played a major role in helping to investigate the cases drawn upon here. He is also grateful to the editors of this volume for very helpful comments on an earlier draft. However, responsibility for the views expressed here and for any remaining errors lies with the author alone.
1. An author has an h-index of n if he or she has n highly cited publications, each of which has earned at least n citations (but the nth + 1 most highly cited publication has earned fewer than n + 1 citations) – see Hirsch (2005).
2. This phenomenon is certainly not confined to academia. In the business world, for example, performance-related pay and large bonuses may encourage top managers to work harder but 'it also incentivizes top managers to cheat or cut corners' (Shi et al. 2016, p. 1354).
3. P-hacking 'occurs when researchers try out several statistical analyses and/or data eligibility specifications and then selectively report those that produce significant results' (Head et al. 2015, p. 1). Using text-mining, Head et al. demonstrate that 'p-hacking is widespread throughout science' (Head et al. 2015, p. 1).
4. Roig (2015) provides a very useful guide to how to avoid plagiarism, self-plagiarism and other questionable research practices. Other helpful resources can be found at http://ori.hhs.gov/research-misconduct-0 (accessed 22 February 2019).
5. For a systematic review and meta-analysis of the extent of research misconduct, see Fanelli (2009). More recent reviews can be found in Macfarlane et al. (2014), Biagioli et al. (2019), and Hall and Martin (2019).
6. For a recent example in management studies, see Harley et al. (2014). Further examples are cited in Martin (2013).
7. See http://grants.nih.gov/grants/research_integrity/research_misconduct.htm (accessed 22 February 2019). Anderson et al. (2013) provide an extensive review of the literature on research misconduct, including: definitions, prominent cases, evidence on prevalence, factors encouraging misconduct, and how best to deal with it.
8. See https://apa.org/research/responsible/misconduct/index.aspx (accessed 22 February 2019).
9. See http://grants.nih.gov/grants/research_integrity/research_misconduct.htm (accessed 22 February 2019).
10. For an account of the misconduct by the individual himself, see Stapel (2014).
11. See http://grants.nih.gov/grants/research_integrity/research_misconduct.htm (accessed 22 February 2019).
12. Tim van der Zee, 'The Wansink dossier: an overview', accessed 22 February 2019 at http://www.timvanderzee.com/the-wansink-dossier-an-overview/.
13. A similar finding was obtained by Masicampo and Lalande (2012) in an analysis of three top psychology journals, and by Ridley et al. (2007, p. 1082) who analysed three leading biology journals and found 'a remarkable excess of probability values being cited on, or just below, each threshold relative to the smoothed theoretical distributions'.
14. See also the discussion in Sterba (2006, p. 315) about 'unethical data manipulations aimed at clipping and preening a sample to move a finding of $p = .06$ ... into the golden area of $p < .05$'.
15. See http://grants.nih.gov/grants/research_integrity/research_misconduct.htm (accessed 22 February 2019).

16. Useful tutorials can be found at https://www.indiana.edu/~istd/ (accessed 22 February 2019), while other examples are given at the end of Roig (2015).
17. Sometimes termed 'dubious research practices', these include:

    taking undeserved credit for intellectual contributions or discoveries; either accepting or awarding 'honorary' or 'gift' authorship of publications; using university equipment, funds, or facilities for private benefit; duplicate publication of data; piecemeal publishing (i.e., deliberately splitting research results into the 'smallest publishable units' to increase the number of one's publications); and keeping sloppy or incomplete research records. (Bedeian et al. 2010, p. 717)

18. See Resnik et al. (2015) for an analysis of the variations in misconduct definitions and policies.
19. Hall and Martin (2019) expand and develop this distinction between misconduct, inappropriate conduct and questionable conduct as part of a formal taxonomy of research misconduct.
20. This section draws extensively on Martin (2013).
21. The practice is again quite widespread, with 86 per cent of US business school faculty reporting 'knowledge of faculty who have "published the same data or results in two or more publications"' (Bedeian et al. 2010, p. 719).
22. An analysis of the extent and causes of self-plagiarism can be found in Horbach and Halffman (2019).
23. See http://www.handelsblatt.com/politik/konjunktur/oekonomie/nachrichten/ulrich-licht enthaler-der-junge-der-alles-richtig-macht/3200312.html (accessed 22 February 2019).
24. Besides self-plagiarism, these offences included (deliberate) omitted variable bias and misreporting the statistical significance of several findings (that is, exaggerated p-values) (see Lichtenthaler 2012).
25. See http://retractionwatch.com/2014/10/10/after-16-retractions-management-professor-licht enthaler-resigns-post/ (accessed 22 February 2019).
26. This is reflected in the bibliography of this chapter, which includes references in journals far from the author's own field.
27. See, for example, http://www.nature.com/authors/policies/duplicate.html (accessed 22 February 2019).
28. National Bureau of Economic Research (NBER) papers often fall into this category; see https://ideas.repec.org/top/top.series.hindex10.html (accessed 22 February 2019).
29. Another questionable research practice relating to conference papers is 'double-dipping', that is, presenting the same paper at another conference when that latter conference explicitly forbids this, a rule that is apparently more honoured in the breach than in the observance (Lewellyn et al. 2017).
30. Hence, if an author is offered the opportunity for a relatively full version of their paper to be published in the conference proceedings, the most sensible response is normally to decline, since there is a considerable potential cost and little potential gain (the status of such conference publications is generally low).
31. This is one situation where the well-known saying 'It's easier to ask forgiveness than it is to get permission' (generally attributed to Rear Admiral Grace Hopper) is reversed. (I am grateful to one of the editors for this observation.)
32. A study of publication bias in strategic management research can be found in Harrison et al. (2017, p. 400), who conclude that 'publication bias affects many, but not all, topics in strategic management research'.
33. See http://aom.org/uploadedFiles/About_AOM/Governance/AOM_Code_of_Ethics.pdf (accessed 22 February 2019). Note that this wording does not mean that an 'author' has to have contributed to the actual writing of the text (he or she may lack the skills or experience required for this), but merely that they should have contributed substantially to the research on which the eventual publication is based.
34. Other examples can be found in Chen (2011), Schminke (2009) and Schminke and Ambrose (2011). (The last of these provides an introduction to a Special Editors Forum in *Management and Organization Review*, in which several of the papers are relevant here.)

In an ironic twist, it was later found that Schminke and Ambrose (2011) contained significant elements of self-plagiarism of Schminke (2009), so it was retracted (see Tsui et al. 2014).

35. Some journals now check further by asking whether other papers have been published from the same dataset. This may elicit information about other related papers that have already been published, but not necessarily about related papers that have been submitted to other journals or those still at an earlier, 'working paper' stage.

36. The standard required for a PhD may be lower than that required for publication in a (leading) journal. Hence, a PhD thesis based on papers may be passed and then become publicly available (that is, a 'publication') before a decision has been reached by a journal concerned as to whether one of the component papers should be published. Here, the exemption mentioned earlier (about not counting a PhD thesis as a 'prior publication') should apply; that is, the existence of a paper (perhaps in an earlier, less developed form) as a PhD chapter should not count in determining the level of originality of the version of the paper being considered by the journal. (I am grateful to one of the editors of this book for making this clarification.)

37. A more detailed analysis of how to deal with the issue of multiple papers from the same dataset can be found in Kirkman and Chen (2011). They, too, conclude with the advice that authors should 'always err on the side of transparency by alerting the editor to the existence of each paper and by proactively sharing their own uniqueness analysis to assist the editor in making an informed decision about the papers' (Kirkman and Chen 2011, pp. 444–5).

38. Another situation in which senior researchers may abuse their position is as referees of research proposals (see, for example, Fong and Wilhite 2017).

39. Elsewhere, I noted that:

    many cases of misconduct are perpetrated by quite senior researchers, often full professors. Their misdeeds tend to involve less obvious encroachments across the boundary between acceptable and unacceptable behaviour. Indeed, often they seem to have convinced themselves that they have not been guilty of any such encroachment – that the boundary is simply in a different location than academic convention would suggest. Moreover, being more experienced, they may be more adept in attempting to cover their tracks. (Martin 2013, p. 1011)

    Moreover, some senior researchers, when confronted with evidence of misconduct, have an unsavoury habit of blaming this on a junior colleague, ignoring that authorship brings with it full responsibility for all aspects of the paper (Schminke 2009, p. 588).

40. For example, for a journal with an impact factor of 2.0, it would be raised to 3.0 by one editorial of this type.

41. For an example of a journal with an unusually large backlog (going back two years), see http://jom.sagepub.com/content/early/recent (accessed on 22 February 2019). Several other top management journals have a backlog of a year or more.

42. Thus, one of the most highly cited recent articles in the case of the journal mentioned in the previous footnote was published online in April 2010 but only appeared in print nearly three years later in February 2013.

43. The acid test is whether the editors involved would feel uncomfortable if they were publicly named. (The interested reader might like to check which high-ranking management journals currently have an online 'queue' of a year or more and hence are benefiting from this JIF-boosting stratagem.)

44. The Supplementary Online Material linked to Wilhite and Fong (2012) names the journals found guilty of this practice; see table S12 at http://www.sciencemag.org/content/335/6068/542/suppl/DC1 (accessed 22 February 2019).

45. For an analysis of the effects of misconduct on scientists' reputations and careers, see Azoulay et al. (2017).

46. See http://publicationethics.org/files/International percent20standards_authors_for percent 20website_11_Nov_2011.pdf (accessed 22 February 2019).

47. Another option when in doubt is to discuss the situation or dilemma with your mentor, peers or respected senior colleagues in order to obtain an outside and more objective perspective.

REFERENCES

Abbott, A. (2007), 'Academic accused of living on borrowed lines', *Nature*, **448** (7154), 632–3.

Anderson, M.S., M.A. Shaw, N.H. Steneck, E. Konkle and T. Kamata (2013), 'Research integrity and misconduct in the academic profession', in M.B. Paulsen (ed.), *Higher Education: Handbook of Theory and Research*, Dordrecht: Springer, pp. 217–61.

Anon. (2015), 'The case of the hypothesis that never was: uncovering the deceptive use of post hoc hypotheses', *Journal of Management Inquiry*, **24** (2), 214–16.

Armstrong, J.S. and K.C. Green (2017), 'Guidelines for science: evidence and checklists', *Scholarly Commons*, 24 January (downloaded from http://repository.upenn.edu/marketing_papers/181 on 22 February 2019).

Autor, D.H. (2011), 'Letter to Professor Bruno Frey', *Journal of Economic Perspectives*, **25** (3), 239–40.

Azoulay, P., A. Bonatti and J.L. Krieger (2017), 'The career effects of scandal: evidence from scientific retractions', *Research Policy*, **46** (9), 1552–69.

Baker, M. (2016), 'Is there a reproducibility crisis?', *Nature*, **533** (7604), 452–54.

Bakker, M. and J.M. Wicherts (2011), 'The (mis)reporting of statistical results in psychology journals', *Behavior Research*, **43** (3), 666–78.

Banks, G.C., E.H. O'Boyle, J.M. Pollack, C.D. White, J.H. Batchelor, C.E. Whelpley et al. (2016), 'Questions about questionable research practices in the field of management: a guest commentary', *Journal of Management*, **42** (1), 5–20.

Basu, S. and H.-U. Park (2014), 'Publication bias in recent empirical accounting research', Fox School of Business Research Paper No. 14-027, Temple University, Philadelphia, PA, accessed 22 February 2019 at http://papers.ssrn.com/sol3/papers.cfm?abstract_id=2379889.

Bedeian, A.G. (2004), 'Peer review and the social construction of knowledge in the management discipline', *Academy of Management Learning and Education*, **3** (2), 198–216.

Bedeian, A.G., S.G. Taylor and A.N. Miller (2010), 'Management science on the credibility bubble: cardinal sins and various misdemeanours', *Academy of Management Learning and Education*, **9** (4), 715–25.

Bergh, D.B., B.M Sharp, H. Aguinis and M. Li (2017), 'Is there a credibility crisis in strategic management research? Evidence on the reproducibility of study findings', *Strategic Organization*, **15** (3), 423–36.

Bhattacharjee, Y. (2013), 'The mind of a con man', *New York Times*, 26 April, accessed 22 February 2019 at https://www.nytimes.com/2013/04/28/magazine/diederik-stapels-audacious-academic-fraud.html.

Biagioli, M., M. Kenney, B.R. Martin and J.P. Walsh (2019), 'Academic misconduct, misrepresentation and gaming: a reassessment', *Research Policy*, **48** (240), 401–13.

Butler, N., H. Delaney and S. Spoelstra (2017), 'The gray zone: questionable research practices in the business school', *Academy of Management Learning & Education*, **16** (1), 94–109.

Camerer, C.F., A. Dreber, E. Forsell, T.H. Ho, J. Huber, M. Johannesson et al. (2016), 'Evaluating replicability of laboratory experiments in economics', *Science*, **351** (6280), 1433–6.

Chen, X.-P. (2011), 'Author ethical dilemmas in the research publication process', *Management and Organization Review*, **7** (3), 423–32.

Edwards, M.A. and S. Roy (2017), 'Academic research in the 21st century: maintaining scientific integrity in a climate of perverse incentives and hyper-competition', *Environmental Engineering Science*, **34** (1), 51–61.

Fanelli, D. (2009), 'How many scientists fabricate and falsify research? A systematic review and meta-analysis of survey data', *PLOS One*, **4** (5), e5738.

Fong, E.A. and A.W. Wilhite (2017), 'Authorship and citation manipulation in academic research', *PLOS One*, **12** (12), e0187394.

Freeman, R., E. Weinstein, E. Marincola, J. Rosenbaum and F. Solomon (2001), 'Competition and careers in biosciences', *Science*, **294** (5550), 2293–4.

Gino, F., S. Ayal and D. Ariely (2009), 'Contagion and differentiation in unethical behaviour: the effect of one bad apple on the barrel', *Psychological Science*, **20** (3), 393–8.

Hall, J. and B.R. Martin (2019), 'Towards a taxonomy of research misconduct: the case of business school research', *Research Policy*, **48** (2), 414–27.

Hardin, G., (1968), 'The tragedy of the commons', *Science*, **162** (3859), 1243–8.

Harley, B., D. Faems and A. Corbett (2014), 'A few bad apples or the tip of an iceberg? Academic misconduct in publishing', *Journal of Management Studies*, **51** (8), 1361–3.

Harrison, J.S., G.C. Banks, J.M. Pollack, E.H. O'Boyle and J. Short (2017), 'Publication bias in strategic management research', *Journal of Management*, **43** (2), 400–425.

Head, M.L., L. Holman, R. Lanfear, A.T. Kahn and M.D. Jennions (2015), 'The extent and consequences of p-hacking in science', *PLOS Biology*, **13** (3), e1002106.

Hirsch, J.E. (2005), 'An index to quantify an individual's scientific research output', *Proceedings of the National Academy of Sciences*, **102** (46), 16569–72.

Hollenbeck, J.R. and P.M. Wright (2017), 'Harking, sharking, and tharking: making the case for post hoc analysis of scientific data', *Journal of Management Inquiry*, **43** (1), 5–18.

Honig, B. and A. Bedi (2012), 'The fox in the hen house: a critical examination of plagiarism among members of the Academy of Management', *Academy of Management Learning and Education*, **11** (1), 101–23.

Horbach, S.P.J.M. and W. Halffman (2019), 'The extent and causes of academic text recycling or "self-plagiarism"', *Research Policy*, **48** (2), 492–502.

Hussinger, K. and M. Pellens (2019), 'Guilt by association: how scientific misconduct harms prior collaborators', *Research Policy*, **48** (6), 516–30.

Ioannidis, J.P.A. (2005), 'Why most discovered true associations are inflated', *Epidemiology*, **19** (5), 640–48.
John, K.J., G. Loewenstein and D. Prelec (2012), 'Measuring the prevalence of questionable research practices with incentives for truth telling', *Psychological Science*, **23** (5), 524–32.
Karabag, S.F. and C. Berggren (2016), 'Misconduct, marginality and editorial practices in management, business and economics journals', *PLOS One*, **11** (7), e0159492.
Kerr, N.L. (1998), 'HARKing: hypothesizing after the results are known', *Personality and Social Psychology Review*, **2** (3), 196–217.
Kirkman, B.L. and G. Chen (2011), 'Maximizing your data or data slicing? Recommendations for managing multiple submissions from the same dataset', *Management and Organization Review*, **7** (3), 433–46.
Leung, K. (2011), 'Presenting post hoc hypotheses as a priori: ethical and theoretical issues', *Management and Organization Review*, **7** (3), 471–9.
Lewellyn, K.B., W.Q. Judge and A. Smith (2017), 'Exploring the questionable academic practice of conference paper double dipping', *Academy of Management Learning & Education*, **16** (2), 217–36.
Lichtenthaler, U. (2012), 'Retraction notice to "The role of corporate technology strategy and patent portfolios in low-, medium- and high-technology firms" [Res. Policy 38 (2009) 559–569] and "Determinants of proactive and reactive technology licensing: A contingency perspective" [Res. Policy 39 (2010) 55–66]', *Research Policy*, **41** (8), 1499.
Macfarlane, B., J. Zhang and A. Pun (2014), 'Academic integrity: a review of the literature', *Studies in Higher Education*, **39** (2), 339–58.
Martin, B.R. (2009), 'Research misconduct – does self-policing work?', in W. Østreng (ed.), *Confluence: Interdisciplinary Communications 2007/2008*, Oslo: Centre for Advanced Study at the Norwegian Academy of Science and Letters, pp. 59–69, accessed 22 February 2019 at http://www.cas.uio.no/Publications/Seminar/Confluence.pdf#page=61.
Martin, B.R. (2012), 'Does peer review work as a self-policing mechanism in preventing misconduct: a case study of a serial plagiarist', in T. Mayer and N. Steneck (eds), *Promoting Research Integrity in a Global Environment*, London: Imperial College Press and Singapore: World Scientific, pp. 97–114.
Martin, B.R. (2013), 'Whither research integrity? Plagiarism, self-plagiarism and coercive citation in an age of research assessment', *Research Policy*, **42** (5), 1005–14.
Martin, B.R. (2016), 'Editors' JIF-boosting stratagems – which are appropriate and which not?', *Research Policy*, **45** (1), 1–7.
Martin, B.R. and other editors of *Research Policy* (2007), 'Keeping plagiarism at bay – a salutary tale', *Research Policy*, **36** (7), 905–11.
Masicampo, E.J. and D.R. Lalande (2012), 'A peculiar prevalence of p values just below .05', *The Quarterly Journal of Experimental Psychology*, **65** (11), 2271–9.
Mumford, M.D., S.T. Murphy, S. Connelly, J.H. Hill, A.L. Antes, R.P. Brown et al. (2007), 'Environmental influences on ethical decision making: climate and environmental predictors of research integrity', *Ethics & Behavior*, **17** (4), 337–66.

Necker, S. (2014), 'Scientific misbehavior in economics', *Research Policy*, **43** (10), 1747–59.
O'Boyle, E.H., G.C. Banks and E. Gonzalez-Mulé (2017), 'The Chrysalis Effect: how ugly initial results metamorphosize into beautiful articles', *Journal of Management*, **43** (2), 376–99.
Resnik, D.B., I.M. Rasmussen and G.E. Kissling (2015), 'An international study of research misconduct policies', *Accountability in Research*, **22** (5), 249–66.
Ridley, J., N. Kolm, R.P. Freckelton and M.J.G. Gage (2007), 'An unexpected influence of widely used significance thresholds on the distribution of reported P-values', *Journal of Evolutionary Biology*, **20** (3), 1082–9.
Roig, M. (2015), 'Avoiding plagiarism, self-plagiarism, and other questionable writing practices: a guide to ethical writing', accessed 22 February 2019 at http://ori.hhs.gov/sites/default/files/plagiarism.pdf.
Ruppert, D. (2006), 'Trimming and Winsorization', in S. Kotz, C.B. Read, N. Balakrishnan, B. Vidakovic and N.L. Johnson (eds), *Encyclopedia of Statistical Sciences*, Hoboken, NJ: Wiley, republished online 2014, accessed 12 August 2019 at https://doi.org/10.1002/9781118445112.stat01887.
Schminke, M. (2009), 'Editor's comments: the better angels of our nature – ethics and integrity in the publishing process', *Academy of Management Review*, **34** (4), 586–91.
Schminke, M. and M.L. Ambrose (2011), 'Ethics and integrity in the publishing process: myths, facts, and a roadmap', *Management and Organization Review*, **7** (3), 397–406; subsequently retracted for self-plagiarism – see Tsui et al. (2014) below.
Shi, W., B. Connelly and G. Sanders (2016), 'Buying bad behavior: tournament incentives and insecurities class action lawsuits', *Strategic Management Journal*, **37** (7), 1354–78.
Simonsohn, U., J.P. Simmons and L.D. Nelson (2015), 'Better p-curves: making p-curve analysis more robust to errors, fraud, and ambitious p-hacking', *Journal of Experimental Psychology: General*, **144**, (6), 1146–52.
Stapel, D. (2014), *Faking Science: A True Story of Academic Fraud*, trans. N.J.L. Brown, accessed 22 February 2019 at https://errorstatistics.files.wordpress.com/2014/12/fakingscience-20141214.pdf.
Sterba, S.K. (2006), 'Misconduct in the analysis and reporting of data: bridging methodological and ethical agendas for change', *Ethics & Behavior*, **16** (4), 305–18.
Tahir, T. (2008), 'Dean dismissed for plagiarism', *The Times Higher*, 6 March 2008, accessed 22 February 2019 at https://www.timeshighereducation.com/news/dean-dismissed-for-plagiarism/400950.article.
Tourish, D. and R. Craig (2018), 'Research misconduct in business and management studies: causes, consequences, and possible remedies', *Journal of Management Inquiry*, online, 5 September, accessed 12 August 2019 at https://doi.org/10.1177/1056492618792621.
Tsui, A.S., A.Y. Lewin, N. Schminke and M. Ambrose (2014), 'Retraction statement for "Ethics and integrity of the publishing process: myths, facts, and a roadmap" by Marshall Schminke and Maureen L. Ambrose', *Management and Organization Review*, **10** (1), 157–62.

Van Noorden, R. (2011), 'The trouble with retractions', *Nature*, **478** (7367), 26–8.
Walsh, J.P., Y.-N. Lee and L. Tang (2019), 'Pathogenic organization in science: division of labour and retractions', *Research Policy*, **48** (2), 444–61.
Wilhite, A.W. and E.A. Fong (2012), 'Coercive citation in academic publishing', *Science*, **335** (6068), 542–3.
Ziman, J. (1978), *Reliable Knowledge: An Exploration of the Grounds for Belief in Science*, Cambridge: Cambridge University Press.

5. Sustaining a publications career*
Mike Wright

INTRODUCTION

We live in a time of turbulence for academic researchers, perhaps especially so for those in management. Politicians question the benefits for business of encouraging management academics to publish in 'obscure US journals' (whether this means obscure European journals are acceptable or beyond the pale is left unsaid). Instead, business school academics are told they should offer more practical help to business. Pressures on internal resources from reductions in public funding and in income generated from executive education undermine budgets to support research. Sharply increased tuition fees for students shift the emphasis to delivering high-quality teaching. Also, submissions to journals have been rising significantly in recent years as a result of a worldwide surge of research activity. With space in most journals remaining unchanged, acceptance rates have been falling sharply and now stand at well below 10 percent, and closer to 5 percent for major management journals. Thresholds to get published have therefore increased, with reviewers and editors becoming more demanding (Clark et al. 2006, 2013). Publication in quality journals has, however, long been recognized to be highly skewed (for example, Podsakoff et al. 2008); few scholars continue to publish in quality journals over a long period.

These trends may mean that publication careers become even more highly skewed. Even though scholars may have published successfully already, they face demands for new skills and need both to be able to identify new opportunities and exploit them more efficiently if they are to sustain a publication career. Accordingly, this chapter sets out to explore the challenges in sustaining a publications career in management and how these challenges may be met.

The chapter unfolds as follows. In the following section I set out the pressure points concerning when scholars need to assess how they can sustain their publications. I then discuss why it is therefore important to develop a publications strategy that is maintained over a longer period. In the fourth section I analyze what scholars can do to develop a sustainable publications strategy by outlining the heterogeneity of publication outlets. The fifth section then addresses how scholars can realize such a strategy by adopting various routes including developing strategic entrepreneurial actions that involve exploring and subsequently exploiting new opportunities for research and accessing the human and social resources required. Throughout the chapter I draw on my career to illustrate one approach to sustaining publications, notably based on experience with the Centre for Management Buyout Research (CMBOR), which was formally created in 1986, although the research opportunity had initially been identified in 1981 as management buyouts were seen as a new entrepreneurial phenomenon (Wright and Coyne 1985). This experience, which covers a publication record of over 30 years, is summarized in Table 5.1. Finally, the chapter presents some conclusions.

WHEN?

There are a number of pressure points where scholars need to (re)assess how they are going to sustain a publications career.

After PhD

As doctoral students we invest considerable effort in a process of research training that involves the development of expertise in a particular domain, theoretical area and methodological tools. This underpins a stream of publications leading up to and directly from the PhD. It may also prompt a number of follow-on publications that help establish an initial reputation. Indeed, evidence indicates that those who publish prior to receiving their doctorate (Park and Gordon 1996) are more likely to continue publishing for up to 10 years afterward.

However, at some point the momentum from this initial topic area will probably begin to run out of steam. Having addressed major paradigm-changing questions, further publications will probably involve more incremental contributions that themselves become harder to publish in good journals as it becomes more challenging to convince reviewers and editors that there is sufficient novelty in the original topic to warrant publication in a good journal. Further, it becomes increasingly difficult to exploit new angles from the dataset gathered during doctoral studies. This dataset, too, is likely to become outdated and at the very least to require more recent observations to be added. New challenges are therefore introduced regarding how or whether a dataset can be extended or whether a new dataset needs to be created.

Table 5.1 An illustration of sustaining publication output

Year/ Period	Topic/Research questions	Theories	Team	Publications	Other spin-off and complementary publications
1981–1985	Review: general descriptive analysis Impact: employment and employee relations		Coyne Coyne, Lockley	Book, practitioner journals IRJ, RS	Management control, industrial relations, state enterprise efficiency auditing
1986–1989	Vendor source: divestment, trading relationships, financial structuring Vendor source: privatization U.K. Review: general impact	Transaction costs, agency theory, resource dependency theory Agency	Thompson, Robbie, Chiplin Mulley, Chiplin, Robbie, Thompson Coyne, Robbie, Thompson	JMS, ABR, JES, BER, PE PMM, FS, APCE LRP, Omega, BAR, JACF	Divestment, marketing financial services and deregulation, regulation and efficiency of state enterprises
1990–1995	Private equity firms: market development Variety (MBOs, MBIs) Vendor source: Bankruptcy Vendor source: privatization U.K., CEE Impact: longevity Impact: employee relations Impact: performance	Agency Agency theory Life-cycle	Thompson, Robbie Robbie Robbie, Ennew Thompson, Robbie, Filatotchev, Buck, Petrin Thompson, Robbie, Romanet, Bruining, Herst Chiplin, Robbie Thompson, Robbie, Ennew	JBV, RS Omega, JMS Omega FAM, CES, EAWM, FS, SS, PAD, IBR, IJTE, JBE, OXRP SMJ, JBFA, ETP, SIJ IRJ BSR, SJPE, ISBJ, EJ	Trade credit, public sector auditing, privatization in general, corporate governance
1996–2000	Vendor source: privatization U.K., CEE Impact: longevity/failure Impact: performance Financial aspects Review articles	Agency theory, stakeholder agency theory, entrepreneurial cognition Agency Agency Contracting	Hoskisson, Filatotchev, Buck, Busenitz, Dial, Grosfeld, Wieser, Wilson, Pendleton Wilson, Robbie, Ennew Wilson, Robbie Citron, Robbie Robbie, Chiplin, Albrighton	AMR, CMR, JDS, JCE, AMP, JWB, EoT, JMS, LGS, APCE, BJIR, EoP, MDE, BSR, JESBF ABR, CGIR JBFA, BH	Corporate governance, VCs (monitoring, syndication, etc.), serial entrepreneurs, divestment and corporate refocusing, employee ownership, emerging economy strategies

59

Year/ Period	Topic/Research questions	Theories	Team	Publications	Other spin-off and complementary publications
2001–2005	Private equity firms: market development and firm behavior Vendor source: privatizations Vendor source: family firms Vendor source: stock market impact Impact: employee relations Impact: MBO firm performance Impact: longevity/failure Review article	Agency theory, entrepreneurial cognition Stewardship Agency Agency	Kitamura, Hoskisson, Bruining, Bonnet, Toms Hoskisson, Busenitz, Filatotchev, Buck, Dyomina Westhead, Howarth Weir Bacon, Dyomina, Bruining, Boselie Siegel, Harris Jelic, Saadouni, Citron, Robbie Filatotchev, Buck	JPE, LRP, MAR, BH AME, VC, JIBS JBV JBFA, AFE BJIR, IJHRM RES JBFA, EFM APCE	Serial entrepreneurs, VCs (syndication, internationalization), divestment and corporate restructuring, academic spin-offs and technology transfer, corporate governance, internationalization, emerging economies, RBV, entrepreneurial teams, journal reviewing and editing
2006–2010	Private equity firms: market development, behavior, partner select Vendor source: family firms Vendor source: stock market firms Impact: employee relations Impact: employment Impact: MBO firm performance Impact: longevity/failure Review articles	Agency, RBV, SE	Renneboog, Scholes, Simon, Meuleman, Manigart, Lockett, Frobisher, Jackson Scholes, Westhead, Bruining, Burrows Renneboog, Weir, Laing, Burrows Bacon, Meuleman, Wood, Bruining, Boselie, Dyomina Amess, Girma Amess, Meuleman, Scholes, Nikoskelainen Citron Siegel, Cumming, Gilligan, Amess, Wood, Weir, Girma	JACF, JMS, JBFA SBE JCF, CGIR, EFM, ABR HR, JIR IJEB JCF, ETP ABR JCF, VC, IJMR, BH, CGIR	Academic spin-offs and technology transfer, VCs, serial entrepreneurs, internationalization, IPOs, returnee entrepreneurs, HRM, RBV, journal editing and publishing, corporate entrepreneurship

2011–	Private equity firm behavior/ internationalization/ negotiation	IT Agency Ethics	Meuleman, Kellermanns	JBV, in progress EFM JBE	Academic spin-offs and technology transfer, VCs, serial entrepreneurs,
	Vendor source: secondary buyouts		Jelic Scholes, Li Scholes, Westhead, Chua, Chrisman, Lloyd	ISBJ, JFBS CGIR, JMG	internationalization and international entrepreneurship, IPOs,
	Vendor source: privatization		Sudarsanam, Huang, Weir Bacon, Meuleman	AMP, IR JCF, JBF, SBE,	returnee entrepreneurs, HRM, RBV, journal editing
	Vendor source: family firms		Wilson, Nikoskelainen, Maula, Bruining, Verwaal, Alperovych	EJOR	and publishing, corporate entrepreneurship,
	Vendor source: stock market firms		Jelic	MDE SBE	management teams, future of entrepreneurship
	Impact: employee relations		Amess, Girma	CGIR, JCF, CC	research, family firms, emerging economies,
	Impact: MBO firm performance		Siegel, Shawky, Wood		corporate governance, entrepreneurial growth,
	Impact: longevity Impact: employment Review articles				directors of entrepreneurial firms Social capital, microfinance

Notes:

Key to Journals: ABR = Accounting and Business Research; AME = Academy of Management Executive; AMR = Academy of Management Review; AFE = Applied Financial Economics; AMP = Academy of Management Executive/Perspectives; APCE = Annals of Public and Cooperative Economics; BAR = British Accounting Review; BER = Bulletin of Economic Research; BH = Business History; BJIR = British Journal of Industrial Relations; BSR = Business Strategy Review; CC= Competition and Change; CES = Comparative Economic Studies; CGIR = Corporate Governance – International Review; CMR = California Management Review; EAWM = Economic Analysis and Workers Management; EFM = European Financial Management; EJ = Economic Journal; ETP = Entrepreneurship Theory and Practice; EJOR = European Journal of Operations Research; EoP = Economics of Planning; EoT = Economics of Transition; FAM = Financial Accountability and Management; FS = Fiscal Studies; HR = Human Relations; IBR = International Business Review; IJEB = International Journal of Economics and Business; IJHRM = International Journal of Human Resource Management; IJMR = International Journal of Management Reviews; IJTE = International Journal of Transport Economics; IR = Industrial Relations; IRJ = Industrial Relations Journal; ISBJ = International Small Business Journal; JACF = Journal of Applied Corporate Finance; JBE = Journal of Business Ethics; JBF = Journal of Banking and Finance; JBFA = Journal of Business Finance and Accounting; JBV = Journal of Business Venturing; JCE = Journal of Comparative Economics; JCF = Journal of Corporate Finance; JDS = Journal of Development Studies; JES = Journal of Economic Studies; JESBF = Journal of Entrepreneurship and Small Business Finance; JFBS = Journal of Family Business Strategy; JIBS = Journal of International Business Studies; JIR = Journal of Industrial Relations; JMG = Journal of Management and Governance; JMS = Journal of Management Studies; JPE = Journal of Private Equity; JWB = Journal of World Business; LGS = Local Government Studies; LRP = Long Range Planning; MAR = Management Accounting Research; MDE = Managerial and Decision Economics; OXRP = Oxford Review of Economic Policy; PAD = Public Administration and Development; PE = Piccola Empresa; PMM = Public Money and Management; RS = Regional Studies; RES = Review of Economics and Statistics; SBE = Small Business Economics; SIJ = Services Industries Journal; SJPE = Scottish Journal of Political Economy; SMJ = Strategic Management Journal; SS = Soviet Studies (Europe-Asia Studies); VC = Venture Capital.

Other abbreviations: CEE = Central and Eastern Europe; HRM = human resource management; IPOs = initial public offerings; MBI = management buyin; MBO = management buyout; RBV = resource based view; SE = strategic entrepreneurship; VCs = venture capitalists.

After Tenure and Promotion

The huge effort required to achieve tenure may leave many scholars with little motivation or energy to maintain a publishing career. Studies tend to show a decline in research productivity post-tenure, although there are variations in the timing and extent of the decline. Harrison (2006) notes that those whose publications are in print when they get tenure are more likely to continue to publish afterwards. Estes and Polnick (2012) notably suggest that reductions in productivity post-tenure are due to reduced motivation, as faculty do not value the outcomes from sustaining higher levels of productivity. During this period in their careers, some faculty may transition into a more mentoring role wherein they guide doctoral students and junior colleagues. However, in countries that have introduced national research assessment frameworks, such as the UK where tenure is absent, there is pressure and incentives to continue to publish at least four good papers every five years or so.

Seeking subsequent promotion after tenure also means there is a need to continue to publish quality research. This may not just mean publishing in top journals, as many scholars publish articles in top journals that have few citations. Accordingly, there is a need to publish in a way to carve out a reputation as a leading scholar in a particular area in order to address the question by promotion committees, 'What is X known for?'

After Career Breaks

Career breaks that affect publishing can take several forms. Major managerial, editorial or other service jobs can place severe time constraints on your ability to publish. Maternity leave likely has a major impact for publishing careers of women faculty. Yet, at a time when academics are expected to make an impact along multiple dimensions, it becomes increasingly difficult to put a stop to a publishing career. The national research assessment and evaluation exercises may still require those performing significant managerial roles to demonstrate a quality publications return (see www.ref.ac.uk, accessed 12 August 2019), although there is some allowance for maternity leave. Many managerial roles, such as head of department, may be for only a limited period of time, after which there is a need to return to normal scholarly activities. While traditionally academics in the hard sciences and engineering may have built large teams of researchers, this is typically less so in the social sciences and in management in particular. Therefore, scholars face major challenges associated with re-entering the publishing process, especially as the literature, the key research questions as well as methods will have moved on.

WHY?

The reasons to maintain a strong publications record are influenced by individual- and environmental-level factors. Apart from personal interest and motivation, my view was that continuing to publish despite the demands of reviewers and editors was a great way to maintain my sanity. Maybe dealing with referees is soul-destroying, but for me the opportunity cost seemed to be a life devoted to interminable faculty meetings and increasingly mindless bureaucracy.

There may be good reasons to maintain a publishing career even after securing tenure or promotion. Annual performance reviews usually take account of publications as one element in setting salary. In addition to an absence of salary enhancement, a lack of publications may lead to compensatory increases in teaching, administration and service loads. Therefore, individuals need to make choices about how they see their career developing.

Environmental level factors can have a huge influence on the need to sustain a publications career. Schools frequently change deans and deans come in with new aims and strategies. On the one hand, having sustained a publications record can provide for mobility if a change of direction by the new dean means that there ceases to be a good fit. On the other hand, a sustained publications record can mean a scholar is well placed if the new dean's intention is to ramp up the research rating in an otherwise under-performing school. Continuing a publications record as a dean or head of department may bring a strong demonstration of leadership in such circumstances.

National research assessment exercises, with their requirements to continue to produce at a specified volume and quality of output, say, every five to seven years, create demands to continue to publish. Some of these exercises are increasingly demanding different forms of output than publication in traditional academic journals. In particular, policymakers are looking for academic research to have a wider impact on society, such as through changing policy and firm behavior. The result of such exercises may be seen by some as pernicious, as they can produce a focus on journal publications to the exclusion of other forms of scholarly output and endeavor. They have typically created a transfer market in academics with publications records that will be judged of high quality by review panels. This can serve to break through rigid salary structures in some contexts that do not fairly reflect performance. However, national evaluation exercises can contain idiosyncrasies and perverse incentives that have implications for sustaining a publications career. For example, if a national assessment exercise constrains authors in the same department from reporting the same piece of co-authored work, it means that there is an incentive to work with colleagues at another university so that an article could be reported twice. By remaining in the same department and continuing to co-author, you may have to publish twice the level of output during the assessment period.

WHAT?

So, there are good reasons to sustain a publications career, but what do you need to do to achieve it?

Develop a Heterogeneous Portfolio for Momentum

Developing a heterogeneous portfolio in the types of publications can be an important means of facilitating a sustained career. Tenure committees focus on publications in a, usually, tightly drawn list of journals. Similarly, national research assessment exercises typically expect to see a specific number of publications per scholar in a set period and reserve their highest evaluation for publications in so-called top journals. Most weight seems likely to be given to rigorously reviewed, theoretical and empirical papers, in some cases to the exclusion of other types of paper let alone other types of output. Yet we know that papers published in what may be regarded as lower-level journals often have higher citation rates than papers published in top journals (Starbuck 2005 and Chapter 7 in this volume). Neglecting second-tier, but still very good, journal outlets may mean that opportunities to publish important contributions are forgone (Clark and Wright 2009). Or, seen from another perspective, a focus solely on publishing in the very top journals will probably lead to a short publications career for many.

It is sometimes thought that authors of highly cited works publish few papers. However, this is not necessarily the case. For example, while Nobel Prize winner Ronald Coase earned his reputation based on his work on transaction costs and the nature of the firm, and the problem of social cost (Coase 1992), he published numerous other papers (http://www.coase.org/coasepublications.htm, accessed 12 August 2019). More general evidence supports this view. Citation classics, in general, appear to emerge as regular parts of a larger research program rather than as one-off pieces divorced from a stream of published articles (Hollenbeck and Mannor 2007). Hence, actively pursuing a sustained publications career can bring the benefits of professional developmental experiences that enhance the overall impact of your research.

Further Empirical/Theoretical Articles

Entering new areas can involve publishing on topics that are related to prior publications, which allows for building upon tacit knowledge and conceptual tools. Alternatively, entering unrelated areas usually requires a bigger investment and dealing with greater competition. Scholars studying a particular managerial phenomenon may enhance the longevity of their research agenda by seeking connections with wider literatures and developing collaborations with teams having expertise in those areas (see below).

For example, my research on management buyouts, while involving a new form of entrepreneurial organization, offered opportunities for new insights and contributions in the finance, strategy, economics and human resource management (HRM) literatures, as I explain in more detail below.

From Traditional Journal Articles to Position/Think Pieces

As scholars, our focus from doctoral studies onwards is on learning how to publish traditional theoretical and empirical articles. However, having developed a reputation in a particular area can create space and open up opportunities for other types of journal articles. Position pieces, keynote articles and contributions to debates provide the opportunity to stand back and say things that are not feasible in a traditional journal article. Often such articles are invited, but some journals allocate space for authors to submit such articles or propose topics for debate. These articles are sometimes in more lowly ranked journals, but not always. For example, when Tim Clark and I were General Editors at the *Journal of Management Studies*, we introduced the 'Point-CounterPoint Section' (PCP) to stimulate debates on emerging topics or to reinvigorate existing areas. The articles are typically subject to development review in order to ensure quality is maintained. They can become highly cited. For example, after I ceased being an editor, Igor Filatotchev and I put together a PCP on governance in multinational corporations in 2011. While the paper by Peter Buckley and Roger Strange analyzed developments in internalization theory, a key theory in international business, the paper by Igor and

I adopted an agency perspective on corporate governance in multinational corporations that challenges the prevailing perspective (Filatotchev and Wright 2011).

As a doctoral student, publishing articles based on a review of the literature can be challenging. This is typically because a literature review article requires more than a summary of the literature. In particular, review articles in good journals that are open to this type of contribution (such as *Journal of Management*, *Journal of Management Studies* and *International Journal of Management Reviews*) require added value in terms of the development of an overarching research framework which helps identify directions for further research. More experienced authors are likely to be able to undertake a review of a particular literature from a position of authority and to be better placed to see the 'road ahead' and/or distil the literature into a framework for further research. Not to be ignored, they may also be better placed to convince journal editors to commission such an article.

Guest editing special issues is a further publication outlet where scholars can build on their experience as an author but also as a reviewer to convince regular editors of the journal to extend the opportunity to bring together articles on an interesting new area (see Chapter 27 in this volume). The role of special issues is usually to open up a new area rather than close down an old one, though the area does need to be sufficiently developed to generate a stream of articles of sufficient quality. As with review articles, writing the introductory article to a special issue provides the guest editor with an opportunity to set out a new research agenda rather than simply summarizing the articles in the special issue. Four special issue introductions that I have co-authored with guest co-editors have become highly cited: Hoskisson et al.'s (2000) introduction to the *Academy of Management Journal* (*AMJ*) special issue on 'Strategy in emerging economies'; Barney et al.'s (2001, 2011) introductions to the *Journal of Management* special issues on the 'Resource based view of the firm'; and Wright et al.'s (2005) introduction to the *Journal of Management Studies* (*JMS*) special issue on 'Challenging the conventional wisdom on strategy in emerging economies'. Note that the *JMS* special issue represents an important dimension of sustaining a publications career as it arose as a direct consequence of profile and collaborative links formed as a result of the *AMJ* special issue. This was further extended when the introduction was selected as a classic *JMS* paper and we were asked to revisit it in 2013 and discuss developments in the area during the intervening period (Hoskisson et al. 2013), with Xu and Mayer (2013) also writing a companion piece assessing the impact of the 2005 article.

Although in an audit culture or for tenure purposes books, particular research monographs, may not count for as much as journal articles, they offer scope to tackle big questions and open up important new areas. These monographs provide an opportunity to bring together previous work and broaden the discussion and contribution. They can become very highly cited and should be seen as an important part of your portfolio of research output. As an example, my journal publications on academic entrepreneurship led co-authors and myself to synthesize and extend the insights gained in an initial book aimed at both a practitioner and research audience (Wright et al. 2007), which itself has become highly cited, and a subsequent book (Link et al. 2015) reflecting on the more mature state of academic entrepreneurship research. Similarly, the work on management buyouts and private equity carried out over a long period lent itself to a book-length retrospective synthesis and assessment (Wright et al. 2018).

A further aspect of sustaining a publications career is to gain impact through reaching a wider audience that includes practitioners and policy-makers (Aguinis et al. 2012; Bartunek et al. 2001). However, a tenure process and evaluation system that focuses on publishing in top-tier academic journals probably downplays the incentive to publish articles in practitioner journals, even though some of these are high quality and articles within them may become highly cited. For example, a practitioner journal such as *Harvard Business Review* features in the approved list of 50 journals that contribute to a school's ranking in the *Financial Times* Top 100 MBA Programs, yet may well be absent from a school's tenure list. Quite apart from the inconsistency in a school's tenure policies and its aims to have its MBA ranked highly, not targeting practitioner journals can undermine efforts to sustain a publications career. Practitioner journals can be viewed as a means of product differentiation that helps extend the publication of research output beyond traditional academic papers. More experienced scholars may be better placed than less experienced co-authors to identify how academic insights can be presented to address the challenges faced by practitioners.

In addition to publications in practitioner journals, engaging with practice through the publication of reports and white papers for industry, professional and governmental bodies may further help sustain a publications career in academic journals. Engagement through social media, while promoting existing research and insights, can also garner useful feedback. This type of engagement can take scholars beyond the closed loop of the academic literature to observe puzzles that challenge existing theory and evidence, as well as the emergence of new phenomena that help identify the boundaries of existing theories. The key is to link these observations to the existing literature in order to develop novel insights. Sometimes this may lead, as Ronald Coase observed in commenting on his contribution during his Nobel Prize Lecture, to the inclusion in our analysis of features so obvious that they have tended to be overlooked but which can become seminal (Coase 1992).

The development of the rigor–relevance debate in the context of the policy debate about the contribution and impact of management research has brought to the fore the importance of interacting with practice (Clark et al. 2013). As a way of sustaining a publications career in a turbulent environment, these interactions need to be seen as complementary to rather than as substitutes for publishing in academic journals.

Throughout the life of CMBOR the strategy has been to publish quarterly reports of market trends in management buyouts and private equity in order to garner media coverage for research funders from the industry. This has led to interviews and invitations to write commentary articles in national and international news media (for example, an interview for a BBC Radio 4 *File on 4* program devoted to private equity). In turn, this profile has attracted further research funding for particular projects (for example, several from the European, Dutch and British Private Equity and Venture Capital Associations). The deliberate strategy has been to approach these projects with a view to being able to subsequently generate further academic journal articles from the research.

Although there was a high level of media interest in reports of trends in the phenomenon, for many years this impact did not count for career enhancement purposes. The last completed Research Excellence Framework in the UK (covering the period 2008–13) belatedly did so and the impact case I produced on CMBOR (available at http://results.ref.ac.uk/Submissions/Impact/1565, accessed 12 August 2019) was rated as outstanding by the review panel, showing that academic journal publications and practice/policy impact can be highly complementary.

HOW?

The key remaining question is how can scholars develop and implement strategies to sustain their publications career?

Being Strategically Entrepreneurial

There may be a tendency to focus on individual papers or projects. Some new areas may garner a lot of interest and generate publications because they happen to be fashionable. However, topics go out of fashion and there is a need to ride the waves of fashion. This may be difficult without adopting a more strategic entrepreneurial perspective that involves envisioning an overarching research program. Developing a research program therefore means thinking about the big questions that need to be addressed in your area (Wiklund et al. 2018) and which will generate your reputation for being an expert in a particular area. That is, the longevity of a publishing career will be influenced by the scope of the initial area the scholar starts with. Scholars therefore need to develop generalized non-tradable assets (Gedajlovic and Carney 2010). These concern the conceptual tools they develop and the empirical contexts they study, but also developing the capabilities for strategic entrepreneurship. Being entrepreneurial involves creating, recognizing and exploiting new opportunities (Alvarez and Barney 2007). Strategic entrepreneurship involves connecting opportunities with the resources needed to deliver on them (Ireland et al. 2003).

We know from evidence on repeat entrepreneurs that the ability to create, identify and pursue new opportunities successfully may be influenced, positively or negatively, by cognitive biases (Ucbasaran et al. 2008, 2009). Repeat entrepreneurs may attempt to use the same 'recipes' that worked well in prior ventures when current environmental conditions require a different approach and may be a new direction. Making a switch to a new area presents challenges. On the one hand, liabilities of newness suggest difficulties in getting up to speed to join an existing 'conversation'. On the other hand, there may be benefits of newness for experienced scholars to enter a new area. The subtlety of wisdom resulting from having learnt how to identify, frame and execute opportunities may help reduce the barriers to entering a new area. However, there is also the need to access the resources to realize these new opportunities, in which the development of social capital and teams has an important role to play.

A schematic development of a portfolio of research programs is shown in Figure 5.1. Doctoral research training provides the basis for an initial research program. This program may come to an end once a PhD dissertation is completed and publications achieved from it. However, it may also be possible to continue and develop this research program over many years. I have found that by making links between a current research program and other emerging areas it is possible to identify and exploit new research opportunities that can be developed into a parallel research program. This continual process of seeking out new research opportunities may lead to the development of new research programs over time. Some may turn out to be limited and wither away after a few

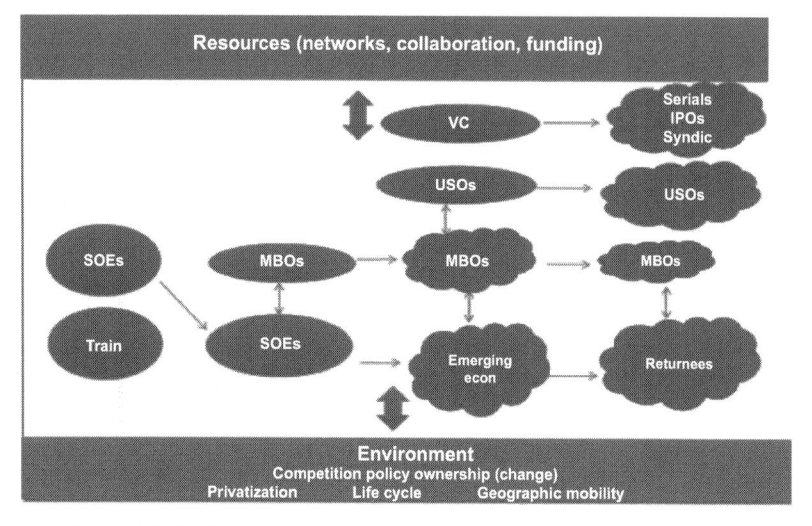

Note: IPOs = initial public offerings; MBOs = management buyouts; SOEs = state-owned enterprises; USO = university spinouts; VC = venture capital.

Figure 5.1 Developing a sustainable publications career

papers. Others may provide a stepping-stone from a declining area and help trigger a resurgence of research activity. You need to curtail research programs when the well is running dry and the publishing opportunities become limited to lower level journals. At this point, the opportunity cost turns in favor of being open to new opportunities. Identifying, building up and sustaining these new research programs requires the development of resources and capabilities, to which we now turn.

Using the case of CMBOR, Figure 5.2 indicates how sustainability was developed from what appeared initially to be a very narrow and transitory phenomenon. The potential longevity of management buyouts as a research agenda was not initially evident. Indeed, as a then junior lecturer (that is, assistant professor) I was told by my head of department that I was wasting my academic career as the phenomenon would disappear once the recession of the early 1980s ended. Fortunately, this was a pre-national research evaluation world, which may well have meant that the research trajectory would not have been pursued. Still, promotion to reader (associate professor), although in the event six years away, would require the demonstration of a publication record in good journals and being known for expertise in a particular area. Over 38 years and multiple millions of dollars research funding later this research is still yielding good journal publications.

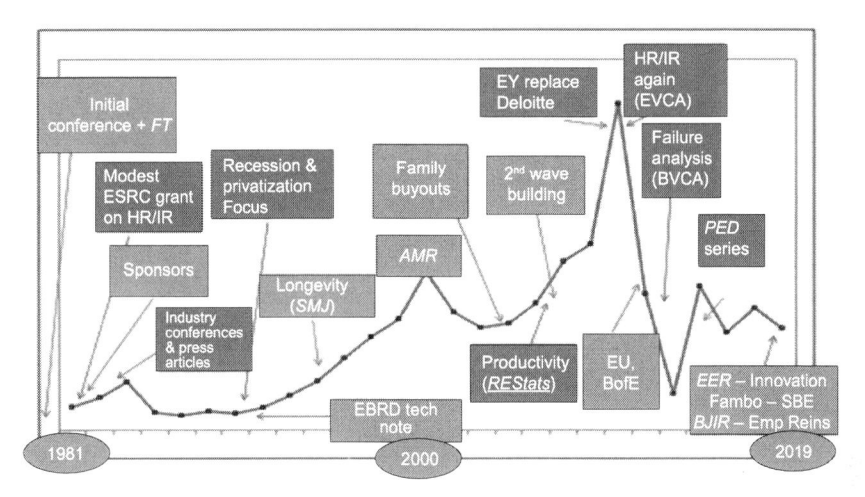

Note: AMR = *Academy of Management Review*; BJIR = *British Journal of Industrial Relations*; BofE = Bank of England; BVCA = British Venture Capital Association; EBRD = European Bank for Reconstruction and Development; EER = *European Economic Review*; ESRC = Economic and Social Research Council; EU = European Union; EVCA= European Venture Capital Association; EY = Ernst and Young; Fambo= Family Management Buyout; FT = *Financial Times*; HR/IR= human relations/industrial relations; PED = *Private Equity Demystified*; REStats = *Review of Economics and Statistics*; SMJ = *Strategic Management Journal*.

Figure 5.2   Thirty-eight years of management buyouts and private equity research

As Table 5.1 and Figure 5.2 show, the focus of the research program evolved over time. Five broad themes were sustained over the period: private equity market and firm behavior; vendor sources of deals; impact of buyouts on employment and employee relations; impact of buyouts on performance and longevity; and review articles.

While exploiting the initial investment in the area, to sustain the research agenda and publications over time, it was necessary to explore new opportunities associated with developments in the management buyout market and to connect to various general literatures and debates.

The evolution of the management buyout phenomenon and related activities over time, notably through waves of activity in the 1980s and from the late 1990s to 2007, led to new research opportunities even within the same broad topic areas, since the research and policy issues have differed over time. For example, the prominence of different vendor sources of buyouts over time generated new dimensions of the phenomenon which enabled links to different literatures to be made. Hence, while management buyouts themselves are narrow, the agenda has been sustained through identifying different dimensions that link to the literatures on entrepreneurship, finance, strategy, economics, employee relations/ HR, international business, ethics, and so on.

These literatures also provided important links to different theoretical tools. In particular, although the finance literature has focused on agency theory, this is a narrow conceptual approach that limits insights on the buyout phenomenon. For example, transaction costs and resource dependency theories could be applied to the observation that some buyouts maintained a trading relationship with their former parent, and entrepreneurial cognition to the observation that some buyouts involved the recognition and exploitation of entrepreneurial opportunities. Both these perspectives sustained the publications agenda as they helped to highlight that buyouts were about more than just downsizing of listed corporations, which had been predominant in the mainstream finance literature.

As regards the impact of buyouts, given the focus on job saving in the recession of the early 1980s, initial academic journal publications were obtained by connecting to the employee relations literature. When the impact of buyouts and private equity on employment and employee relations came to the fore again from 2007 onwards, this earlier research provided a basis for comparison and stimulated a new research agenda (Bacon et al. 2019).

As the buyout market and the associated literature evolved, review articles developed from general articles based on explaining the phenomenon, to more detailed surveys covering a wider and deeper body of literature that could be published in better journals over time.

Together with the management buyout work specifically, publications have been made in related areas that have helped sustain publications output. To some extent there has been a two-way flow of insights and identification of opportunities for projects and papers. Notably, the closeness of management buyouts and private equity to venture capital lent itself easily to the development of this area as a related core program. Studying the concept of an entity being transferred from being part of one organization to becoming an independently owned firm also meant that it was a relatively short step to recognizing the research opportunities of academic spin-offs from universities. Research in this area has developed into a further core program (Siegel and Wright 2015). A more recent extension of this work is to explore entrepreneurship at universities in the guise of ventures created by students, as we noticed from teaching developments that this was becoming an important yet under-researched area (Wright et al. 2017, 2019).

Initially, my interest in management buyouts involved riskier exploration activity, while at the time I was exploiting previous investments in work on management control systems (I taught management accounting and was collaborating with an electrical engineering colleague) and, separately, efficiency and accountability in state-owned enterprises (I had previously worked in a state-owned firm and had written a Master's dissertation on inflation accounting and performance in the gas industry). These early core research areas declined as privatization took hold.

While these topics were at some distance from management buyouts there were subsequent opportunities to make connections that at first were not remotely envisaged. For example, the development of state enterprise privatizations in the UK from the mid-1980s and, subsequently, in former centrally planned economies after the fall of the Berlin Wall saw an important role for management and employee buyouts. This policy development and CMBOR's unique track record in buyouts opened up opportunities for policy and practical impact through advice that led to the publication of reports aimed at these audiences as well as academic publications. A growing profile and reaching out from studying buyouts in emerging economies led to connections being made with other researchers interested in strategy in emerging economies and, subsequently, returnee entrepreneurs. This research led to the development of a new core area of research and the development of an extended team of researchers and collaborators (Buck, Filatotchev, Hoskisson, Liu, Lu, Honig, Drori, Peng and Pruthi), as summarized in Table 5.2. More recently, questioning the impact of privatization and political changes has led to a reassessment of the role of government in industry and the emergence of a state capitalism research agenda (Wood and Wright 2015).

Social Capital

Developing your social capital can provide a basis for unlocking new opportunities and accessing complementary expertise. Social capital represents the resources associated with individuals' networks of relationships (Gedajlovic et al. 2013). Scholars build their social capital initially through working with supervisors, attending doctoral colloquia, presenting at conferences, and so on. However, the paradox of embeddedness in existing social relationships is well-known (Meuleman et al. 2010; Uzzi 1997). For example, family firms may benefit from the social capital of

Table 5.2 Emerging economies research

• 2000 AMJ Special Issue	➢ Broadening out of recognition
• 2005 JMS Special Issue	
• 2006: BA Funded survey	➢ Builds on EE program
• 2008: ETP SI University vs non-university location choice & asset complementarity	➢ Ground clearing survey of returnees only; cross-section, ltd measures
• 2009: JIBS Exporting & knowledge transfer	
• 2009: ETP SI Transnationals; SEJ SI IE	
• 2010: JIBS Knowledge spillovers	➢ Broaden agenda
• 2011: SEJ Networks & spillovers	➢ Archival database
• 2012: ResPol Knowledge spillovers and mobility	
• 2013: Book ch. Resources	
• 2013: SEJ SI SE in EE	➢ Recognition
• 2013: ISBE Returnees, transnationals & entry networks in India	➢ Broadening agenda
• 2013: IBR TMT and diversification	➢ Extending context & RQs
• 2014: JIBS Int experience & home/host institutions	➢ Returnees just one aspect of TMT human & social capital
• 2014: ISBJ Learning and returnees	
• 2014: JMS Classic Paper	

Notes: AMJ = Academy of Management Journal; BA = British Academy; EE = Emerging Economies; ETP SI = Entrepreneurship Theory and Practice Special Issue; ISBE = Institute for Small Business and Entrepreneurship; ISBJ = International Small Business Journal; IBR = International Business Review; JIBS = Journal of International Business Studies; JMS = Journal of Management Studies; ResPol = Research Policy; SE in EE = Strategic Entrepreneurship in Emerging Economies; SEJ = Strategic Entrepreneurship Journal; SEJ SI IE = Strategic Entrepreneurship Journal Special Issue on International Entrepreneurship; TMT = top management teams.

the founder but this may lead to inward looking behavior, missed opportunities for growth and, ultimately, a threat to the survival of the firm (Steier et al. 2009; Wilson et al. 2013). For family firms and scholars alike, new social capital may need to be built in order to break out of the straitjacket of existing trajectories.

How can you build new social capital? Social capital through collaboration with actual or potential team members can be built by delivering quality contributions on time. A reputation for delivery can mean team members will want to work with you again (see Chapter 15 in this volume). Providing timely, detailed and insightful informal comments on colleagues' working papers or on papers of scholars working in your area also builds social capital. Supervising doctoral students is a way to build social capital for the future as those students go on to become faculty members.

Some activities while potentially being onerous or seen as purely altruistic can generate significant benefits for sustaining a publications career. A willingness to contribute to learned societies by, for example, organizing and participating in doctoral and junior faculty colloquia, such as those run by the divisions of the Academy of Management at the annual conference, can both build social capital and provide exposure to emerging ideas.

Taking on editorial and reviewing roles, and performing them effectively, can help sustain a publishing career. For example, the social capital that is developed can make editors more predisposed to accept proposals for special issues as they know that scholars will be able to deliver a quality contribution that fits with that particular journal's expectations. These activities also generate advance exposure to emerging ideas and methods that can help extend expertise and, without involving plagiarism, suggest new directions for existing research agendas.

Team Building

There is little doubt that building teams of collaborators is a key way to developing a sustained publications career. There is clear evidence that the mean number of authors per journal paper has been increasing over time. For example, analysis of trends in the *Journal of Management Studies* since it was founded in 1964 shows that in the first five years, over four-fifths (81.3 percent) of articles published were single authored. In contrast, during 2005–09 only a quarter (25.1 percent) of articles were single authored and the number of triple-authored papers also exceeded the number of single-authored papers, with the number of papers with four authors also noticeably increased (Clark et al. 2014). This trend is perhaps not too surprising given the demands for papers to show novel contributions, conceptual development and high-quality data and analytical techniques.

Team working helps maintain momentum on projects and papers, particularly in the face of other demands on scholars' time that emerge as careers develop. A number of writers have stressed the importance of maintaining momentum in sustaining a publishing career, such as setting aside regular parts of each day to write, rather than waiting for some mythical ideal of a dedicated block of time (Boice 1992). Moreover, even if a sabbatical period is secured, planning momentum ahead of time can help optimize the eventual output. If a co-author is unable to devote large blocks of time during a particular period, having team members who can push the work forward can be very useful. Even being able to work briefly on a paper, before passing it on in a timely manner to co-authors, can help maintain momentum.

Building a team also brings complementary expertise. Such complementarity is not just in relation to conceptual and empirical expertise. Complementarity can also extend to the different perspectives that team members bring to bear on a research question that can contribute to novel syntheses. Further, a team member who is able to position and frame a paper in relation to the literature, and who is able to draw out the contribution of a paper, possesses an important skill. While often under-recognized, such expertise can make the difference between whether a paper is published or not. Unless a paper's contribution to addressing an important research gap is clearly articulated in the introduction, editors and reviewers may not be convinced (see Chapter 13 in this volume). More experienced team members may be better placed to perform this role and this too can enable them to extend their publishing career.

As scholars' research agendas develop, the nature of research teams may also evolve. The composition and dynamics of an initial team may change and new teams may be formed either instead of or alongside the original team. From my own experience, the development of new research avenues beyond the initial work on management buyouts involved building different teams of co-authors with knowledge and empirical skills in these new areas as well as with junior colleagues. Colleagues in these other areas had the incentive to collaborate as the topic offered access to a novel dataset and research question that had not previously been addressed in their area. This approach included developing collaborative links with colleagues when I was at Nottingham, as it was necessary to understand what was required to publish in journals in these areas. For example, research on employee relations aspects of buyouts involved the development of a collaborative team including Nick Bacon, at that time a professor of industrial relations, and Louise Scholes, at that time a researcher in CMBOR. Similarly, work on management and employee buyouts in Eastern Europe involved building a research team comprising Igor Filatotchev and Trevor Buck who had expertise in former centrally planned economies and corporate governance.

Some team members have been co-authors of mine for over 20 years (Thompson, Filatotchev, Bruining, Wilson, Hoskisson, Manigart and Westhead), while others are much shorter-term or even one-off collaborators. Some team members' involvement has ebbed and flowed as the agenda has changed over the different waves of buyouts and private equity (Wilson). Some team members have continued the collaboration in other areas beyond management buyouts. For example, collaboration with Filatotchev on privatization buyouts in emerging economies has evolved into research on both initial public offerings (IPOs) and returnee entrepreneurs.

Various conflicts can arise which undermine the longevity of teams. Author order on papers can be especially contentious, especially for authors concerned about promotion or who, like me, happen to have a family name towards the end of the alphabet. There are various ways to alleviate this problem that should be addressed at the outset. For example, authors may agree to include a note that authors are listed alphabetically but all contributed equally. For teams that work successfully together over a sustained period, one practical solution that enables each team member to be first author is to take the lead in turn in writing the first draft of a paper, even if it is only a rough draft, and to be responsible for driving a paper to completion. This was a strategy we adopted, for example, in the team with Buck and Filatotchev.

Perceived or actual contributions that fall short of other members' expectations can seriously undermine team cohesion. Before this leads to irretrievable breakdowns, open discussion of the problems may help resolve those problems. It may be that unexpected and unavoidable demands have meant that a team member is unable to deliver at the expected time that was initially promised. Where there is a continuing research program, it may be feasible to delineate a subset of areas where particular team members may contribute rather than having an expectation that all members will contribute equally to all outputs. In this way, the composition of teams may be fluid.

Some teams may be maintained over long periods while others may be just one-off or short lived. The longevity of a team's collaborative efforts may not be evident at the outset. An initial team collaboration may be viewed as taking out an option for future collaborations, which may or may not be exercised. What the subsequent opportunities will be may not be known at the outset, and may only emerge as a result of the collaboration.

Over time, team members may want or need to pursue other interests and projects but may still be able to continue working together. Some members may need to carve out their own trajectory to provide a clear signal of their contribution to a field to tenure and promotions committees. Pursuing other opportunities can be beneficial, too, in bringing new insights that can reinvigorate an initial research collaboration.

Professional Development

How a sustained publishing record can be delivered involves professional development of scholars. Much of the focus of training has typically been on doctoral students and junior faculty through colloquia at conferences such as the Academy of Management Conference. However, mid-career academics also need continuing support. The bar to get into top journals rises significantly over time. Meeting increases in the industry standard quantitative and qualitative research methods expected of papers aimed at top journals may be particularly critical. However, the need for professional development goes further as editorial and reviewer demands regarding the framing and contribution of papers also change over time.

Research Grants

Obtaining research grants can result in additional resource in terms of time, as they may allow for buyouts from teaching and administration, as well as providing for the recruitment of researchers. Research grants from governmental funding bodies increasingly require evidence that the work will have an impact in addition to academic journal output. Research grants from governmental funding bodies are typically highly competitive and therefore less likely to be achieved as rejection rates are high. Research funding from industry and commerce is also increasingly difficult to come by and may rely very much on the researcher having established a reputation in a particular area. The objectives of research funders in industry and commerce may be specific, focused on issues of immediate concern, and involve confidentiality issues. However, the trick is to design studies that allow access to novel data that, while meeting the needs of commercial funders, can also allow novel research questions to be addressed that will be publishable in top journals. In an environment where there is a need to demonstrate research impact, this type of research funding can be a useful source.

For example, building on the reputation we had developed on private equity and management buyouts, the European Private Equity and Venture Capital Association commissioned CMBOR in 2008 to conduct a survey of employee relations in private-equity backed companies. This was driven by concerns being raised by trade unions and the European Parliament about the supposed adverse impact on union recognition and consultation following a private equity backed buyout. Our study, which involved putting together a team including myself and others with expertise in private equity and those with expertise in industrial relations and HRM, provided rigorous evidence to counter the critics but also enabled us to publish several papers in academic journals (notably *Human Relations*, *Industrial Relations* and *Academy of Management Perspectives*), as well as being able to construct an impact case study for the UK Research Excellence Framework exercise in 2013.

CONCLUSIONS

In this chapter I have attempted to analyze how the challenges in sustaining a publications career can be addressed. Sustaining a publications career involves taking a wider view of what publication means that goes beyond traditional academic articles in the field you began with to include other complementary forms of publication and diversification into related domains. Sustaining a publications career also requires scholars to engage in strategic entrepreneurship that involves both the continual creation and recognition of publishing opportunities and the development of the resources to realize such opportunities. This strategic entrepreneurship is facilitated by the development of both adaptable human capital and a broadly based social capital.

Undoubtedly, there are different routes to sustaining a publications career. The analysis presented here provides some insights into how scholars at different stages in their careers can map out a route that fits their interests and circumstances.

NOTE

* A shorter, family firm research-orientated version of this chapter was published as Wright and Sharma (2013).

REFERENCES

Aguinis, H., I. Suarez-González, G. Lannelongue and H. Joo (2012), 'Scholarly impact revisited', *Academy of Management Perspectives*, **26** (2), 105–32.
Alvarez, S.A. and J.B. Barney (2007), 'Discovery and creation: alternative theories of entrepreneurial action', *Strategic Entrepreneurship Journal*, **1** (1–2), 11–26.
Bacon, N., K. Hoque and M. Wright (2019), 'Is job insecurity higher in leveraged buyouts?', *British Journal of Industrial Relations*, **57** (3), 479–512.

Barney, J.B., D.J. Ketchen Jr. and M. Wright (2011). 'The future of resource-based theory: revitalization or decline?', *Journal of Management*, **37** (5), 1299–315.

Barney, J., M. Wright and D. Ketchen Jr. (2001), 'The resource-based view of the firm: ten years after 1991', *Journal of Management*, **27** (6), 625–42.

Bartunek, J., S. Rynes and R. Daft (2001), 'Across the great divide: knowledge creation and transfer between practitioners and academics', *Academy of Management Journal*, **44** (2), 340–55.

Boice, R. (1992), *The New Faculty Member*, San Francisco, CA: Jossey-Bass.

Clark, T. and M. Wright (2009), 'So farewell, then … reflections on editing the *Journal of Management Studies*', *Journal of Management Studies*, **46** (1), 1–9.

Clark, T., S.W. Floyd and M. Wright (2006), 'On the review process and journal development', *Journal of Management Studies*, **43** (5), 655–64.

Clark, T., S.W. Floyd and M. Wright (2013), 'In search of the impactful and the interesting – swings of the pendulum?', *Journal of Management Studies*, **50** (8), 1358–7.

Clark, T., M. Wright, Z. Iskoujina and P. Garnett (2014), 'The shifting nature of management research: a longitudinal analysis of the content of the *Journal of Management Studies* 1964–2010', *Journal of Management Studies*, **51** (1), 19–37.

Coase, R. (1992), 'The institutional structure of production', *American Economic Review*, **82** (4), 713–19.

Estes, B. and B. Polnick (2012), 'Examining motivation theory in higher education: an expectancy theory analysis of tenured faculty productivity', *International Journal of Management, Business and Administration*, **15** (1), 1–7.

Filatotchev, I. and M. Wright (2011), 'Agency perspectives on corporate governance of multinational enterprises', *Journal of Management Studies*, **48** (2), 471–86.

Gedajlovic, E. and M. Carney (2010), 'Markets, hierarchies and families: toward a transaction costs theory of the family firm', *Entrepreneurship Theory and Practice*, **34** (6), 1145–72.

Gedajlovic, E., B. Honig, C. Moore, T. Payne and M. Wright (2013), 'Social capital and entrepreneurship: a schema and research agenda'. *Entrepreneurship Theory and Practice*, **37** (3), 455–78.

Harrison, J. (2006), 'Post-tenure scholarship and its implications', *University of Florida Journal of Law and Public Policy*, **17**, 139–64.

Hollenbeck, J. and M. Mannor (2007), 'Career success and weak paradigms: the role of activity, resiliency, and true scores', *Journal of Organizational Behavior*, **28** (8), 933–42.

Hoskisson, R., L. Eden, C.M. Lau and M. Wright (2000), 'Strategies in emerging markets', *Academy of Management Journal*, **43** (3), 249–67.

Hoskisson, R., M. Wright, I. Filatotchev and M. Peng (2013), 'Emerging multinationals from mid-range economies: the influence of institutions and factor markets', *Journal of Management Studies*, **50** (7), 1295–321.

Ireland, R.D., M.A. Hitt and D.G. Sirmon (2003), 'A model of strategic entrepreneurship: the construct and its dimensions', *Journal of Management*, **29** (6), 963–89.

Link, A.N., D.S. Siegel and M. Wright (2015), *The Chicago Handbook of University Technology Transfer and Academic Entrepreneurship*, Chicago, IL: University of Chicago Press.

Meuleman, M., A. Lockett, M. Manigart and M. Wright (2010), 'Partner selection decisions in interfirm collaborations: the paradox of relational embeddedness', *Journal of Management Studies*, **47** (6), 995–1019.

Park, S. and M. Gordon (1996), 'Publication records and tenure decisions in the field of strategic management', *Strategic Management Journal*, **17** (2), 109–28.

Podsakoff, P.M., S.B. MacKenzie, N.P. Podsakoff and D.G. Bachrach (2008), 'Scholarly influence in the field of management: a bibliometric analysis of the determinants of university and author impact in the management literature in the past quarter century', *Journal of Management*, **34** (4), 641–720.

Siegel, D.S. and M. Wright (2015), 'University technology transfer offices, licensing, and start-ups', in A.N. Link, D.S. Siegel and M. Wright (eds), *The Chicago Handbook of University Technology Transfer and Academic Entrepreneurship*, Chicago, IL: University of Chicago Press, Chapter 1.

Starbuck, W. (2005), 'How much better are the most prestigious journals? The statistics of academic publication', *Organization Science*, **16** (2), 180–200.

Steier, L.P., J.H. Chua and J.J. Chrisman (2009), 'Embeddedness perspectives of economic action within family firms', *Entrepreneurship Theory and Practice*, **33** (6), 1157–67.

Ucbasaran, D., P. Westhead and M. Wright (2008), 'Opportunity identification and pursuit: does an entrepreneur's human capital matter?', *Small Business Economics*, **30** (2), 153–73.

Ucbasaran, D., P. Westhead, M. Wright and M. Flores (2009), 'The nature of entrepreneurial experience, business failure and comparative optimism', *Journal of Business Venturing*, **25** (6), 541–55.

Uzzi, B. (1997), 'Social structure and competition in interfirm networks: the paradox of embeddedness', *Administrative Science Quarterly*, **42** (1), 35–67.

Wiklund, J., M. Wright and S. Zahra (2018), 'Conquering relevance: entrepreneurship research's grand challenge', *Entrepreneurship Theory and Practice*, **43** (3), 419–36, doi.org/10.1177/1042258718807478.

Wilson, N., M. Wright and L. Scholes (2013), 'Family business survival and the role of boards', *Entrepreneurship Theory and Practice*, **37** (6), 1369–89.

Wood, G. and M. Wright (2015), 'Corporations and new statism: trends and research priorities', *Academy of Management Perspectives*, **29** (2), 271–86.

Wright, M. and J. Coyne (1985), *Management Buyouts*, Beckenham: Croom Helm.

Wright, M. and P. Sharma (2013), 'Sustaining a publications career', *Family Business Review*, **26** (4), 323–32.

Wright, M., P. Mustar and D. Siegel (2019), *Student Entrepreneurship*, Singapore: World Scientific (in press).

Wright, M., D. Siegel and P. Mustar (2017), 'An emerging ecosystem for student start-ups', *Journal of Technology Transfer*, **2** (4), 909–22.

Wright, M., K. Amess, N. Bacon and D. Siegel (2018), *The Routledge Companion to Management Buyouts*, London: Routledge.

Wright, M., B. Clarysse, P. Mustar and A. Lockett (2007), *Academic Entrepreneurship in Europe*, Cheltenham, UK and Northampton, MA, USA: Edward Elgar.

Wright, M., I. Filatotchev, R. Hoskisson and M. Peng (2005), 'Strategies in emerging markets: challenging the conventional wisdom', *Journal of Management Studies*, **42** (1), 1–34.

Xu, D. and K. Meyer (2013), 'Linking theory and context: strategy research in emerging economies since Wright et al.', *Journal of Management Studies*, **50** (7), 1322–46.

6. Why publish in Asian management journals?

Daphne W. Yiu

INTRODUCTION

Traditionally, region-focused journals are viewed as a secondary or second-tiered outlet for publication of marginalized research that carries a theme of a regional phenomenon and/or uses regional data. Nonetheless, with the fast growth and increasing significance of Asian countries in the global economy, Asian management journals have recorded skyrocketing numbers of manuscript submissions and increasing impact factors in recent years. For example, the *Asia Pacific Journal of Management* (*APJM*) has a five-year citation impact factor of 3.00 as stated in the ISI Journal Citation Reports for 2013. The 2013 impact factor places the *APJM* as the twenty-fourth most influential management journal among all 172 tracked management journals. The *APJM* receives over 800 manuscripts per annum and publishes 35–40 articles.

This chapter aims to provide a general discussion of the similarities and differences in publishing Asian research in Asian management journals compared with in North America as regards publication-related issues viewed and experienced by myself as author, reviewer and editor at Asian management journals in the past decade. I particularly use *APJM* as the focal Asian management journal in my illustrations. In addition, to echo the recent advocacy on the future direction of Asian management journals, I discuss if and how Asian management journals publish more indigenous research.

ASIAN MANAGEMENT JOURNALS VERSUS WESTERN MANAGEMENT JOURNALS

The Rules of the Game

When tracing the development of the *APJM*, it is interesting to observe the resemblance to an indigenous local firm undergoing a gradual internationalization path. Founded in 1983, the *APJM* was a journal established by the dean of the business school at the National University of Singapore as an in-house publication for Master in Business Administration (MBA) and graduate students (Lee 2007). Subject to tremendous barriers and pains during its childhood and adolescence, the *APJM* started to catch international attention and, in 1998, it was formally accepted as the official affiliate of the Asia Academy of Management, with a mission to 'encourage contextualized management research with Asian relevance towards contribution to global scholarship' (Lau 2007, p. 401). Since then, the *APJM* has grown to be highly reputable and the most prestigious journal in Asian management research (for the achievements of the *APJM*, see Peng 2007).

With such a historical development, together with the development of Asian business schools towards the American system, recruitment of faculty members from North America, a reward system striving for publishing in higher-ranked journals that are often US based, affiliation with American academic associations and collaboration with US publishers, Asian management journals such as the *APJM* highly resemble many of the top-tiered US management journals. As commented by Leung (2007, p. 512), 'the downside of the adaptive response to the pressure to publish in highly cited journals is that virtually all Asian management research falls within the confines of well-known Western theories'. The adaptation and institutionalization process has resulted in conformity in how editors and reviewers evaluate publishable research, as well as academic stakeholders having to make sense of what a top-tiered Asian management journal should look like. In particular, Pfeffer (2007) highlighted that what seems to signal quality of a research or journal rank is the attraction to theory and methodological sophistication. To gain legitimacy, many Asian management journals are run just like the American and other global management journals, and the expectations of quality are very similar; for example, novelty and importance of research questions, theoretical contributions, logical adequacy and consistency, empirical rigor and coherence between theory and empirics, and relevance and implications to academic and practitioner communities.

Regional relevance, global impact

Does Asian management matter? How distinct is Asian management from management elsewhere? This question has been pondered by many Asian management scholars, editors, and reviewers in the publication process of Asian management journals. In his reflection on Asian management in the twenty-first century, Hofstede (2007, p. 412) commented, 'management problems basically have remained and will remain the same over time, and that their solutions differ less from period to period than from part of the world to part of the world, and even from country to country'. Given that management problems themselves do not change over time but management thinking differs from one country to another as a function of the local culture, universal solutions to management problems do not exist. So, the key for Asian-based management research to contribute to global management is to study the contextual boundaries of management knowledge, and researchers need to trade ideas across borders and the cultural limits of their own thinking (Hofstede 2007; Meyer 2006).

As stated in the objectives of the *APJM*, two out of the three key features of the journal are about regional relevance – focusing on key management and organizational trends in the region, and being the first and most prominent management journal published in and about the fastest growing region in the world. Given the trajectory of the fast-growing economies with substantial economic turbulence and institutional upheavals in Asia, timely research on emerging business phenomena and management issues that can provide explanations, predictions and insights are important in their own right. To facilitate regionally relevant research, an effective and efficient way is to organize special issues of the journal on timely local phenomena that may contribute to global understanding of the Asian context. For example, after the Global Economic Crisis in 2008, a special issue 'Varieties of Asian capitalism: toward an institutional theory of Asian enterprise' was published in 2009, which challenged the often presumed superiority of the liberal market model of capitalism and restated how alternative models of capitalism may be preferable for developing economies in Asia (Carney et al. 2009). The concept and view of varieties of capitalism (VoC) have also addressed the limitations of institutional theory that has yet to explain the immense variations within and between national economies and provides a third leg to examine institution–firm relationships. The VoC perspective can be fruitfully applied in the Asian context by delineating the complex institutional dynamics existing in Asian capitalism, thus realizing the full potential of regional relevance. Also, through the theory-building process, by contextualizing the institution–firm phenomenon from a co-evolutionary and actor-centered view, the VoC model presents a challenge to mainstream scholars investigating traditional capitalism in a Western context, thus exerting global impact on the rethinking of the Western model of market capitalism.

A special issue, 'Asia & poverty: closing the great divide through entrepreneurship & innovation' (Bruton et al. 2015), was launched to address the poverty problem in Asia, a topic that has been largely unexplored by business scholars in spite of the close links between business and poverty, and over half Asia's total population living on approximately $2 a day. As entrepreneurship is a fundamental engine of economic growth (Baumol et al. 2009), Bruton et al. (2015, p. 5) advocated that entrepreneurs should move beyond subsistence entrepreneurship, which they refer to as 'ventures in settings of poverty in which a new venture offers little in terms of the potential to significantly improve the entrepreneur's life or that of the entrepreneur's family', to create new entrepreneurial ventures and initiatives, such as microlending, social entrepreneurship and base of the pyramid (BoP) initiatives, to empower the poor to break out of poverty. This special issue is the pioneer in management journals to publish research on poverty. Not only has it laid the foundation for future pursuit of entrepreneurship as a solution to poverty, but it has also undoubtedly provided new approaches and insights to policymakers and entrepreneurs regarding the formation of entrepreneurial growth policies in different countries. This indicates a strong dedication of the *APJM* to be the first to publish on underexplored yet important business issues that are of critical relevance to the business community and region.

Puffer et al. (2013) demonstrated how to bridge local relevance and global impact in their special issue on 'Favors in the global economy', exploring and demonstrating how a seemingly regionally salient, culturally specific construct plays an important role in global business transactions. This sounds like an old topic but it has never systematically been examined in the management discipline. The construct of favors is found to be multidimensional and complex, conveying different meanings and expectations across different cultures. The special issue focuses attention on a timely topic that fits with a concurrent special issue and conference theme in the broader management academy, including the Special Research Forum 'West meets East: new concepts and theories' in the *Academy of Management Journal* and the theme 'The informal economy' of the Academy of Management annual meeting in 2012.

In conclusion, as compared with top-tiered international business and management journals in the West, Asian management journals seem to give more weight to publishing context-relevant research with topics that are timely and of growing importance in the region, and which spur global awareness and tighten connection with practice.

Contributions: the rigor/relevance tradeoff?
Asian management research has been treated more as an area of study that relies heavily on applying Western management theories, and rarely on the development of new theories (Lau 2002; Tsui et al. 2004; White 2002). The lack of theoretical contribution and questioning about the generalizability of research findings are often the main reasons for reviewers to suggest a rejection in Asian management journals. This raises a fundamental question that has been asked by many Asian management researchers: is the notion of making theoretical contributions a hindrance to publishing interesting and novel research that is of high local or regional relevance content? Theoretical contribution often refers to the addition of knowledge to mainstream theories that are developed using Western logic, measurements developed and validated in the West, as well as data and samples collected in the West (Lau 2006; Leung 2007, 2012).

We can expect that the role of theory did not carry significant weight at the early stage of Asian management publications. Nonetheless, in the past decade or so, there have been numerous reflections on and suggestions for the levels of the theoretical contributions of publications in Asian management journals, such as the classifications into theory application, theory extension and development of a new theory by Lau (2006), contextualizing theory (theories in context) and theorizing about context (theories of context) by Whetten (2009), and context-insensitive (contextualization in what), context-sensitive (contextualization in how) and context-specific (contextualization in why) by Jia et al. (2012). With an objective for Asian management journals to produce more high-impact publications, and the tremendous efforts given by associations including the Asia Academy of Management (AAOM) and the International Association of Chinese Management Research (IACMR) to blend Asian management research with that of the West, the research skills of Asian management scholars, especially the younger generations, have been elevated substantially and quickly in the past decade (Leung 2007). There are signs that more Asian contributions are appearing in mainstream management research, both in terms of extending management theories with contextualized constructs and variables, and developing contextualized theories to examine context-specific phenomena, although the latter has accounted for a much smaller portion so far (Jia et al. 2012; Lau 2006; Whetten 2009). In general, the tradeoff between rigor and relevance is getting smaller.

TOWARDS THE NEXT ERA OF ASIAN MANAGEMENT RESEARCH

Leong and Leung (2004) predicted that the adopted Western approach, owing to institutional pressure to publish in high-impact journals in the West in many Asian business schools, will eventually prevail in Asia, while the Asian approach, focusing on indigenous research, will be marginalized and the integration approach will be difficult to implement. Such a claim has been realized in the past decade with the swing moving towards adopting Western theories using Asian context. A significant drawback of such an internationalization or Westernization approach is that the value-added of Asian management research is diminishing. Leung (2009) criticized the adaptive approach that has shaped Asian researchers to imitate publications in top-tier management journals in the West, with expectations such as favoring deductive rather than inductive research, deriving research ideas from well-known mainstream theories in the West instead of nascent theories, and demonstrating as much methodological rigor as possible. As a consequence, 'Asian researchers tend to publish on research topics that are well known in the West' (Leung 2007, p. 512). It is also my observation over the past few years that the style and findings of Asian management research cannot be distinguished from mainstream international business research published in the West. That is, do we need to continue to claim that 'Now the Chinese can produce a Xiaomi that looks very much like an iPhone?' The 'homogenizing tendencies of organizational studies' (March 2005, p. 5) may adversely affect the development of global management knowledge and even hamper scientific progress (Tsui 2007).

There has been increasing call for making Asian management research more contributory by conducting more indigenous, context-specific research (Jia et al. 2012; Leung 2012; Meyer 2006; Tsui 2013; Whetten 2009). So, it sounds as though the swing is shifting back to the emphasis on regional and local relevance. In Tsui's (2009, p. 1) editorial introduction, she advocated that 'Based on the principle of autonomy of inquiry and heeding the warning of the constraint of normal science, the Chinese management research community can shape its own future by engaging in research that may contribute to global management knowledge and address meaningful local management problems'. I completely share her view that we definitely need high-impact research, but what we need more is the researcher's pure pursuit of scientific discovery and theoretical innovations that can develop more new and global knowledge.

Many editorial teams of Asian management journals are discussing how to make Asian management journals stand out more and be more distinguishable from Western journals. A defensive reason for this is the huge competition for quality manuscripts and the challenge of how to create differentiation from both mainstream international business and regional-focused journals. A more proactive reason is that journals such as the *APJM* have matured and are well recognized in the international arena; therefore, the time is right for them to make a more ambitious move. Editors and established scholars are increasingly calling for developing truly universal theories by conducting indigenous management research in the region. I conclude by providing three suggestions for how we can approach such an ambitious move.

Understand the Context Deeply

Undoubtedly, the soul of Asian management research is its context. However, Asian management researchers thus far have not treated the unique context of Asia seriously and rigorously. Why should we treat the context seriously? Previously, I have restated Hofstede's (2007) comment on the importance of Asian management research, in that research and theories coming out of one cultural context may not be applied to other cultural contexts. Owing to the context-dependent assumptions of theories (Whetten 2009), there is a need to conduct indigenous research in order to develop a theory that can best explain regional or locally relevant phenomena (Leung 2012). How do we treat the context rigorously? The Asian economic ascendance provides ample opportunities for exploratory research in Asia. If we can thoroughly understand emerging and newly developed business phenomena, and examine them rigorously, it is possible that an exploratory, indigenous theory can contribute to the development of truly universal theories. According to Leung (2009, 2012) and Whetten (2009), there are several ways that Chinese or Asian researchers can develop original and trail-blazing universal theory: demonstrating the boundary conditions of a Western theory when applying it in the Asian cultural context, showing the superiority of an indigenous theory developed in Asia over a Western theory in the Asian context, and identifying what indigenous theories developed in Asia can be applied to another cultural context and where. By synthesizing indigenous research from diverse cultural contexts, we may ultimately arrive at truly universalistic theories (Yang 2000).

Ambicultural Approach

To instill new ideas and perspectives into global management, Chen and Miller (2011) proposed an ambicultural approach to bridge the global divides between East and West by integrating the best practices of the East and the West – self–other integration – identifying commonalities and applying universalities in both Eastern and Western settings, and transcending paradigmatic differences and integrating extremes. By so doing, Asian researchers can be enlightened by expansive new paths of scholarly, managerial and human pursuits. The ambicultural approach echoes Mao Zedong's key message in 'On contradiction' (Zedong 1967), in which he highlighted that the fundamental cause of the development of a thing lies in the contradictoriness with it. Instead of choosing one of the two contradictory paths, it is critical to take both simultaneously because it is in the tension between the two that new insight is most often generated. Barney and Zhang (2009) suggested that this may also be the case with the evolution of Chinese and Asian management research. To facilitate the process of integrating Eastern and Western management research, Asian researchers should not criticize those who are focusing on extending Western management theories to the Asian context or those who are dedicated to deriving logics and formulating theories from local context. Instead, it is through the continuous efforts of studying contextual differences that we may develop new and universal theories.

Uphold the Spirit of Scholarship

Finally, Asian researchers are strongly encouraged to undertake the purest pursuit of scientific discovery. As Tsui (2009, p. 3) suggested, 'it is time for the Chinese management research community to chart its own course in developing valid knowledge and contributing to scientific progress, thus achieving both rigor and relevance, the dual criteria of good applied science'. The same is true for Asian management scholars, who should leave the ivory tower and be critical of the relevance and usefulness of the research questions, theories and methods in addressing phenomena in their own contexts (Pfeffer 2007; Tsui 2009). It is interesting to learn from the former editor of *APJM* that many of the few exploratory research papers were not published because the research did not provide an answer to the research question (Ahlstrom 2011). Therefore, despite standing firm against the strong current, Asian management communities should be more courageous in striving for scientific discoveries and the development of Asian-based universal theories (Leung 2009; Tsang, 2009).

To end the chapter, I offer the following, more concrete guidance to authors who are dedicated to making meaningful contributions to Asian management research.

- Explore and discover substantively important yet under-studied phenomena in the context that can bring new insights to the field of organization and management in general. What makes Asian research stand out from context-free studies is always its context-specific nature, which will inform the academic community about timely management and organizational issues in the Asian context. It is not surprising to find manuscripts submitted to Asian management journals in which the authors did not show any relevance to the Asian context in the study motivation or state the implications of their findings for the Asian management context.
- Theorizing versus theoretical contributions. Most of the typical manuscripts received by Asian management journals are about theorizing a phenomenon in a context, with a solid literature review and employing mainstream management theories from which they develop a set of concrete hypotheses. Nonetheless, theoretical contributions are lacking. Authors are often reminded to ask if their hypotheses still hold if the country context is omitted in their hypothesis statements. Authors are strongly recommended to make use of the context to challenge and/or modify existing theories, or even to build an original and universal theory from the context.
- Crafting and writing. Many Asian management journals are developmental and have a mission to train Asian scholars towards a universal standard of publication. This, to a large extent, is owing to the lack of crafting and writing skill development in the education background of universities in Asia. Therefore, authors are strongly recommended to devote their efforts to strengthening and fine-tuning their skills in crafting their manuscripts. Editors and reviewers often have to guess what the true motivations and contributions of the study are. Effective communication from the authors would certainly keep readers' attention and interest in reading the manuscript.

REFERENCES

Ahlstrom, D. (2011), 'On the aims and scope of the *Asia Pacific Journal of Management*: what does APJM really seek to publish?', *Asia Pacific Journal of Management*, **28** (2), 215–19.

Barney, J.B. and S. Zhang (2009), 'The future of Chinese management research: a theory of Chinese management versus a Chinese theory of management', *Management and Organization Review*, **5** (1), 15–28.

Baumol, W.J., R.E. Litan and C.J. Schramm (2009), *Good Capitalism, Bad Capitalism, and the Economics of Growth and Prosperity*, New Haven, CT: Yale University Press.

Bruton, G.B., D. Ahlstrom and S. Si (2015), 'Entrepreneurship, poverty, and Asia: moving beyond subsistence entrepreneurship', *Asia Pacific Journal of Management*, **32** (1), 1–22.

Carney, M., E. Gedajlovic and X. Yang (2009), 'Varieties of Asian capitalism: toward an institutional theory of Asian enterprise', *Asia Pacific Journal of Management*, **26** (3), 361–80.

Chen, M.J. and D. Miller (2011), 'The relational perspective as a business mindset: managerial implications for East and West', *Academy of Management Perspectives*, **25** (3), 6–18.

Hofstede, G. (2007), 'Asian management in the 21st century', *Asia Pacific Journal of Management*, **24** (4), 411–20.

Jia, L., S. You and Y. Du (2012), 'Chinese context and theoretical contributions to management and organization research: a three-decade review', *Management and Organization Review*, **8** (1), 173–209.

Lau, C.M. (2002), 'Asian management research: frontiers and challenges', *Asia Pacific Journal of Management*, **19** (2–3), 171–8.

Lau, C.M. (2006), 'Achievements, challenges and research agendas for Asian management research studies', *Asian Business & Management*, **5** (1), 53–66.

Lau, C.M. (2007), 'The first decade of the Asia Academy of Management', *Asia Pacific Journal of Management*, **24** (4), 401–10.

Lee, S.A. (2007), 'APJM and NUS, 1980–90', *Asia Pacific Journal of Management*, **24** (4), 395–6.

Leong, F.T.L. and K. Leung (2004), 'Academic careers in Asia: a cross-cultural analysis', *Journal of Vocational Behavior*, **64** (2), 346–57.

Leung, K. (2007), 'The glory and tyranny of citation impact: an East Asian perspective', *Academy of Management Journal*, **50** (3), 510–13.

Leung, K. (2009), 'Never the twain shall meet? Integrating Chinese and Western management research', *Management and Organization Review*, **5** (1), 121–9.

Leung, K. (2012), 'Indigenous Chinese management research: like it or not, we need it', *Management and Organization Review*, **8** (1), 1–5.

March, J.G. (2005), 'Parochialism in the evolution of a research community: the case of organization studies', *Management and Organization Review*, **1** (1), 5–22.

Meyer, K.E. (2006), 'Asian management research needs more self-confidence', *Asia Pacific Journal of Management*, **23** (2), 119–37.

Peng, M.W. (2007), 'Celebrating 25 years of Asia Pacific management research', *Asia Pacific Journal of Management*, **24** (4), 385–93.

Pfeffer, J. (2007), 'A modest proposal: how we might change the process and product of managerial research', *Academy of Management Journal*, **50** (6), 1334–45.

Puffer, S.M., D.J. McCarthy and M.W. Peng (2013), 'Managing favors in a global economy', *Asia Pacific Journal of Management*, **30** (2), 321–6.

Tsang, E.W.K. (2009), 'Chinese management research at a crossroads: some philosophical considerations', *Management and Organization Review*, **5** (1), 131–43.

Tsui, A.S. (2004), 'Contributing to global management knowledge: a case for high quality indigenous research', *Asia Pacific Journal of Management*, **21** (4), 491–513.

Tsui, A.S. (2007), 'From homogenization to pluralism: international management research in the academy and beyond', *Academy of Management Journal*, **50** (6), 1353–64.

Tsui, A.S. (2009), 'Editor's introduction – autonomy of inquiry: shaping the future of emerging scientific communities', *Management and Organization Review*, **5** (1), 1–14.

Tsui, A.S. (2013), 'The spirit of science and socially responsible scholarship', *Management and Organization Review*, **9** (3), 375–94.

Whetten, D.A. (2009), 'An examination of the interface between context and theory applied to the study of Chinese organizations', *Management and Organization Review*, **5** (1), 29–55.

White, S. (2002), 'Rigor and relevance in Asian management research: where are we and where can we go?', *Asia Pacific Journal of Management*, **19** (2), 287–352.

Yang, K.-S. (2000), Monocultural and cross-cultural indigenous approaches: the royal road to the development of a balanced global psychology', *Asian Journal of Social Psychology*, **3** (3), 241–63.

Zedong, M. (1967), *Selected Works of Mao Zedong*, Beijing: Foreign Languages Press.

7. Squeezing lemons to make fresh lemonade: how to extract useful value from peer reviews[*]

William H. Starbuck

A GOLDEN RULE

Many years ago, feedback from an editor induced me to formulate a rule that proved very valuable, so valuable that after some years, I began to call it my golden rule. Other authors will find this rule useful. It states:

> No reviewer is ever wrong!

This rule is valuable partly because it makes an assertion that seems patently ludicrous and bizarre. Any human being, even an editor or reviewer, may err. Sometimes editors or reviewers make comments that appear stupid or they recommend changes that are unethical or methodologically incorrect. Occasionally reviewers seem arrogant, disrespectful and even nasty. Therefore, to declare that reviewers' comments are never wrong might appear irrational, but this apparent irrationality draws attention to a more fundamental truth: editors and reviewers are only reporting what they thought when they read your paper and every editor and every reviewer is a potentially useful example from the population of potential readers. A reviewer is likely to be a better source of information than is a typical reader in that a reviewer probably reads more carefully than a typical reader does and nearly every reviewer plows through an entire paper instead of giving up in disgust after a few pages.

The central purpose of my golden rule is to remind me to regard reviewers' comments not as judgments about the value of my research or the quality of my writing, but as data about potential readers of my paper. If a reviewer interprets a statement differently than I intended, other readers, possibly many other readers, are also likely to interpret this statement differently than I intended, so I should revise the statement to make similar misinterpretations less likely. If a reviewer thinks I made a methodological error, other readers, possibly many of them, are also likely to think that I made this error, so I should revise my paper to explain why my methodology is appropriate. If a reviewer advises me to cite literature that I see as irrelevant, some other readers are also likely to think this literature is relevant, so I should explain why it is not relevant. In general, I should attend very conscientiously to the honest reactions of anyone who has read my words carefully. These are much more realistic data than the polite but superficial comments of close colleagues, who may have read hastily and who do not want to hurt my feelings. Valid data about readers' reactions are hard to obtain and good data can never be wrong.

My golden rule does not ask me to follow reviewers' advice blindly. Editors and reviewers often give bad advice. Their advice derives from their interpretations of what they thought I was trying to say, which may not be what I actually intended to say. Often, reviewers conflict with each other or what reviewers advise conflicts with advice from my colleagues, so I have to decide what advice is more useful. Most of the time, reviewers' advice also conforms to widely accepted but incorrect beliefs about proper methodology. Reviewers and especially editors often see radically deviant ideas as incorrect or implausible. Indeed, there would be no point in doing research if all widespread beliefs were reliably correct.

Editorial practices have serious deficiencies, the main deficiency being the assumption that reviewers should select papers for publication. The act of rendering judgment creates a hierarchical relationship between a reviewer and an author that benefits neither of them and that often keeps innovative research from appearing in prestigious journals.

Peer review should mean that reviewers and authors are equals. However, most editors and most reviewers act as though reviewers have more competence than do authors, and as though reviewers' evaluations have more validity than do authors' evaluations. Editors also typically act as if they themselves have the wisdom and knowledge to impose constraints on papers. Such behaviors create power differences that not only contradict the concept of peer review, but also invite reviewers and editors to indulge their idiosyncrasies. As Lord Acton's hoary dictum implies, editorial power tends to corrupt and absolute editorial power ... . Very few editors or reviewers can refrain from thinking: 'I could say this better', 'I see a more interesting problem' or 'I could design a better study'.

Authors also find it extremely difficult to look upon editors or reviewers as peers. For authors, feedback from journals has implications for social status, job security and self-image. Thus, authors defensively tend to interpret all editorial comments as critical judgments. Even when a reviewer intends to say 'perhaps this might be a useful suggestion', the author is likely to hear 'do this or I will recommend that the journal reject your paper' (see also chapters 19 and 20 in this volume).

Before, during and after my period as the editor of *Administrative Science Quarterly* (*ASQ*), a botanist copy-edited the accepted papers. *Administrative Science Quarterly* employed this botanist as a way to foster effective communication with an interdisciplinary audience, the premise being that a management paper that a botanist could understand would also be understandable to a wide variety of readers. Over time, however, the botanist made ever more detailed demands of authors and grew increasingly disdainful of authors' own writing. Authors sometimes protested against the botanist's style preferences or the tone of the botanist's remarks. A crisis arose when the botanist wrote on the paper of a very famous and distinguished author, 'This looks like the ramblings of a senile old man speaking before a Rotary Club!' Thereafter, with every copy-edited paper sent back to an author, I sent a letter explaining (1) that the copy-editor was a botanist, (2) that *ASQ* used a botanist to copy-edit precisely because the botanist might not understand nuances and jargon, and (3) that the author was free to ignore the botanist's suggestions and comments because they were merely suggestions. I also told the botanist what I was telling the authors. The botanist's comments developed a different tone and authors never again complained about the botanist's suggestions, yet it appeared that authors were following those suggestions more thoroughly than before. More tactful and explanatory editorial suggestions were persuading authors who had the right to ignore the suggestions unless they improved the papers.

Editorial processes might be more effective if editors would frequently tell authors to regard the ideas of reviewers – and of the editors themselves – as mere suggestions for possible improvement rather than as commands.

The next section of this chapter summarizes studies of editors and reviewers. These studies indicate that reviewers usually disagree with each other and give mutually inconsistent advice to authors and reviewers make inaccurate predictions about the impacts that papers will have on their fields. Reviewers' biases imply that they go beyond the actual texts of papers and take account of data that may signal authors' competence. Two ensuing sections propose how authors should think about and react to feedback from journals. A final section suggests the possibility of a better future for peer review.

EVALUATIONS BY EDITORS AND REVIEWERS HAVE EARNED SKEPTICAL READING

Editing *ASQ* also exposed me to statistical evidence about the unreliability of reviewers' judgments. As an author, I had received several pairs of reviews that contradicted each other, but I had interpreted these contradictions as mere variations in personal experience. As an editor, however, I took note of the very high frequency with which pairs of reviewers gave me inconsistent advice about publication and desirable changes. After I had accumulated reviews of several hundred papers, I observed that about 25 percent of the reviewers recommended acceptance, 25 percent recommended revisions and 50 percent recommended rejection. I also calculated the correlation between reviewers' recommendations to accept, revise or reject. The correlation between reviewers was only 0.12. Thus, knowing the recommendations of one reviewer gave no basis for predicting the recommendations of a second reviewer.

I have found six instances in which editors published the frequencies of reviewers' recommendations (Starbuck 2005). Acceptance recommendations ranged from 9 percent to 14 percent, revision recommendations from 25 percent to 44 percent and rejection recommendations from 46 percent to 66 percent.

I have also found 15 instances in which editors published statistics about the agreement between reviewers (Starbuck 2003, 2005). These correlations ranged from 0.05 to 0.37, with an average of 0.18. Further, Gottfredson (1977, 1978) found that psychologist reviewers distinguish between the quality of a paper and its probable impact on its field, but reviewers' ratings of impact correlate only 0.14 with later citations. The practical correlation is nil because reviewers' ratings of impact correlate only 0.03 with later citations for papers that receive few citations, implying that positive correlations between reviewers arise entirely from above-average papers. Since citations and ratings of papers have lognormal distributions, positive correlations between reviewers are attributable to only about 20 percent of the papers (Starbuck et al. 2008).

A graph may clarify the practical implications of these statistics. Figure 7.1 is a graph of the agreement–disagreement for 1000 pairs of simulated reviewers whose evaluations resemble the published data about real reviewers. The figure shows finely measured evaluations by these imaginary reviewers just before they convert their evaluations into discrete recommendations about readiness for publication. The circular area formed by most of the dots indicates that the correlation between reviewers is near zero for papers that reviewers evaluate as near or below average. However, there is an overall positive correlation between reviewers, because agreement about the good and excellent papers produces the conical projection to the upper right of the graph.

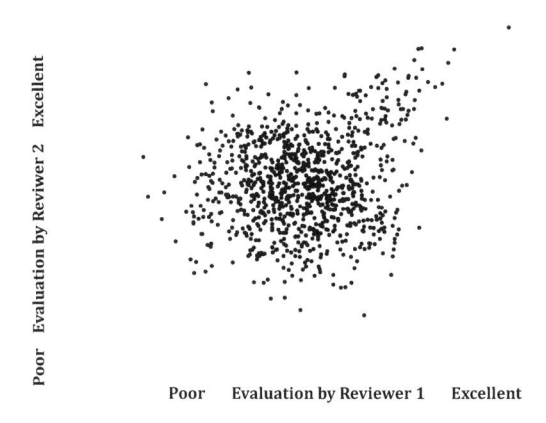

Figure 7.1 Simulated evaluations of 1000 papers by pairs of reviewers

Table 7.1 shows the data from Figure 7.1 in a different way – with the reviewers' evaluations converted into recommendations to accept, revise, or reject. The frequencies of these recommendations approximate the frequencies published by journals.

Table 7.1 Reviewers' recommendations to editors

Recommendations by two reviewers	Percentage of manuscripts
Accept–accept	6
Accept–revise	6
Accept–reject	13
Revise–revise	8
Revise–reject	37
Reject–reject	30

The published statistics imply that, on average, journals reject over half of the best papers that they receive. Journals having more prestige receive more submissions, which gives them more opportunities to publish the best papers, so they publish more of the best papers. However, erratic publication decisions mean that all journals, including the most prestigious, often reject superior papers while choosing to publish those that are inferior. The most prestigious 20 percent of journals publish almost half of the best papers they review and they publish less than one-seventh of the worst papers they review (Starbuck 2005). Also, erratic publication decisions cause about half of the best articles to appear in second-tier or third-tier journals.[1]

Undoubtedly, some editors and reviewers make erratic evaluations and provide incorrect feedback because they devote insufficient time to reading papers and writing clear comments about them. However, the main reason editors and reviewers make disparate evaluations is that the reviewing tasks are too difficult. Although most reviewers and editors are trying, their evaluation tasks exceed their cognitive and communication abilities. Calculations indicate that reviewers' advice to editors is so unreliable that having evaluations from five reviewers would yield no better editorial decisions than having evaluations by two reviewers.

Two factors make highly unreliable evaluations both desirable and necessary. First, social scientists disagree about the nature of knowledge, the purposes of scholarly publication, the character of good research methodology, the social functions of scholarly journals and the proper roles of editors and reviewers (Starbuck 2014). Many behavioral scientists concede that human knowledge is socially constructed, but some believe they are creating knowledge that will have a very stable value and relevance for decades or centuries, whereas others see their research as updating reports about current events or as translations of ancient generalizations into contemporary language. In addition to publishing excellent papers, journal editors seek to gain circulation, to earn readers' respect, to nurture inexperienced authors and to bring about changes in scholars' beliefs and methods (Starbuck et al. 2008). Very often authors misrepresent how they conducted research by saying they derived hypotheses by reading previous studies before they gathered data, whereas they actually analyzed their data before they proposed hypotheses, then they searched for previous studies to support these *ex post* hypotheses (Bedeian et al. 2010; Bones 2012; Kepes and McDaniel 2013). Authors also overstate the validity of their inferences by making numerous calculations under differing assumptions but then they disregard the implications of this data mining when they calculate statistical significance (Simmons et al. 2011). One result is that researchers claim to have found convincing support for 75–90 percent of their hypotheses (Mazzola and Deuling 2013).

Since so many researchers violate the assumptions underlying their published statistical tests, high percentages of their claimed findings are incorrect and unreproducible (Ioannidis 2005a). These deceptions turn claims about the significance or meaningfulness of findings into hollow charades, yet scholars defend the charades by saying 'This is standard practice in our literature', or something similar (Starbuck 2014). Open use of such justifications suggests that many scholars may see research as a way to demonstrate membership in a social group rather than as a way to generate useful knowledge. If people cannot agree about what they should be trying to accomplish, it is better for them to disagree with each other and thereby portray the diversity of values they hold and the goals they pursue.

Secondly, scholarly papers have many and diverse properties: authors' writing skill, authors' prestige, the prestige of authors' employers, the structures of logical arguments, the amounts and relevance of reviewed literature, the currency of topics, researchers' access to relevant data, various properties of data, implications for practices and implications for past or future research. Gottfredson (1978) identified 83 distinct properties that 299 reviewers mentioned in their comments. Although some of these correlate with each other, the properties do not fall into a logical hierarchy. Every paper has some properties that can elicit reviewers' dissatisfaction. Every paper contains some poorly phrased statements. Every paper fails to mention some relevant literature. Every paper makes some arguments that have unclear reasoning. Every theory overlooks some potentially important contingencies. Every design for a study has some defects. All data have some limitations and defects. Every analytic technique makes some unrealistic assumptions. Every useful study demonstrates its own inadequacy by revealing some aspects of the studied situation(s) that the researchers did not anticipate. One finding of every empirical study is that the study had some limitations and authors point these out. As a result, for a large majority of papers, reviewers find it much easier to complain about liabilities than to praise assets. However, reviewers do not agree with each other about which liabilities warrant complaints.

Gottfredson (1978), Gottfredson and Gottfredson (1982) and Wolff (1970) found that reviewers for psychological journals agree strongly that papers ought to exhibit some general, qualitative properties: Mainly, the research should address an important and interesting problem, not a trivial, ho-hum problem. Research should not have glaring errors. Also, the paper should exhibit a good writing style and it should discuss findings, not merely report them. However, when reviewers react to specific papers, their agreement plummets, as they focus on different properties of the paper and they assign different priorities to these properties. The properties that draw the strongest agreement from reviewers when stated as generalities are also the properties that draw the weakest agreement from reviewers when they characterize specific papers (Gottfredson 1978). Reviewers are especially prone to disagree about whether research is interesting or important and about what researchers have done wrong. The result is erratic quality for the range of published papers: Mazzola and Deuling (2013) found that many published papers had tested unstated hypotheses, had failed to test stated hypotheses or had drawn inferences about hypotheses that they neither stated nor tested. If people cannot agree about the relative importance and qualities of stimuli, it is better for them to make mutually inconsistent judgments that reveal the uncertainty surrounding their evaluations.

Studies of evaluations by editors and reviewers have disclosed biases that suggest they supplement the information they gain from merely reading papers. These studies imply that authors receive feedback that is more favorable if they say they have had other papers accepted for publication, write in idiomatic English, use mathematical formulas, even if nonsensically, report findings that support widely held beliefs and have return addresses at highly prestigious schools.

Reviewers seem to be groping for clues about authors' excellence or mediocrity. Nylenna et al. (1994) found that reviewers gave higher ratings to a paper in English than to the same paper in the native language shared by the author and reviewers. Mahoney et al. (1978) inferred that reviewers were more likely to render favorable evaluations about papers that cited in-press studies by the papers' authors. Eriksson (2012) reported that readers with backgrounds in the humanities or social sciences gave higher evaluations to abstracts that included a sentence about a mathematical model that had no relevance to the research; readers with backgrounds in the physical sciences did not show such a bias.

Perhaps the most discussed and controversial study of peer review was that by Peters and Ceci (1982), who resubmitted 12 papers to the journals that published them just 18 to 32 months earlier. All 12 journals were highly regarded and all of the papers had authors who worked in prestigious psychology departments. However, the resubmitted papers had fictitious authors with return addresses at obscure schools. The resubmissions went to 38 editors and reviewers. Three of these 38 people recognized that the papers had already been published, which cut the sample to nine papers and 18 reviewers. Sixteen of the 18 reviewers recommended rejection and the editors rejected eight of the nine papers.

The most prevalent reasons for rejection were 'serious methodological flaws', including inappropriate statistical analyses and faulty study design.

Reviewers' comments about research methodology may cloak other biases. Mahoney (1977, 1979) submitted five papers to 75 people who had recently reviewed for the *Journal of Applied Behavior Analysis*. The papers were nearly identical except that some of them reported negative results, some reported positive results and some reported mixed results. Mahoney chose reviewers whose own publications suggested they would prefer positive results and, indeed, these reviewers did generally give higher ratings of scientific contribution to papers that reported positive results and they were much more likely to recommend acceptance or minor revision of papers that reported positive results. The inter-rater correlations were 0.30 for recommendations about publication and ratings of scientific contribution, but close to zero for ratings of methodology, relevance and the quality of discussion. The evaluated papers all had identical methodology, yet the ratings of methodology correlated 0.94 with recommendations about publication. That is, reviewers found methodological faults in studies presenting evidence that contradicted the reviewers' own published work and they applauded the methodology of studies offering evidence to support the reviewers' own published work.

Junior and senior scholars may have different biases when they act as reviewers. One junior scholar told me in private:

> When I first started reviewing, I was terrified of two kinds of errors: giving a negative evaluation to a 'good' paper, and giving a good evaluation to a 'bad' paper; either result, I feared, would lead me to look incompetent in the eyes of the editor. My fellow junior scholars privately expressed the same fears.

Senior scholars may think of themselves as experts, and experts often make less accurate predictions than non-experts do. Various studies have documented this pattern for predictions about conflict resolution, economic trends, ecological changes, political trends, tennis victories and stock investments. One factor is that experts' predictions often overemphasize a few specific details while underemphasizing general patterns. Thus, reviewers and editors who regard themselves as experts may make inaccurate predictions about papers' impact and importance. McBride et al. (2012) provide a long bibliography.

Editors may be more likely than reviewers to make significant evaluation errors. Whereas reviewers can focus solely on properties of the manuscript before them, editors have to attend to the social status and financial viability of their journals, which implies that editors must demonstrate conformity to widespread social norms. For example, a reviewer can advise an author to use an unconventional statistical analysis, whereas an editor – aware that methodology is a formal ritual that persuades readers to have respect for researchers' work – may recommend using a statistical analysis that matches readers' expectations (Starbuck 2014). Editors generally know authors' names and institutions, and authors and everyone else knows the editors' names and institutions. Thus, editors have reasons to protect their personal reputations and social relationships. As established scholars, editors are more likely than are many reviewers to encounter papers that relate to their own prior research. Bedeian (2008) has reported that many editors force authors to include statements in their papers with which the authors disagree.

Laband (1990) studied comments by editors and reviewers, and authors' reactions to these comments, for 89 papers that had appeared in top journals. He inferred that reviewers' comments had significantly increased the numbers of citations of the published papers, but editors' comments had not affected citations. He concluded that editors add little value to manuscripts except by choosing reviewers well.

Silera et al. (2015) studied 1008 papers that authors had once submitted to three prestigious medical journals; 808 of these papers eventually appeared in various journals. The editors of the prestigious journals had desk-rejected 772 papers and had not sent them to reviewers; after 571 of these desk-rejected papers appeared in other journals, they averaged 70 citations. Of the papers sent to reviewers for the prestigious journals, the editors rejected 187; these rejected papers averaged 95 citations after publication in other journals. Thus, Silera et al. inferred that the papers chosen for review were better, on average, than those that editors had desk-rejected. However, the editors performed very poorly as evaluators of the most outstanding papers. Nearly all of the published papers attracted comparatively few citations, but 14 papers had drawn many more citations than the others had. Of these 14 papers that drew many citations, editors of the most prestigious journals had desk-rejected 12 and one of these heavily cited papers was desk-rejected by the editors for two of the most prestigious journals. Silera et al. (2015, p. 365) opined,

> it seems that distinguishing poor scientific work is easier than distinguishing excellent contributions. However, the high rate of desk-rejections among extremely highly cited articles in our case studies suggests that although peer review was effective at predicting 'good' articles, it simultaneously had difficulties in identifying outstanding or breakthrough work. In turn, the complexity of science appears to limit the predictive abilities of even the best peer reviewers and editors.

Although the inferences by Silera et al. (2015) seem plausible, they may overstate editors' aversion to research that attracts many citations. Silera et al. did not investigate whether later studies had confirmed the findings reported in the highly cited papers. Ioannidis (2005b) found that subsequent research had failed to confirm the findings of 36.8 percent of highly cited papers, compared with 24.4 percent of a random sample that had not been highly cited. Thus, highly cited papers were about 50 percent more likely to have reported findings that were overstated or wrong.

Laband and Piette (1994) investigated the effects of favoritism by editors. Papers by authors having personal connections with editors were more likely to become lead papers, and these papers attracted significantly more citations after publication. Laband and Piette (1994, p. 194) inferred that 'although journal editors occasionally publish subpar papers authored by colleagues and former graduate students, on balance their use of professional connections enables them to identify and "capture" high-impact papers for publication'. Medoff (2003, p. 434) drew a similar conclusion:

> [a]rticles authored by those with editorial connections, particularly serving on the publishing journal's editorial board, are both statistically and numerically of higher quality. ... The empirical results support the proposition that journal editors, in order to reduce the search costs involved in identifying high-quality manuscripts, use personal ties and institutional connections to persuade high-quality authors to submit their papers to them. Journal editors/coeditors attract these submissions by inducing high-quality authors to serve on their editorial boards as well as by offering constructive comments and suggestions on a high-quality author's paper, reducing the author's transaction cost of publishing.

The next two sections of this chapter offer some thoughts on the implications of the foregoing studies and propose how authors might deal with reviewers' comments.

WHY SUCH STATISTICS MATTER

Of course, everyone who has submitted several papers to journals has experienced inconsistent reviews and every academic has heard many stories about the inconsistent reviews received by colleagues. Nevertheless, such experiences inevitably leave authors wondering if they are especially unfortunate, if other authors of more talent and greater skill receive helpful, positive reviews. The overall negative tone of editorial feedback induces some scholars to withdraw from publishing altogether and the difficulty of satisfying editors and reviewers persuades scholars to eschew publication in prestigious journals. After Gans and Shepherd (1994, p. 165) asked 140 leading economists what they thought about review processes, many respondents told stories about very influential papers that journals had rejected, and some wrote 'several blistering pages'.

Statistical studies put individual experiences in perspective and provide evidence that almost all authors must deal with conflicting demands, some of which seem to be unwise. Reviewers rarely agree about what researchers did wrong or the importance of research topics; they agree weakly about papers' scientific contributions and worthiness for publication; and their ratings of scientific contribution correlate very weakly with later citations of published papers.

The reactions to this situation have been remarkably diverse, as demonstrated by the numerous commentaries accompanying the papers by Cicchetti (1991) and by Peters and Ceci (1982). Peer review arouses strong emotions, beliefs and ambitions. It angers, it reassures, it intimidates, it tramples egos and it puffs them up. For some people, peer review demonstrates the vacuousness and unreliability of social science, whereas other people see peer review as evidencing the substance and reliability of social science. Responses range from abstract to quibbling, from idealistic to pragmatic and from outraged to philosophical (Baumeister 1990; Bedeian 1996a, 1996b; Holbrook 1986). There has also been much writing, research and discussion about the advantages and disadvantages of using citation counts as evidence about peer review, paper visibility, paper quality, journal prestige and journal quality; Osterloh and Frey (2015) provide a long bibliography.

Harnad (1986, p. 24) opined that attitudes about peer review depend on whether people believe that most published research is 'significant and essential' or 'neither significant nor essential'. However, this phrasing understates the role of social construction. It is people, acting collectively, that define 'significant and essential'. Processes of communication, social influence and consensus building transform the insignificant into the significant, the inessential into the essential, the irrelevant into the interesting, perceptions into facts, conjectures into theories and beliefs into truths. Davis (1971) inferred that influential contributions to sociology have presentational ingredients that create tension in readers and make the topics seem 'interesting'.

Debates about what is significant and essential have strong effects on the development of widely shared perceptions and beliefs. Kuhn (1970) argued that some scientific fields develop around stable paradigms that state criteria for choosing problems and methods of research; a new paradigm emerges only when doubt about an existing paradigm grows strong and spreads widely. This is not the world of management thought, however, where paradigms are multitude, vague and ever changing. Researchers do not behave as if consensus declares certain beliefs and perceptions to be true or correct. Editors insist that studies must make theoretical contributions rather than demonstrate the effectiveness of existing theories. Therefore, almost every author dismisses prior findings and claims to have discovered support for new hypotheses. Minor revisions of existing theories get distinctive names and attract enthusiastic adherents (Starbuck 2009).

One consequence is that research ideas tend to follow dialectic trajectories: a new assertion elicits a contrary assertion; indeed, merely stating a hypothesis may be sufficient stimulus to elicit a contrary hypothesis. The ensuing debates often yield syntheses that combine the opposing hypotheses in more complex frameworks; such integration expands perceptions. Nevertheless, until these syntheses occur, the proponents of alternative viewpoints continue to quarrel about terminology and methodology. Partly because researchers have not agreed about what they know, knowledge has not accumulated and today's theories have no more explanatory power than do those in use 50 years ago (Webster and Starbuck 1988).

HOW AUTHORS CAN DEAL WITH THIS ENVIRONMENT

The statistical evidence about editors and reviewers can be liberating because it shows that ultimate decisions about what is right must come from inside authors, expressing their own expertise, ways of thinking and ethics. Editors and reviewers are unreliable judges of the value of scholarly papers; the more prestigious journals publish better papers mainly because authors submit better papers to them. Although authors should pay careful attention to the comments of editors and reviewers, authors dare not depend on editors and reviewers to tell them what to do. We are peers, even though social roles induce some of us to behave as if they are superiors.

Since comments from editors and reviewers rouse strong emotions, authors may find it useful to follow a step-by-step procedure that distributes the issues over time.

Issue 1

Did the editor desk-reject the paper? If so, did the editor state a reason for this action? A desk-reject may mean little except that an overloaded editor made a mistake. Even so, you should reduce the probability of another mistake of the same sort. You might have sent the paper to the wrong journal. Does the paper cite several recent studies in that journal? Does the paper make a meaningful contribution to an ongoing conversation in that journal? If the answers are 'yes', the current version of the paper does not present itself effectively. You ought to rewrite the paper's title, abstract and introduction to clarify the paper's importance and contribution.

Issue 2

Are you ready to act calmly and analytically? Coping with editorial feedback requires managing yourself – your ego and your emotions. You are disappointed and possibly offended; you want to protest or correct misunderstandings. However, it is a mistake to undertake revisions while you are feeling this way. Wait several weeks and reread the reviewers' comments about once a week. Eventually, you will be able to regard the reviewers' comments as data about your potential audience, and you will see why the reviewers are not wrong. They are just fallible humans struggling with difficult tasks.

Issue 3

You should analyze reviewers' comments carefully and make corresponding changes in your paper no matter what the editor said about publishing the paper – accept, revise or reject. Those comments reveal how readers reacted to the paper; if you do not like those reactions, you have to change the stimuli that evoked them.

How should you react to the reviewers' comments? Examine each sentence, asking why the reviewer made that statement and then make a corresponding change in the paper. Every comment by a reviewer warrants changes. Make notes about every change you make and why you made it. What is the reviewer's interpretation? An alternative phrasing might help. You might need to add detail or to explain an assumption. If a reviewer suggests there is something you do not know, show your knowledge, but first consider the possibility that you ought to read some additional literature. If a reviewer says you used the wrong methods, explain why you used those methods, but first consider the possibility that the reviewer might know better methods.

Beware, however, of a lurking trap. Reviewers' comments generally encourage authors to add to their papers. These additions can make the paper too complex, too difficult to read and lacking in a main theme. Ultimately, your paper must have a clear topic and clear findings.

As an editor, I observed that only about half of the authors who received invitations to revise actually submitted revised manuscripts that differed noticeably from their earlier manuscripts. The other half of these authors either submitted very superficial revisions or never resubmitted. Thus, authors' motivation and belief in their work play large parts in determining whether their papers make it into print. Some authors respond to feedback by withdrawing or refusing to comply, whereas other authors respond by demonstrating persistence and a degree of compliance.

Issue 4

Should you send the revised paper back to the journal that rejected it? An editor's decision to reject a paper may be worthy of appeal (see Chapter 21 in this volume). A central question is whether you had submitted the paper to the best possible journal. If you did, then you should resubmit it to the same journal. Before doing so, however, you should make very conscientious efforts to satisfy the reviewers, either by correcting problems or by explaining better why these are not actually problems. Many editors are willing to listen to tactful and rational appeals of their decisions. Of my four most cited papers, two were rejected by the journals that later published them.

Issue 5

If you are sending the revised paper back to the original journal, have you explained your revisions well? Editors and reviewers expect to receive detailed explanations of the revisions authors made in response to their comments (Liu 2014). These explanations are partly symbols of deference, but they also serve to focus reviewers' attention on elements that they challenged earlier, which makes it less likely that the reviewers will raise entirely new issues on the next iteration.

Issue 6

If you are not sending the revised paper back to the original journal, where should you submit it? What is the most appropriate journal? Match the properties of your paper against the properties of typical papers in each candidate journal. Has this journal recently published papers on related topics? Do papers in this journal use statistical methods or qualitative methods?

The foregoing procedures are useful in today's publication environment, but the environment has been changing and appears likely to change even more over the coming years. The final section of this chapter points to the possibility of more useful peer review.

PEER REVIEW COULD HAVE A BETTER FUTURE

In this changing academic publication environment, technology is challenging journals to show that they can be useful. However, unreliable peer review is an Achilles heel that could, perhaps should, put journals out of business.

Peer review originated because publishing was expensive. Each published page had a significant cost, so editorial budgets limited the numbers of pages. Libraries had to choose which journals to purchase. Journal publishers held editors to annual page limits. University administrators and scholars generally interpreted peer review as a mild validation of the quality of scholarly publications.

Then, peer review gained financial leverage. In the late 1980s, popular magazines began to publish ratings of schools and colleges, and some of these ratings took account of the journals in which professors published. Publication in prestigious journals had some influence on students' applications and donors' willingness to give. Around 2000, word spread that the wealthiest and most prestigious departments and schools were placing great emphasis on publishing in the most prestigious journals – 'so-called A journals' (Starbuck 2005, p. 180).

Publishing no longer has to be expensive. Scholars read journals online and libraries provide computer terminals instead of printed books and journals. Additional pages online cost almost nothing. Many scholars are making their papers available through online databases (for example, SSRN and ResearchGate) and their universities' websites. New journals are appearing daily and the total number of journals is exploding. In early 2014, Forgues and Liarte (2014) reported that open-access journals numbered around 10 000 and that 68 percent of these charge nothing for their services.

So, what value can editors and editorial boards offer? As long as university administrators see journal prestige as a very important factor in attracting donations and students, scholars will seek to win endorsements from editorial boards composed of prestigious editors and reviewers (Davis 2014). However, that seems to be an embarrassingly poor rationale in the face of evidence about the ineffectiveness of editors and reviewers.

Improved communication would be a more promising rationale for the existence of editors and reviewers. Instead of focusing on whether to publish, editors could focus on how to make papers clearer, more persuasive and more interesting. Although editors and reviewers sometimes use criteria that are not legitimate and they may have concealed motives, improved editorial practices could moderate both tendencies. For example, editors could make doubly sure that nothing in a paper hints at the author's identity, place of employment or previous publication history. Editors could tell reviewers that they should phrase their comments to authors as suggestions for improvement, not as necessary changes. Editors could tell authors that they should only follow reviewers' advice if they believe changes will improve their papers. Editors could act less as authorities or judges and more as coaches and peers. Then peer review could become what it claims to be.

NOTES

* This chapter is an updated revision of a paper that appeared in the *Journal of Management Inquiry* (2003), **12**, 344–51. However, this chapter differs substantially from the earlier paper. Thanks to Jeffrey Gish, Andrew Nelson, Andreas Schwab and the editors of this book.
1. Search engines have been making less prestigious journals more visible. Acharya et al. (2014) reported that whereas the non-elite journals published only 27 percent of the most cited papers in 1995, the non-elite journals published 47 percent of the most cited papers in 2013. In addition, authors have been using online media to attract readers to their papers.

REFERENCES

Acharya, A., A. Verstak, H. Suzuki, S. Henderson, M. Iakhiaev, C. Chiung et al. (2014), 'Rise of the rest: the growing impact of non-elite journals', Cornell University, 8 October, accessed 13 August 2019 at https://arxiv.org/abs/1410.2217.

Baumeister, R.E. (1990), 'Dear journal editor, it's me again: sample cover letter for journal manuscript resubmissions', *Dialogue*, **5** (Fall), 16.

Bedeian, A.G. (1996a), 'Thoughts on the making and remaking of the management discipline', *Journal of Management Inquiry*, **5** (4), 311–18.

Bedeian, A.G. (1996b), 'Improving the journal review process: the question of ghostwriting', *American Psychologist*, **51** (11), 1189.

Bedeian, A.G. (2008), 'Balancing authorial voice and editorial omniscience: the "It's my paper and I'll say what I want to"/"Ghostwriters in the sky" minuet', in Y. Baruch, A. Konrad, H. Aguinis and W.H. Starbuck (eds), *Opening the Black Box of Editorship*, Basingstoke: Palgrave Macmillan, pp. 134–42.

Bedeian, A.G., S.G. Taylor and A.N. Miller (2010), 'Management science on the credibility bubble: cardinal sins and various misdemeanors', *Academy of Management Learning and Education*, **9** (4), 715–25.

Bones, A.K. (2012), 'We knew the future all along: scientific hypothesizing is much more accurate than other forms of precognition – a satire in one part', *Perspectives on Psychological Science*, **7** (3), 307–9.

Cicchetti, D.V. (1991), 'The reliability of peer review for manuscript and grant submissions: a cross-disciplinary investigation', *Behavioral and Brain Sciences*, **14** (1), 119–86 (includes 33 pages of comments by others and a response by Cicchetti).

Davis, G.F. (2014), 'Editorial essay: why do we still have journals?', *Administrative Science Quarterly*, **59** (2), 193–201.

Davis, M.S. (1971), 'That's interesting! Towards a phenomenology of sociology and a sociology of phenomenology', *Philosophy of Social Science*, **1** (2), 309–44.

Eriksson, K. (2012), 'The nonsense math effect', *Judgment and Decision Making*, **7** (6), 746–9.

Forgues, B. and S. Liarte (2014), 'Academic publishing: past and future,' *M@n@gement*, **16** (5), 739–56.

Gans, J.S. and G.B. Shepherd (1994), 'How are the mighty fallen: rejected classic articles by leading economists', *Journal of Economic Perspectives*, **8** (1), 165–79.

Gottfredson, D.M. and S.D. Gottfredson (1982), 'Criminal justice and (reviewer) behavior: how to get papers published', *Criminal Justice and Behavior*, **9** (3), 259–72.

Gottfredson, S.D. (1977), 'Scientific quality and peer-group consensus', *Dissertation Abstracts International*, **38** (4-B), 1950–51.

Gottfredson, S.D. (1978), 'Evaluating psychological research reports: dimensions, reliability, and correlates of quality judgments', *American Psychologist*, **33** (10), 920–34.

Harnad, S. (1986), 'Policing the paper chase', *Nature*, **322** (6074), 24–5.

Holbrook, M.B. (1986), 'A note on sadomasochism in the review process: I hate when that happens', *Journal of Marketing*, **50** (July), 104–6.

Ioannidis, J.P.A. (2005a), 'Contradicted and initially stronger effects in highly cited clinical research', *JAMA*, **294** (2), 218–28.

Ioannidis, J.P.A. (2005b), 'Why most published research findings are false', *PLoS Medicine*, **2** (8), e124.

Kepes, S. and M.A. McDaniel (2013), 'How trustworthy is the scientific literature in industrial and organizational psychology?', *Industrial and Organizational Psychology*, **6** (3), 252–68.

Kuhn, T.S. (1970), *The Structure of Scientific Revolution*, 2nd edn, Chicago, IL: University of Chicago Press.

Laband, D.N. (1990), 'Is there value-added from the review process in economics? Preliminary evidence from authors', *Quarterly Journal of Economics*, **105** (2), 341–52.

Laband, D.N. and M.J. Piette (1994), 'Favoritism versus search for good papers: empirical evidence regarding the behavior of journal editors', *Journal of Political Economy*, **102** (1), 194–203.

Liu, L.A. (2014), 'Addressing reviewer comments as an integrative negotiation', *Management and Organization Review*, **10** (2), 183–90.

Mahoney, M.J. (1977), 'Publication prejudices: an experimental study of confirmatory bias in the peer review system', *Cognitive Therapy and Research*, **1** (2), 161–75.

Mahoney, M.J. (1979), 'Psychology of the scientist: an evaluative review,' *Social Studies of Science*, **9** (3), 349–75.

Mahoney, M.J., A.E. Kazdin and M. Kenigsberg (1978), 'Getting published', *Cognitive Therapy and Research*, **2** (1), 69–70.

Mazzola, J.J. and J.K. Deuling (2013), 'Forgetting what we learned as graduate students: HARKing and selective outcome reporting in I–O journal articles,' *Industrial and Organizational Psychology*, **6** (3), 279–84.

McBride, M.F., F. Fidler and M.A. Burgman (2012), 'Evaluating the accuracy and calibration of expert predictions under uncertainty: predicting the outcomes of ecological research', *Diversity and Distributions*, **18** (8), 782–94.

Medoff, M.H. (2003), 'Editorial favoritism in economics?', *Southern Economic Journal*, **70** (2), 425–34.

Nylenna, M., P. Riis and Y. Karlsson (1994), 'Multiple blinded reviews of the same two manuscripts: effects of referee characteristics and publication language', *JAMA*, **272** (2), 149–51.

Osterloh, M. and B.S. Frey (2015), 'Ranking games', *Evaluation Review*, **39** (1), 102–29.

Peters, D.P. and S.J. Ceci (1982), 'Peer-review practices of psychological journals: the fate of published articles, submitted again', *Behavioral and Brain Sciences*, **5** (2), 187–255 (includes 50 pages of comments by others and a response by Peters and Ceci).

Silera, K., K. Leeb and L. Beroc (2015), 'Measuring the effectiveness of scientific gatekeeping', *PNAS (Proceedings of the National Academy of Sciences)*, **112** (2), 360–65.

Simmons, J.P., L.D. Nelson and U. Simonsohn (2011), 'False-positive psychology: undisclosed flexibility in data collection and analysis allows presenting anything as significant', *Psychological Science*, **22** (11), 1359–66.

Starbuck, W.H. (2003), 'Turning lemons into lemonade: where is the value in peer reviews?', *Journal of Management Inquiry*, **12** (4), 344–51.

Starbuck, W.H. (2005), 'How much better are the most prestigious journals? The statistics of academic publication', *Organization Science*, **16** (2), 180–200.

Starbuck, W.H. (2009), 'The constant causes of never-ending faddishness in the behavioral and social sciences', *Scandinavian Journal of Management*, **25** (1), 108–16.

Starbuck, W.H. (2014), 'Why and where do academics publish?', *M@n@gement*, **16** (5), 707–18.

Starbuck, W.H., H. Aguinis, A.M. Konrad and Y. Baruch (2008), 'Tradeoffs among editorial goals in complex publishing environments', in Y. Baruch, A. Konrad, H. Aguinis and W.H. Starbuck (eds), *Opening the Black Box of Editorship*, Basingstoke: Palgrave Macmillan pp. 250–270.

Webster, J. and W.H. Starbuck (1988), 'Theory building in industrial and organizational psychology', in C.L. Cooper and I. Robertson (eds), *International Review of Industrial and Organizational Psychology 1988*, Chichester: Wiley, pp. 93–138.

Wolff, W.M. (1970), 'A study of criteria for journal manuscripts', *American Psychologist*, **25** (7), 636–9.

8. Managing a research pipeline
Brian L. Connelly

There comes a time in the life of a management academic when a terrifying reality hits. It occurs sometime after you are hired but before your colleagues vote on your tenure and promotion. You took the job with a newly minted PhD, high hopes for the publication of your dissertation and a quiet contentment that comes with knowing you have embarked on a career path that is the envy of your industry colleagues. Somewhere around two years into the job, though, your dissertation has (hopefully) been published, perhaps a project you began in your PhD program has also come to fruition, and then it happens: you realize that your tenure vote rests on the successful publication of a paper that you have not yet even started. Panic ensues.

Getting published in the best management journals is difficult, but the real challenge lies in doing so repeatedly. Certo et al. (2010, p. 593) empirically investigated the extent to which individuals 'publish five top-tier publications in 5 years (approximating tenure requirements) and ten top tier publications in 10 years (approximating requirements for promotion to full professor)'. The conclusion of their study is straightforward: few actually meet these lofty standards. As Professor Adrienne Colella informed me at the start of my PhD program, the median number of top-tier publications for a management professor in the US is zero.

I decided to dig further into these numbers by empirically examining how many management scholars publish more than once in the best management journals. To do so, I downloaded all the articles over the past 20 years from six management journals that my own institution, Auburn University, considers to be elite. The six are the *Academy of Management Journal* (*AMJ*), the *Academy of Management Review* (*AMR*), the *Journal of Management* (*JOM*), the *Administrative Science Quarterly* (*ASQ*), the *Strategic Management Journal* (*SMJ*), and the *Journal of Applied Psychology* (*JAP*). Figure 8.1 reveals that about 5700 individuals have published at least once in these top journals during that period. However, fewer than half that many are authors on at least two articles. Moving on to multiple articles reveals a waterfall curve, such that if you were able to publish ten or more articles in those years (that is, one every other year) you could count yourself among the top 250 most productive management scholars in the world. The hidden truth in these numbers and Figure 8.1, though, is a corollary to Professor Colella's rule: most people who publish in the best management journals will not do so twice.

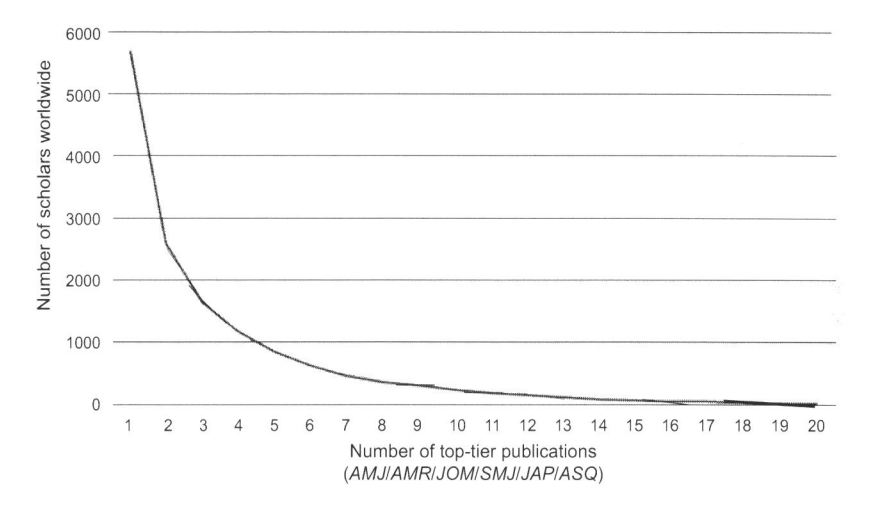

Figure 8.1   Management scholars with multiple top-tier publications

THE RESEARCH PIPELINE

There is a solution to the challenge of attaining a multi-publication research record that most management academics try to implement but with varying degrees of success. The answer lies in nearly every job talk, and it is called a 'research pipeline'. Some academics discuss their research pipeline at the beginning of their job talk, others wait until the end. Some call it a pipeline, others a funnel and still others an agenda. Some utilize a cute graphic to depict the flow from beginning to end, or top to bottom, one way or another showing projects moving from idea to publication. Regardless of the terminology or chosen analogy, the message is the same: the individual has a plan to work on specific projects that will get their publishing record from where it is now to where it needs to be for them to advance to the next stage of their career.

Many academics use some form of visualization for their research pipeline. This might comprise a spreadsheet or document on the researcher's computer or it might be prominently displayed on a whiteboard. I do both. Figure 8.2 shows the way I view a research pipeline, as listed on the whiteboard in my office and in the spreadsheet on my computer. The whiteboard allows for quick and readily accessible assessment of the current state of the pipeline. The spreadsheet allows me to incorporate more information about each paper in the pipeline, such as the action editor that is handling the paper, a history of conferences where it has been presented and a star rating system for my own guess about the current prospects for the paper. In addition to being an informative view of my work that comes in handy for annual reviews, I find both the whiteboard and spreadsheet to be motivational. There must be some chemical released in the brain when we check off a task from a to-do list or, in this case, show a project as having advanced from one stage to the next in our research pipeline.

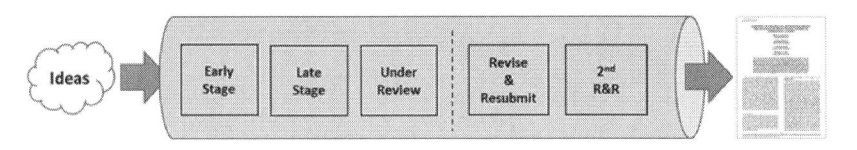

Note: R&R = revise and resubmit.

Figure 8.2 The research pipeline

While visualizations are helpful, in this chapter I dig deeper into unpacking the process of managing a research pipeline. The motivation for doing so is that some management scholars fall into the trap of thinking that simply listing a number of potential studies at various stages of completion is tantamount to managing a research pipeline. However, this type of practice could lead to a false sense of security because there is a temptation to think we have mastered something after we have applied a label to it. Applying a label to the studies that we plan to publish, with an underlying assumption that a miracle occurs to turn those studies into publications, is not pipeline management. Successfully managing a research pipeline requires a systematic approach to establishing priorities, balancing limited resources and filtering out the noise that distracts scholars from their main career objective.

EARLY-STAGE PROJECTS

The first stage of the research pipeline is the most fluid. This is the early stage, and projects might come and go from this stage with some regularity. I list projects as early stage when there is some kind of commitment to exploring an idea. Perhaps it is a personal commitment to myself or maybe it is a commitment to co-authors that we will examine some relationships. Ideas are always flowing. They may emerge over lunch with colleagues, while reading an academic article or the *Wall Street Journal*, or in personal times of reflection. Ideas, though, do not enter the research pipeline as an early-stage project until you have a mental or verbal contract with yourself or others to pursue the idea. The question to ask at this stage is, how do you know when to allow an idea to enter the research pipeline as an early-stage project?

There are two distinct philosophies about this issue: Shookarian and McNamarian. In the Shookarian view (named after management researcher Christopher L. Shook) a large number of ideas can enter the research pipeline. The driving force behind this view is exemplified in Shook's response to a doctoral student who asked, 'What percent of projects that you work on are eventually published?' Shook's answer was '100 percent!' That is, when Shook starts a project, he sees it through to completion so the project eventually finds a home in an appropriate journal. (Shook was only referring to projects where there are results to report; he was not suggesting that researchers will always find results for all their ideas.) The underlying assumption in this view is that Shookarians will continue to submit their work to publication outlets of diminishing prestige until the article ultimately filters down to the journal where it belongs. This means that Shookarians can allow a large number of projects to enter the research pipeline because some might be aimed at lower-tier journals and hence demand less effort and attention. This approach works well for those at institutions that reward researchers for publishing in a wide range of journals.

In the McNamarian view (named after management researcher Gerry McNamara), researchers are highly selective about which ideas enter their research pipeline. The driving force in this view is exemplified in McNamara's response to a personal inquiry, 'When do you let a project go and stop working on it?' McNamara's answer was, in effect, 'after it has been rejected by the top journals in the field'. At that point, he turns his attention to other projects. McNamarians, therefore, must be judicious about the projects to which they are willing to commit, because it is a huge commitment of time, energy and resources to work on a paper from idea through to submission to a top journal. McNamarians cannot afford to make those commitments if the paper is not going to stand a chance at a top-tier journal, because there is no recourse if the paper does not make it at the top. They must devote considerable effort, therefore, to the selection process to ensure that projects in their research pipeline have a reasonable shot at being published at an elite management journal. This approach works well for those at institutions that reward researchers for publishing in a narrow subset of the best management journals.

Regardless of whether you fall in the Shookarian or McNamarian camp, there is one guiding question that will help you decide when an idea should enter your research pipeline as an early-stage project, but that guiding principle changes over the course of your career. In the early stages of your career, the guiding question should be: 'who would I be working with?' The reason this is so important is that, in the early part of your career, it is imperative to learn the craft of publishing. To do so, it is extremely helpful to work with people that will help shape you as a researcher. For example, in my early years I worked with senior scholars who taught me key research habits, such as carefully matching data with theory and crafting revisions with responses in mind. In the early years, your co-authors are thus a key determinant of whether you should allow a project to enter your research pipeline at the early stage. Later in your career, as you develop the skills required to be a lead researcher, you can shift your guiding question to: 'what will I be working on?' This shift allows you to focus more on a subset of specific topics to become an expert on those topics. For example, I am at the point in my career now where I usually only allow an idea to enter my research pipeline if it has to do with corporate governance or competitive dynamics.

LATE-STAGE PROJECTS

I was recently working with a capable young assistant professor on an early-stage project, and noticed that he was peeking into my office each day to look at my whiteboard and check the status of our project. We had been working on the project for some time, and one day he simply asked, 'what does it take to move from early stage to late stage?' The answer is that papers move from early stage to late stage when the ideas, hypotheses and data are fixed. Early-stage projects can change direction in a heartbeat. It could be that you do not find the expected results. In that scenario you might just drop the project. There is no guarantee that early-stage projects will ever become late-stage projects. Alternatively, when things do not go as originally planned, you could take the paper in another direction. As you collect and analyze data, you may uncover important boundary conditions that change the nature of your study. You might have an idea for a new predictor that did not dawn on you until the project was under way. When all of these things are settled and you are no longer changing core aspects of the paper, you will have a late-stage paper.

If I glance at my whiteboard and want to know how heavy my workload is at the moment, I count up everything that is late stage and beyond. There is a fundamental difference between the two stages because early-stage papers might never make their way through the research pipeline, but one way or another every late-stage paper is going to go from beginning to (hopefully fruitful) end. As a result, I do not even count early-stage papers because they could disappear, but the late-stage papers are concrete and will be part of my workload for years into the future. Moving from early stage to late stage is non-trivial, which is why late-stage papers form the basis of the entire research pipeline.

A distinguishing characteristic of moving papers from early stage to late stage is that there is no time pressure to make that transition, nor should there be. The focus on making it to the late stage is on getting it right, not getting it fast. Papers should stay in the early stage for as long as they need in order to become solid papers that have a good chance of finding their way into a top management journal. When a paper is in the early stage, there are no demands for completion. These early-stage projects can be residual claimants of your research time and energy. When you move a paper to the late stage, though, you start a clock. There are still no external demands for completion, but the hypotheses, arguments and data are almost fixed so you cannot allow it to sit for too long because it may become obsolete or get scooped by others working in your area. The clock is ticking on late-stage papers, so wait until the papers are ready before moving them there.

A related issue with late-stage papers is what a senior scholar describes as having quality shots on goal. This is imperative in sports such as soccer or hockey, where many factors including luck and serendipity could determine the success or failure of any one shot. It is also imperative in the publishing process because researchers cannot fully control all the determinants of a paper's success or failure. They can, however, put papers in a position to be successful. To that end, late-stage projects are not just about shots on goal, they are about quality shots on goal. I have seen many instances where researchers did not attend to the quality part but, instead, allowed mediocre and underdeveloped projects to advance in their research pipeline. This is a mistake that is tantamount to a soccer player lazily lofting a slow-rolling ball in the direction of the goal. Those shots rarely, if ever, score and they hurt the team because now they must devote their energy and attention to getting the ball back. The same may be said of papers that prematurely advance to the late stage: they gobble resources and divert the researcher's attention away from what he or she should be working on. Researchers who allow bad projects to advance to the late stage find themselves trying to turn inferior papers into satisfactory papers. It is important to let early-stage projects germinate and grow to what they need to be before deciding to move the project to the late stage, since late-stage projects are going to demand your attention for a very long time.

UNDER REVIEW

The third stage of the research pipeline, journal submission, is the final stage of the process that is almost completely under the researcher's control. Determining when a paper is ready for journal submission is as much art as science, but researchers should be aware of at least two main errors that occur at this juncture. The first is a type I error, a false positive, where we think a paper is ready for submission when it is not. This is by far the most common error. You will know you made this mistake when you submit a paper and the decision letter comes back with words such as premature and under-developed. The best researchers learn from their mistakes so that they do not continually make this error. One effective way to help prevent this from occurring is to get a friendly review of your work. Even if you have co-authors on the paper, friendly reviewers provide a different perspective because these individuals approach the paper without any prior knowledge of your work, much like the real reviewers will.

The second type of error is a type II error, a false negative, where we think a paper is not ready for submission when we probably should have already submitted it. The problem with this error is that you continue to make changes to the paper, but the changes do not make the paper better, only different. I do not think I have ever made this kind of error, but there are people who do this. Statisticians suggest type I errors are about four times more grievous than type II errors. The delays associated with type II errors are costly in terms of time lost, but the rejections associated with type I errors are even more costly because you only get one shot at submitting your work to a particular journal.

The first step in moving a paper from the late stage to being under review is to write a rough draft of the first sentence of every paragraph. This is the most important step because it creates a path dependence for the paper. The result of drafting all the first sentences will be an outline. The main advantage of starting with the first sentences is that it forces you to carefully consider the logic of your arguments and how the entire paper fits together. Writing the first sentence of each paragraph, and nothing else, is an extremely difficult exercise. It is even harder when you finish and give the sentences to co-authors or friendly reviewers to ensure the logic is water-tight. Time spent at this stage of the project will save you time, effort and worry at every subsequent stage. Moreover, I can assure you that if you do this well, it will be the single best thing you can do to maximize your chances of publishing success.

With your first sentences in hand, the rest of writing the paper becomes straightforward, since there is a corollary to the rule of beginning with the first sentence of every paragraph, which is that every sentence in a paragraph should support the first sentence. Once you have established the first sentences, you already know exactly what you want to say, so it becomes almost automatic at that point to insert the arguments in support of your first sentence. This approach to structuring paragraphs might sound remedial to you, but most management researchers have not mastered the skill of first-sentence logic and paragraphs that support the first sentence. You will know that you have not mastered the skill if your decision letters and reviews come back to you with words such meandering and hard to follow. In contrast, when you have carefully attended to this rule and its corollary, you are likely to begin receiving decision letters and reviews that praise the clarity and logic of your arguments. They might not agree with your arguments, but at least they will know precisely what you are saying.

Finally, there are two ways in which authors often misallocate their attention when moving papers from the late stage to being under review. The first is they devote considerable attention and effort to high-level arguments but insufficient attention to detail. This is a mistake because being meticulous in areas that are visible to editors and reviewers communicates to them that you were equally careful about matters that are less observable. Further, attention to detail facilitates their review and decision-making because they can focus on things that matter as opposed to being distracted by unforced errors. There are many details to which authors must attend, such as ensuring the accuracy of citations and references, eliminating grammatical errors or typographical errors and rigorously following the journal's submission guidelines. I am not suggesting that the paper be excellent in these matters, I am suggesting it should be almost perfect.

The second misallocation is that authors devote diminishing amounts of attention to parts of the paper that they write last, which usually include the discussion section. By the time they get to the end they have no energy left for drawing conclusions. This, too, is a mistake because reviewers and editors will be assessing the potential consequences of your work. The classic problem that occurs is that authors devote all their creative energy to the front end of the paper and tack on a discussion section that mostly just repeats that which appeared earlier in the paper.

Discussions should be creative. One way to ensure you are writing a value-added discussion is to highlight every sentence of your discussion that already occurs in the paper. There should be very little highlighting.

REVISE AND RESUBMIT

This stage is slightly different than the others because there is nothing you can do to move a paper from being under review to getting a revise and resubmit (R&R). On my whiteboard, as seen in Figure 8.2, a dashed line separates the first three stages from the remaining stages. The whole goal is to get over the dashed line. However, once you submit your paper for review, there is nothing you can do to advance your work to the next stage in the research pipeline. An action editor will make the decision about whether your paper advances or not. You can request a particular action editor, which is probably a good idea, given that not all editors at the best management journals are equally qualified. As a result, if you leave the editorial assignment to chance, there is a possibility you might end up with an editor who is not well suited to your work.

If you receive an R&R, it should become the most important thing in your academic life. Indeed, if you have an R&R and you are reading this chapter, go work on your R&R. For everyone else, understand that when you receive an R&R it is the first time in the life of a paper that you have time pressure from an external audience. Journals will usually give you a few months to complete a revision, and you can request a few more, but this stage in the publishing process is the time to set all other projects aside to focus on the R&R. From time to time when working on an R&R I will receive a message from a co-author that they will work on it after they finish X, where X is some late-stage project they are trying to get under review or some early-stage project where they are collecting and analyzing data. This does not make sense to me. The R&R should not just be the highest priority, it should be the only priority, except for other R&Rs.

In addition to getting squeezed out by other projects, another danger is allowing an R&R to get delayed by a plethora of other academic responsibilities. John Hollenbeck at Michigan State University calls this 'death by a thousand ant bites'. Teaching, service and outreach are important, but an R&R is the path toward a management researcher's primary career objective. Recently, I was juggling several R&Rs, and as a motivational tool I listened to Lin-Manuel Miranda's award-winning song 'Non-Stop' every morning on the way to work. It is a masterpiece. The song is about Alexander Hamilton's singular focus when he was writing

The Federalist Papers in defense of the new US Constitution, and he encourages his listeners to write 'like you're running out of time'.

A final recommendation about the R&R stage in the research pipeline is that this is an excellent place to add a co-author. Researchers often do not think of doing this, but it is an outstanding strategy for adding talent to your research team. One reason it is so helpful at this particular juncture is that the paper now has an end goal. Adding co-authors in earlier stages can sometimes unintentionally yield a deadweight author who may have been well suited to an earlier version of the paper but as the paper evolved it moved away from his or her expertise. Responsible co-authors who find themselves in a situation where they no longer contribute much to a paper should offer to drop themselves from the authorship team, but this rarely happens. As a result, it is important in earlier stages of the research pipeline to consider leaving an authorship slot open for a later addition at the R&R stage. I have added co-authors to an R&R who have specific expertise with a reviewer-recommended methodology, are well versed in a reviewer-recommended theory and have access to reviewer-recommended data. This strategy is an all-around win. Reviewers like it because the new co-author enables you to be highly responsive, the existing authorship team likes it because it expands their experience in the specific direction the paper needs to go, and the co-author you invite onto the project likes it because he or she can add a project that is already well on its way down the research pipeline.

SECOND REVISE AND RESUBMIT

Moving an R&R to a request for another revision is hard work, and that work begins with the responses to reviewers. Write these first. Some authors prefer to revise the paper first and prepare the responses after they have finalized the revision. I believe starting with the responses is better because it imposes a structure on the revision process. In the first three stages of the research pipeline, the paper could conceivably go in any direction you want it to go. The end product could be anything, it is totally up to you and your co-authors. Once you jump over the dotted line (Figure 8.2) to an R&R, though, there is one specific direction in which the paper should go. The reviewers have, at least to some degree, told you what the end product should be. Starting with the responses to reviewers, therefore, forces you to begin with the end in mind. If you begin the revision process by revising the paper, you might find yourself solving problems you do not have. If you begin with the responses to reviewers, then by the time you turn your attention to revising the paper you will have a clear set of guidelines for what you should be revising.

When preparing the responses to reviewers, fix every problem they mention. Sometimes authors will respond to a three-paragraph comment with a response that only broadly addresses the main issue. That is not what reviewers want to see. There is a reason the reviewer wrote the review in detail. Therefore, it is important to respond to every concern, including comments within comments. It is acceptable to say you could not do something, or you tried to do something but it did not work, but at least acknowledge that you read, understood and considered every comment. Researchers adopt different philosophies about responding to reviewers. Some suggest only implementing changes that you think are for the better. It might sound crazy at first, but I think authors should implement all the reviewer recommendations they possibly can, even if they might disagree with the recommendation (with a caveat that they should not implement changes where they believe the reviewer is wrong). The rationale is that, on the whole, papers that reflect the collective wisdom of authors and reviewers are likely to be better than papers that only selectively allow for reviewer influence. Thus, in my view, comprehensively responding to reviewer concerns is not just a matter of improving the likelihood of publishing success, it is also the best approach to improve the substance of our work.

CONCLUSION

In summary, managing a research pipeline is largely about moving projects from one stage in the pipeline to the next. The whole point of the pipeline is to focus on movement. In Table 8.1 I summarize some of the key points in this chapter that describe how to move a project from one stage in the research pipeline to another. The key is to not let the pipeline get blocked at any one stage.

Ultimately, you want to manage a battery of projects such that enough of them result in an eventual acceptance. There could be intermediary steps of a second or third revision before a paper is accepted, or some studies might skip the second R&R and go straight to conditional acceptance. People sometimes ask how many projects should be in their pipeline. To arrive at the answer, you probably need to work back from how many acceptances you need, and take into account that not all projects will be successful (it is difficult to predict which projects will ultimately be successful). Also, people sometimes wonder how long it takes to move from the start of the research pipeline to the end. The

Table 8.1 Summary of recommendations for moving projects from one stage to the next

Pipeline flow	Key thoughts
From idea to early stage	Adopt a Shookarian or McNamarian approach to taking on new projects Consider who you will be working with (in early career) Consider what you will be working on (in later career)
From early stage to late stage	Finalize the hypotheses, logic, data and analyses Take your time, there is no hurry yet Quality shots on goal, not just shots on goal
From late stage to under review	Avoid Type I error (you think the paper is ready, but it is not) Avoid Type II error (you think the paper is not ready, but it is) Structure paragraphs to reflect the flow of your logic Allocate resources to the whole paper, including detail and discussion
From under review to R&R	Prioritize revisions over other projects Devote all your professional attention here Add an appropriately skilled co-author to your research team
From R&R to second R&R	Begin with the responses Fix every problem, and tell them how you fixed it

fastest I have seen that happen, in my own case, was two years. The slowest was nine years. I would guess the median for my projects is about four years to move from an early-stage project to acceptance. Given the attrition rate for projects that do not succeed and the time required to traverse the entire research pipeline, it is imperative to maintain a sufficient quantity of projects in the pipeline to attain your career goals. Following the guidelines described here might help you maximize the chances of successfully moving those projects through your research pipeline and, hopefully, be an exception to the rule that most people who publish in the best management journals will not do so twice.

REFERENCE

Certo, S.T., D.G. Sirmon and R.A. Brymer (2010), 'Competition and scholarly productivity in management: investigating changes in scholarship from 1988 to 2008', *Academy of Management Learning & Education*, **9** (4), 591–606.

9. Everything you always wanted to know about research impact

Anne-Wil Harzing

Academics and universities worldwide have increasingly been subjected to monitoring and evaluation of research outputs. Research impact has become a buzzword, and the use of metrics for research evaluation has become an integral part of the academic landscape. The adverse impact of this audit culture is well documented (Adler and Harzing 2009; Mingers and Willmott 2013). A reversal of this trend, however, is unlikely; it is therefore important for academics to be aware of these debates. This chapter provides a brief introduction into research impact, based on my academic research in the area, over 12 years of user support for Publish or Perish (Harzing 2007) – a free software program for citation analysis – and my presentations and blog posts on the topic.

WHAT IS RESEARCH IMPACT AND HOW IS IT MEASURED?

The answer depends on whom you ask. Ask a bibliometrician and they will probably tell you it's the extent to which an academic publication is cited by other academics. This is what we refer to as academic impact, the way in which our research influences the research of other academics. Ask a research dean in the UK involved in a Research Excellence Framework (REF) submission and they will instantly refer to impact case studies that show how academic research impacts on the world outside academia. This non-academic impact might be felt in industry and public policy, as well as in society generally. Ask an academic who is passionate about teaching and they are likely to mention the way our teaching impacts on the lives of our students. All three of them are right; impact is all of these things. Ideally, any academic should have an impact in every one of these areas, although possibly with a different level of emphasis for different career trajectories and different career stages. This chapter, however, centres on academic impact, which is typically operationalized as citations. Chapter 1 in this volume focuses on other elements of research impact.

WHAT IS THAT THING CALLED THE H-INDEX?

Beyond citations, the research metric that is most commonly used to measure academic impact is the h-index. It is defined as 'A scientist has index h if h of his/her Np papers have at least h citations each, and the other (Np-h) papers have no more than h citations each' (Hirsch 2005, p. 16569). An h-index of 20 thus means that 20 of the articles that an academic (or journal) has published have at least 20 citations each. The advantage of the h-index is that it combines an assessment of quantity (number of papers) and quality (impact, or citations to these papers). An academic cannot have a high h-index without publishing a substantial number of papers. However, this is not enough. These papers need to be cited in order to count for the h-index.

Therefore, the h-index is said to be preferable over the total number of citations as it corrects for one-hit wonders, that is, academics who might have authored (or even co-authored) one or a limited number of highly cited papers, but have not shown a sustained and durable academic performance. It is also a preferable measure over the number of papers, as it corrects for papers that are not cited. Hence the h-index favours academics that publish a continuous stream of papers with lasting and above-average impact. Although by no means an undisputed measure of academic impact (see, for example, Costas and Fransen 2018), it has become influential.

WHY SHOULD I BE BOTHERED WITH CITATION IMPACT?

Why should you even care if other scholars cite your work? I would ask, why publish if nobody cites your work? To me, not publishing is a bit like being mute, not being cited is a lot like talking without anybody listening. Your academic work might be used by students, managers or other academics who do not publish themselves. In my view, however, academic research should also aim to contribute to the academic discourse in a particular field of knowledge.

Knowing how much and where your work is cited also helps you to prepare for your confirmation or tenure application, your promotion application, your yearly performance appraisal or, more generally, your case for academic impact. Being familiar with citation analysis also makes it easier to influence your dean – or other senior academics that might influence your future – on this topic.

Most importantly, by paying attention to your citations you can learn who is building on your research. Depending on their level of engagement with your work – granted some citations can be superficial or even incorrect (see Harzing 2002) – these people might well be future collaborators. It is also exciting to see how others are using your research; you might get new ideas for research through it. Finally, citations – which will typically occur far more frequently than publications – are a nice ego boost. We do not get much positive feedback in academia, so it is nice to know someone has, presumably, read your work and found it important enough to refer to it.

HOW CAN I IMPROVE MY CITATION IMPACT?

There are quite a lot of things individual academics can do to improve the chances of their work being cited. Please note that this does not mean adopting an instrumental, let alone an unethical, approach to getting cited. It simply means ensuring that your academic publications – which have taken you a lot of blood, sweat and tears to complete – achieve the impact they deserve. Although this chapter deals solely with academic impact, many of the recommendations in it are also likely to help you achieving greater societal impact. You can increase the likelihood that your academic work is cited by paying attention to what I have called the four Cs of citations: competence, collaboration, care and communication (Harzing 2017d).

Competence, Collaboration and Care

First, impact starts with competence, that is, publishing high-quality work. Although all of us can name exceptions, as a general rule shoddy work will attract few citations and high-quality, meaningful work is more likely to be cited.

Second, collaborate! Collaboration not only makes doing research more fun. It often leads to better quality research, especially if you ensure your collaborators have complementary skills in areas where you are not that strong. Having a co-author also means that there is always someone to read your paper critically before it is subjected to the, often harsh, journal review process, thus again improving its quality. Importantly, it also ensures more motivation to finish your papers – procrastination is harder to justify to someone else. Apart from the quality boost, and thus indirect positive citation effect, there is another reason why co-authored papers are often cited more frequently: each author has their own network of academics that follow and potentially cite their work. In addition, your collaborators are likely to cite your co-authored work in their other projects.

Third, care. Care for your own academic reputation and never engage in questionable research practices. Nobody wants to cite the work of someone they don't respect. Don't think nobody will notice, academia is a small world and academics gossip just as much as the next person. Most importantly, care for others. Building high-quality networks based on trust and reciprocity (rather than instrumentality) helps the dissemination of your research. This means not rejecting review requests unless you really have to, keeping the promises you make at conferences, alerting collaborators and academic friends to useful information, and congratulating them on their achievements; in short, being a good academic citizen.

Communication

The fourth and final C is communicate. This is probably the most important aspect of getting cited (see also, Harzing 2018a). It makes sense. Academics cannot read and cite your work if they cannot find it. So why do some academics make it so terribly difficult to find their work? This might have been excusable in times before the Internet, but these days there are so many ways in which you can make your work available.

Create a personal website. I have been running a personal website since 1999 and it is the best thing I have ever done. You can put pre-preprints of all your papers online, provide an up-to-date list of publications and offer an accessible write-up of your research programmes. Having a good online presence ensures that your papers are found easily when someone searches in Google for a topic relating to your research. You need a content-rich website to achieve this and you cannot build this up in just a few years, so start early in your career.

If having your own website sounds like too much work, listing your work in online repositories is an excellent alternative. This could be your own university repository, ResearchGate, SSRN, arXiv or Academia.edu. You do not need to use all of these services, just pick one or two, and make sure you keep them up to date, otherwise people might assume you have not published anything for years. Having no profile is almost better than an out-of-date publication list that gives an 'in press' designation for articles published five years ago.

At the very least create a Google Scholar Citation (GSC) profile. Unless your name is very common, it only takes a few minutes to set it up and it ensures that everyone can find an up-to-date list of your publications. This is even more important if you have a common name as most citation databases have very poor author disambiguation (Harzing 2015). Make sure you keep your profile clean and up to date. A very easy way to clean up a messy GSC profile is to use Publish or Perish to search for your GSC profile (see Harzing 2018b). By sorting the results in a variety of ways you can easily spot mistakes or inconsistencies in your profile that you can then fix.

Attend conferences, present your work and *talk* to people. Avoid mixing only with your friends. Volunteer to participate in, or even organize, professional development workshops, act as a discussant or as a session chair. This gives you the opportunity to introduce yourself to a dedicated and captive audience; give them a few lines about your own research and impress them with your comments and organizational skills. This is particularly important for young academics who need to gain name recognition.

Does all this conference networking sound too hard for you? Are you an extreme introvert? (Most academics are introverts; they are just pretending to be extroverts for the duration of the conference.) Are you unable to travel for family or financial reasons? In that case, being active on social media can be a good alternative (see Harzing 2018c, 2019). Consider using Twitter to obtain relevant information in your field and to tweet about any new research findings or publications. I originally thought Twitter was utterly stupid; it certainly does have its limitations. However, I have gained a great deal of useful information through it that would have taken me a lot longer to gather through other sources. Tweeting about my papers and blog posts typically increases readership fivefold or tenfold, sometimes much more – not bad for a 2-minute, 280-character post.

If you are really keen, start writing blog posts about your research. It can be very enjoyable to write up the key findings of your research in a format that is accessible to a larger audience than just for your own micro-tribe. Especially if you have accumulated a body of work on a certain topic, this can be a good way to diffuse it more widely. As an example, refer to my blog post on 'Challenges in International survey research: illustrations and solutions' (Harzing 2017b). You do not need to be a senior academic to do this. Two of my junior co-authors – Shea Fan and Helene Tenzer – wrote great guest posts about their research on expatriate identity and managing multilingual teams, respectively (Fan 2018; Tenzer 2016). They are now approaching companies for new research projects and are using these blog posts to give them an accessible summary of their academic work. This works much better than sending them long emails or – horror of horrors – journal articles.

Finally, there is nothing wrong with the old-fashioned way of communicating about your research, sending an email. Are you reading an unusually interesting paper in your own field? Email the author to tell them what you liked about it and send them one or two of your own related papers. There is no need to be shy about sending academics your own papers; most of them appreciate it, as it is hard for everyone to keep up to date with the literature. However, make sure you do not become an academic spammer (Harzing 2016).

If all of this sounds unfair to you and makes you think 'But surely if my work is good academics should read and cite it?' and 'Why should publicity and name recognition matter?', I can only agree wholeheartedly, but the days of academics having the time and ability to keep up with all of the good work published in their field are well and truly behind us. Most academics have a pressured existence and the volume of publications is rising rapidly. Marketing, publicity, and reputation are important in almost any area of life these days and academia is no exception. Most academics still appreciate and recognize substance over packaging, but why not make it easier for them to appreciate the substance of your work?

HOW DO I GET ACCESS TO CITATION DATA?

Until 2004 there was only one way to get access to citation data: consult the Web of Science, also known as ISI, a subscription-based database originally established by Eugene Garfield and later run by Thomson, before morphing into Thomson-Reuters, and now reincarnated as Clarivate Analytics. Many academics, especially those who have been in academia from the time when the Web of Science was the only source available, are still firmly wedded to this data source. The problem is that the Web of Science's level of coverage is very different across academic disciplines; it is much more comprehensive in the life and natural sciences than in the social sciences and humanities, with coverage in engineering in between these two extremes.

In 2004, two new data sources were launched: Scopus and Google Scholar. Scopus, provided by Elsevier, is subscription-based and, similar to the Web of Science, relies on manual data curation, that is, journals need to be selected to be included in these data sources. Although initially its coverage only went back to 1996, it has since dramatically expanded its back catalogue and now typically provides a better coverage than the Web of Science, especially for the social sciences and humanities.

Google Scholar was launched in 2004 as the academic equivalent of the Google search engine and allows users to search the academic literature. Google Scholar crawls academic websites and indexes the full text or metadata of academic publications. As a result, some non-scholarly citations, such as student handbooks, library guides or editorial notes may slip through, and there might be some overestimation of the number of scholarly citations in Google Scholar. However, in my view this is preferable to the significant and systematic underestimation of scholarly citations in the Web of Science or Scopus for many disciplines (see Harzing 2017a). In 2012 Google Scholar introduced Google Scholar Profiles, which enables academics to create and curate an online profile with their publications (see Harzing 2018b).

In the past few years, the research evaluation landscape has been constantly evolving and new, largely free, sources of citation data are launched almost every year. The most important of these free data sources are Crossref, Microsoft Academic (Harzing 2017c) and Dimensions. Just like Google Scholar, these data sources retrieve their publication and citation data from sources that are available online. This means that their level of accuracy might be slightly lower than the manually curated databases Scopus and the Web of Science. However, I have found all three to provide cleaner data than Google Scholar.

All of these data sources are accessible through Publish or Perish (Harzing 2007), making it easy to compare metrics across data sources. Table 9.1 provides an overview of how metrics might differ across data sources, using my own publication record as an example. For Google Scholar I used my manually curated Google Scholar Profile in which I have merged stray citations with their master record[1] and removed non-scholarly records. The column 'Other' includes working papers, white papers, blog posts, professional articles, software and data.

Table 9.1 Research metrics across data sources, February 2019

Data source	Citations	h-index	No. of journal articles	No. of books	No. of book chapters	No. of conference papers	Other
CrossRef	5 323	39	84	1	11	8	0
Dimensions	5 758	39	83	1	4	8	0
Google Scholar Profile	15 722	58	84	5	24	17	21
Microsoft Academic	13 756	55	84	4	11	9	7
Scopus*	5 852	39	80	0	2	2	0
Web of Science*	3 558	32	61	0	2	0	0

Note: * General search option, that is, only includes publications listed in these data sources.

HOW DO CITATION LEVELS DIFFER BY CAREER STAGE AND DISCIPLINE?

Both overall citation levels and summary statistics such as the h-index increase with age. It can easily take five to ten years after an academic's first publication before seeing a significant number of citations materialise. This is particularly true for the social sciences and humanities, where the publication process is generally more drawn-out than in the other disciplines, with many rounds of revisions. Even accepted publications can take years to finally appear in print. Taking my own case as an example, my current Web of Science citation record puts me in the top 0.2 per cent of most cited academics in my field. However, my citations took a long time to take off. My first publication appeared in 1995; by 2000 I had about 12 publications printed or in press. However, at the start of 2000 I only had nine Web of Science citations (with 20 new citations in 2000 and 27 new citations in 2001). If I had been asked to make my tenure case after just five years, I would not have had much to show in terms of citation impact.

Moreover, citation levels are typically substantially higher in the life sciences and the natural sciences than in engineering, the social sciences and humanities. This is partly caused by the lack of comprehensive coverage of publications in the latter three disciplines in the two most commonly used databases: the Web of Science and Scopus. As we will see, disciplinary

Everything you always wanted to know about research impact 135

differences in citation levels are much smaller in Google Scholar. Most of these differences are caused simply by differences in publication patterns. Academics in the life sciences and natural sciences typically publish significantly more papers than academics in the other disciplines. However, these papers are typically shorter, have a much less tortuous review process and have significantly more co-authors. Therefore, professional bibliometricians typically work with field-corrected citation data.

CAN I COMPARE CITATION LEVELS ACROSS CAREER STAGES AND DISCIPLINES?

Unfortunately, the field-corrected citation data that are used by professional bibliometricians are not typically available to individual academics. Therefore, Harzing et al. (2014) introduced an easily accessible h-index variant that corrects for differences both across career stages and across disciplines: the hI,annual (or hIa for short). It is calculated as follows and is one of the standard metrics reported by Harzing's Publish or Perish (2007):

$$hIa: hI,norm/academic\ age,$$

where:

- hI,norm = normalize the number of citations for each paper by dividing the number of citations by the number of authors for that paper, and then calculate the h-index of the normalized citation counts; and
- academic age = number of years elapsed since first publication.

The hIa-index thus measures the average number of single-author equivalent h-index points that an academic has accumulated in each year of their academic career. An hIa of 1.0 means that an academic has consistently published one article per year that, when corrected for the number of co-authors, has accumulated enough citations to be included in the h-index. Most academics' hIa will be below 1.0 as it is difficult to keep up a stream of high-impact publications over a sustained period of time. Based on two studies of high-performing academics, Harzing and Mijnhardt (2015) suggest that an hIa above 1.0 should be considered to reflect excellent performance. An hIa above 1.5 might be considered to reflect outstanding performance, and an hIa above 2.0 can be seen as truly exceptional. Someone who co-publishes with others will not need to publish more articles to achieve the same hIa as an academic who publishes single-authored articles. However, the co-authored articles will need to gather more citations to become part of the hIa, as the article's citations will be divided by the number of co-authors.

Harzing et al. (2014) and Harzing and Alakangas (2016) illustrate the use of the hIa in a study of 146 academics at the associate or full professor level in 37 different sub-disciplines in the life sciences, sciences, engineering, social sciences and humanities. To demonstrate the effect of the hIa in terms of correcting for career length differences, Table 9.2 ranks the top ten most highly ranked academics for both the h-index and the hIa. The top ten by h-index includes mainly full professors, with an average academic age of 34.4 years. The top ten by hIa is perfectly balanced in terms of level of appointment, and the average academic age is much less, at 20.7 years. This demonstrates that the h-index is strongly influenced by longevity, whereas the hIa provides a more level playing field for younger academics.

Table 9.2 Level of appointment (full professor/associate professor) and academic age of the top ten academics ranked by h-index and hIa-index

Top ten by h-index		Top ten by hIa-index	
Level	Age	Level	Age
Prof	21	Prof	17
Prof	41	Prof	23
Prof	24	Assoc	27
Prof	37	Assoc	21
Prof	35	Prof	29
Prof	37	Assoc	13
Prof	30	Prof	19
Prof	43	Prof	21
Assoc	27	Assoc	18
Prof	29	Assoc	19
Average h-index 38		Average hIa-index 0.75	

Source: Adapted from Harzing et al. (2014).

Figures 9.1 and 9.2 illustrate the effect of using the hIa rather than the h-index when comparing research metrics across disciplines. They also show the differential levels of coverage across disciplines for the three

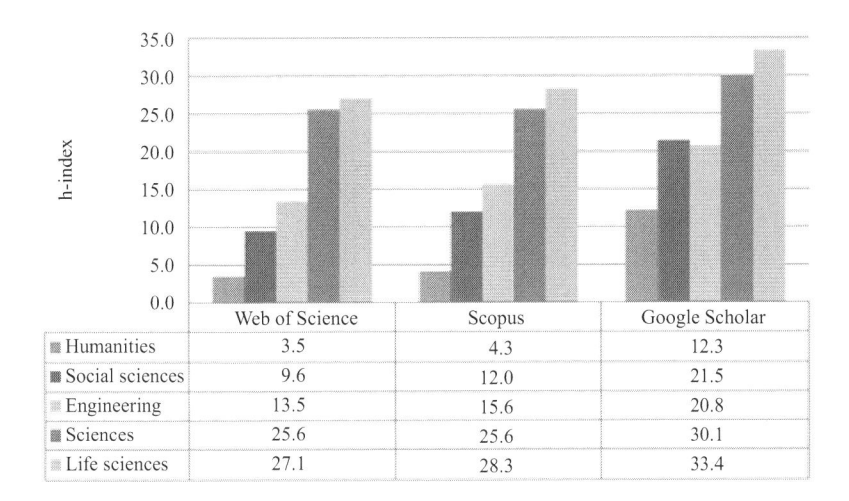

Everything you always wanted to know about research impact 137

	Web of Science	Scopus	Google Scholar
Humanities	3.5	4.3	12.3
Social sciences	9.6	12.0	21.5
Engineering	13.5	15.6	20.8
Sciences	25.6	25.6	30.1
Life sciences	27.1	28.3	33.4

Source: Harzing and Alakangas (2016).

Figure 9.1 Average h-index per academic for five different disciplines in three different databases, July 2015

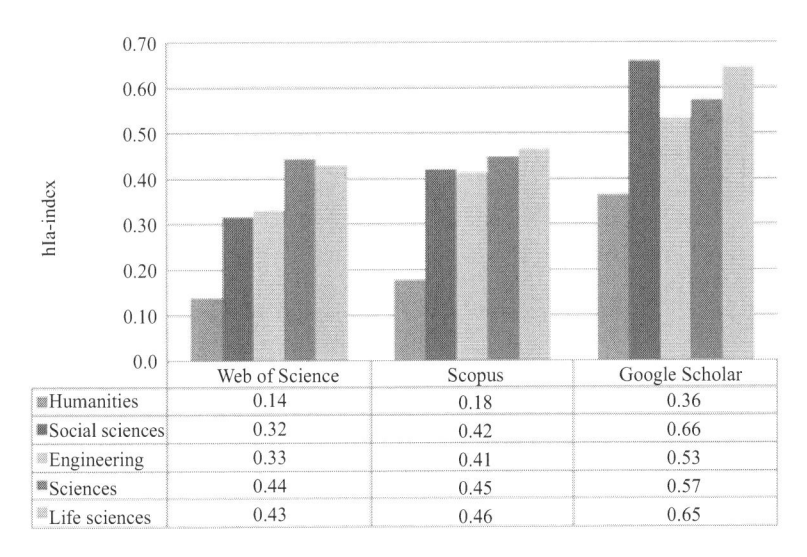

	Web of Science	Scopus	Google Scholar
Humanities	0.14	0.18	0.36
Social sciences	0.32	0.42	0.66
Engineering	0.33	0.41	0.53
Sciences	0.44	0.45	0.57
Life sciences	0.43	0.46	0.65

Source: Harzing and Alakangas (2016).

Figure 9.2 Average hIa per academic for five different disciplines in three different databases, July 2015

main sources of citation data: Web of Science, Scopus and Google Scholar. Disciplinary differences between the databases are substantial. In the Web of Science, the h-index of the average life sciences academic is nearly eight times as high as for the average humanities academic, and nearly three times as high as for the average social scientist. In Google Scholar these differences are reduced to 2.7 times as high for humanities and only 1.5 times as high for social sciences.

An even more striking picture appears when, instead of the regular h-index, we compare disciplines using the hIa. Using this metric dramatically reduces the differences between disciplines for any database. Even in the Web of Science, the difference between science and life science, on the one hand, and social science and engineering academics on the other, is now relatively small, the latter only showing 25 per cent lower metrics. In Scopus, four of the five disciplines now have very similar scores, whereas in Google Scholar the average for the social sciences is even marginally higher than the life sciences average, and substantially higher than the average for engineering and the sciences.

I WANT TO KNOW MORE. CAN YOU SUGGEST ANY FURTHER RESOURCES?

There are plenty of easy-to-read blog posts in the reference list at the end of this chapter. In addition, this is a list of freely accessible books, white papers and blog posts on topics more generally related to research impact and research evaluation, which provide an easy-to-read introduction to the field and plenty of academic references in case you want to dig deeper:

- https://harzing.com/popbook/index.htm – a free online version of the Publish or Perish Book;
- https://harzing.com/resources/publish-or-perish/tutorial – a free online version of the Publish or Perish tutorial;
- https://harzing.com/publications/free-bibliometrics-articles – a list of my articles in the area of bibliometrics that are freely accessible from the publisher;
- https://harzing.com/publications/free-articles-on-journal-rankings – a list of my articles in the area of journal rankings that are freely accessible from the publisher;
- https://harzing.com/blog/2019/01/fostering-research-impact-through-social-media – a recording – courtesy of Middlesex University – of a 1.5-hour presentation on the four Cs of getting cited and an eight-step workflow on how to effectively disseminate your research;

- https://harzing.com/blog/2017/10/to-rank-or-not-to-rank – overview of my research in the field of journal rankings, university rankings and citation rankings;
- https://harzing.com/blog/2017/09/citation-analysis-tips-for-deans-and-other-administrators – recommendations for deans and senior administrators for fair and equitable research evaluation;
- https://harzing.com/blog/2016/11/presenting-your-case-for-tenure-or-promotion – this demonstrates how to make your case for tenure or promotion by comparing your record with that of a relevant peer group;
- https://harzing.com/blog/2017/11/making-your-case-for-impact-if-you-have-few-citations – advice on strategies to demonstrate impact with a very low citation level;
- https://harzing.com/blog/2017/09/bank-error-in-your-favour-how-to-gain-3000-citations-in-a-week – this shows how even commercial data sources such as the Web of Science can contain inaccurate data;
- https://harzing.com/blog/2016/08/sacrifice-a-little-accuracy-for-a-lot-more-comprehensive-coverage – an invited prologue for a book on Google Scholar.

CONCLUSION

In this chapter I have provided a brief introduction into the world of academic impact. Its main conclusions can be summarized as follows:

- There are many forms of research impact, of which academic (citation) impact is only one. Other forms include impact on policy, industry (managers), society and students.
- Although by no means undisputed, the h-index is often used as a quick summary of an academic's research impact.
- There are many reasons to care about citation impact, including instrumental reasons such as performance evaluation and educating your dean, and intrinsic reasons such as contributing to academic discourse and finding collaborators.
- An academic can improve their citation impact through using the four Cs of citation analysis: competence, collaboration, care and communication.
- There are many sources for citation data (Web of Science, Scopus, Google Scholar, Microsoft Academic, CrossRef, Dimensions) and their respective coverage differs substantially by discipline.

- Citation levels vary dramatically across career stages and disciplines.
- Comparing citation data across career stages and disciplines is possible with the use of the hIa, a citation metric that corrects for differences in academic age and co-authorship patterns.
- There are many free resources that can help academics to find out more about the topic of their chapter.

NOTE

1. It is important to note that stray citation records are not unique to Google Scholar. They are, for instance, also prevalent in the Web of Science if you use the 'Cited Reference' search function (which includes references to books and non-ISI listed journals) rather than the general search function. I need to submit data change reports to Clarivate almost every week to ask them to merge stray citations for my work in their relevant master records. Likewise, Scopus has well over 400 secondary document results for my name, so many that I don't usually bother to submit data change reports.

REFERENCES

Adler, N. and A.W. Harzing (2009), 'When knowledge wins: transcending the sense and non-sense of academic rankings', *Academy of Management Learning & Education*, **8** (1), 72–95.

Costas, R. and T. Franssen (2018), 'Reflections around "the cautionary use" of the h-index: response to Teixeira da Silva and Dobránszki', *Scientometrics*, **115** (2), 1125–30.

Fan, S.X. (2018), 'Managing expatriates' identity: subtle desire, big impact', Harzing.com blog, 1 November, accessed 15 August 2019 at https://harzing.com/blog/2018/11/managing-expatriates-identity-subtle-desire-big-impact.

Harzing, A.W. (2002), 'Are our referencing errors undermining our scholarship and credibility? The case of expatriate failure rates', *Journal of Organizational Behavior*, **23** (1), 127–48.

Harzing, A.W. (2007), 'Publish or perish', accessed 15 August 2019 at https://harzing.com/resources/publish-or-perish.

Harzing, A.W. (2015), 'Health warning: might contain multiple personalities. The problem of homonyms in Thomson Reuters Essential Science Indicators', *Scientometrics*, **105** (3), 2259–70.

Harzing, A.W. (2016), 'Don't write mass emails (1): distributing your work', Harzing.com blog, 18 May, accessed 15 August 2019 at https://harzing.com/blog/2016/05/dont-write-mass-emails-1-distributing-your-work.

Harzing, A.W. (2017a), 'Google Scholar is a serious alternative to Web of Science', Harzing.com blog, 28 February, accessed 15 August 2019 at https://harzing.com/blog/2017/02/google-scholar-is-a-serious-alternative-to-web-of-science.

Harzing, A.W. (2017b), 'Challenges in international survey research: illustrations and solutions', Harzing.com blog, 3 April, accessed 15 August 2019 at https://harzing.com/blog/2017/04/challenges-in-international-survey-research-illustrations-and-solutions.

Harzing, A.W. (2017c), 'Microsoft Academic is one year old: the phoenix is ready to leave the nest', Harzing.com blog, 26 June, accessed 15 August 2019 at https://harzing.com/blog/2017/06/microsoft-academic-is-one-year-old-the-phoenix-is-ready-to-leave-the-nest.

Harzing, A.W. (2017d), 'The four C's of getting cited', www.harzing.com white paper, 22 August, accessed 15 August 2019 at https://harzing.com/blog/2017/09/the-four-cs-of-getting-cited.

Harzing, A.W. (2018a), 'How to ensure your paper achieves the impact it deserves?', Harzing.com blog, 15 January, accessed 15 August 2019 at https://harzing.com/blog/2018/01/how-to-ensure-your-paper-achieves-the-impact-it-deserves.

Harzing, A.W. (2018b), 'Google Scholar citation profiles: the good, the bad, and the better', Harzing.com blog, 24 November, accessed 15 August 2019 at https://harzing.com/blog/2018/11/google-scholar-citation-profiles-the-good-the-bad-and-the-better.

Harzing, A.W. (2018c), 'How to promote your research achievements without being obnoxious?', Harzing.com blog, 1 December, accessed 15 August 2019 at https://harzing.com/blog/2018/12/how-to-promote-your-research-achievements-without-being-obnoxious.

Harzing, A.W. (2019), 'Fostering research impact through social media', Harzing.com blog, 3 January, accessed 15 August 2019 at https://harzing.com/blog/2019/01/fostering-research-impact-through-social-media.

Harzing, A.W. and S. Alakangas (2016), 'Google Scholar, Scopus and the Web of Science: a longitudinal and cross-disciplinary comparison', *Scientometrics*, **106** (2), 787–804.

Harzing, A.W. and W. Mijnhardt (2015), 'Proof over promise: towards a more inclusive ranking of Dutch academics in economics and business', *Scientometrics*, **102** (1), 727–49.

Harzing, A.W., S. Alakangas and D. Adams (2014), 'hIa: an individual annual h-index to accommodate disciplinary and career length differences', *Scientometrics*, **99** (3), 811–21.

Hirsch, J.E. (2005), 'An index to quantify an individual's scientific research output', *Proceedings of the National Academy of Sciences of the United States of America*, **102** (46), 16569–72.

Mingers, J. and H. Willmott (2013), 'Taylorizing business school research: on the "one best way" performative effects of journal ranking lists', *Human Relations*, **66** (8), 1051–73.

Tenzer, H. (2016), 'How to manage multi-lingual teams?', Harzing.com blog, 17 November, accessed 15 August 2019 at https://harzing.com/blog/2016/11/how-to-manage-multilingual-teams.

10. Positioning papers for publication*
Jay B. Barney

There is continuing interest in how to write and publish papers in top management journals. Some authors have focused on how the content of papers affects their publication (Corley and Gioia 2011) – are they creative (Weick 1989) and interesting (Davis 1971), with well-defined constructs (Suddaby 2010), clear boundary conditions (Busse et al. 2017) and provocative implications (Whetten 1989)? Others have focused on how theories and results are presented in a paper – is the paper written clearly (Ragins 2012), is its macrostructure logical (Fulmer, 2012) and is its style consistent with a particular journal (Fulmer 2012)? Yet other authors (Smith and Hitt 2005) have focused on the processes that scholars have used to develop influential bodies of work. Taken as a whole, this work – whether focused on content, presentation or process – has generated important insights into writing and publishing papers in top management journals.

However, many of these insights remain abstract and difficult to implement. A paper must be creative and interesting, but how do you develop such papers? A paper must also be written in a clear and understandable way, but so often what is clear and understandable to an author may turn out to be opaque and incomprehensible to some readers. While some commonalities in the process of developing influential bodies of work have been identified (Hitt and Smith 2005), there are almost as many ways to develop this kind of work as there are examples of it – providing young scholars with little guidance in identifying processes likely to work for them. Thus, while informative about publishing papers, in principle, much of this prior work remains difficult to apply when it comes to actually writing the papers.

The purpose of this chapter is to present one approach to writing one part of a paper – the introduction – that is less abstract and, thus, more applicable than prior work. This approach is not an algorithm for writing an introduction; its application still requires creativity, a commitment to clarity and a great deal of work. Nevertheless, its application can help authors accomplish one of the most important tasks in writing a publishable paper: positioning a paper in a way that makes its contribution to theory evident to its readers (Huff 1999).

A SIMPLE FRAMEWORK TO POSITION PAPERS FOR PUBLICATION

This approach to positioning a paper is presented as a simple framework that divides the introduction into several parts. This framework was used in writing the introduction to this chapter, so readers can use this example to see how to implement it.

First Sentence: Introducing the Paper to the Reader

Whether a paper is designed to significantly extend a received theory or to develop a new theory (Barney 2018), the ideas developed in it are part of an ongoing conversation in the literature (Huff 1999). Before attempting to make a contribution to that conversation, an author must tell the reader what conversation their paper proposes to join. Thus, the first sentence of the paper must identify the broad conversation it proposes to join. In the case of this chapter, that conversation focuses on 'how to write and publish papers in top management journals'.

Choosing the conversation a paper wants to join is often not straightforward, yet its consequences can be profound, especially in terms of the reviewers that are chosen for a paper. For example, in the field of strategic management, a paper that seeks to join the 'strategic alliances' conversation is likely to get different reviewers than is a paper that seeks to join the 'governance choice' conversation, and this will probably get different reviewers than a paper that seeks to join the 'theory of the firm' conversation – even though all three conversations are closely linked and build on similar theoretical concepts. Thus, writing the first sentence of a paper is also about choosing the kinds of scholars that will review the paper.

Given its importance, it is not unusual for authors to write several different first sentences, examining the implications of how joining different conversations in the literature affect the evolution of the rest of the introduction, as well as the rest of the paper. Stephen King, the noted novelist, recognized the importance of this type of experimentation in beginning his books:

> When I'm starting a book, I compose in bed before I go to sleep. I will lie there in the dark and think. I'll try to write a paragraph. An opening

paragraph. And over a period of weeks and months and even years, I'll word it and reword it until I'm happy with what I've got. If I can get the first paragraph right, I'll know I can do the book. Because of this, I think, my first sentences stick with me. They were a doorway I went through [to write a novel].[1]

Typically, papers published in management journals start by specifying the theoretical conversation they are joining. This applies to both theoretical and empirical papers. However, it can be appropriate to start a paper with a brief description of the phenomenon that is being studied. This is particularly the case for inductive empirical papers. However, most papers are about contributing to theory. They typically frame the discussion in the introduction around theory and theoretical issues. Even if a paper initially emphasizes a phenomenon, the language of the introduction should quickly change to focus on the theory (or theories) that try to explain this phenomenon, rather than on the phenomenon per se.

The Rest of the First Paragraph

After identifying what conversation their paper proposes to join, authors must convince the reader – especially a reader with expertise in this conversation – that they have been paying attention to this conversation's main findings and conclusions. This does not require a literature review but two or three sentences that summarize a conversation's main research traditions, together with the most important results associated with those traditions.

Armed with a computer and a reasonable bibliographic database, almost anyone can generate a long list of papers that address a particular research topic. This is different from knowing the literature well enough to distill its essential features into two or three sentences, in the first paragraph of the introduction. This distillation will typically be enough to show what at least one unresolved theoretical issue in the literature is, why this issue is important and how this paper is going to resolve it – elements of the introduction discussed below.

In the case of this chapter, the first paragraph asserts that prior work on 'how to write and publish papers in top management journals' has focused on (1) the impact of the content of these papers, (2) the presentation of these ideas in a paper and (3) the process by which these ideas are developed. The paragraph ends by asserting that all these streams on publishing papers have generated important insights.

First Word, Second Paragraph

The purpose of the second paragraph in the introduction is to identify an unresolved theoretical issue in the received literature and then to demonstrate why this unresolved issue is important. This purpose is signaled by the first word in the second paragraph. Often, the word 'However' is sufficient.

The Rest of the Second Paragraph

While not denying the importance of the work cited in the first paragraph, the second paragraph must establish a legitimate theoretical reason for writing a new paper. Usually, that reason is to resolve a theoretical or empirical issue that has not been resolved in the received literature. Thus, the rest of the second paragraph must first identify this issue and then explain why it is important.

There are a variety of reasons why addressing a previously unresolved theoretical or empirical issue may be important. For example, sometimes important empirical implications of a theory may have not yet been articulated, or if articulated, they may not have been empirically examined. Other times the implications of a theory's boundary conditions may not have been fully identified, for example, how relaxing some of its underlying assumptions may fundamentally change the implications of a theory. Also, the implications of one theory for another theory (or theories) may not have been discussed yet in the literature. All these, and many others, are reasons why a particular unresolved theoretical or empirical issue needs to be resolved (Davis 1971).

One unacceptable reason why a theoretical or empirical issue is important is that it has not been addressed in previous literature. Some management disciplines call this finding a gap in the literature. There are literally thousands of gaps in the literature. Many have not been studied because they are not likely to generate any particularly noteworthy theoretical or empirical insights. This second paragraph must explain why, from among all these gaps in the literature, a particular unresolved theoretical or empirical issue is especially important.

In this chapter, the issue identified in the second paragraph is that prior work on how to write and publish papers in top management journals has often been abstract and difficult to apply. Since conversations in the literature on how to publish papers are designed to help authors write and publish these papers, that the papers are abstract and difficult to apply is an important issue in the prior work that needs to be addressed.

First Sentence, Third Paragraph

The first sentence of the third paragraph starts with, 'The purpose of this paper is ...'. This is where authors present the central research question their paper seeks to answer. This is done without subtlety, using a simple, short, declarative sentence that tells the reader what question the paper is going to answer. The answer to this question – to be developed in the paper – must resolve the important theoretical or empirical issue identified in the second paragraph.

Some authors may find it difficult to summarize their research question in a single, simple, declarative sentence. Usually, this is because these authors do not fully understand what their research question is. Other authors may find it difficult to identify just one research question in their paper.[2] This is usually because they are not clear about the specific theoretical or empirical issue they are trying to resolve. In general, papers that are about two or more research questions are usually about no research questions.[3] Finally, some authors believe that they cannot introduce a research question until after an exhaustive literature review.[4] This is often because these authors are not sufficiently familiar with a body of literature to identify its central elements in two or three sentences in the first paragraph.

The Rest of the Third Paragraph

The rest of the third paragraph provides a preview of how the paper answers its research question and some of the critical implications of this answer. It is important that this preview not attempt to summarize, in detail, the paper's entire theoretical or empirical argument. If this argument could be summarized in a single paragraph, it probably is not much of an argument.

Instead, the preview in the third paragraph begins by simply stating the answer to the paper's research question; for example, 'The purpose of this paper is to examine the implications of X for Y. It concludes that X has an important impact on Y'. The rest of the third paragraph highlights a small number of important implications of the answer to this research question. These implications further help clarify the importance of a paper's theoretical or empirical argument.

In its third paragraph, this chapter promises a less abstract and more applicable approach to writing one section of theory papers – the introduction – and warns that this approach is not an algorithm but that it can nevertheless be applied to help establish how a paper makes a contribution to the received literature. The inability to identify clearly how a paper makes such a contribution is widely seen as the most important determinant of whether a paper is published in a top management journal (Rynes 2002).

At this point in the introduction, many authors feel compelled to use several paragraphs to explain their paper's numerous contributions. In general, if the introduction is written correctly, the central contribution of the paper – that it resolves an important theoretical issue – will be obvious. Listing several other contributions – to other research questions, to practice and for teaching – simply draws attention away from a paper's central contribution and will be self-evident if the introduction is written correctly.

A paper may have other implications. It is acceptable to mention, typically in a series of short sentences, these other implications in the third paragraph of the introduction. However, these implications will usually be explored in more detail not in a paper's introduction, but in the paper's discussion section.

The Length of an Introduction

In well-written papers the full introduction is approximately one and a half manuscript pages.[5] This length reflects both style and practical considerations.

From the perspective of style, shorter is almost always better than longer. Constraining yourself to one and a half manuscript pages will almost always generate more precise writing than will introductions that go on for two or three manuscript pages. When writing papers, authors should generally write a first draft, cut it by 20 percent and then cut it by another 20 percent. The results of this draconian editing are almost always positive.[6]

In practice, authors only have a page or a page and a half to convince readers that their paper is worth the time and effort to read in detail. Readers have little patience with papers that force them to wade through page after page of prose, only to find the paper's research question on page seven, if at all. In these settings it would not be surprising for readers to ask themselves, 'Why am I doing all the work to try to understand what this paper is about? Wasn't it the author's responsibility to explain the importance of this paper to me?'

COMMON MISTAKES IN WRITING AN INTRODUCTION

Over decades of reviewing papers and editing journals, I have developed a taxonomy of common mistakes authors make in writing introductions. This taxonomy is discussed here. I do not claim that this taxonomy is complete; I am constantly surprised by the new ways that authors can write bad introductions. However, this taxonomy does include many of the most common mistakes made in writing introductions, which reduce the probability that a paper will ultimately be published.

First Paragraph Literature Reviews

One of these most common mistakes in writing introductions is trying to put an entire literature review in the first paragraph of the introduction. Recall that the purposes of the first paragraph are, first, to let the reader know (in the first sentence) what conversation a paper is joining and, second, to show those that have been part of this conversation that the authors have been listening. The purpose here is not to demonstrate that the authors have read every important paper that has ever contributed to this conversation – although this should have occurred – by citing and summarizing the findings of all these papers. Instead, the purpose in the first paragraph is to abstract from these numerous papers to describe the important elements of the broader conversation.

In practice, putting the entire literature review in the first paragraph almost guarantees that an introduction will be longer than one and a half pages. It also will make completely redundant the actual literature review later in the paper.

Second Paragraph Summaries of Theoretical and Empirical Arguments

A second common error in writing introductions is to try to summarize the entire theoretical or empirical arguments in the second paragraph. Recall that the purpose of the second paragraph is to identify an unresolved theoretical or empirical issue in the received literature and explain why it is important. Readers need to understand what this issue is and why it is important before they are willing to spend the time needed to understand a paper's entire theoretical or empirical arguments. Explaining how you resolve an issue in the literature before explaining what it is and why it is important is putting it in the wrong order.

There are two indicators that a paper is prematurely summarizing its theoretical and empirical arguments in the second paragraph. First, this paragraph will be very long, often well over a page – an innovative style of prose for William Faulkner, but not acceptable in an academic publication. Second, most of the content of the paragraph will be repeated in the theory development section of the paper.

Third Paragraph Summaries of Theoretical and Empirical Arguments

The third error is related to the second – trying to summarize the entire theoretical or empirical arguments of the paper in the third paragraph. Authors often think so much of their theoretical or empirical analyses that they cannot wait to share the details of their complex and subtle reasoning with readers. However, by the third paragraph, readers are still deciding whether or not they are going to continue reading the paper. What they are looking for is a reason to do so, or not. Detailed argumentation, whether it is conceptual or empirical, does not draw readers into the paper as effectively as a higher level, and short, statement of the research question, the paper's answer to that question and a brief discussion of how the paper's conclusions change the received literature. At the end of the third paragraph, readers should want to read more, to work through the details of a paper's theoretical and empirical arguments.

A surprisingly common third-paragraph mistake is to focus on methods and statistical models. The most egregious example of this error is identifying the statistical package that was used to estimate the models in a paper. Less egregious, but still problematic, is spending several sentences in this paragraph describing a sophisticated, yet relatively common, modelling technique that was applied in the paper. Some authors emphasize that the implications of a particular theory have never been examined in a paper's unique sample – an argument that devolves into the gap filling 'because it has never been done before' logic. Unless the contribution of a paper really is the method or models, these items should get no more than one sentence in paragraph three.

Disconnecting Radical New Theories from Prior Conversations

As an editor, I periodically receive papers that seek to supplant the entire received literature in an area of work with a completely new way of theorizing. These papers start by dismissing the received view as irredeemably misguided, and offer a new set of concepts, assumptions and propositions that, they assert, will change the way we all think about the research area in question. Rarely are these papers convincing.

The problem with these papers is not their new, radical arguments; some of these arguments may be logical, well-articulated and have the potential to generate important new insights. The problem with them is that they often fail to position their radical new ideas vis-à-vis the received literature. Until a reader understands the weaknesses of a received approach to theorizing and what the theoretical, empirical and policy implications of those weaknesses are – at least from the point of view of a radical critique – it is difficult to evaluate the advantages (and disadvantages) of a radical new approach. Without this theoretical context, these papers fail to explain why their theoretical arguments are important and instead devolve into denunciations of the received view and pronouncements about the new approach.

Thus, while at first glance it may appear that the three-paragraph model of writing introductions presented in this chapter is designed mostly for marginal theoretical and empirical contributions to established research conversations, the same model can be applied to writing papers that call for radical changes in current research. If, for example, a paper briefly summarizes the received literature (in paragraph one), identifies one or two critical weaknesses of this literature and why these weaknesses are important (in paragraph two), and then identifies the research question of trying to understand the implications of addressing these weaknesses (in paragraph three), it is set up to introduce a radical new approach to theorizing. However, this new approach does not dismiss the prior literature; it shows how addressing limitations of the prior literature open a radical new way of thinking about a class of research questions.

Introductions Longer than One and a Half Pages

Over the years, I have heard many authors complain about the one and a half page requirement for 'good introductions', and there are probably a few examples of excellent introductions that go beyond this limit. However, the page and a half is more than just an arbitrary constraint. It represents an intellectual discipline that forces authors to clearly state the main findings in a literature (paragraph one), important limitations of that literature (paragraph two) and how they intend to address these limitations through answering their research question (paragraph three). If there is no way to accomplish these tasks in one and a half pages, try again. If absolutely necessary, take two pages, maybe even four paragraphs, but do not put the research question on page seven and expect anyone to read the paper.

The issue here is not just a page and a half; it is about being a disciplined writer who knows exactly what the paper is (and is not) about, and keeps the paper focused on answering that question.

DISCUSSION

This chapter presents a simple framework for writing introductions to papers that helps establish how these papers contribute to the received literature. Obviously, this is not the only way to write an introduction. However, the discipline that underlies this particular framework is probably common across other ways of writing introductions to theory papers.

Also, writing a good introduction – using this or some other approach – does not guarantee that a paper will make an important theoretical or empirical contribution. The rest of the paper has to deliver on the promise of the introduction. Moreover, the paper must be easily comprehensible, with a logical macrostructure and consistent with a journal's style. However, while writing a good introduction does not guarantee that a paper will get published, writing a bad introduction, which does not make a paper's contribution to the literature obvious, virtually guarantees that it will not get published.

NOTES

* This chapter is based on a 'From the editor' essay originally published in the *Academy of Management Review* (2018) 43 (3), 1–4. The content of this chapter is based on a presentation given to many audiences, in many venues, around the world. Most recently, it was presented to the AMR Paper Development Workshop held on 10 February 2018, at the Haas School of Business, University of California at Berkley and to the AMR Theory Development Hackathon on 21 February 2019 at the IESE Business School, University of Navarra, Barcelona.
1. www.theatlantic.com/entertainment/archive/2013/07-why-stephen-king-spends-months-or-even-years-writing-opening-sentences/278043/ (accessed 19 March 2019).
2. If a paper should have only one main research question, it does not mean that a paper can have only one research proposition. It does mean that the multiple propositions in a paper must all speak to multiple dimensions of a single research question. Also, a single research question may have multiple parts that must be addressed if the implications of answering that question are to be fully resolved.
3. Sometimes it is possible to introduce a second or even third research question in the discussion section of the paper. However, typically, the main purpose of including these research questions in the discussion is to call for additional research.

4. 'Exhaustive' can also be read as 'exhausting'.
5. There should be no cheating – no micro-fonts and no quarter-inch margins.
6. I have applied this standard to my own writing, including to this chapter. I am reminded of the quote attributed to French Philosopher Blaise Pascal in 1657: 'If I had more time, I would have written a shorter letter.'

REFERENCES

Barney, J.B. (2018), 'Editor's comments: theory contributions and the *AMR* review process', *Academy of Management Review*, **43** (1), 1–4.

Busse, C., A. Kach and S. Wagner (2017), 'Boundary conditions: what are they, how to explore them, why we need them, and when to consider them', *Organizational Research Methods*, **20** (4), 574–609.

Corley, K. and D. Gioia (2011), 'Building a theory about theory building: what constitutes a theoretical contribution?', *Academy of Management Review*, **36** (1), 12–32.

Davis, M. (1971), 'That's interesting! Towards a phenomenology of sociology and a sociology of phenomenology', *Philosophy and Social Sciences*, **1** (4), 309–44.

Fulmer, I.S. (2012), 'Editor's comments: the craft of writing theory articles – variety and similarity in *AMR*', *Academy of Management Review*, **37** (3), 327–31.

Hitt, M. and K. Smith (2005), 'Introduction: the process of developing management theory', in K. Smith and M. Hitt (eds), *Great Minds in Management*, Oxford: Oxford University Press, pp. 1–8.

Huff, A. (1999), *Writing for Scholarly Publication*, Thousand Oaks, CA: Sage.

Ragins, R. (2012), 'Editor's comments: reflections on the craft of clear writing', *Academy of Management Review*, **37** (4), 493–501.

Rynes, S. (2002), 'From the editors: some reflections on contribution', *Academy of Management Journal*, **45** (2), 311–13.

Smith, K. and M. Hitt (eds) (2005), *Great Minds in Management*, Oxford: Oxford University Press.

Suddaby, R. (2010), 'Editor's comments: construct clarity in theories of management and organization', *Academy of Management Review*, **35** (3), 346–58.

Weick, K. (1989), 'Theory construction as disciplined imagination', *Academy of Management Review*, **14** (4), 516–31.

Whetten, D. (1989), 'What constitutes a theoretical contribution?', *Academy of Management Review*, **14** (4), 490–95.

PART II

Resolving Practical Key Issues

Section II.I

Becoming a scholar

11. Rules of the game redux 2.0

Denny Gioia

The original 'Rules of the game' was published in this volume's predecessor, in 2016 (Gioia 2016). A tweaked version of that chapter was subsequently published in *Journal of Management Inquiry* in 2018, where it drew a number of appreciative compliments, but also a stinging rebuke from a number of women on Twitter, who argued that my description of the rules of the publishing game represented an overly masculine view – portraying the process as a solitary, adversarial type of competition for scarce journal space (see Greenhalgh 2019). They therefore contributed their own, more gender-neutral, set of rules for getting published.

For someone whose longstanding self-image has been that of an advocate for women and feminism, I was a bit taken aback by the characterization of the piece as fundamentally masculine in tone. Such labelling would never have occurred to me because … I'm a guy. Now, these 46 women had me on at least one point – all my rules were named after guys (except those that were either unattributed or attributed to corporate entities, such as Nike). Therefore, in the spirit of redressing a hidden bias, I offer all the original rules of the game, plus four (well, five) additional rules that come from women. I have been using all these rules in my publishing workshop at various times, so perhaps I can save a little face by confessing to a sin of omission, rather than engaging in an attempt to deny a sin of commission. Here, then, is a more complete set of rules of the publishing game, beginning with the original introduction and rules, with the new (mostly gender-neutral) rules interspersed.

* * *

Isaac Newton – a semi-modest man despite his genius – once said that, 'If I have seen far, it is because I have stood on the shoulders of giants', Pablo Picasso – not quite so modest, but just as insightfully clever – said 'Good artists copy; great artists steal', by which he meant that great artist's take the essence of a good idea and transform it in their own image. I have an undeserved foot in both these august camps. I stand tippy-toed on a lot of broad shoulders to survey the mindscape of our field, but I also consider myself an equal-opportunity kleptomaniac. I will steal from anybody. Well, not exactly steal, but I am prone to borrowing the spirit of others' wisdom and transmogrifying it for my own purposes.

When I started out in the field, the whole business of publishing in the organization sciences was an intimidating and intriguing mystery. Having come from a doctoral program that did not emphasize publishing only made uncovering the arcane secrets of the process even more mysterious. How to begin to decipher a figurative Rosetta Stone? As a faux ethnographer, I began to ask various published scholars for their insights, their heuristics, their received wisdom and their rules of the game of publishing. In addition to my own colleagues, anytime a visiting scholar showed up at Penn State I would make it my business to pick their brains (which is what I do for a living anyway – see Gioia 2004). Over the years, I have assembled a lot of informal rules. I at least had the good sense to steal with a tip-of-the-hat attribution to the person from whom I stole the spirit of a rule worth internalizing.

Here, then, is a selection from my assemblage of rules, named in honor of the person from whom I purloined it – even if these rules are my (probably bastardized) interpretations of what they actually said. All have a specific theft victim's name, except in the first and last instance, because the first, 'Somebody's Statement,' has achieved the status of received folk wisdom that is woven into the fabric of our field, and the last, 'Nike's Rule,' is named for a mythological figure whose name was swiped by a corporate entity (thus demonstrating that I am not the only thief in the realm). A small bit of, probably unnecessary, commentary accompanies each entry. You should forgive the forced alliteration in the names of the rules. Sometimes I just can't help myself.

Somebody's Statement: *Publish or perish!* It is worth beginning with this old cliché, because publishing is the currency of the realm and you ignore this hackneyed (if nonetheless wise) counsel at your peril. My old professor, Bill Hodge's, perennial advice was 'always have options'. Publishing is the best way to keep your options open in this field.

Susman's Standard (named for Gerry Susman): *Two good publications per year keep the wolf away from the door.* Earlier in his career Gerry would close up his writing shop for the year as soon as he had two good hits (an 'A' and a something else reputable). I wish I didn't have the publishing disease and could bring myself to live by this wisdom. Might make for a more balanced life.

Gray's Gold (Barbara Gray, with inspiration from Mother Teresa): *Collaborate until it hurts.* Mother Teresa actually said: 'If you love until it hurts, there can be no more hurt, only more love'. A similar notion applies to collaboration. Collaboration is mutually generative. Most good ideas do not come from the classic loner sitting at a desk dreaming great dreams. Great ideas come from interacting with your colleagues, using them as sounding boards, piggybacking on things they say, and taking inspiration and motivation from them.

Manz's Method (Chuck Manz): *More shots on goal means more goals.* No, it's not cynical. It's actually insightful. The metamessage here is to be prolific. However, remember, the product has your name on it, so you cannot try to foist off garbage.

Mejia's Model (Luis Gomez-Mejia): *Target every manuscript to a specific journal.* Pay attention! Don't be oblivious! Journals have hallmarks. Look for what they're looking for.

Bassiri's Barometer (Mehrnaz Bassiri): *Celebrate small wins; achieve big goals.* Too early in my career I encouraged people to shoot for publishing in the best journals. Predictably enough, that was a recipe for a demoralizing rejection. Instead, start smaller; learn how to play the game in the minor leagues before you shoot for the majors. Celebrate the small successes to build a path to achieving your larger ambitions.

Sims' Statute (Hank Sims): *Work on the things that are closest to publication.* A dose of pragmatic wisdom. Most of us are easily distractible. Too many balls in the air. Which one to snare, chew on and polish? (Somebody call the mixed metaphor abuse hotline, quick!) Sims' statute solves this problem with a simple heuristic.

Locke's Law (Ed Locke): *Don't take no for an answer.* Never give up on a paper. Never, never, never give up, as some famous Englishman so famously said.

Roosevelt's Reflection (Eleanor Roosevelt): *When you cease to make a contribution, you begin to die.* The name of the publishing game is always, always, always contribution. Reviewers ask for it; editors ask for it; readers ask for it. Give it to them, but simplify your message. All readers, even academic readers, can be semi-obtuse (or, like me, just tired of reading academese, when straightforward English will do nicely, thank you).

Meyer's Maxim (Alan Meyer): *You want to be read, not just published.* A really good observation. Do it like you mean it. Intend not just to get it published; intend for people to read it. I'll even add a corollary: do it so people will cite it. Yes, you want to be published, you want to be read, but more importantly, you want to have other scholars use your work in their work.

Brass's Bylaw (Dan Brass): *The best predictor of future performance is past performance.* How do you know you're good at this game? You keep doing it and doing it and doing it the best you can.

Weick's Wisdom (Karl Weick): *There are few truly new ideas. Focus instead on finding a different way of seeing.* Coming up with the Grand Shazzam just isn't very likely. Instead, take an interesting idea and play with it. Look at what everyone thinks they know in a different way. Revisit Davis's (1971) pointers for what leads people to say 'That's interesting!' and build those attributes into your projects and your papers.

Ginsberg's Guideline (the notorious RBG – Ruth Bader Ginsberg): *If you're going to change things, you have to work with the people who hold the levers*, and ***Mead's Motto*** (Margaret Mead): *Never doubt that a small group of thoughtful, committed citizens can change the world; indeed, it's the only thing that ever has.* Despite the apparent contradiction in advice, both women are right. We all work within institutionalized systems fraught with inertial, path-dependent power structures. Power holders are not inclined to give up their power, so would-be change agents need to find ways to take it from them. Rebellion is sometimes required; cooperation always is. Are you frustrated by the existing publishing power structure? Then change it, either by confrontation or collaboration. Better both together, though.

Gioia's Judgments (My name is pronounced as 'Joya,' so you should forgive the necessary use of a homonym here, as I am not quite clever enough to come up with a term beginning with 'g' that alliterates 'Gioia'.) When you set out on a project to steal other peoples' wisdom, you develop a few rules of your own. Here's a selection that have served me well:

- *The academic world can be divided into knowledge generators and knowledge disseminators. Better to be a knowledge generator.* You probably wouldn't be reading this little chapter if you saw yourself primarily as a disseminator of other people's ideas (a teacher), rather than a generator of ideas (a theorist/researcher).
- *The academic world can be divided into readers and writers. Better to be a writer.* Question 1: do you (a) think to write or (b) write to think? The effective people who publish answer with (b). Question 2: do you (c) read to write or (d) write to read? Guess which tactic the effective publishers use? (If you think it's (c), rethink it).
- *Rhetoric matters.* In our field argumentation matters most. Data/results/findings can mean lots of different things to lots of different people. In the face of the kind of ambiguity associated with our field, you need to learn to structure ambiguity for others (I call that

sensegiving). You do *that* in a manuscript by arguing well. And you do that by becoming a rhetorician.
- *Write something every day. Writing is rewriting. Revise, Revise, Revise.* Writing for publication is a craft honed by deliberate practice (Colvin 2008). The key to my professional identity is my sense that, among my many identities, above all I am a writer. So I write something every day (even if some days it's just a well-crafted email).
- *It's all personal but you can't take it personally.* If you take yourself seriously as a writer, you are putting yourself out there whenever you submit a paper for publication. Your work is who you are. Odds are, however, that you're going to be rejected, sometimes even with a dreaded RwS (Rejection with Scorn). *Illegitimi non carborundum!* (loosely translated as 'Don't let the bastards get you down!').

I conclude with two pearls that have served as my metaguides.

Castaneda's Counsel (Carlos Castaneda): *Find a path with a heart.* This was the core message from Castaneda's *The Teachings of Don Juan*. It sounds like a new-age idealistic platitude, but it is nonetheless good counsel. It's also not that easy to do. Successful publishing too often seems like opportunistic publishing – joining in on any project that might look like it has publication potential. Don't do that. A small witticism around my shop is that we counsel junior faculty that having three streams of research is too many and having one stream is too few, so ... do the math. In the end, you want to be known for something. You can't be known for something if you're acting like you want to be known for everything. Find a path with a heart. Be known for that.

Nike's Rule (Corporate America): *Just do it!* (Yes, I will even steal from disembodied entities who are quasi-people.) Here's why I have chosen this simple, pragmatic rule of the game as my parting shot: I am often amazed at how many procrastinators and seeming perfectionists there are in academia. Both procrastination and perfectionism are diseases that are inhibitors. First, you gotta discipline the execution of your craft by finding your own ways of working on your work without constantly putting if off. Just do it. Second you gotta stop using the pursuit of perfection to enable your procrastination. Get off your duff. Just do it!

REFERENCES

Colvin, G. (2008), *Talent Is Overrated: What Really Separates World-Class Performers from Everybody Else*, New York: Penguin.

Davis, M.S. (1971), 'That's interesting: towards a phenomenology of sociology and a sociology of phenomenology', *Philosophy of Social Science*, **1**, 309–44.

Gioia, D.A. (2004), 'A Renaissance self: prompting personal and professional revitalization', in P.J. Frost and R.E. Stablein (eds), *Renewing Research Practice: Scholars' Journeys*, Stanford, CA: Stanford University Press, pp. 97–114.

Gioia, D.A. (2016), 'Rules of the game', in T. Clark, M. Wright and D.J. Ketchen, Jr. (eds), *How to Get Published in the Best Management Journals*, Cheltenham, UK and Northampton, MA, USA: Edward Elgar, pp. 109–12.

Greenhalgh, T. (2019). 'Twitter women's tips on academic writing: a female response to Gioia's rules of the game', *Journal of Management Inquiry*, **28** (4), 484–7.

12. Learning by walking through the snow

R. Duane Ireland

Those close to my age (this means we are a part of the oldest segment of the baby boomers) may recall that walking through the snow to attend school as a youth was thought to represent a true hardship. If lucky, a person received responses of heartfelt concern from others when telling a story about wearing boots while traipsing through snow-laden streets to arrive at school. Indeed, I did walk through the snow to attend elementary school in the Midwestern US city in which I was born and raised.

With hindsight, I realize that walking in the snow was a positive experience in that I quickly learned the value of patience. In particular, when confronted by heavy amounts of snow, the young student is not able to reach school quickly. Also, snowdrifts and accumulations of snow challenge the walker to carefully plan the route to take. Part of an effectively constructed walking route is specification of alternate paths to take when adjustments are required to deal with unexpected conditions (such as encountering ice underneath piles of snow). My experiences reveal that both developing and executing snow-walking plans requires patience.

So it is with us as scholars. I believe that each of us must learn to be patient as we design and execute research projects. However, this is difficult for us, given our desire to quickly (after we complete our degrees) and continuously (throughout our careers) contribute to the literature and potentially to inform managerial practice in the process of doing so. This is understandable in many ways, given the reality that, for most of us, research productivity is critical to our short- and long-term academic success. Patience is particularly difficult to develop for untenured faculty who have little time to publish their scholarship as the foundation for becoming legitimate in the eyes of their colleagues and employing institution. The infamous tenure-clock is ticking! The reality though is that high-quality research – the type that finds a home in top-tier outlets and that commonly is foundational to earning a promotion with tenure – is a product of carefully constructed designs and executions of them. As I explain next, there are multiple parts of the research process for which patience is critical.

Specifying an interesting research question is the foundation on which impactful scholarship is built. Paraphrasing Murray Davis (1971), the first criterion people use to judge work is whether it is interesting or not. The parameters of interesting research are expansive and include organizing a study around counterintuitive arguments, using novel methods, developing an unusual dataset and using theories to creatively examine an intriguing question of the current time. To me, the informal economy, changing corporate mechanisms, determining the meaning of organizational size in an increasingly digitized world and strategic entrepreneurship are examples of currently-interesting phenomena. Being able to identify important questions requires us to be patient enough to take the time and energy required to integrate multiple theories and methods within the context of contemporary phenomena that are of interest to a particular audience.

The journal to which scholarly work is to be submitted is an important audience to consider. Each journal has a mission statement that describes the type of research it seeks to publish. Scholars should patiently analyze various journals' missions to find the one that is the closest match to the research project with which they are involved. Submitting manuscripts featuring research that rests outside a journal's mission wastes precious time, given that the review process is unlikely to yield the scholar's desired outcome. Similarly, scholars should carefully read articles, especially those related to their research domain, that are published in a journal to which they intend to submit their work. Journals develop different cadences in how the research they publish is presented. The journal's mission, editorial review policies and copyediting practices are examples of influences on a journal's cadence. Becoming familiar with the nature of published work in a journal increases the likelihood of preparing a manuscript that is consistent with what a journal commonly publishes.

Assuming the mindset of a reviewer while designing and completing a study, and then writing a manuscript to describe the study, is another action requiring patience. However, doing this can lead to very positive outcomes. Carefully studying our own work as we anticipate a reviewer will do once he or she receives our paper from an editor increases the probability that we will proactively identify problems with our work. Once recognized, we can deal with those problems prior to submitting our work for review. Aggressively challenging our work as we complete it occurs only when we are able to disassociate ourselves from knowing that we are the scholar being challenged. Also, we would take the time and energy needed to identify and correct problems ourselves, rather than have those problems be the source of a rejection.

There are other actions we can take to improve the chance of our work being positively received by reviewers and editors. Asking colleagues to isolate weaknesses in our arguments before we initialize work on a project, studying the latest methods to see if a recently developed method is highly appropriate for our analyses, and seeking constructive feedback from colleagues prior to submitting a manuscript are examples of actions we can take. Learning how to write concisely also benefits our scholarly work. We should develop skills through which we are able to explicate carefully in one to two pages the research question our work addresses and its importance. When conducting empirical studies, using theory parsimoniously as a foundation for specifying the relationships we test generates reviewers' interest. Each of these actions, too, requires patience. Exercising the patience needed to consistently take the actions proposed in this commentary has the potential to lead to publishing success. As with carefully planning the route to take to walk to school through snow-laden territory, being patient enough to craft our research as effectively as possible can result in scholarly success. To develop patience as a scholar, each of us must be confident that doing so is a path to publishing impactful research.

REFERENCE

Davis, M.S. (1971), 'That's interesting: towards a phenomenology of sociology and a sociology of phenomenology', *Philosophy of Social Sciences*, **1** (4), 309–44.

13. It's all about contribution! Using the discussion to define and develop your paper's contributions

Donald D. Bergh

INTRODUCTION

The discussion section of a paper provides important insights into that paper's contribution; it is where readers learn how a paper's story adds uniquely to existing knowledge. An effective discussion will identify the research purpose, the paper's new insight, and then provide an elaboration of the contribution's meaning and implications. If your paper offers a new advance, the reader should find it in the discussion. If your paper does not offer a new contribution, the reader will find that out by reading the discussion. The discussion is the most critical part of your paper because that is where you define and develop its contribution and unique value-added. All too often, discussions rehash empirical findings and go no further – a big red flag that the authors have not thought their way through the contribution. This is why I read the discussion first whenever I review a submission.

In the following sections, I offer some suggestions on how you can use the discussion to identify and develop your paper's contributions.

SUGGESTION 1: OBJECTIVE

Consider first your motivation for writing a paper. If the purpose of writing your paper is just to publish it, or make some use of existing data, then you might not invest the effort in making it interesting and novel, and your lack of enthusiasm may become apparent to reviewers and editors. If you are not interested in the work per se, then why expect the readers to become so?

When authors are passionate about their work, the motivation, argumentation and implications become exciting. Ask yourself how you can make your paper's story poignant and compelling. If your purpose is to offer a strong, unique and confident voice to a conversation, then your story is going to be more engaging for the paper's evaluators. What is interesting about your research? Does it have broad appeal? Does it pertain to a critical social issue? Think about what makes your research interesting. Be mindful that reviewers will assess the breadth and depth of your paper's contribution, and whether it is surprising and of importance (Rynes 2002). You might think, too, about whether your paper may have a competitive advantage in the marketplace of ideas; what is rare and valuable about your paper's story (Bergh 2003)? All this begins with a clear definition of your work's objective and why it is important.

Imagine what discussion sections look like when the authors are not vested in the work versus when they are. If the discussion is boring and repetitive, focuses on empirical findings instead of on developing a story and does not proclaim the advance and its merits, do you really think the reviewers and editors are going to spend their time seeking out the paper's diamond?

SUGGESTION 2: MATURITY

Many papers are submitted prematurely; the new conceptual stories are not developed. Within the discussion, the content tends to focus on findings rather than link them to supporting a story. I recommend that you prioritize your paper's story and use the data and findings in a supporting role. Think about it like this: the evidence is used to substantiate the contribution and is not a substitute for it. Think long and hard about what the findings and arguments really mean in terms of supporting a novel and valuable conceptual story before submitting the paper. Let your ideas ripen. Think, too, about what future research might emanate from your story.

Closely related to this issue is when authors submit their papers to journals in the hope of receiving a revision outcome or feedback, so they can revise the paper for submission elsewhere. Such objectives seem to ignore the main reasons why we read papers in the first place and why some succeed in the peer review process. If the contribution is not well developed, then authors will be unlikely to receive comments on the most important aspect of their paper, will waste the time and resources of everyone involved, and will destroy the chance to resubmit to that journal.

SUGGESTION 3: MOTIVATION

Contributions need to be built upon strong foundations. This goes for both the paper's introduction and discussion. Different types of foundations exist and typically fall into one of two categories: theories or findings. Most new submissions focus on the latter. However, if you are attempting to make a compelling case for your paper, the motivation for the contribution is generally more convincing if it is rooted in revising or expanding explanations and understandings. Can you challenge conventional wisdom?

I mentioned the problems with empirical motivations. Many submissions report a motivation of resolving differences in reported empirical findings as the reason for their study. This approach sets off alarm bells in my mind. I remember in graduate school being told by Professor Luis Gomez-Mejia to not add a pebble to a pile of rocks. Papers whose motivations are based on resolving differences in empirical findings can lose sight of addressing bigger issues in explanations and descriptions. If you are really interested in addressing differences in empirical results, then adding another study to the mix is likely to be considered as just another pebble to support one side over the other. If that is what you want to do, then consider a meta-analysis that synthesizes a literature and empirically assesses the strength of moderators existing across a set of studies. Keep in mind that reconciling different theoretical explanations for a relationship elevates the conversation.

I see motivation as having different levels. Empirical motivations are lower and less interesting than theoretical motivations based on data, which help us explain phenomena and behaviors. In the latter case, the data take a supporting role.

SUGGESTION 4: STRUCTURE

A strong contribution will typically have four features. First, it will be clearly articulated relative to a research question. Second, the contribution will be defined, explained and developed. Third, it will be positioned relative to existing thinking so the reader can understand how the paper's unique story extends or revises current knowledge. Fourth, it will set a foundation for future research. Collectively, the development of the contribution within the discussion will help reviewers and editors understand your paper's value-added and help them to offer you their reactions to it if you provide a clear organization of the advance and its implications. I suggest you organize discussion sections in that way.

SUGGESTION 5: TARGETING

Contribution can take different forms and types. At least three exist: (1) a new advance for theory and topic; (2) a new advance for topic, but not theory; and (3) a new advance to theory, but not to topic (Bergh 2008). The type of contribution offered by your paper needs to align with the journal's objective. Realize that journals seek to publish specific kinds of contributions. If you are targeting a top academic journal, then your paper probably needs to offer an advance for both theory and topic (see type 1 above). If you are targeting the next level of journals, then your paper might apply extant theory in order to derive a new insight into a topic (see type 2). Many, if not most, papers are rejected because the type of contribution that they can offer does not align with what the journal seeks to publish. From my experience, some papers can be shifted among these types, so that a paper's publication prospects can be significantly enhanced. This development often occurs during a revision process involving highly engaged authors and reviewers working together (Bergh 2006).

CONCLUSION

In closing, new submissions often do not include several of the above points. Become an expert in discussion sections. Read them closely so you, and your readers, can better understand what any paper offers the literature. Think of the discussion as helping you add your voice to an existing conversation.

REFERENCES

Bergh, D.D. (2003), 'Thinking strategically about contribution', *Academy of Management Journal*, **46** (2), 135–6.
Bergh, D.D. (2006), 'Editing the 2004 AMJ Best Article Award winner', *Academy of Management Journal*, **49** (2), 197–202.
Bergh, D.D. (2008), 'The developmental editor: assessing and directing manuscript contribution', in Y. Baruch, A.M. Konrad, H. Aguinis and W.H. Starbuck (eds), *Opening the Black Box of Editorship*, London: Palgrave Macmillan, pp. 114–23.
Rynes, S. (2002), 'Some reflections on contribution', *Academy of Management Journal*, **45** (2), 311–13.

14. 'You miss 100% of the shots you don't take'

Annette L. Ranft and Anne D. Smith[*]

This famous quote – 'You miss 100% of the shots you don't take'[1] – by ice hockey Hall of Fame player Wayne Gretzky captures what we want to address in this short chapter: the need to get your papers out and under review! Let's be clear – we are not advocating against getting friendly reviews or feedback from conferences in order to strengthen your paper. (In our roles as associate editors, we have certainly seen many desk rejects of papers that needed much more work before submission.) Yet, just as some may have the propensity to submit to a journal too soon, we know there are others who are slow to send their manuscripts to a journal, if they send them at all. These are researchers who take weeks, months or years to tinker with a manuscript, scrapping whole sections or the entire paper, collecting more data, reading one more book or stream of research, and/or rethinking the theoretical frame. We are addressing our comments to these colleagues whom we know well – those who are tinkerers, perfectionists, slow, or simply never 'take a shot' by sending a paper to a journal. We have found that this paralyzing stultification can occur at many points in a career – from a first-year assistant professor who is no longer focused on deadlines imposed by a dissertation chair, to a senior researcher who has endured a spate of harsh, negative reviews about his or her stream of research or methodological approach. Our objective in this chapter is to articulate why getting a paper under review is critical. We provide suggestions to help overcome the tendency to hold on to a manuscript.

In ice hockey, if you don't take shots, you become a weak member of a team, and your playing time and marketability subsequently decrease. So, too, in academic institutions, not getting papers out leads to lower productivity which not only hurts your chances for promotion but also decreases your market value if you want or need to move. In addition, in many streams of research, there is a window in which papers on a topic are sought after. Further, delaying getting your manuscript under review opens the door to be scooped by another academic. Instead of trying to perfect a manuscript, it would be better to get a good manuscript under review and allow reviewers to provide direction towards publication. As Golden-Biddle and Locke (2007) noted, reviewers in many cases become similar to co-authors, providing clear direction on the types and degree of changes needed. A high-risk revise and resubmit can often require additional data, a new theory lens and substantial new analyses; yet rarely does a researcher need to start over with a blank screen for a revision. Finally, being good enough for a review should become your mantra instead of getting it perfect.

If you have a colleague or co-author (or see parts of yourself) in the above description, here are some suggestions to help move from manuscript to submission

- Use deadlines to force you to submit. Special issues have built-in deadlines for submission and review cycles. Use these externally derived deadlines as your own. Conference deadlines provide an opportunity to complete and submit a draft. However, moving from conference paper to journal submission many times requires creating a deadline for yourself. Committing to that deadline publically to your colleagues, co-authors, spouse, anyone who will listen and ask you about it again later, will enhance the effectiveness of your self-imposed deadlines.
- Publicly stating your commitment to meet a deadline can spur you to action. While the deadline commitment can be made orally, we suggest also making a public reminder by using a whiteboard in your office that identifies which manuscripts are targeted to which journals with hard deadlines. Discuss the whiteboard with colleagues (you might find some common interests). At the very least, you create personal accountability from these visible commitments. No erasing allowed! If you must alter a deadline for submission, strike through the old deadline and put in a new deadline – again no erasing allowed!
- Identify colleagues who are productive and have a strong publication track record, and learn from their habits. How do they spend their time? How do they approach readying a manuscript for submission? Find out if one of these colleagues would be willing to work with you. You will learn about their work habits and approach to deciding when a manuscript is ready to send out. Even if the topic areas don't naturally overlap, most academic researchers enjoy collaborating and connecting over intriguing ideas. You bring

the deep topic knowledge, and they bring the process to getting the manuscript out of the door.
- Write daily and work with one or two colleagues during two or three distinct times of the week. Many graduate students we have known have used this approach – writing with another graduate student on Saturday or every other day at specified times. Consider creating a 6 a.m. to 8 a.m. writing time in the office with another early-morning colleague. Share manuscripts, ask for advice, commiserate over coffee and, in effect, hold one another accountable. This regular routinized approach to writing not only helps to build communities and hold you accountable, but it also makes the process of writing and revision less lonely.
- Listen to colleagues who shoot straight but not to kill. All manuscripts could benefit from another set of eyes and feedback. On manuscripts that are for initial journal submissions, give the paper to a colleague who may not know a lot about the topic to see if he or she can discern what the project is about. Ask someone in the same knowledge domain as the manuscript's subject to provide input, both about the manuscript and about guidance on where to submit the manuscript. Take the feedback as input but not unchangeable directives, and set a time limit for your revision. This becomes your submission goal date. For significant and material criticisms, it may be that the project should be narrowed or perhaps, if enough negative input, the project should be cancelled. There is nothing worse than having a black cloud of a lingering project hanging over your head.
- Revisions are tricky, so get some advice. The initial deadline for yourself is to send the manuscript to a journal. Once you have done so, and you have received that glorious revise and resubmit decision, a new deadline is in place for the revision. There is no time to blame the reviewers for not understanding your study or theory and no time to process emotional reactions to the lack of enthusiastic support for your obvious creativity and intellect. We often receive advice to put the reviews aside for 24 hours. This is good advice, but also ask for a friendly read of reviewer comments during that time. This can be invaluable whether you are a new assistant professor or seasoned full professor. Some authors who are slow to send papers out for review may perceive a large-scale revision as needed in the comments, whereas another will identify that the editor is calling for less substantial changes. Before heading down the path of collecting more data or scrapping the methods, ask for advice and interpretation of editors' comments

about a revision (and congratulate yourself for the revision from the journal, which brings us to our last point).
- Tell the negative mouse to be quiet. Michael Lubatkin, a prolific strategy scholar, described having a mouse on either shoulder – one with helpful thoughts ('That is a great insight!' 'Congratulations on the revision!' 'You can do this!') and the other a (usually louder) negative mouse ('You only wrote a paragraph today?' 'That is just BS.' 'You will never finish this manuscript'). These negative thoughts slow you down and are not helpful. Confidence is not built overnight, but getting manuscripts out is a visible sign that the negative mouse's arguments were curtailed.

We hope that our suggestions help you to 'take a shot' and submit your manuscript in a timely fashion to journals.

NOTES

* Equal authorship.
1. http://www.forbes.com/sites/actiontrumpseverything/2014/01/12/you-miss-100-of-the-shots-you-dont-take-so-start-shooting-at-your-goal/ (accessed 19 January 2014).

REFERENCE

Golden-Biddle, K. and K. Locke (2007), *Composing Qualitative Research*, Thousand Oaks, CA: Sage.

15. Why I don't want to co-author with you and what you can do about it

David J. Ketchen, Jr.

INTRODUCTION

Time is the most precious resource that each of us manages in our professional lives. Those of us who have been fortunate enough to advance through our careers from assistant professor to associate professor to full professor and finally to chaired professor generally find that the demands on our time seem to grow as we move up the proverbial academic ladder. This forces us to make hard choices and to say 'no' more than we would like. Who to embrace or reject as co-authors is one of the important choices that all academics, and especially senior faculty, must make.

My goal in this chapter is to offer some useful tips on how to be a more appealing potential co-author. In doing so, I draw inspiration from a 1985 book chapter by Dick Daft entitled 'Why I recommend that your manuscript be rejected and what you can do about it'. Daft analyzed his experiences as a reviewer for premier journals and distilled some guidelines for authors about how to improve their chances of having their journal submissions accepted. As a doctoral student in the early 1990s, this chapter provided me with a behind-the-scenes perspective on the review process that helped me understand what research success requires. Similarly, I hope to offer some candid advice about co-authorship based on my experiences writing 160 or so co-authored articles across the past three decades.

YOU FIND IT, YOU FIX IT

Few co-author behaviors are more frustrating than identifying a problem and then expecting others to fix it. Quite a few times I have heard from friends who were infuriated because a co-author simply pointed out a deficiency without attempting to solve the problem that was identified. Instead of quickly firing off an email saying 'this abstract you wrote doesn't reflect our paper's contents', take the time to try rewriting the abstract instead. This sends a positive signal about your approach to collaboration and you might even come up with a great abstract. A co-authored paper is a bit like a row boat – each person with an oar in the water needs to make a good-faith effort if the boat is to reach its destination with everyone still smiling. Don't just tell me how bad something is, make it better!

A related problem is responding to a co-author's requests for help by not being helpful. A few years ago, a friend asked a more methodologically sophisticated co-author for assistance with addressing a technical question raised by a reviewer. Instead of drafting a response to the reviewer's inquiry, the co-author emailed PDFs of one or more of his or her past articles and simply stated that the answer can be found in the attached articles. You should not treat a co-author as you would a student in your class.

DON'T SANDBAG

In golf, a sandbagger is someone who cheats his or her opponents by pretending to be a worse golfer than he or she really is. This often involves, for example, inflating their handicap so that they are put in a better position to win a tournament where handicaps are factored into players' scores.

Academic sandbagging occurs when someone fails to do his or her best in their role as a co-author. I was guilty of this once as a doctoral student, although naive logic rather than ill-intent was behind it. My doctoral advisor at Penn State (Jim Thomas, who later became dean there) and I were working on a revise and resubmit for a modest journal. If accepted, this would be my first refereed article. I struggled with one of the sections that Jim had asked me to draft and I turned it over to him to fix. As an experienced writer, he could tell that it was not the best work of which I was capable. When he asked for an explanation, I noted that he could fix in a few minutes what would take me hours or even days to resolve. His face then turned an unrecognizable shade of red as he roared at me: 'How do you expect to become good at this if you don't work your way through it?' I slunk out of his office, did my best on the passage in question and never sandbagged anyone again.

I have been on the receiving side of sandbagging a few times. I tend to be more forgiving when a sandbagger confesses to the crime. However, if the same person sandbags on a series of projects over time, my goal becomes to stop co-authoring with them. If a person has a reputation as a sandbagger, I avoid agreeing to co-author with them in the first place.

SAVE THE DRAMA FOR YOUR MAMA

An old saying wonders 'why buy trouble when you get enough for free?' We all have drama in our life, whether controversies at home, conflicts with our supervisor, a mid-life crisis or any number of other types of angst. Given that some drama in life is inevitable, it makes sense to avoid it in areas where it is not inevitable, such as the selection of co-authors. Indeed, one of the attractive aspects of doing academic research is that we generally get to pick our co-authors as opposed to being assigned them.

A few years ago, a tenured professor sent me this email regarding a doctoral student (edited slightly to disguise the guilty):

> Joe shows up at my office and says he wants to 'update me' on a research project we agreed to do together. I haven't heard anything from him in over a year. After hearing him out, I tried to gently tell him that he needs to stay in touch more, and he got all defensive. Weird!

Understandably, the professor was not excited about pursuing this project – or any other project – with the defensive doctoral student. Worse yet, the same student had shirked his work without apology on a previous project with the same professor.

Another situation involved both drama and sandbagging – double trouble. A lead author did a poor job writing a section of a paper. It was obvious, based on past good performance, that she had not done her best work. When gently called out on the sandbagging by a male co-author, the response was not 'OK, you got me, I'll do better'; instead, the male was accused of gender bias. This came as a shock to the male, who is generally viewed by his colleagues as a strong supporter of female faculty. In the early 1990s, he encouraged his fiancée to keep her last name when they got married – that is, he was a feminist when feminism among men was not cool. Behaviors like those of the lead author are horribly damaging to individuals and to the profession; they draw attention away from actual gender bias and they discourage people from collaborating with others who differ from them demographically, especially in the context of today's toxic 'torches and pitchforks' social media culture.

In 2010, Mike Buckley and I wrote an article on workplace divas and how to manage them. Lest the above anecdote be misinterpreted, let me state unequivocally that males and females are equally capable of being workplace divas. Based on our experiences with other academics and an informal survey of professionals in other fields, we suggested that workplace divas tend to have some combination of seven attributes: attention seeking, temperamental, blame avoiding (seen starkly in the above anecdote), lack of perspective, overly demanding, self-important and self-promoting. Supervisors often try to ignore or appease this type of behavior; these strategies rarely work. In the research context, however, we can avoid divas and the associated drama by refusing to work with them. I count several of my regular co-authors among my dearest friends. I would be foolish to take time away from them and devote it to co-authoring with a workplace diva.

KEEP YOUR PROMISES

This one is simple. Do what you say you are going to do. If you say you will send a co-author a draft by Tuesday, do whatever it takes to send the draft by Tuesday. Unexpected glitches are inevitable and no reasonable person will be mad if a deadline is missed because a hard drive crashes or a child gets sick, but if the reason for lateness is along the lines of 'I was too busy' or 'I was overcommitted', then your stock as a co-author will sink. Moreover, a series of missed deadlines will undermine your attractiveness as a co-author regardless of how legitimate any individual excuse might be.

Before you break a promise, keep in mind that your co-author's work time is limited and precious. From his or her point of view, any time that he or she wastes on a bad co-author (that is, you) could have been invested in a good co-author. A tenured scholar typically has enough quality co-authors available that there is little incentive to take a chance on 'damaged goods'. Also, since past performance is the best predictor of future performance, a scholar who becomes viewed as an undesirable co-author will have a very difficult time reversing this perception.

CONCLUSION

In summary, being an attractive co-author does not require a stellar curriculum vita or an exceptional level of brilliance. Instead, the basic recipe is simple: act in good faith, always do your best, keep drama and other negative emotions out of the research process, and live up to your promises. Academics that fulfill these four criteria always will have collaborators eager to work with them.

REFERENCES

Daft, R.L. (1985), 'Why I recommended that your manuscript be rejected and what you can do about it', in L.L. Cummings and P.J. Frost (eds), *Publishing in the Organizational Sciences*, Thousand Oaks, CA: Sage, pp. 193–209.

Ketchen, D.J., Jr. and M. Buckley (2010), 'Divas at work: dealing with drama kings and queens in organizations', *Business Horizons*, **53** (6), 599–606.

Section II.II

Getting your methods right

16. Are your results really robust?

Bruce T. Lamont and Gonzalo Molina Sieiro

Scholars with PhDs are trained to develop theory, collect data to test it, run analyses, write up the results and send the paper to a journal for publication consideration. Under time pressures to get manuscripts under review, however, many scholars do not take the time to collect additional data to address potential endogeneity, alternative measures of their constructs or other theories that may account for their anticipated findings. Nor do many scholars assess the sensitivity of their results to their sensible but possibly arbitrary methodological choices, or explore why all of the results did not turn out as expected.

Why would they? What we just outlined sounds like a lot of work and would take a lot of time. That is true. However, it is also necessary if the goal is to publish in top-tier journals. By not taking these matters into consideration in the design and execution of a project, researchers are setting themselves up for failure. Without thoroughly assessing alternative explanations for your findings, it is impossible to know if the stated interpretation is correct. More importantly, reviewers at our best journals are not likely to believe it, with increased attention being placed on methodological rigor (Bettis et al. 2014). If the hurried researcher's paper makes it through the first round of review, the data and results are not likely to survive the review process without significant alterations, possibly taking the author in directions the original theory may not support, leaving him or her with a modest or uninteresting contribution and an unpublishable paper, at least in a great journal. Our purpose in this brief contribution is to detail a few of things we have found useful to consider before you collect data, and while you are analyzing data, for a project. The aim is to improve the odds that your data and results are robust enough to survive a rigorous review process.

BUILDING A ROBUST DATASET

Beyond the primary variables for a study, there are a few data collection issues to consider, not the least of which is endogeneity. Unless you are planning a laboratory study, most management research exists in an endogenous world (Hamilton & Nickerson, 2003). It is far better to consider this while designing your study and data collection strategy than afterwards. If endogeneity is a foreign term, there are useful reference sources (for example, Hamilton and Nickerson 2003; Larcker and Rusticus 2010; Semandeni et al. 2014; Shaver 2019; Wooldridge 2010). Two of the more common forms of endogeneity are when the sample is composed of firms or people who made a choice that underlies their inclusion (sample selection bias) or when managers choose the independent variables (IV) for specific reasons to affect the dependent variable (DV), that is, there are omitted variables correlated with the IV and DV.

Selection and omitted variable bias may affect your results. For example, suppose you were interested in how social networks of entrepreneurs affected their firms' performance, and you plan to collect a data set of social network factors (IVs) and firm performance (DV) for a sample of entrepreneurs in a particular industry. These data would have both types of endogeneity problems noted above. Entrepreneurs choose to be entrepreneurs and may be different from non-entrepreneurs. Their social networks may be built for a number of reasons, one of which might be to help the performance of their firm.

The corrections for endogeneity all require additional data on predictors of the sample-selection bias (that is, being an entrepreneur) and/or the endogenous variables. Correcting for sample-selection bias requires data on the sampled firms and non-sampled firms (that is, non-entrepreneurs) on variables that are likely to distinguish between the two groups. The two-stage Heckman (1979) selection correction uses predictions of the group membership as the first stage to generate an inverse Mills ratio (IMR) in the second stage as a control (Certo et al. 2016), where the primary IVs of interest (for example, networks) are used to predict the primary DVs of interest. Correcting for endogenous variables requires data on predictors of these variables, named instrumental variables, which satisfy the appropriate assumptions and restrictions: exclusion, monotonicity, exogeneity (that is, independence) and relevance (Wooldridge 2010). So, the data requirements for addressing sample-selection bias and endogenous variables are best to address upfront when you can best get the data.

There are two basic approaches to estimate instrumental variables: two (or three) stage estimators and control function estimators (Wooldridge 2010). The multi-stage approach uses the predicted values from the first stage as the predictor of interest in the second stage. The three-stage models are typically used to refine the instrument from the second stage; but we have found them rarely justified. The control function approach uses the residual values from the first stage as a control variable in the second stage. It is particularly appropriate when your endogenous IV takes on multiple functional forms (for example, linear and quadratic) or interacts with other variables. It is also important to note that when using any instrumental variable estimation approach, it is best practice to estimate the variance–covariance matrix of both stages concurrently, or to bootstrap both stages to obtain the best estimate of the instrument and the uncertainty around it in order to make the most appropriate inferences.

When you get to using and assessing the adequacy of your instrumental variables, but find that they are not very good instruments despite your planning ahead, as is often the case (Didelez et al. 2010), we have found the approach outlined in section 7 of Larcker and Rusticus (2010) to be very helpful. They show how to estimate the sensitivity/robustness of your results to uncontrolled endogeneity. We have usually found that when we cannot control for endogeneity, the results would not be substantively different if we were able to do so. That may not always be the case, as Shaver (1998) demonstrates, but the maximum effect of endogeneity can be logically estimated using the Larcker and Rusticus procedure. You should routinely perform such a sensitivity analysis when using instrumental variable methods, given the possibility that the chosen instruments may not be valid

For the case where your IV is categorical (or can be construed as such) and involves sample selection bias and is endogenous (for example, an acquisition event or an individual being a smoker), we have found that propensity-score matching procedures can be an effective way to address both biases simultaneously. These methods predict the propensity of a unit (for example, a firm or an individual) being in a treatment (for example, an acquisition or a smoker) or control group (for example, a non-acquirer or a non-smoker) using a set of covariates that represent important differences between the two groups that are likely to affect both their membership in their respective groups and the relationship between the endogenous IV (for example, acquisition event) and DV of interest (for example, performance). These propensity scores are used to match and balance the observations in the two groups (Imbens and Rubin 2015). Then multiple regression is used to estimate an unconfounded effect of the IV on the DV of interest using the matched sample.

Propensity-score matching has both advantages and disadvantages over the use of the combined Heckman and instrumental variable methods. The advantages of these methods are that they address sample selection and endogeneity biases simultaneously, and require less stringent assumptions than some other methods. For example, there is little cost to adding covariates to the propensity score estimation stage, while the same is not the case for the two-stage instrumental variable methods (Stuart 2010). Therefore, it is normally preferable to include an irrelevant covariate in the estimation of the propensity score than to exclude a potentially important covariate (Imbens 2004). Nevertheless, propensity score methods are more sensitive to the choice of covariates, particularly when the number of first-stage covariates is small, than are control function estimators, which only create a control term in the second stage without influencing the sample structure on the second stage (Heckman and Navarro-Lozano 2004). Therefore, we have found it quite helpful to control for as many covariates as is feasible in propensity-score matching to reduce the variability in the estimates. Unfortunately, this increases the amount of data to be collected.

There are other data collection issues that should also be included in the design stage (Shaver 2019). For example, alternative measures you could use for your main variables should be included to assess the sensitivity of your results to alternative specifications. Authors rarely develop strong rationales for the measures they choose. Reviewers view these choices as arbitrary, and frequently ask authors to consider and collect additional data for other measures. These measurement issues are most economically addressed in the design stage. Also it is very helpful to push your thinking about alternative theories that might be relevant to your study. These alternate theories might suggest other predictors, potential moderators or possible mediators you might find useful to explore in a future study, but would be excellent controls in this study. We have frequently found these indirectly relevant data to emerge as very relevant once we get to the data analysis stage. As you may be beginning to see, we do not believe you can ever have too much data; and you should rarely rely on single measures.

CONDUCTING ROBUST ANALYSES

Once you have your data, get to know it well, very well. Use the alternative measures that you collected. Examine subsamples of the dataset. Try different arbitrary choices (for example, five-year averages instead of three years or a cut-off of $500 million instead of $100 million). Use different analysis techniques. Try different endogeneity corrections. Verify their adequacy. Test your primary and alternate theories. We typically like to push the analyses in multiple ways to see which results or patterns in the results are robust and when and why any unstable results are unstable. When you find something completely unexpected (for example, significant findings in the opposite direction of previous research or insignificant results when several other studies consistently find positive results), we would strongly suggest doing *post hoc* analysis (and reporting it as such), possibly with additional data, to explore logical possibilities for why you found these counterintuitive or unexpected results.

All of this data manipulation is not to be confused with data mining or what Bettis (2012) has called 'the search for asterisks'. What we are advocating is a discovery process to learn why you found what you found and how stable the results may be to alternative specifications. This is useful information that will help you in the positioning of your paper and its contribution. Also, reporting the various approaches to analyzing your data in a robustness section of your paper goes a long way to convincing the reviewer that what they are seeing is important or at least reliable. It also means that your results are likely to remain, regardless of the direction your paper may take in the review process. There will be no need to collect further data, conduct additional analyses or use alternative measures, because you will have already done these.

Interesting data with truly robust results put you in an excellent position to publish in our top management journals. Getting robust results can be systematic. It requires foresight in the design of a research project and diligent execution in the analyses. Always consider sources of possible endogeneity, alternate theories and alternative measures in the design of your data collection strategy. Also, always push your analyses to identify the systematic, non-spurious results in your data, those that withstand endogeneity corrections, the inclusion of various controls from other theories, and the use of alternative measures and analysis procedures. By doing this, you will dramatically boost your odds of publishing in our best management journals.

We end, however, with a cautionary note and challenge following from Shaver (2019). It is important for all of us, as authors (and reviewers and journal editors), to remember that there are limitations to all data, measures, endogeneity corrections and analyses, and we can only understand true relationships through the accumulation of evidence across multiple intentionally well-designed and well-executed, albeit imperfect, research efforts. We have tried to highlight things we have found helpful in improving the design and execution of our own research, knowing that there will always be some degree of uncertainty in the reporting and interpretation of the results of any particular study. Still, careful and thoughtful research design and execution are better than the alternatives, should bolster confidence in your reported findings and their interpretation, and generally aid the accumulation of evidence in management research. Therefore, we encourage you to take the substantial time and effort that is required to make your results truly robust.

REFERENCES

Bettis, R. (2012), 'The search for asterisks: compromised statistical tests and flawed theories', *Strategic Management Journal*, **33** (1), 108–13.

Bettis, R., A. Gambardella, C. Helfat and W. Mitchell (2014), 'Quantitative empirical analysis in strategic management', *Strategic Management Journal*, **35** (7), 949–53.

Certo, S.T., J.R. Busenbark, H.S. Woo and M. Semadeni (2016), 'Sample selection bias and Heckman models in strategic management research', *Strategic Management Journal*, **37** (13), 2639–57.

Didelez, V., S. Meng and N.A. Sheehan (2010), 'Assumptions of IV methods for observational epidemiology', *Statistical Science*, **25** (1), 22–40.

Hamilton, B. and J. Nickerson (2003), 'Correcting for endogeneity in strategic management research', *Strategic Organization*, **1** (1), 51–78.

Heckman, J. (1979), 'Sample selection bias as a specification error', *Econometrica*, **47** (1), 153–61.

Heckman, J. and S. Navarro-Lozano (2004), 'Using matching, instrumental variables, and control functions to estimate economic choice models', *Review of Economics and Statistics*, **86** (1), 30–57.

Imbens, G.W. (2004), 'Nonparametric estimation of average treatment effects under exogeneity: a review', *Review of Economics and Statistics*, **86** (1), 4–29.

Imbens, G.W. and D.B. Rubin (2015), *Causal Inference in Statistics, Social, and Biomedical Sciences*, Cambridge: Cambridge University Press.

Larcker, D. and T. Rusticus (2010), 'On the use of instrumental variables in accounting research', *Journal of Accounting and Economics*, **49** (3), 186–205.

Semadeni, M., M. Withers and T. Certo (2014), 'The perils of endogeneity and instrumental variables in strategy research: understanding through simulations', *Strategic Management Journal*, **35** (7), 1070–79.

Shaver, J.M. (1998), 'Accounting for endogeneity when assessing strategy performance: does entry mode choice affect FDI survival?', *Management Science*, **44** (4), 571–85.

Shaver, J.M. (2019), 'Causal identification through a cumulative body of research in the study of strategy and organizations', *Journal of Management*, 26 April, accessed 19 August 2019 at https://doi.org/10.1177/0149206319846272.

Stuart, E.A. (2010), 'Matching methods for causal inference: a review and a look forward', *Statistical Science*, **25** (1), 1–21.

Wooldridge, J.M. (2010), *Econometric Analysis of Cross Section and Panel Data*, Cambridge, MA: MIT Press.

17. The reviewers don't like my sample! What can I do?

Brian K. Boyd

INTRODUCTION

Let me start with the caveat that most of what I write is macro empirical research. While my examples will draw from strategy articles, the concepts are applicable to other management specialties, and other disciplines, as well. I have served on a wide variety of editorial boards, including those with both a generalist (for example, *Academy of Management Journal* (*AMJ*), *Journal of Management* and *Journal of Management Studies*) and specialist (for example, *Organizational Research Methods* and *Strategic Management Journal*) focus, as well as those with interdisciplinary (for example, *Corporate Governance: An International Review*) and international (*Management & Organization Review*) emphases. Also, given my background, the vast majority of papers that I review are empirical. Regardless of the focus, one question consistently surfaces when I read a new manuscript: 'If I were to design a study to test these research questions, is this the ideal sample?' As the answer is most often 'No', the second question is whether the sample is adequate. In some cases, the answer is still 'No', and at other times it is the grudging acceptance of an imperfect, yet workable sample. In the majority of cases, though, the answer is 'Hard to tell', as authors may not provide sufficient information about the sampling process or characteristics of the data. Depending on the severity of reviewer concerns, sampling issues can be a fatal flaw that triggers a rejection, or can be enough of a problem to render an entire results and discussion section moot.

There are two sets of tactics available to authors. The first is preventive, and aimed at keeping the sample questions from entering the reviewer's consciousness. The second set is reactive, such as responding to an editor's high-risk revision invitation that emphasizes reviewer skepticism as to the validity of your data.

PREVENTATIVE TACTICS

Benjamin Franklin is credited with the aphorism 'An ounce of prevention is worth a pound of cure'. Aguinis and Vandenberg (2014) drew on Franklin's wisdom to develop a checklist of research design considerations that authors should address well before collecting the first piece of data, some of which relate to sample issues (Table 17.1). These ideas are also consistent with Toyota's second paradox (Ward et al. 1995): that delaying the start of a project to spend more time on development and consideration of alternatives will lead to faster completion time, accompanied by better quality and lower cost. Consequently, the best approach that authors can take when considering their sample is to 'hurry slowly'.

Table 17.1 Checklist for sample design preparation

Topic	Key questions
What are the sampling norms for this type of research?	Are the norms different depending on how I frame the point of comparison? For example, would there be different norms based on the methodology versus the topic?
	Are the norms different based on the target journal? Consider that you will often not publish in your first choice outlet, but possibly second or third choice
What are the relevant statistical power considerations?	What are the effect sizes of relevant work – small, medium or large?
	Measurement error affects power. Do my power considerations include the effects of attenuation?
	What are the method-specific power considerations?
	If reviewers request alternative analyses, do I still have sufficient power?
Response rate	What are the typical response rates for this topic?
	What steps can I take to optimize the potential response?
	When combining response rate, power issues, and attenuation, what is my target for data collection?
Response bias	What analyses will I conduct to assess response bias?
Worst-case scenario planning	How much bias would be needed to skew my results? This can be explored empirically through simulation (Rogelberg and Stanton 2007)
	How feasible is it to replicate or create a different sample if required by reviewers?

To start, prospective authors should understand what the norms are for the research question of interest. This includes not only sample size, but data collection processes, sample characteristics, and so on. For example, if you are designing a new study of a strategic management topic, how large a sample size is needed? The answer is 4523. This number is the mean sample size for a pool of roughly 500 empirical articles published in *Strategic Management Journal* during its first 30 years (Boyd et al. 2012). That number is an intentional misrepresentation, for several reasons. First, sample sizes in this article pool vary widely for studies using survey data, where samples of 200–400 are common; versus archival studies, which have much larger samples. In addition, the average sample size for archival-based studies in this pool has more than quadrupled since the early 1980s. If your topic was strategic consensus, the sample size in prior work ranged between 19 and 252, with a mean sample size of 93, and a substantially higher mean of 151 in more recent papers (Gonzalez-Benito et al. 2012). Your goal as an author is to more than convince reviewers that the sampling process is not weak, but is outstanding. For Gonzalez-Benito and colleagues, their sample of 102 observations was average for the overall pool of work on this topic, but smaller than the norm for more recent studies. Thus, a challenge for their manuscript was to convince reviewers that their sample was still sufficient for the research questions being posed.

Sample size is not the only characteristic of a good sample. Other aspects, such as response rate, and generalizability also are considerations. Again, norms may vary depending on the line of inquiry. For example, what is a good response rate? For a strategy study, the answer is 12 percent. This is based on the often cited Hambrick et al. (1993) article which suggested that response rates of 10–13 percent for executive surveys are typical. Again, this is an arbitrary guideline. Not only is this a dramatically different norm than from employee surveys (which often yield 50 percent response rates), but content analyses of executive-based surveys reveal that the true response rate is about one in three, and that response rates are declining over time (Cycyota and Harrison 2006; Slater and Atuahene-Gima 2004). For Gonzalez-Benito et al. (2012), their response rate was around 25 percent, but also based on multiple respondents per firm, which sets a higher bar. They also conducted comparisons of multiple archival variables as well as wave analysis (comparison of early and later respondents) to assess response bias. In addition, they addressed social desirability bias, common method variance and the similarity of key findings relative to prior work to infer generalizability. To sum up the first set of tactics, authors should present as much descriptive information as possible in the methods and results sections to benchmark the robustness of their sample. In addition to the topics mentioned here, other sample-related questions include statistical power, measurement precision and implications for attenuation, as well as analytic considerations.

REACTIVE TACTICS

Possible response bias is often raised as a concern by reviewers, particularly if your response rate is low. This issue can be addressed by authors both before and after data collection. On the preventive side, factors such as survey length, endorsement of the project by opinion leaders and other considerations can enhance the likelihood that senior executives will respond to survey invitations (Bednar and Westphal 2006; Cycota and Harrison 2006). Research in other topic areas can help to provide best practices for a target audience. Subsequent to data collection, there are many options available to assess the generalizability of a respondent pool. Rogelberg and Stanton (2007) provide a review and assessment of the main techniques. While in the design stage of your project, you should identify multiple avenues for analysis, and be able to justify why you chose your tool. For example, Rogelberg and Stanton (2007) characterize wave analysis as a weaker tool. As a reviewer, I would ask for additional tests if wave analysis was the only test for response bias reported in a manuscript. If it were one of several tests, though, I would be less concerned.

Statistical power deserves special attention as a preventive measure. Unsupported hypothesis tests are common in management research. For instance, content analyses of transaction cost economics and the resource-based view each found that, on average, about half of hypotheses were supported (David and Han 2004; Newbert 2007). While many of the non-significant tests may reflect the absence of any substantive relationship, weak statistical power is a far more plausible explanation. However, in the manuscripts that I review, authors very rarely rule out power issues when reporting a nonsignificant hypothesis test. Power is affected by many factors, including the underlying effect size, alpha levels, sample size and statistical test being used. Power problems are also exacerbated by attenuation associated with imprecise measurement. While in the planning stages, prospective authors should conduct power analyses and report this information in the manuscript.

Despite these efforts, authors will still be criticized for their samples. What are some tactics for addressing these concerns in a revision? The following are a number of options.

Triangulating to Previous Studies

One way of demonstrating the suitability of your sample is to make formal comparisons with related work. There are two sets of tactics here. The first approach is to conduct a small-scale content analysis that compares aspects of your sample design with other studies. Following the earlier discussion of general tactics, a key step is to carefully articulate related work – it can be based on subject matter, methodology or even by journal. For example, in an upper-echelons study, reviewers questioned our sample-size decision. We performed a content analysis focused on the target journal for a recent period, and included all articles using the same methodology (structural equation modeling). We then compared sample size, model complexity (number of indicators) and the ratio of observations to indicators to benchmark our sample and model. To support these comparisons, we also ran additional models on our own data, and re-ran some models using the published correlation matrix of another study. Together, the combination of comparisons and supplementary models provided a strong justification for our sample.

A second form of triangulation is to compare data or results to prior articles. These can be simply means of key statistics, or more substantive comparisons. For example, in a study of research norms among strategy faculty, reviewers were justifiably concerned whether a single discipline sample would be representative of the broader universe of management faculty. There was a prior *AMJ* article that reported a mean of 1.2 (standard deviation of 2.39) articles per faculty member ten years post-PhD. We were able to replicate their coding scheme, and came up with a corresponding estimate for our sample of 1.1 (standard deviation of 2.66) articles during the same time period. Thus, comparisons with norms in other studies, published statistics or databases can be useful. A more powerful approach is to replicate findings in prior work. As another example, in one paper we tested a relationship that was not related to our hypotheses, but had been studied in other settings and drew on variables used in our model. We then identified prior tests of this relationship, conducted a meta-analytic summary of these findings and demonstrated how our result closely mirrored the entire stream of related work. Mechanisms to front-load these comparisons in your study include the inclusion of consistently performing control variables in your model, and to include some relationships which are well established previously between the independent and outcome variables, and stating that they are included for purposes of replication and comparison.

A Second Sample

In many cases, no amount of triangulation will convince reviewers that your sample is meaningful. This situation is more common when using single-industry data, less mainstream international samples, rarely used databases and other unique sources of data. What you might see as an innovative sample, reviewers might see as suspect. For example, we used a sample of hospital executives to develop and validate a measure of strategic planning processes. Part of our rationale was that this setting offered strong comparison to prior work for our tests of predictive validity of the new measure. However, reviewers posed a critical question of whether strategic planning activities in this industry, which has many unique features, would be applicable to Fortune 500 or other firms. In this case, the editor counseled us that a new sample was probably the only option that could satisfy reviewer concerns. Subsequently, we constructed a new survey based on a cross-industry sample of for-profit businesses, which strongly validated our original findings.

Holdout samples are often used as a preventive tool to forestall questions about generalizability. This entails collecting additional data using the same sampling process, and replicating results across the two subsets. However, there are many limitations with holdout samples, including inefficiency (that is, they do not use all available data to test hypotheses), and that they often fail to capture actual differences across subsets (Murphy 1983). More critically, the holdout sample will have the same flaws and weaknesses. Thus, if reviewers are unsatisfied with the main sample, they will be equally nonplussed about the holdout sample. I have two main suggestions for this option: first, in the design stage, authors should brainstorm – and brainstorm widely, in the spirit of the Toyota second paradox – different ways that they might develop a second sample. Second, when reviewers push for a second sample, embrace the idea versus fight it. While the effort of a new dataset is substantial, it can add tremendous value to your manuscript.

CONCLUSION

In a review paper (Hitt et al. 2004), we compared empirical research with Porter's value chain, which is broken into primary and support activities. We characterized the research question and data as primary activities: given sufficient data at the outset, you can always redefine or refine measures, or try different statistical analyses. Without an appropriate sample and meaningful research question, though, every other aspect of the manuscript is suspect. Inter-rater reliability among reviewers is notoriously low (see Chapter 7 in this volume). However, I hope that these suggestions will get you closer to a 'Yes' when a reviewer asks: 'If I were to design a study to test these research questions, is this the ideal sample?'

REFERENCES

Aguinis, H. and R.J. Vandenberg (2014), 'An ounce of prevention is worth a pound of cure: improving research quality before data collection', *Annual Review of Organizational Psychology and Organizational Behavior*, **1** (1), 569–95.

Bednar, M.K. and J.D. Westphal (2006), 'Surveying the corporate elite: theoretical and practical guidance on improving response rates and response quality in top management team survey questionnaires', in D. Ketchen and D. Bergh (eds), *Research Methodology in Strategy and Management*, vol. 3, New York: Elsevier, pp. 37–55.

Boyd, B.K., K.T. Haynes, M.A. Hitt, D.D. Bergh and D.J. Ketchen Jr. (2012), 'Contingency hypotheses in strategic management research: use, disuse, or misuse?', *Journal of Management*, **38** (1), 278–313.

Cycyota, C.S. and D.A. Harrison (2006), 'What (not) to expect when surveying executives: a meta-analysis of top manager response rates and techniques over time', *Organizational Research Methods*, **9** (2), 133–60.

David, R.J. and S.K. Han (2004), 'A systematic assessment of the empirical support for transaction cost economics', *Strategic Management Journal*, **25** (1), 39–58.

Gonzalez-Benito, J., H.A. Aguinis, B.K. Boyd and I. Suarez-Gonzalez (2012), 'Coming to consensus on strategic consensus: a mediated moderation model of consensus and performance', *Journal of Management*, **38** (1), 1685–714.

Hambrick, D.C., M.A. Geletkanycz and J.W. Fredrickson (1993), 'Top executive commitment to the status quo: some tests of its determinants', *Strategic Management Journal*, **14** (6), 401–18.

Hitt, M.A., B. Boyd and D. Li (2004), 'The state of strategic management research: a view of the future', in D. Ketchen and D. Bergh (eds), *Research Methodology in Strategy and Management*, vol. 1, New York: Elsevier, pp. 1–31.

Murphy, K. (1983), 'Fooling yourself with cross-validation: single-sample designs', *Personnel Psychology*, **36** (1), 111–18.

Newbert, S.L. (2007), 'Empirical research on the resource-based view of the firm: an assessment and suggestions for future research', *Strategic Management Journal*, **28** (2), 121–46.

Rogelberg, S.G. and J.M. Stanton (2007), 'Understanding and dealing with organizational survey nonresponse', *Organizational Research Methods*, **10** (2), 195–209.

Slater, S.F. and K. Atuahene-Gima (1993), 'Conducting survey research in strategic management', in D. Ketchen and D. Bergh (eds), *Research Methodology in Strategy and Management*, vol. 1, New York: Elsevier, pp. 227–49.

Ward, A., J.K. Liker, J.J. Christiano and D.K. Sobeck (1995), 'The second Toyota paradox: how delaying decisions can make better cars faster', *Long Range Planning*, **36** (3), 43–61.

18. When being normal is not enough: a few thoughts about data, analyses and (the storm of) re-analyses

Philip L. Roth and Wayne H. Stewart, Jr.

INTRODUCTION

Good research is hard to do. Getting accepted for publication is harder still. So, when the editors of this book asked us to contribute a short chapter, we turned to Pooh and asked, 'What should we write about?' Pooh mumbled something about honey, ice cream and being the perfect weight for a bear a foot taller than he was, and then sort of wandered off to worry about more important issues in the world of bears. This left us with only a few other personalities in our own heads with which to brainstorm ideas. After talking among (all of) ourselves, we decided to extol the virtues of not being entirely normal when it comes to data and analyses.

A number of years ago, we published a meta-analysis (Stewart and Roth 2001) on the relationship between entrepreneurial status and risk propensity (Pooh was not interested in that either). We found that individuals who were entrepreneurs were more likely to have higher levels of risk propensity than were managers, a difference magnified if the entrepreneurs were growth orientated. We were not very surprised when two researchers asked for our data (Eeyore did predict doom and gloom ...), but we were surprised when a rather spirited attack on our original meta-analysis appeared in the *Journal of Applied Psychology* (Miner and Raju 2004). It was at this point that we were very glad that we were not entirely normal.

OBSESSIVE-COMPULSIVE AND PARANOID

We were thankful that we had been obsessive-compulsive and paranoid in several aspects of our research. Particularly, we were very glad that we

192

had obsessed over the research question in which we clearly defined entrepreneurs (and operationalized our definitions of entrepreneurs in two ways) and contrasted their risk propensity to those of managers. We are also big proponents of drawing out research models to obsess on clarity and exactness of the research model when needed (even if you have to borrow a pencil from Piglet).

We were also obsessive about identifying primary studies and generating the meta-analytic data (we thought about this as creative paranoia). To ensure our data were of high quality, both authors coded every article in the meta-analysis. This is uncommon, as many meta-analyses have one author code all the data and a second author code a percentage of the data to establish some estimate of reliability. We are also big believers in getting your hands dirty in analyzing the data (which is much better than washing your hands again and again ... we prefer getting them dirty again and again). So, we entered all the data ourselves, ran descriptive statistics on everything, and mulled over various aspects of the data, including large samples, influential cases, measurement and watching for dependent data.

We were also paranoid about analyses. We literally thought about what someone else would think about how we ran the analyses (this is where multiple personalities come in handy as one can write and the other can question ...). So, we kept all of our original analyses, with notes on what we did and how we handled various cases. We felt like Owl setting up a detailed list for finding Roo.

Finally, we were careful to consider the 'So what?' question in our thinking and writing. We were sure we would get a reviewer as on some past papers. We were anxious to avoid reviewers such as Dr O.B. Tuse, as failing to answer the 'So what?' question can sink a manuscript. So, we thought our original submission was on solid ground when it was accepted by dealing with a critical issue in entrepreneurship research.

CONCLUSION

As Eeyore warned, a dark day came for us with the article by Miner and Raju (2004). It came with a vengeance, with a past president of the Academy of Management and an award-winning research methodologist teaming up against us. Fortunately, their arguments were not based on obsessive-compulsive and paranoid thinking. Instead, they engaged in fuzzy thinking in terms of the definition of entrepreneurs, use of unconventional measures of risk propensity, and use of dependent samples in their critique and re-analysis of our study (Stewart and Roth

2004). The good news was that Miner and Raju discovered no errors in our analyses, but only added dubious data to the situation (mixing Heffalumps and Woozles can be very confusing).

We happened upon an extremely well-known meta-analyst at a professional meeting after our exchange in the literature. He said, 'I read your reply to Miner and Raju ... devastating'. At that point, we were extremely glad to have been far from normal. We were thankful for all the care we put into formulating the research question, extracting the data and conducting the analyses. That is why we did everything we could to do the research right. At the end of the day, we heard the little voices in our heads saying, 'Are you paranoid if they really are out to get you?'

REFERENCES

Miner, J.B. and N.S. Raju (2004), 'Risk propensity differences between managers and entrepreneurs and between low- and high-growth entrepreneurs: a reply in a more conservative vein', *Journal of Applied Psychology*, **89** (1), 3–13.

Stewart, W.H. and P.L. Roth (2001), 'Risk taking propensity as a distinctive entrepreneurial characteristic: a meta-analysis', *Journal of Applied Psychology*, **86** (1), 145–53.

Stewart, W.H. and P.L. Roth (2004), 'Data quality affects meta-analytic conclusions: a response to Miner and Raju concerning entrepreneurial risk propensity', *Journal of Applied Psychology*, **89** (1), 14–21.

Section II.III

Navigating the review process

19. Selling your soul to the devil? Mistakes authors make when responding to reviewers[*]

Pamela L. Perrewé

Publishing in the organizational sciences is not for the faint of heart. First, as authors, we all need to cope with rejection occasionally (sometimes all too often). If you are not used to receiving decision letters that begin with 'thank you for your submission, however ...', start steeling your nerves now. Second, many management scholars believe publishing involves unfair politics. Although I am not convinced this is true, I do know that prolific authors often are asked to contribute their work to a special issue of the journal or a book. Thus, prolific authors become even more prolific. Is that politics? I will let you decide that. The point is that in order to be asked to write for books or special issues, you will need to have a strong research and publication reputation. In this chapter, I help authors overcome rejection by learning to respond to reviewer and/or editor comments.

If you have an opportunity to revise a manuscript and you are currently responding to editor and reviewer comments, congratulations! This is great news! It means that the door is still open for a possible publication. Even if the decision to allow a revision is high risk (most editors and associate editors use this phrase), I encourage all researchers to work hard at their revision. As Jim Carrey remarked in the classic film, *Dumb and Dumber*, 'So you're telling me there's a chance ... . Yeah!'

It is a myth to believe you must agree with and make every suggested change made by reviewers. Often reviewers have excellent suggestions to help your research appeal to more scholars, to improve the rigor of your data analysis, to deepen your theoretical contributions, and so on. However, there are times when reviewers ask for changes that are simply not needed or that take away from the primary message of your research. For example, if a reviewer suggests changing the focus of the article to hone in on one specific finding rather than examining your entire conceptual model, it is appropriate to thank the reviewer but to politely argue that the meaningfulness of your message may be lost if the focus is specific to only one finding. It might be possible to discuss this finding that the reviewer found interesting in a bit more detail – everyone is happy. Also, it is a good idea to write to the editor or the action editor to explain why you are not accommodating every change.

Regarding the role of editors and action editors, it is appropriate to ask for guidance if reviewers conflict in their suggested changes. However, try to read between the lines of the revision letter, as good editors and action editors often offer suggestions to authors and, perhaps, tip their hat to one reviewer suggestion over another. Editors always have an opinion. Further, there may be times when it is clear you will never appease a reviewer (for example, the reviewer finds your research topic uninspiring or not unique enough). If other reviewers find the topic interesting and offer suggestions to strengthen your article, you may want to contact the editor or action editor about the reviewer of concern.

I once had a second revision on a paper and it was very clear to me that one reviewer 'did not think it made enough of a contribution'. I contacted the editor stating I was inclined to withdraw the paper as, after two revisions of the paper, I was not able to convince this reviewer that my work made a significant contribution to the literature. The editor asked me not to withdraw the paper, but to focus on all of the comments I could address. The editor then told me that he has been known to go against a reviewer now and again. I thanked him, made the changes, and even though one reviewer was not satisfied, my research was eventually published because the editor saw value in it.

A final note regarding the role of the editor or action editor is that editors often choose to become an additional reviewer. Thus, authors may receive comments from two or three reviewers as well as additional comments from the editor or action editor. Editors vary in their involvement in the review process, but remember they do have a right as well as an obligation to try to make the research paper the best it can be. However, tensions can arise when the advice from an editor goes well beyond navigating the reviews and the editor becomes another reviewer (except with veto powers). Not long ago, I had an article that went through several reviews despite the editor's concern about my statistical effect size. The editor allowed me to revise my research paper and I did my best to address the effect size issue. After three rounds of revisions and appeasing all the reviewers (they all accepted the paper with no additional changes), the editor decided not to publish the article owing to the effect size that was deemed too low. Although ultimately this is the editor's call, I was disappointed that I was encouraged to continue to revise my paper if the editor believed that the statistical effect size was a fatal flaw from the beginning.

On a brighter note, I once had an editor who saw something positive in my research and, even though the reviewers were brutal, he called me and helped me to reframe my research paper to make a more obvious contribution to the literature. The editor's insight helped me to reframe and better position my arguments for a wider audience and the reviewers eventually liked my contribution. The paper was eventually published in a top journal and, to this day, I think about this editor's initiative, guidance and care as he helped me navigate through the review process.

A mistake authors too often make is to be overly emotional or defensive in their responses to reviewer comments. The anonymity of the review process can, at times, allow some rather caustic remarks to be made by reviewers about a research paper. Try not to take the negative reviews too personally. However, if a reviewer does get the better of me, I have no problem responding with snide remarks initially (but privately – I never send these; it just allows me to vent and get rid of the emotion). After I calm down (it might take several days), I delete everything I wrote, and work on addressing the comments with kindness, political skill and humility. It does absolutely no good to allow the tone of reviewer comments to affect the tenor of your responses to those comments, as a negatively toned response to reviewers can anger them and result in them taking an even more critical view of your manuscript. Further, after my defensiveness goes away, I often find some good suggestions in the review, even though I could have done without the caustic tone.

Do not summarize reviewer comments or paraphrase their comments in an easy-to-read table with your responses. Summarizing reviewer comments and putting them in a table is popular in some fields, but not in the management field. Summarizing comments and putting these comments into your own words annoys reviewers as their entire comment is not apparent in the response to the reviewers. I suggest you copy and paste the entire comment and then respond to this comment so that the reviewers see their entire comment as well as your response. For example, there might be an aspect of a comment that is important to a reviewer that you inadvertently omit in your paraphrasing. Even if you paraphrase perfectly, the reviewer might not trust that you did paraphrase perfectly. Including the entire comment is the safest and easiest way to proceed.

Reviewers will often suggest new analyses to better flesh out some potential intriguing findings in your research. Although the intent is good, this also has the potential of increasing the length of the paper as well as taking away from the main message of the paper. Clearly, conducting the suggested analyses may well be warranted, however, authors do not necessarily need to put the new analyses and results in the text of the paper. These new analyses and results can be included in the response to reviewer comments with the caveat that if the reviewer and the editor or action editor would like to see these additional *post hoc* analyses in the paper, the authors are happy to include them in a subsequent revision of the manuscript.

Including additional analyses, or working another suggested theory into your paper, is fine as long as you do not 'sell your soul to the Devil'. Tweaking titles, bringing in additional theory, or even collecting additional data, is all within the realm of a revision. However, be careful not to change the message you want to, and know you should, convey. I once heard another academic, talking at a major management conference, saying that he would do anything a reviewer or editor wanted in a revision in order to get a publication. Yikes! There needs to be integrity in research because, even when the pressures of publishing to obtain promotions or raises are strong, research needs to be honest.

For example, a reviewer might want you to cut out part of your findings and conclusions for the sake of parsimony. Seldom should we be in favor of reducing the amount of information in a research article. However, if we are convinced this helps the message of the research, we may be amenable to the suggested changes. If the suggested changes affect the meaning of the research (for example, taking out findings and conclusions), you might want to reconsider the reviewer comment. Sometimes reviewers will have a vested interest in not having something published that does not support their own research. This happens rarely, but be careful to convey the message you know you should convey. The integrity of our research is tied closely to our personal scholarly reputation and to our own integrity – no publication is worth risking that.

In conclusion, responding to reviewer comments is somewhat of an art form. First, even if the revision is a high risk, it is almost always worth the effort to revise your research paper as the door for publication has been left open. Second, be respectful in your tone and make all the suggested changes or, at a minimum, explain why you did not make the change. Third, never hesitate to contact the editor or action editor for clarification; this is particularly important if reviewers seem to be at odds as to how best to frame the paper or reanalyze the data. Further, do not get overly emotional, arrogant or defensive in your responses; there is no advantage in upsetting your reviewers. Finally, do not 'sell your soul to the Devil' in your revision. Your scholarly reputation depends upon it and integrity is the key to meaningful research in our field.

NOTE

* The author would like to thank Jeremy D. Mackey, B.P. Ellen III, Charn P. McAllister, and D.J. Steffensen for their comments on this topic and chapter.

20. Respond to me – please!

James G. Combs

Dear Author,

I am a busy person. My spouse and kids want my time. My university places ever greater teaching and service demands on me. I believe in our profession and that what we do matters. As such, I am active in the Academy, and I serve as an editor, on editorial review boards, and as an *ad hoc* reviewer. Amid all this, I keep an active portfolio of research projects and I work hard to keep these projects moving toward publication. It is in this context that I sat down one evening to read your paper, and spent much of the following day writing comments that I thought you needed to hear if you are to bring your research to a successful outcome. Your action editor read my comments and those of the other reviewers and gave you an opportunity to have your successful outcome at *this* journal: congratulations to you, more work for me!

When it came time for me to open your revised paper and response document, I did so with mixed feelings. On the one hand, the combined document is 90 pages – it's going to be a long night! On the other hand, I am invested in your paper and eager to see where it is going. We reviewers are not all alike in how we approach a revision, but I think that many are like me in that we start with your response document. I do this to remind me what your paper is about and what my concerns were. I also want to get a general feeling for how you changed the paper in response to the review team's comments.

At first, I am relieved to find that your formatting makes sense. You smartly put the review team's comments in bold italic with your responses in normal print following each comment. Some authors put their own responses in bold and the review team's comments in normal print, which signals that the authors think too highly of themselves. You also weren't afraid to split my comments when I brought up more than one issue in a single numbered comment. Reviewers sometimes ramble and it is usually easier to split a comment then to have a long multi-part response. I should note that some journals now force response documents into web-based windows – where all the formatting goes out the window (pun intended). The only way to keep the reviewers on track is to use ALL CAPS (that is, EDITOR COMMENT #1 ... RESPONSE TO EDITOR'S COMMENT #1). You can also use spacing to your advantage in these cases by double spacing between comments and responses, and triple spacing between responses and the next comment. Fortunately, that was not a problem here.

I am glad you got the formatting right because it goes downhill from there. I started with the Editor's letter hoping to find a summary of the key issues and your solutions. Nope. Whereas the editor summarized the key issues raised by the reviewers and teed up a chance for you to summarize the changes, you ignored this opportunity by telling us to look for detailed responses below. Okay, I get it. These documents can get crazy long, and there is no need to be redundant, but can't you at least give me the broad strokes here while saving the details for the individual reviewer responses? I am frankly too lazy to go jumping around the response document. Another (perhaps better) approach is to simply start with an 'executive summary.' I have only seen a few of these and my heart leaps for joy when I see them. There it is: the three big issues raised by the review team summarized for me along with a brief overview of how these issues were dealt with in the revision. Alas, you didn't do this either.

At this point, I am a little grumpy, but I am still eager to see how you responded to my comments. A good reviewer will list comments roughly in order of importance; my first comment was that your initial submission named three related theories in the introduction but you did not explain any of these or use them as the theoretical logic for your hypotheses. Also, none of these formed a theoretical frame dictating which hypotheses to include. What I was hoping for in your response was for you to tell me which theory you decided to use in the revision, and to describe how you used that theory to ground your contribution and tie together all of your hypotheses. What I got was a two-page, single-spaced review of the three theories (or perspectives, really) and how they relate to each other.

Now I am getting frustrated – big time. Yes, I want you to review the relevant theory in your paper. But in the responses, I just want you to make it clear that you heard me and to explain what you did in the revision. I am looking for phrases like 'we made the following changes in the revision ...' or 'We did not change ... in the revision as you suggested because ...'. What I don't want is a long diatribe on the history of a theory (or three theories) and all the prior research that pertains to this phenomenon. I plan to read your paper, and it's ultimately the paper

I am going to judge – not the response document. When you either dump text from the paper into the response document (which is partially out of context for me) or try to engage me in a lengthy discussion of all the issues related to my comment, what you *actually* did in the paper tends to get lost – and that's ultimately all I care about. This is subtle, but powerful. I want you to *describe* the changes in the revision as they pertain to each of my comments. I don't want you to actually give the changes to me here. Often, you will have details or analyses to justify the changes you made. This material can go after your succinct description (that is, 'the reason we went this direction is …') or in an appendix to the response document. Just be sure to first succinctly describe the changes. That way, *what* you did won't get lost in a long defense of *why* you did it – and I can skip the latter if I want.

Well, I'm done. I read your lengthy responses to my first two comments and found them overwhelming. I never got a clear sense of how you approached the problem. You buried me in detail and minutia. I learned not to expect much, so I am now going to read through the rest of my comments while skipping over your responses. I might also look at the other reviewers' main comments. Then it's on to your paper, sour mood and all. Even though you were unable to explain succinctly in the response document exactly how you responded to my concerns, with a little luck, perhaps you put all of your mental energies into the manuscript where you did indeed respond to my concerns. If so, all will be forgiven, your paper will delight me and I will be pleased to see that the big issues from your initial submission are mostly resolved. If not, my frustration will grow as I see that your lack of response carries over into the actual paper.

Either way, I write you this letter because otherwise you will probably never know how frustrated I was by your response document, or how useless I found it for quickly digesting the changes that you made. All I really want is for you to acknowledge that you understand my comment, tell me briefly what you changed and, if necessary, explain why. Don't waste my time trying to engage me in 'interesting' discussions or making me re-read your paper in the response document. I truly hope that my advice here benefits those reviewers who will read your future response documents, of which I hope there will be many.

Sincerely,

M.A. Reviewer

PS. Stop with: 'thank you for this insightful comment' at the beginning of each response. Let's be honest; some of my comments made you angry, and you're not fooling anyone with false praise. If one of my comments helps you make real and significant improvements in your paper, thank me *after* telling me how. Then I will be gratified to see that some of my comments mattered.

PPS. Don't under-value Reviewer #3. Reviewers are *not* assigned numbers that represent their importance. Manuscript Central assigns numbers as the reviews come in. More often than not, I bet that the last review in is from a busy senior scholar, not from an eager junior scholar trying to win a seat on the editorial board.

21. Challenging the gods: circumstances justifying the protest of a journal rejection decision

Gerald R. Ferris

Young scholars, new to the organizational sciences field, learn early on about the process through which their research gets published in scientific journals. It is called the peer review process, has been in operation for decades and is used in virtually all academic disciplines. The publication fate of scholars' work typically rests in the hands of an associate editor and several anonymous reviewers, who presumably are knowledgeable about the subject matter of the scholars' work. It is their collective judgments about the quality of the work being reviewed, and perhaps its subsequent revisions, that determine whether the research is published in the journal or rejected. Therefore, the field grants great deference (or even omniscience) to the evaluations of research by these 'gatekeepers' in the peer review process.

Given this process, and the esteem it is granted by the field, it might seem inappropriate to question or challenge/protest a decision to reject your paper. I would agree that, in most cases, scholars need to accept the outcome of the peer review process concerning the research paper they submitted for review – whatever that decision might be. However, I am arguing in this chapter that there are situations or circumstances that arise where it is legitimate to challenge or protest a rejection decision by a journal editor or associate editor. I mention some of these circumstances, and then provide an example from my own experience, over the past 35 years, of an associate editor's decision to reject my manuscript that I challenged.

A FEW HINTS ON WHEN TO CHALLENGE A REJECTION DECISION

In trying to better understand the peer review process, it is helpful to know a little about the context within which these decisions get made, and thus the mindset of the decision makers reviewing submitted manuscripts. With the ever-increasing volume of manuscript submissions to the top journals in our field, the mindset of reviewers is similar to that of employment interviewers – it is a search for negative information. That is, reviewers are not focused as much on the positive features of a manuscript that might lead to an acceptance, but instead search for flaws and negative features that might result in rejection. Papers are accepted for publication less as a result of possessing many positive attributes, and more for reviewers' failure to detect a sufficient number of negative features to warrant rejection. However, rejection decisions in many if not most cases are warranted, but sometimes they are not and it is appropriate to challenge or protest the decision. I see the following as some circumstances that might warrant the protest of a journal article rejection decision:

1. When decision makers get things factually wrong, owing to their misinterpretation of the results, or lack of understanding of the subject matter of the manuscript.
2. When decision makers render what appears to be a largely unsupported decision to reject, after at least one or more rounds of revisions, when the reviewers appear to indicate that the authors responded acceptably to their concerns.
3. When there are large discrepancies between what you see the reviewers saying, and what conclusion is reached by the associate editor or editor.

EXAMPLE OF A CHALLENGED REJECTION DECISION

Several years ago, I (and several co-authors) submitted a paper to a journal in our field (not one of the very top or A journals, but a solid, respectable A– or B+). The associate editor handling the review process sent us the evaluations and comments of three reviewers, and the decision was to invite us to submit a revision of our paper that responded to each of the reviewers' and the associate editor's comments. We did this, and in the next round, the associate editor and reviewers felt we still had some work to do in better addressing some of the comments, so we were given another revise-and-resubmit decision.

We prepared and submitted another revision of our manuscript, and the reply we received from the associate editor was interesting in that it presented a dilemma for me. The reviewers felt that we had done a good job with almost all of their comments and concerns, and each only mentioned one or two points on which they still wanted a little more information, but they all were minor issues that could be dealt with easily. Thus, we expected that the associate editor was going to give us a 'conditional acceptance', but instead the manuscript was rejected for what appeared to be no good reason at all, other than a statement that indicated that the associate editor did not think we would be able to address the remaining concerns.

My co-authors were angry, but felt there was nothing to be done, so already were discussing to what other journal we might consider sending our manuscript. After re-reading the reviewer comments and the associate editor's email, I suggested to my co-authors that there were no fatal flaws in our paper and the reviewers' remaining comments all were doable. Therefore, I suggested that we respectfully challenge the associate editor's decision, and request another round of reviews where we would prepare another revision that responded to the remaining concerns. I was not confident that the request would be granted, so I was pleasantly surprised to hear back from the associate editor granting our request, and that they would evaluate another revision of our manuscript that was responsive to the remaining concerns. I must say that we took great care in our responses to this final set of reviewer concerns, and when we re-submitted the revision, the associate editor replied within just a few weeks accepting our manuscript for publication in the journal.

CONCLUSION

The ideas outlined in this chapter are meant to suggest situations when it might be appropriate to question, challenge or protest a journal rejection decision. However, I emphasize that these should be rare cases that occur where a protest is appropriate, and I believe most scholars who have been in the field for many years would agree that it is not a frequent occurrence. Although some scholars in our field might elevate journal editors and associate editors to a God-like status, they are human beings and sometimes make mistakes. When you feel mistakes have been made in the review of your manuscript, it is appropriate to question the process handled by those involved. Yet, whether we like it or not, the peer review process is the best system we have for determining publication status in our journals, until someone can come up with something better (which does not seem likely).

22. Beginner's muck: maximizing your paper's chances of success with a novice editor

Kevin G. Corley and Beth S. Schinoff

> You can always tell a novice rider; they aren't comfortable in the saddle and have to hang on. (Harry Carey Jr., movie actor in westerns)

What do an actor who has to ride a horse, a first-time parent and a just-appointed editorial team member have in common? While at first glance it would seem like not much (except maybe a reliance on luck and a lack of sleep?), as we worked with several editorial teams on a research project looking at how editors make sense of theoretical contribution (see Corley and Schinoff 2017), we realized that they have one very important commonality – they are novice experts. Novice experts are 'individuals expected to make expert judgments without the necessary experience or knowledge to qualify as experts' (Corley and Schinoff 2017, p. 5). The actor is expected to ride a horse as comfortably as would the character being played, the new parent expected to know instantly how to keep a baby alive and thriving, and the new editorial team member expected to make reject or revise-and-resubmit decisions on manuscripts from day one.

NOVICE EXPERT? SOUNDS SCARY! DON'T WORRY, IT'S NOT

Knowing what differentiates a novice expert editor from an experienced expert editor will help you better understand how to navigate the review process. Our research suggests two very important differences. First, novice expert editors have limited experiences and knowledge to draw on when determining if a manuscript clears the bar for publication (or, more likely, the bar for an invited revision). One of the more enduring legends about publishing in academic journals is the result of this inexperience.

As the lore goes, a new editorial team is more likely to reject papers at the beginning of their editorial term than they are later in the term. Similarly, new editors are less likely to accept papers than experienced editors, even when serving on the same editorial team. This phenomenon is appropriately named first-term bias. Why does this occur? Until novice editors have taken several submitted manuscripts all the way through to acceptance (and have thus developed some expertise), they will have nothing to compare your manuscript to other than the finished articles published in their journal, and that is a very high bar for a first submission to clear. Just think about how most manuscripts go through anywhere from two to four or more revision cycles before publication. One new editor-in-chief we spoke with believed in the impact of first-term bias so much that she took explicit steps at the beginning of her team's term to encourage revise-and-resubmit decisions and combat the bias (with some notable success too).

The second key difference is that novice expert editors tend to depend on reviewers' comments much more than experienced editors. We heard from many of the new editors we interviewed that relying on reviewers granted legitimacy to their decisions in a way that perhaps only experience could have provided otherwise. It also made it slightly easier to manage reviewers as an audience. After all, editors are the only non-anonymous party in the review process. Given that reviewers volunteer, editors spoke often about paying tribute to the hard work of the review team. For novice editors, who are also just establishing themselves as worthy of the editorial role, managing the relationship between themselves and reviewers appeared especially salient.

TIPS FOR PUBLISHING IN A JOURNAL WITH NOVICE EXPERT EDITORS

Given these differences, what can you do? In conversations with other academics, we often heard, 'I never submit to a journal with new editors in their first year'; but who has the luxury to wait for the editors to move past their novice expert stage? Based on our research, we believe there are concrete actions to take that will help ensure a manuscript submitted to a novice editor will be treated similarly as a manuscript submitted to an experienced editor.

- Polish that paper until it's the shiniest car on the block. One of the best things you can do to help your chances with a novice editor is to submit a manuscript that looks as much like a polished paper as possible. This means, at a minimum, that it is well-written, well-argued and engaging; having all of your (proverbial and literal) i's dotted and t's crossed. Why will this help? One of the first things a new editor learns about their role is that you want good papers to be published in your journal. Unlike reviewers (often reviewing for multiple journals and not necessarily identified with a specific journal) who tend to have a rejection mindset ('What's wrong with this paper? Why should it be rejected?'), editors need to think about what is best for their journal and, thus, have an acceptance mindset ('What's good about this paper? How could it eventually be publishable?'). A well-written, well-argued and engaging manuscript signals to the editor not only that you are experienced and know what a good paper should look like, but also that you are capable of handling an invitation for revision. It gives the novice editor a sense that the paper is good, could eventually be publishable and that you are capable of taking that paper from its current state to a publishable one. First impressions – even spelling/grammar errors and leaving off a citation – do matter, perhaps even more so with a novice expert.

- Make the mission possible to understand. Make sure your manuscript aligns strongly with the mission of the journal you are submitting to, and does so in an explicit way. As with most new-role occupants, novice editors have more recently finished whatever formal socialization they go through than have more experienced editors. They have just recently been trained in what the journal is trying to accomplish and what types of papers they should be looking for to fit that mission. For most top management journals, the mission currently is about advancing theory, either empirically or conceptually; other top outlets are interested in methodological contributions or advancing managerial/executive practice. Regardless, it is to your advantage to be very clear about how your manuscript meets that journal's mission in order to (again) signal to the novice editor that you have the ability to take this manuscript to a publishable place. Thus, explicit statements about how your findings or theorizing challenge current thinking in the theoretical (or methodological or practical) area you are targeting and how you are advancing theory (methods/practice) are necessary components to the front- and back-ends of your manuscript.
- And the people's choice goes to … . Although it might seem counterintuitive or intimidating to suggest reviewers for your manuscript, the editors we spoke with generally found it helpful. You (as

the author) have a much better understanding of the major players in your content/method area than the editor does. Since novice experts rely on these reviewers' comments and recommendations more than experienced editors do, use your submission cover letter to suggest reviewers who would provide developmental feedback on your paper (we would suggest no more than three). This not only helps the novice editor with a challenging part of his or her job, but also increases the chances that the reviewers of your paper will appreciate and understand your research. That said, not all editors will use suggested reviewers (especially if it is obvious that you are just suggesting friends or colleagues), but it does not hurt to try.

- A little reviewer kindness could go a long way. Finally, a word about dealing with a revise and resubmit manuscript under a novice expert editor. One of the interesting side effects of the many rejected papers that occur in the beginning of an editor's term is that new editors might not give their first revise and resubmit to a manuscript for quite some time. So, even after several months in the editorial role, editors are still very much novices when assessing revised manuscripts. This is why we believe paying close attention to the original decision letter is so important, as our findings revealed a crucial difference in how novice and experienced editors wrote revision letters. Namely, novice editors tended to rely heavily on reviewer feedback in justifying their decision, often quoting reviewers' comments directly; whereas experienced editors synthesized reviewer feedback with their own opinion of the paper to create new insights for strengthening the paper. Thus, when responding to the revise-and-resubmit decision of a novice editor, our findings suggest that it is worth the time and effort to pay extra attention to reviewers' comments. This can mean going out of your way to acknowledge when a reviewer's comment spurred a particularly important change in the manuscript and explicitly noting in the replies-to-reviewers document how the reviewer concerns were handled in the paper.

As the size of today's editorial teams continues to increase (to keep up with the ever-increasing number of submitted manuscripts), it is likely that the editors at top management journals are novice experts when they join the editorial team of a journal. Our hope is that by helping you understand the unique challenges these novice editors face, you can use our suggestions to ensure that your manuscript not only gets the editorial attention it deserves, but also that your chances of receiving a favorable assessment on your submitted manuscript improve as well. Good luck!

REFERENCE

Corley, K.G. and B.S. Schinoff (2017), 'Who, me? An inductive study of novice experts in the context of how editors come to understand theoretical contribution', *Academy of Management Perspectives*, **31** (1), 4–27.

Section II.IV

Understanding the journals

23. Publishing in the top journals: the secrets for success

Michael A. Hitt

INTRODUCTION

Having your research published in top scholarly journals is one of the crowning achievements in our profession. It is exciting and satisfying to have your work published in one of these journals with other high-quality scholarly research. Most of these top journals accept 5–10 percent of the manuscripts submitted. Therefore, they truly represent the crème de la crème of the research in the field. Publishing work in these top journals is challenging, given the large amount of competition for journal space and high standards enforced by these journals (evidenced by the low acceptance rates). Therefore, the publication process can also be frustrating at times. Yet, there are actions that we can take to increase the probability that our work will be published in these journals.

First and foremost in my view is the development of the capacity to excel. Most of us believe that only the most talented people are able to publish their work in the top journals. These people have strong intellectual capabilities and are well trained at top research institutions. Yet, research across fields shows that individual talent (for example, intellectual capability) and experience play only a small role in success. The research in fields such as medicine, science, sports and music shows that outstanding performance is based on intense, prolonged and highly focused efforts to improve your current performance (Baron and Henry 2010). Researchers refer to this as deliberate practice. Deliberate practice expands individuals' domain-specific knowledge and skills, and enhances their basic cognitive capabilities. Perhaps, the simplest analogy to understand is from sports. The top athletes often are talented but only those who practice tenaciously and are highly skilled, owing to that deliberate practice to excel. This suggests that, in our field, people must practice deliberately to develop their skills in conducting research and in the development of manuscripts (especially the writing).

CONDUCTING THE RESEARCH

Publishing in top scholarly journals begins with the conduct of good research. This means developing a strong theoretical base and a strong research design with methodological rigor. Quality research, though, is catalyzed by a valuable research question. The research question should be derived from a gap in the literature. While a void in the literature is necessary, it is also insufficient to qualify as a valuable research question. Answering the question must add value to our knowledge. Thus, it is an important research question.

The next concern is building a strong theoretical framework that leads to hypotheses, assuming the research is an empirical study. Kurt Lewin once said that '[n]othing is so practical as a good theory' (Van de Ven 1989). Most empirical research is designed to add to our theoretical knowledge but not create new theory. Developing new theory commonly involves development, feedback and refinement over a period of time (often years) (Smith and Hitt 2005). Yet, some research may be designed to build theory (for example, good qualitative research). Smith and Hitt (2005) found that many of the highly respected theorists in our field developed their theories only with significant time and feedback from others' work that allowed them to continuously refine their ideas. Therefore, most of us use existing theory. However, to publish research most scholarly journals require a contribution to theory. This normally entails extending our knowledge of an existing theory. To do so requires considerable thought and care in developing the theoretical framework and in explaining how the research extends our understanding of that theory.

Concomitant to enriched theory is the need for methodological rigor in the design (for example, sampling, measurement) and in the analytical process. One concern is the use of random samples. Short et al. (2002) found that only 20 percent of published research used random samples. It is difficult to select random samples because it is often challenging to identify the universe from which they are to be drawn. Therefore, most samples are convenience samples. Sometimes this is absolutely necessary but it must be justified to the editors and reviewers. Non-random samples create the potential for sampling biases that lead to potential errors in the results and interpretation (Heckman 1979). A common concern often noted in strategic management research is that of endogeneity, for example.

Another potential concern is that of statistical power. Boyd et al. (2005) criticized a great deal of the empirical research in strategic management because of the lack of attention to the statistical power in their studies. They suggested that statistical power can affect both type 1 and type 2 errors. Interestingly, most of the top scholarly journals are most concerned about type 1 errors (that is, weeding out poor research designs). However, in doing so they often overlook potential type 2 errors (Hitt et al. 2004) in which papers may be rejected when they contain valuable ideas that should be in the literature. Also, authors may have excellent ideas but fail to follow through on some basic processes to assure the editors and reviewers that they have conducted quality research.

Boyd et al. (2005) noted that macro researchers are often guilty of not paying adequate attention to measurement quality. They found that a significant number of studies used single-item indicators for constructs which are highly vulnerable to measurement error. Therefore, researchers can increase the probability of publishing their work in top scholarly journals if they pay careful attention to sampling, avoiding type 1 errors and avoiding (or constraining) measurement error.

DEVELOPING QUALITY RESEARCH

For quality empirical research, no shortcuts in the methodology should be taken. This is exceptionally important because almost any shortcut will be identified in the review process, and often serve as the reason that the manuscript is rejected. It is important to have a novel and valuable message. The manuscript should tell a story that explains the novelty and the value of the research done and its contributions. This explanation should be placed early in the manuscript and reiterated and reinforced in the discussion section. Key constructs should be defined early in the paper (the first time they are identified). Defining these constructs early avoids confusion on the part of the reader and will reduce questions from reviewers about the theoretical arguments, hypothesized relationships, construct measures and interpretation of the results.

The hypotheses must be supported by strong theory-based arguments. This means that the theoretical underpinnings must be clearly and thoroughly (yet concisely) presented. The theory (or theories) being used and, hopefully, extended by this research needs to be clearly identified and clearly explained.

The methodology also requires thorough explication. If there are any weaknesses (and most assuredly there are no perfectly designed studies in our field), they should be acknowledged, justified and explained. For example, the author should acknowledge a non-random sample and explain why the sample could not be randomly selected. Furthermore, the authors need to discuss (and probably test) the representativeness of their sample.

Normally, manuscripts should be developed over time using a patient refinement process. This process involves review by colleagues who provide feedback with which to further develop the manuscript. This feedback will help to avoid potential errors or lack of clarity in critical areas noted earlier, which could prohibit a positive decision. Thus, peer review and feedback is needed, even though it often requires extra time and delays submission to a journal. In addition, it requires clear and concise writing (and rewriting); there is no substitute for good writing. Therefore, deliberate practice can be quite helpful.

DOING RESPONSIBLE RESEARCH

There is a movement promoted by major business schools, major management scholars and the Association to Advance Collegiate Schools of Business (AACSB) to encourage and value responsible research, which has the characteristics emphasized as important in the two previous sections. This movement also promotes attributes that include the impact on society, valuing plurality, and multidisciplinary thinking and contributions. In addition, it seeks to motivate and value both basic and applied research. Considering the value of any research project for society (and businesses) is likely to be a criterion used in the evaluation of research by business schools and journals in future years. Indeed, the US National Science Foundation now uses a criterion regarding the impact on society in the evaluation of research proposals submitted for funding from the organization (Glick et al. 2018). Therefore, management researchers would do well to consider this criterion in the development and implementation of research projects. Research that has greater value for society is likely to be more positively evaluated by multiple stakeholders and therefore will have a larger positive impact on the researcher's professional development, rewards and career over time.

CONCLUSIONS

Everyone in our profession can publish their work in top scholarly journals if they develop the capacity to excel, identify a valuable research question (for the field and for societal stakeholders), build a strong theoretical framework, and ensure methodological rigor in the design of their research and rigor in the development of the manuscript. When people engage in this process they achieve a higher probability of having a long-term impact on the field. Scholars using this approach view their research using a longer-term lens. Therefore, instead of focusing on 'low-hanging fruit', these scholars will attempt to address important research questions that add value to our knowledge and for society more generally. Undoubtedly, the competition for journal space has increased considerably and probably will continue to do so. There is a greater balance in the research capabilities of scholars throughout the world and many scholars in other parts of the world, such as Asia and Latin America, are engaged in developing their capacity to excel.

REFERENCES

Baron, R.A. and R.A. Henry (2010), 'How entrepreneurs acquire the capacity to excel: insights from research on expert performance', *Strategic Entrepreneurship Journal*, **4** (1), 49–65.

Boyd, B.K., S. Gove and M.A. Hitt (2005), 'Construct measurement in strategic management research: illusion or reality?', *Strategic Management Journal*, **26** (3), 239–57.

Glick, W., A. Tsui and G. Davis (2018), 'The moral dilemma of business research', *BizEd*, **17** (3), 32–7.

Heckman, J.J. (1979), 'Sample selection bias as a specification error', *Econometrica*, **47** (1), 153–61.

Hitt, M.A., B.K. Boyd and D. Li (2004), 'The state of strategic management research and a vision of the future', in D. Ketchen and D. Bergh (eds), *Research Methodology in Strategy and Management*, Amsterdam: Elsevier, pp. 1–31.

Short, J.C., D.J. Ketchen and T. Palmer (2002), 'The role of sampling in strategic management research on performance: a two-study analysis', *Journal of Management*, **28** (3), 363–85.

Smith, K.G. and M.A. Hitt (eds) (2005), *Great Minds in Management: The Process of Theory Development*, Oxford: Oxford University Press.

Van de Ven, A.H. (1989), 'Nothing is quite so practical as a good theory', *Academy of Management Review*, **15** (4), 486–9.

24. Hitting your preferred target: positioning papers for different types of journals

Yehuda Baruch

INTRODUCTION

Our role as academic scholars is to generate (and disseminate) new knowledge. Academic knowledge is considered new if it is published in an academic outlet. As a rule of thumb, the more prestigious the outlet, the more acclaimed the scholar and contribution. Publish or perish is thus a cliché based on the true nature of academic work and careers (Baruch and Hall 2004), and scholars aim to publish their work in the best possible outlet. When scholars write papers, they need to decide on their target journal. Two questions then arise: which journal to target, and how to maximize the prospects of publications in the chosen journal.

In this chapter, I analyse this decision process to help scholars, setting out a series of considerations to provide guidance to optimize cost–benefit returns, where the costs are emotional, time and energy – clear outcomes of a misjudgement. The need for such a contribution is growing due to a significant acceleration in the number of academic scholars and their output (supply), and the limited set of quality journals (demand) (Edwards and Smith 2010). There are very few top journals, and there is a constant pressure to publish in top journals as a key factor for academic employability (first) and promotability (at a later stage).

What do academic scholars look for? The answer is publications, and in particular, publications with impact. The expected impact would usually vary across types of writing. Those who wish to publish in *Harvard Business Review* aim at top executives, and in many cases, if successful, develop their articles into books, some of which become best-sellers: the impact here would be measured in terms of business and management practice. Scholars who target *Academy of Management Review* aim at academics interested in theoretical developments. They may publish scholarly books, typically not best-sellers, and their impact is confined to the research community. The target audience may be very specific, restricted to scholars with interests in a particular topic or a certain methodological approach. Further, not all journals are considered top journals, and subject to the strength of the message (contribution, relevance, and so on), scholars may better target a second-tier journal to optimize the impact. In this case, it is better to publish in a second-tier journal than receive rejections and lose time by trying to aim too high. The purpose of this chapter is to help scholars to make these decisions.

In this chapter, I consider three main issues: (1) which journal to opt for; (2) how to evaluate the fit between the manuscript and the journal, and (3) practicalities, including dealing with an invitation for a revision, special issues, which arguments to avoid and how to gain insider knowledge. Finally, I return to the main point – publish or perish.

THE 'HOW TO' QUESTION FOR CHOOSING A TARGET JOURNAL

How to position a manuscript for the appropriate journal? The triad to decide:

- What is your target journal (and who is your target audience)?
- The fit of the manuscript to the target journal:
  - The nature of the paper, for example, conceptual versus empirical, qualitative versus quantitative methodology; academic versus practitioners; general versus domain specific versus interdisciplinary.
  - The topic, for example, how closely does the paper relate to the core mission statement of the journal?
  - Quality and reputation, e.g. strength of the paper vs. strength and reputation of the journal; how big the message is and how significant the contributions are.
- Practicalities, for example, style (language, length and referencing), the audience (readership), past coverage of the topic in the journal; past experience with the journal (self and of others) and costs (in time, money and emotion).

WHICH JOURNAL?

One of the issues to consider, as early as when you start writing your manuscript, is which journal(s) to target. Looking for a journal when the manuscript is ready for submission – or so you think – is far too late. No two journals are alike; no two editors are alike. The choice of your targeted journal (and the fall-back options) should guide your writing. Your first choice should be the best possible journal where the manuscript realistically may be accepted.

You may identify a cluster of journals that the manuscript may fit. Often a manuscript is rejected by the first-choice journal; thus, it would be appropriate to consider in advance not only your initial target journal, but also one or two possible fall-back options. In revising a paper that was rejected by your first choice, you need to be open to required changes, including revising the style and settings of the manuscript for the new target journal.

Choice of Journal and Desk Reject

A very strong indication that you have made the wrong choice is if you receive a desk rejection. Desk rejection rates have increased owing to many more submissions, few top journals and the challenge facing editors to identify reviewers who will not decline invitations to review. Editors try to avoid burdening reviewers with manuscripts that are clearly not suitable. Therefore, around 50 percent or even more submitted manuscripts do not make it even to the review process. There is debate about how appropriate and ethical are the reasons for desk rejections (Rupp 2011), but it is a reality you should be aware of.

Why are papers being desk rejected? Apart from poor-quality manuscripts, the most common reasons for editors to desk reject are lack of fit with the journal and poor preparation of manuscripts. In a recent conference session, the Editor of the *International Journal of Management Reviews* advised that some 30 percent of the submissions to their journal consist of empirical papers. These receive an outright desk-rejection decision. The lack of fit may relate to the topic, field or discipline, the methodology or, even, the style. The issue of poor preparation of manuscripts can be avoided by, initially, rigorous attention to the particularities of the journal: its mission statement, target population and requested style of presentation (use of headlines, section numbering and lack thereof, and in particular its referencing style). In addition, scholars should subject their final version to professional proof-reading and editing before submission, especially those for whom English is a second language.

FIT OF MANUSCRIPT

Nature of the Paper

There are many types of papers, and different papers will fit different journals. A paper may be conceptually or empirically orientated (empirical papers may offer conceptual contribution too). Some journals will accept only non-empirical contributions; for example, the *Academy of Management Review* or the *International Journal of Management Reviews*. Others will consider only empirical, evidence-based contributions, for example, the *Academy of Management Journal* (*AMJ*) whereas some journals, such as the *Journal of Management* or the *Journal of Management Studies*, would accept both contributions.

As regards empirical papers, the chosen methodology may also matter for the fit between manuscript and journal. Studies may be qualitative or quantitative, or employing mixed methods. Authors should recognize that many journals have preferences over methodology, whether qualitative or quantitative. Advice for scholars on this ground can be found in a number of editorial notes (for example, the *AMJ*, among many). There are also books with specific advice for specific types of manuscripts. For example, Cooper and Burgoyne (2006) discuss qualitative submissions, Baugh et al. (2006) discuss quantitative submissions and Puffer et al. (2006) give worthy advice on scholarly practitioners' journals. These authors provide useful indications of how your reviewers may evaluate your manuscript.

Another distinction is between academic journals and practitioner journals. Breakthroughs in the latter are particularly difficult, as these journals often have strong preferences for authors from particular institutions (for example, papers by authors from Harvard University who publish in the *Harvard Business Review* are out of proportion compared with their representation in the academic community or in other top management journals). However, belonging to a clique is one element; to make it into top journals authors must have the ability to articulate and present a paper that will attract executives to read it.

The prescription is simple: before submitting, check for fit. When there is not a 100 percent fit, adjust the paper. Do not expect the journal to adjust to your work. However, the question remains: how should fit be evaluated? This is largely a tacit knowledge, and asking learned colleagues, in particular your mentor, can provide good suggestions. You can also learn much from open material. What can you identify yourself? What should you leave for others to point out? You can (and should) read the journal web page to learn its mission statement, aim(s) and scope. Then, read some recent papers that were published in that journal. Can you see your manuscript sitting well with such papers? Do you cite papers published in the journal? This can be one indication that the manuscript fits the journal.

Still not sure? Editors are there to serve their community. You are entitled to consult editors when in doubt. When and how should you consult an editor? Both Feldman (2006) and Rynes (2008) provide general and specific advice for authors regarding the issue of how to communicate with editors. You should have a strong reason to approach an editor to enquire about whether or not to submit to their journal, but if you do have a good reason, do not hesitate. If you have an administrative issue (for example, length, how long it typically takes for a decision or the time from decision to print), it may be better to check with the managing editor or with the journal's secretary.

The Topic

Luckily, this is usually straightforward. Does the topic of the manuscript correspond with the research area and mission statement of the journal? As a scholar, you should know your field and identify if related work has already featured in this journal. Sometimes, a paper combines two theoretical perspectives, so it is unclear if a paper should be sent to, for example, human resource management journals or to industrial psychology journals. Also, there are journals that are general in nature and open to a wide variety of contributions (for example, the *AMJ*, the *Journal of Management* and the *Journal of Management Studies*), whereas others are specific to their field (for example, the *Strategic Management Journal* or the *Journal of Finance*). Authors need to decide whether to opt for a general or specific journal. Interdisciplinary papers pose a challenge; try a generalist journal or one of the disciplines, but which one to choose? The guiding line is the fit for the audience – the readership.

Quality and Reputation

How can you know the quality, strength and status of a journal? How can you know the quality of your manuscript? Both evaluations are needed to match the right manuscript with an appropriate journal.

Knowledge of the quality of a journal is both tacit and explicit. There are several journal rankings that can provide some guidance, but any such ranking can, at best, offer only a proxy for the relative importance and relevance of a journal within a specific field. One journal ranking is the Institute for Scientific Information (ISI) Impact Factor ranking, which uses a formula related to citation levels. Currently, there are over 200 journals in the ISI Management and Business rankings, and even these comprise just a fraction of all available journals in the field. More exclusive is the Financial Times 50 ranking that lists only 50 major journals (until recently, 45), whereas a more inclusive list is the Vienna List with around 1000 journals. There are national rankings, such as the UK ABS list (labelled as the International Guide to Academic Journal Quality) or the CNRS French list, and there are many other rankings offered by various institutions (for a detailed source of such lists see http://www.harzing.com/jql.htm, accessed 22 August 2019).

The problem is that any journal ranking is politically influenced by various factors, such as who decides to include the journals listed, or evaluates their worthiness. However, most of these various rankings tend to be strongly correlated. Thus, the recommendation here is to acquaint yourself with more than one ranking, the journals of interest and the preferences of your employing institution.

The next question is how to judge the strength of the manuscript. The main factor that should determine the worth of the manuscript is its contribution – to theory and to practice (or to both). Self-evaluations are often biased; positively, if you are a strong believer in yourself, or negatively, if you are truly humble and tend to underestimate your own work.

Feedback can help. For example, whether an earlier version was accepted for a prestigious conference (and what feedback the audience gave), what trusted colleagues say about it, as well as your own estimation – the authors should know, for instance, if the empirical results are robust. In empirical studies, for example, cross-sectional data structure is less well regarded than longitudinal, or data collected from multiple sources (avoiding common method bias); sample type and size are also important indicators. Are there enough observations to enable valid and robust analysis? Are there enough participants? See for example Saunders and Townsend (2016) for norms in number of interviews in qualitative studies. Response rate is also important – for norms, see Baruch and Holtom (2008). Data, though, is not enough. How did you analyse the data? Did you compare means? Did you test correlations? ANOVA? Regression? Structural equation modelling (SEM)? Bayesian analysis? Did you use the latest software (for example, for

SEM, you can use LISREL, AMOS or MPlus). How significant are the results (statistically, for quantitative work; reaching saturation, for qualitative studies)? How meaningful are the results? With a sample large enough, even negligible differences will be statistically significant, but not worthy (Allison 1999). Going beyond the data and analysis, you should know if this is a confirmation of existing theory, refinement of theory or a major theoretical breakthrough. There is a difference between an evolutionary refinement to theory and a revolutionary conceptual innovation.

When in Doubt

The advice is 'Aim at the right level'. I would say: 'Aim high, be sensible'. You should aim high, but you have to be realistic too. Submitting a problematic paper to a top journal is futile. It will cost you time, particularly if the editor invites a review. You would need to wait a number of months, just to have a rejection decision. The feedback might be useful, but the price is high. It is not just the cost in time. There is also reputation. You do not want editors to consider you a time-waster, or that you typically submit substandard work. Finally, even if you expect a high prospect of a rejection, receiving a rejection will not add to your feel-good factor.

Alternatively, aiming too low may gain you a quick journal publication, but you would waste a valuable opportunity to publish well. If a manuscript submission was accepted very quickly and with minor corrections, it might be an indication that you aimed too low.

Practicalities

While academic competence and rigor are the critical factors, some exogenous factors can hinder the process. Authors must pay attention to style (language, length and referencing). Match the style, the language, the spelling, in particular USA or UK (for example, organization, labor or organisation, labour). It is unfair on institutions with low resources, but paying for professional proof-reading can be the best practice in terms of return on investment.

Consider the readership. Check for your own and others' past experience with the journal (time to respond, quality of feedback); and, finally, consider the costs (in time, money and emotion).

OTHER ISSUES AND SPECIFIC TIPS

Resource Optimization

It is good to have several papers in the pipeline, but this requires an optimization of submissions, as resources are limited. Authors may need to juggle across different stages of manuscript (in writing, under revise and resubmit, rejected and revising for another journal, and so on). It is important to know when to invest in a new project, when to abandon a failed manuscript, what to do in cases of invitation to revise and resubmit, is it worth considering special issue calls, to mention a few opportunities. Institutional policies and expectations would be a factor – some schools will want only publication in the most prestigious outlet, others will be happy with a wider range of outlets.

Great News: Revise and Resubmit – What Now?

It is very rare for a high-quality journal to accept a submission as is – the best you can hope for is an invitation to revise and resubmit. What should you do if this is the case? The custom, and usually the appropriate action, is to revise and submit it to the journal which invited you to do so. However, there can be exceptions, such as trying other journals, of higher or lower quality, with or without revising first (Altman and Baruch 2008). It might be that the reviewers are asking for too much (in your opinion) or for something you cannot do (for example, collect more data or run an analysis for which you are technically unqualified). Even if this is the case, it would make more sense and show integrity to consult the editor (with whom the decision ultimately lies). The editor can suggest, for example, what is essential, what is 'nice to have' or, even, something more specific – 'I am open to a revision based on the current data' or 'you will definitely need to increase the sample size'. They will also ask for a time limit for resubmission, which is another consideration to bear in mind (although such a time limit can be negotiated if you cannot make it by the suggested date). Then you can make an informed decision about your next step. Again, in most cases, the best option would be to revise and resubmit to the original target journal, in particular because your chances of acceptance are probably reasonable.

Opportunities

Special issues – should you try?
Special issues can be a great opportunity. However, there is also a dilemma – you can never know if this is a 'stitched' system. There have been rumours that guest editors know in advance which papers they are going to accept, so it would be futile for others to try. However, my experience suggests that such a phenomenon is not prevalent, but you should read between the lines – how inviting is the call? Is it based on papers presented in a certain conference track, and do they expect you to attend a special (possibly costly) seminar before approving it? In leading journals, this gaming is rare or non-existent. On the positive side, the odds of acceptance in special issues are typically (though not always) better than in regular issues.

Personal connections
You know (or think that you know) the editor (or the associate editor); you may even consider him or her to be a friend or colleague. This is not a good reason to target the journal. Do not think it will help; it might backfire. However, these contacts can be a good source of sincere feedback. A good friend, whether an editor or a colleague, may help you to direct your manuscript to an appropriate journal (and perhaps to the journal where your friend is the editor).

How to gain insider knowledge about your target journals?
When you go to conferences, attend 'Meet the editors' sessions; network with people who are involved with the journal or published there. When you correspond with an editor (see Feldman 2006 or Rynes 2008), you may learn things that are not official open knowledge. For example, that the journal is trying to enter a new field or that the editor is tired of too many articles in a certain field. It is legitimate to use this knowledge as a further input for the decision to submit (or refrain from submission).

Another great way to learn about journals is by reviewing for them. As a reviewer, you learn from the experience of others (Sullivan et al. 2010; Tjosvold 2014). You see both why certain manuscripts do not make it, and why others are more successful. Typically, you will be sent the comments of the other reviewers to compare with your own and gain further learning experience. Learning from failure of others can help you to avoid similar mistakes. Just learning from successes (reading only papers that were published) would not give you the full picture.

Rejection

Rejection is not the end of the world. It is part of life, and academic life in particular. Really there is no such a thing as 'rejection'. I would advise to take a reject decision as an invitation to revise and re-submit to another journal. The first thing to consider when receiving a rejection letter is not to take it as a personal insult – the reviewers and the editor do not dislike you; they just do not agree with your ideas, methods or conclusions. See what you may learn from the commentary, and start from the beginning – which journal to try next? Read the comments and respond by revising the paper appropriately, otherwise the same criticism may come from the second (and third) journal. If you are upset by the rejection, I recommend reading the suggestions of Nancy Day (2011). Remember, Barney's (1991) theoretical study on the resource-based view was rejected from several journals before making it to print, as was the case for many fine contributions, including Nobel Prize-winning contributions. Thus, persistency and self-belief are critical ingredients for successful publication.

FINAL NOTE

The main messages of this chapter are summarized in Table 24.1.

Table 24.1   Take-aways

Advice	Rationale
Which journal?	
Consider target journal early in the process of writing	Improve the fit, less work in revising or re-writing to fit the journal later
Have in mind one fall-back option or more	The chance of acceptance in the first journal is fairly low
Consult colleagues and editors when needed	Use their experience and knowledge
Know your target journals and their level of prestige as reflected in your own 'community'	Different schools, different countries, different scholarly communities have divergent views on the prestige of journals

Table 24.1 (continued)

Advice	Rationale
Consider new journals backed by prestigious professional associations and/or edited by leading scholars	You may have better chances at these journals, which may later become high-flier journals (for example, the *Academy of Management Annals* or the *Strategic Entrepreneurship Journal*)
Fit for manuscript	
Be attentive to the respective natures of your manuscript and the journals in your field	So you can identify a successful match
Be honest when evaluating your manuscript: (1) subject prominence, (2) strength of theoretical contribution, (3) strength of data and the analysis	Overestimating your manuscript may lead to disappointment and loss of time when the inevitable rejection arrives
Consider specialist journals, even if not ranked as high as other outlets	Specialist journals might grant better fit and have high appeal to particular audiences
Aim high, be reasonable	Use logic, not wishful thinking
Practicalities	
Submit when you feel that the manuscript is ready	Perfectionism will lead you to never submitting. Remember, the enemy of the 'good' is the 'better'
Don't trust your own proof-reading	This is a separate professional job, even when English is your mother tongue – certainly, if it is not
Check journal's web page for style; use the latest edition of the guidelines	If not, expect a desk rejection
Consider both journal and publisher reputation	In particular, journal reputation is a major factor
If rejected, revise and readjust before trying an alternative journal	Benefit from the free advice of reviewers – they might have had good reasons for recommending rejection
Do not submit prematurely if you believe that the manuscript may be publishable in a better journal	Good ideas might not receive due attention if published in lower-ranked journals
Do not let one or two rejections discourage you	There is always an element of luck in the process
Sometimes, it is appropriate to bin a manuscript. Give up if you get the thumbs down from too many	Some manuscripts are just not good enough for publication. Beware of the trap of emotional sunk costs

Advice	Rationale
Miscellaneous	
Review for your target journals	Gain insider knowledge
Have more than one manuscript in the pipeline	With a high rate of rejection, this is advisable
Look for special-issue calls	The acceptance odds may be better than in a regular issue, if there is a good fit
Be resilient: rejection decision is not catastrophic outcome	Better to expect the worst and hope for the better
Ask practitioners to read your manuscript	They can often have a clearer judgement, reflect on managerial implications and be less tolerant of academic jargon

Do not be afraid, but be reasonable. When you write a paper, you want it to be published and become part of contemporary knowledge. Do not keep papers to yourself, make them public knowledge by publishing them. Choose wisely and effectively. Learn from others – from both their successes and failures.

Think – why am I here? What is my 'calling' (Hall and Chandler 2005)? How will this be translated into my quest of progressing academic knowledge? Then, follow your heart, but apply a measure of logic before submission.

Good luck in this quest!

REFERENCES

Allison, P.D. (1999), *Multiple Regression: A Primer*, Thousand Oaks, CA: Pine Forge Press.

Altman, Y. and Y. Baruch (2008), 'Strategies for revising and resubmitting papers to refereed journals', *British Journal of Management*, **19** (1), 89–101.

Barney, J. (1991), 'Firm resources and sustained competitive advantage', *Journal of management*, **17** (1), 99–120.

Baruch, Y. and D.T. Hall (2004), 'The academic career: a model for future careers in other sectors?', *Journal of Vocational Behavior*, **64** (2), 241–62.

Baruch, Y. and B. Holtom (2008), 'Survey response rate levels and trends in organizational research', *Human Relations*, **61** (8), 1139–60.

Baugh, S.G., J.G. Hunt and T.A. Scandura (2006), 'Reviewing by numbers: evaluating quantitative research', in Y. Baruch, S.E. Sullivan and H.N. Schepmyer (eds), *Winning Reviews: A Guide for Evaluating Scholarly Writing*, Basingstoke: Palgrave Macmillan, pp. 156–72.

Cooper, C.L. and J. Burgoyne (2006), 'Reviewing for academic journals: qualitative-based manuscripts', in Y. Baruch, S.E. Sullivan and H.N. Schepmyer (eds), *Winning Reviews: A Guide for Evaluating Scholarly Writing*, Basingstoke: Palgrave Macmillan, pp. 143–55.

Day, N.E. (2011), 'The silent majority: manuscript rejection and its impact on scholars', *Academy of Management Learning & Education*, **10** (4), 704–18.

Edwards, D. and T.F. Smith (2010), 'Supply issues for science academics in Australia: now and in the future', *Higher Education*, **60** (1), 19–32.

Feldman, D.C. (2006), 'Communicating more effectively with editors: strategies for authors and reviewers', in Y. Baruch, S.E. Sullivan and H.N. Schepmyer (eds), *Winning Reviews: A Guide for Evaluating Scholarly Writing*, Basingstoke: Palgrave Macmillan, pp. 236–50.

Hall, D.T. and D.E. Chandler (2005), 'Psychological success: when the career is a calling', *Journal of Organizational Behavior*, **26** (2), 155–76.

Puffer, S.M., J.C. Quick and D.J. McCarthy (2006), 'Reviewing for scholarly practitioner journals', in Y. Baruch, S.E. Sullivan and H.N. Schepmyer (eds), *Winning Reviews: A Guide for Evaluating Scholarly Writing*, Basingstoke: Palgrave Macmillan, pp. 173–95.

Rupp, D.E. (2011), 'Ethical issues faced by editors and reviewers', *Management and Organization Review*, **7** (3), 481–93.

Rynes, S.L. (2008), 'Communicating with authors', in Y. Baruch, A. Konrad, H. Aguinis and W.H. Starbuck (eds), *Opening the Black Box of Editorship*, Basingstoke: Palgrave Macmillan, pp. 56–67.

Saunders, N.K.M. and K. Townsend (2016), 'Reporting and justifying the number of interview participants in organizational and workplace research', *British Journal of Management*, **27** (4), 836–52.

Sullivan, S.E., Y. Baruch and H. Schepmyer (2010), 'The why, what, and how of reviewer education: a human capital approach', *Journal of Management Education*, **34** (3), 393–429.

Tjosvold, D. (2014), Reflecting on reviewing: applying conflict management research', *Journal of Organizational Behavior*, **35** (8), 1079–92.

25. Targeting journals: a personal journey

Franz W. Kellermanns

When asked by the editors to contribute a chapter to their book on how I position family business research in targeting different types of journals, I thought that this would be a simple task. Codifying intangible knowledge, however, is easier said than done. Thus, I searched my memory to find where this intangible knowledge comes from and how I have established my publication pattern.

When I was a doctoral student at the University of Connecticut, I was interested (and still am) in both strategy process and family business research, and have tried to thread these passions throughout my work. At the time, I was exposed to and strongly influenced by the work of my dissertation chair, Steven Floyd, and by the groundbreaking work on family firm research by Michael Lubatkin and Bill Schulze. A series of papers (Schulze et al. 2001, 2003a, 2003b), as well as the establishment of the theory of family firm conference (Chrisman 2003), led me and the field of management (and finance) to develop a strong interest in family firm research. Specifically, studies by Schulze et al. highlighted that classical agency theory assumptions (for example, Eisenhardt 1989; Jensen and Meckling 1976) did not hold for the family firm context. That some papers were published in mainstream journals (Lubatkin et al. 2005; Schulze et al. 2001, 2003a) as opposed to family business journals (*Family Business Review*) or entrepreneurship journals (for example, *Entrepreneurship Theory and Practice*, *Journal of Business Venturing* and *Journal of Small Business Management*) drew substantial attention to family business research, which previously had been minimal (Debicki et al. 2009).

My first academic position was at Mississippi State, one of the leading family firm research universities (Debicki et al. 2009), where I met Jim Chrisman, who became a mentor and friend. Mississippi State had a clearly defined journal list, and publishing in mainstream management journals was not necessarily required to gain tenure. However, advice given to me early in my career by Gregory Dess influenced me then and influences me still. He suggested trying to establish a record of publications aimed not at obtaining tenure at your current institution, but at allowing movement to other institutions. In my case, this meant that I needed to target both entrepreneurship/family business and general management journals. With this in mind, my comments are based on three themes: publishing for tenure, assessing contribution, and learning from co-authors and reviewers. I conclude with specific examples of the positioning of three of my papers to illustrate some of the points made throughout the chapter.

PUBLISHING FOR TENURE

While many of us deeply love research, we ultimately need to be employable and tenure-able. Although elite institutions may require multiple top-tier publications in general management journals, most institutions are satisfied with a mix of journal articles at various levels published in both general and niche journals. For faculty not at an elite institution, focusing only on top-tier publications is a dangerous proposition. As a general rule, higher-level journals have more stringent standards and the publication process takes longer. Publishing in a few such journals presents the opportunity to move to other institutions. More often than not, however, this strategy seems to result in a portfolio that is insufficient for tenure and often insufficient to pursue other academic positions at another comparable institution. Therefore (as reflected in my own record), I am a proponent of the 'shotgun' approach, which targets both general and specialty journals at different levels and allows papers rejected by higher-level journals to move to lower-level journals. I am a firm believer that investing significant time in a paper should lead to publication. This approach allows that papers are published at lower levels and the effort put into the paper is not entirely wasted. The shotgun approach also increases the likelihood (at non-elite institutions) of achieving tenure or being able to move to a different school. In the next section, I approach the question of how to target journals by their varying level of contribution in more detail.

ASSESSING CONTRIBUTION

What constitutes a contribution has been widely discussed (for a more family firm specific guide, see Reay and Whetten 2011 and particularly

Whetten 1989). Generally, in order to publish a niche topic in a general management field, the contribution needs to be substantial and of general interest; that is, it adds more than incrementally to the topic and speaks to the wider management audience. This is most easily accomplished if the paper also advances a theory that is already well accepted. For example, Schulze et al.'s (2001, 2003a) work not only contributes to the family firm literature, but also to agency theory. Although a contribution to mainstream theory is required, it does not have to be dominant. For example, a previous paper (Eddleston et al. 2008) makes a contribution to both the family firm and resource-based view literature, yet is clearly focused on a family firm contribution. Publication in general management journals is also possible, but is less likely to occur if the paper develops a new theory (for example, Gómez-Mejía et al. 2007) or makes a substantial contribution to the literature in this particular niche (for example, Zellweger et al. 2012). It is often harder for the latter to be accepted, as the editor/reviewer will have to judge whether the topic is of interest to the wider journal audience in addition to making a strong contribution. However, even substantial contributions to a sub-discipline are often published in more specialized journals (for example, Astrachan et al. 2002; Habbershon and Williams 1999; Klein et al. 2005).

If a paper meets wider journal quality assumptions (for example, sample size and study design) but reviewers fail to see a substantial contribution, the likelihood of publication in higher-level general management journals decreases; therefore, more niche-specific journals should be targeted. Usually, a paper targeted at a general management journal may be considered by a more niche-specific journal, but a paper that was initially written for a niche journal is almost impossible to place at a general management journal. Targeting a niche journal does not imply that the paper is not important; it simply indicates that the interested audience is likely to be more narrowly defined (see, for example, Eddleston and Kellermanns 2007; Kellermanns and Eddleston 2004). On the positive side, however, papers in these specialized journals may receive much more attention from interested scholars since they have higher visibility in the niche area (the following papers which I co-authored illustrate this: Kellermanns et al. 2008; Zellweger et al. 2010).

CO-AUTHORS AND REVIEWERS

The more papers you get published, the more papers you get rejected. If this relationship is not true for you, then you need to target higher-quality journals. While we want every paper to be successful at the first attempt, it should not. If you hit every *Academy of Management Journal* (*AMJ*) or *Administrative Science Quarterly* (*ASQ*) you submit to, your time is better spent writing another article rather than reading this chapter.

Taking the assessment of the paper's contribution into account, the journal should be targeted by the impact of the paper and in relation to journal quality. In general management, particularly in the United States, a publication in *Organization Science* or *Journal of Management* is more highly regarded than a publication in *Journal of Management Studies*, which, in turn, is more highly regarded than *Journal of Business Research*. Yet, there are some contextual exceptions to this rule; in the United Kingdom, *Journal of Management Studies* due to a stronger focus on the 'Financial Times 50' list may be a more highly regarded publication than the *Journal of Management*, which only was added to the 'Financial Times 50' list during its last expansion. Similarly, in entrepreneurship, *Journal of Business Venturing* and *Entrepreneurship Theory & Practice* are considered higher-level journals than *Journal of Small Business Management* or *Small Business Economics*, and *Family Business Review* is more highly regarded than *Journal of Family Business Strategy*. Although publication in any of these journals (and many others) constitutes an excellent publication, the field values certain journals more than others and the submission process needs to reflect this. When in doubt, the Social Science impact factor is a good, albeit not flawless, guide, as are journal rankings (for example, Chrisman et al. 2008; Harzing 2015).

Journal submission decisions should also be guided by the input of co-authors and (friendly) reviewers. Although more experienced co-authors may have a better feeling for the level of journal that the paper might hit, they are not always right in their assessment of where the paper will ultimately get published. There is an element of luck in the submission decision (for a general discussion of luck, see Barney 1986), as the blind review process relies on reviewers who have different knowledge-sets and preferences. If working with less experienced co-authors, asking for feedback from other authors in the field helps to assess the contribution of a paper and the level of journal. The article on which I obtained the most feedback from a large number of senior scholars and which I consider one of my strongest papers was also my most rejected paper before acceptance. Unfortunately, it is not among my most cited works (Kemmerer et al. 2007). Thus, this approach does not guarantee the desired outcomes.

Finally, while a negative review (and a rejection from a journal) does not mean that the paper cannot be successful at another same-level journal, consistent (negative) feedback indicates that lower-level journals or more niche-specific journals should be targeted.

POSITIONING EXAMPLES

The first paper I published on family firm research (Kellermanns and Eddleston 2004) focused on conflict among family members. It took established constructs from conflict theory and used this literature to provide a theoretical foundation to the abundant conflict often observed in family firms. Yet, to that date, the discussion about conflict in family firms was void of theory and was mostly anecdotal. We then supplemented the conflict theory with family firm-specific constructs and grounded the paper in the family firm literature. This positioning was clearly intended to make a contribution to the family firm literature. While it showed that conflict theory has unique moderators in a family firm context, this contribution would probably have been insufficient for a general management journal and thus the paper was targeted for and published in *Entrepreneurship Theory and Practice*.

Another family firm paper of mine (Eddleston et al. 2008) was targeted at a general management journal. If you read the contribution section in the introduction, the first contribution targets the resource-base view. We suggest that in addition to just having resources (Newbert 2007), it is how these are leveraged that is important. Also, we apply this theory to the realm of family firms and make a family firm contribution. Thus, this paper is of interest to both the general management audience as well as family firm researchers, and was published in *Journal of Management Studies*.

Finally, let me comment on a paper of mine that extends the notion of 'familiness' (Zellweger et al. 2010). This paper was specifically written for the *Journal of Family Business Strategy*. As a theoretical paper that focuses on a family firm specific construct (that is, familiness), it would be very difficult if not impossible to publish it in a general management journal. Yet, the contribution to this family firm specific construct by introducing the importance of identity in the development of familiness was important for the field, and the paper is widely read and cited.

CONCLUSION

Similar to my suggestion to use a shotgun approach in the publication process, I recommend mixing ambition (junior faculty) with experience (senior faculty). Articles written with other junior faculty members firmly establish your contribution to the field (for an early publication of mine with an at the time junior faculty member, see Kellermanns and Eddleston 2004). Articles written with senior faculty members or your chair, although providing exposure to great skill-sets and increasing your overall ability to publish, do not allow you to establish an independent identity. I was fortunate to publish (and continue to do so) with Kim Eddleston, another junior scholar, as well as with senior scholars (most notably, Steven Floyd and Jim Chrisman). By focusing on a research area and working with a variety of co-authors, you will acquire tacit knowledge about article positioning over time, which will increase your chances to publish. Rejections, however, are part of the publication process. While extremely frustrating, particularly early in an author's career, it happens to the best authors and papers. If a paper is rejected, take the reviewers' advice that you find useful and try to resubmit it quickly. Unlike good wine, most papers do not get better with age.

REFERENCES

Astrachan, J.H., S.B. Klein and K.X. Smyrnios (2002), 'The F-Pec scale of family influence: a proposal for solving the family business definition problem', *Family Business Review*, **15** (1), 45–58.

Barney, J.B. (1986), 'Strategic factor markets: expectations, luck, and business strategy', *Management Science*, **32** (10), 1512–14.

Chrisman, J.J., J.H. Chua and L.P. Steier (2003), 'An introduction to theories of family business', *Journal of Business Venturing*, **18** (4), 441–8.

Chrisman, J.J., J.H. Chua, F.W. Kellermanns, C.F. Matherne and B.J. Debicki (2008), 'Management journals as venues for publication of family business research', *Entrepreneurship Theory and Practice*, **32** (5), 927–34.

Debicki, B.J., C.F. Matherne, F.W. Kellermanns and J.J. Chrisman (2009), 'Family business research in the new millennium: an overview of the who, the where, the what, and the why', *Family Business Review*, **22** (2), 151–66.

Eddleston, K. and F.W. Kellermanns (2007), 'Destructive and productive family relationships: a stewardship theory perspective', *Journal of Business Venturing*, **22** (4), 545–65.

Eddleston, K., F.W. Kellermanns and R. Sarathy (2008), 'Resource configuration in family firms: linking resources, strategic planning and technological opportunities to performance', *Journal of Management Studies*, **45** (1), 26–50.

Eisenhardt, K.M. (1989), 'Agency theory: an assessment and review', *Academy of Management Review*, **14** (1), 57–74.

Gómez-Mejía, L.R., K.T. Haynes, M. Núñez-Nickel, K.J.L. Jacobson and H. Moyano-Fuentes (2007), 'Socioemotional wealth and business risk in family-controlled firms: evidence from Spanish olive oil mills', *Administrative Science Quarterly*, **52** (1), 106–37.

Habbershon, T.G. and M. Williams (1999), 'A resource-based framework for assessing the strategic advantage of family firms', *Family Business Review*, **12** (1), 1–25.
Harzing, A.-W. (2015), 'Journal quality list', accessed 21 March 2015 at http://www.harzing.com/jql.htm.
Jensen, M.C. and W.H. Meckling (1976), 'Theory of the firm: managerial behavior, agency costs and ownership structure', *Journal of Financial Economics*, **3** (4), 305–60.
Kellermanns, F.W. and K. Eddleston (2004), 'Feuding families: when conflict does a family firm good', *Entrepreneurship: Theory & Practice*, **28** (3), 209–28.
Kellermanns, F.W., K. Eddleston, T. Barnett and A.W. Pearson (2008), 'An exploratory study of family member characteristics and involvement: effects on entrepreneurial behavior in the family firm', *Family Business Review*, **21** (1), 1–14.
Kemmerer, B., F.W. Kellermanns, J. Walter and V.K. Narayanan (2007), 'Empirical validation of resource-evaluation frameworks: a judgment analysis perspective', working paper, Society of Entrepreneurship Scholars Conference and Manuscript Boot-Camp, Ohio State University, Columbus, OH.
Klein, S.B., J.H. Astrachan and K.X. Smyrnios (2005), 'The F-PEC scale of family influence: construction, validation, and further implication for theory', *Entrepreneurship: Theory & Practice*, **29** (3), 321–39.
Lubatkin, M.H., W.S. Schulze, Y. Ling and R.N. Dino (2005), 'The effects of parental altruism on the governance of family-managed firms', *Journal of Organizational Behavior*, **26** (3), 313–30.
Newbert, S.L. (2007), 'Empirical research on the resource-based view of the firm: an assessment and suggestions for future research', *Strategic Management Journal*, **28** (2), 121–46.
Reay, T. and D.A. Whetten (2011), 'What constitutes a theoretical contribution in family business', *Family Business Review*, **24** (2), 105–10.
Schulze, W.S., M.H. Lubatkin and R.N. Dino (2003a), 'Exploring the agency consequences of ownership dispersion among the directors of private family firms', *Academy of Management Journal*, **46** (2), 179–94.
Schulze, W.S., M.H. Lubatkin and R.N. Dino (2003b), 'Toward a theory of agency and altruism in family firms', *Journal of Business Venturing*, **18** (4), 473–90.
Schulze, W.S., M.H. Lubatkin, R.N. Dino and A.K. Buchholtz (2001), 'Agency relationships in family firms: theory and evidence', *Organization Science*, **12** (2), 99–116.
Whetten, D.A. (1989), 'What constitutes a theoretical contribution?', *Academy of Management Review*, **14** (4), 490–95.
Zellweger, T.M., K.A. Eddleston and F.W. Kellermanns (2010), 'Exploring the concept of familiness: introducing family firm identity', *Journal of Family Business Strategy*, **1** (1), 54–63.
Zellweger, T.M., F.W. Kellermans, J.J. Chrisman and J.H. Chua (2012), 'Family control and family firm valuation by family CEOs: the importance of intentions for transgenerational control', *Organization Science*, **23** (3), 851–68.

26. 'Read the damn article', or the appropriate place of journal lists in organizational science scholarship

M. Ronald Buckley and John E. Baur

One of us (Buckley) received a call from a colleague who could best be described as crestfallen. Buckley had known this professor for well over 10 years as this professor had completed his PhD with one of Buckley's dearest friends. The reason the colleague felt this way was owing to a recent conversation he had with an administrator (dean, associate dean or department chair in the United States of America) in his business school in which he was told 'you don't publish in journals we value around here'. Buckley asked where this had come from and was told by the colleague that it was due to the notion that he did not publish in the journals that were at the top of the journal list of his college. Buckley tried to assuage his colleague's negative emotions by telling him that he had a fine record and some really well cited publications. Buckley hoped he felt better, but the conversation forced us to think of that most recent shibboleth that we are increasingly witnessing in business schools around the world today – the dreaded journal list – which outlines the quality of publications in the absence of reading said publications. Journal lists have been with us for a number of years but their importance continues to increase as we rely on them as a crutch to determine meaningful scholarship.

Let us share with you our bias. In his farewell address to the nation, President Ronald Reagan said something profound: 'It is as true as a law of physics – when government expands liberty contracts.' Our opinion on journal lists, with apologies to President Reagan, is this – 'When our reliance on journal lists expands, scholarship contracts'. It is ridiculous that these journal lists, which frequently have come to be the keystone by which to determine scholarly activities, seem to serve only administrative purposes (so no one has to actually read the article) and facilitate a situation whereby nascent scholars are forced to follow local college norms (which often do not align with the norms of our profession). Too often we are incentivized to target and publish our life's work in journals merely because someone at one time in history published in the journal, served on the editorial board or otherwise had an affinity for the journal and thus placed the outlet high on a journal list. In doing so, we fall into the system that overlooks the true value and impact of our work to instead count 'quality pubs'. The belief that this is an appropriate and fair system would certainly be recognized as management lore.

This is reminiscent of a presentation from a well-known scholar in which he proudly proclaimed, 'I have five of those and six of those and three of those …'. We have no idea what his scholarly contribution was, how these publications impacted and directed future research, or whether this work was his own or a senior co-author's research – only that he had more of the 'baseball cards' than many of our colleagues (Do you remember saying: 'Got 'em, got 'em, need 'em' when we were collecting baseball cards as children? That is what he was doing – collecting top publications, defined as being on 'the journal list'). He obviously was not acquainted with the quote often attributed to Einstein: 'Not everything that can be counted counts, and not everything that counts can be counted.'

Let us offer an example of how the journal list mentality might fail to recognize high-quality scholarship. The article written by Jay Barney (1991) in which he outlines the tenets of the resource-based view was published in the *Journal of Management*. At the time of writing this chapter, Barney's article has 62 453 Google Scholar hits. While the *Journal of Management* has had a positive trajectory over the years, it has only recently been recognized as a pre-eminent outlet at many universities. Had the same stringent journal lists that faculty are expected to publish in today been mandated at the time, this work would not have been treated as a premiere journal article, nor would it have been ranked as a premier journal article in Professor Barney's annual review. Therefore, although the citations of this one article are nearly double the aggregated citations for all articles published in the *AMJ*, a widely-recognized elite business journal, during the same year (38 202) and dwarf the average cites (849) per article and even the most highly cited article (8365), it would have deprived Professor Barney of the global recognition he has achieved from the impact demonstrated by this fine piece of work.

In spite of this, significant mentors of ours (for example, Achilles Armenakis, Art Bedeian, Phil Benson and Kevin Mossholder) and our friends at the Southern Management Association impressed upon us the high quality of the *Journal of Management*, and that it is a premiere journal in the organizational science field. Those 62 453 Google Scholar hits for that one *Journal of Management* article are more than the aggregated Google Scholar hits of a high percentage of entire business schools around the world (this is a fact, as we have looked it up). Likewise, Baron and Kenny's (1986) fundamental work outlining the standard procedures for testing mediation and moderation has 79 712 Google citations. While the *Journal of Personality and Social Psychology* is a fine journal, would these authors be recognized for their exceptional work that has probably influenced a majority of our field more than most others, or would it still not be considered a 'top-tier pub'? While the field continues to advance and statistical techniques have allowed for more exacting techniques, these authors laid the cornerstone for the analyses of many of the hypotheses published in top-tier journals. Furthermore, as evidenced by their very name, journal lists are biased toward publications in academic, peer-reviewed journals and often overlook other scholarly works (for example, books and chapters in a series) entirely. Many of the seminal thinkers in our field (for example, Peter Drucker, Philip Zimbardo, Jeffrey Pfeffer, Howard Aldrich, Stanley Milgram, James Thompson, Karl Weick, John Galbraith, Richard Cyert and James March) would have unduly low research evaluations based on this standard. For example, most of Peter Drucker's contributions were made through his books, which would be devalued by the 'keepers' of the journal list, yet no one can seriously doubt Drucker's influence on our profession and practice.

One of our students was recently on the job market, and we discussed the journal lists of his potential employers as he received campus-visit invitations. What we quickly realized is that there is a wide range of positions that universities today seem to be taking on this issue of journal lists. At one extreme, a university with a doctoral program reported that they did not have a journal list, but that when it comes to tenure, 'you tell us what the good journals in your field are'.

Other journal lists were so politically charged that they were undoubtedly created by neither the norms of the field nor the scholarly impact of the journals. Instead, these lists seem to be motivated and created by certain list creators or political players were able to publish, and then successfully lobbied for those journals to be included on the list for their institution. This frequent process often results in animosity and bitterness as confounding influences (for example, power and political skill) skew the rankings away from their intended outcomes. Over the years, we have witnessed this phenomenon first hand, and have heard from some of our colleagues who related similar stories of the 'annual lobbying for journal quality' process. How can we observe such a process and then regard journal quality as an objective reality when it clearly is a socially constructed reality?

Alternatively, we saw that some journal lists were older and less current, and thus failed to appreciate the advancement of certain journals to elite levels in our field. This is a systemic problem that is not unique just to journal lists that were created many years ago, but to all similar attempts to measure scholarly achievements through a count of numbers. Often committees are created that seek to encompass the myriad interests throughout a business school and thus include committee members from various fields and domains, all with a vested interest in what is created. This process usually takes several months, if not years, until, perhaps through a war of attrition, some determination of an algorithm is agreed upon and thus journals are ranked. While doing this is supposed to create a fair, consistent and accurate reflection of the relative prominence of the various journals both within and across the disciplines, by the time the process is agreed upon, enacted and then voted into the college standards, the rankings are often already outdated. This type of process creates a static snapshot at one time and does not reflect the dynamic and changing status of journals.

The problem is only reinforced when the effort and time required to create the original journal list demotivates faculty from reinvesting the resources required to update it as needed in order to reflect the current journal standings. Our senior faculty are often tasked with these central service roles, yet journal lists impact them the least. Consequently, junior faculty are not only most directly impacted by journal lists (that is, promotion and tenure) but also have the smallest voice in their development and maintenance.

Is there a rational or logical pattern here that is developing with regard to these journal lists and, if so, what is it? Interestingly, and perhaps perplexingly, some widely established top-tier journals were not reflected in many of the journal lists and on other lists many high-quality journals were omitted, whereas significantly lower-level scholarly journals were well represented. Further, many exceptional niche journals (for example, *The Leadership Quarterly*, *Journal of Business Ethics* and *Human Resource Management Review*) either did not appear on these journal lists or were placed well below what the field norms and metrics would suggest, even though they may be a premier outlet for researchers in those areas. We hope you are noticing the confusion here, because we are laying it on pretty thick! The student and I then had the local norms versus national norms of our profession discussion, and we are confident he will produce high-quality research, according to the norms of our profession.

Many of the journal lists imply that only premier journal articles are acceptable (that is, counted in your favor for promotions, tenure, and so on), and anything else is categorized under the 'journals we don't value around here' category, relegating those publications to such inferior status as to sometimes even be regarded as worthless. We reject this position, which many in the field seem to be taking today, as they promote their distinguished and selective lists of journals. As Kerr (1975, 1995) noted, developers of reward systems must be careful of incentivizing erroneous outcomes. In recent conversations with editors and associate editors at many of the premier journals, the current system is not only problematic to our colleagues (for example, stress, anxiety and burnout) but also for the journals that are bombarded with ever-increasing numbers of manuscripts to review. Further, such a tournament-style approach may reward unethical behaviors from both sides – researchers engaging in falsified data and p-hacking as well as journals that pad their stats by strongly 'suggesting' their papers should be cited frequently in new submissions. The aforementioned is far from the trunk (that is, premier publications) and branches (that is, other quality publications) strategy impressed upon us by our fine mentors. We are partial toward the advice of our mentors (that is, the aforementioned Achilles, Art, Phil and Kevin), as it has served us well in our pursuits, and we are confident that the same advice will serve our students very well in their career progress and achievement.

So, we say to our administrative colleagues (and, yes, these journal lists typically are the creations of deans and department chairs, who are trying to convince their constituencies that they are running an elite, high-quality business school, represented by premier scholarly faculty who publish only in select, high-quality journals): 'Give yourself some credit, because you are intelligent, and can understand research.' *Read the damn article* before you judge it according to any journal list. We would wager that the administrator in the example presented in the introduction to this chapter would have found some value if he had read the articles of the crestfallen colleague. Furthermore, where does such an administrator derive the chutzpah to say such a thing? If Jay Barney, Peter Drucker, Achilles, Art, Phil or Kevin made such a statement to us, we would be worried. If administrators lacking in research productivity themselves say it, we will consider the source.

We all need to understand that not all research is destined for a premier journal, but also that publications in journals not appearing on the journal lists are still of value in your overall research program and development as a contributor to our scholarly pursuits. Focusing only on an exclusive subset of journals in this manner not only ignores quality work but also does not recognize a researcher's work in totality. To rely on this approach rather than to assess the actual work based on its own merits is not only malfeasance and a dereliction of duty by those responsible for evaluations of performance, but it is also an admission than an often ill-created ranking can somehow be a heuristic for our unwillingness to engage in the same intellectual inquisitiveness (that is, 'reading the damn article') that drew us into this profession in the first place.

To our junior colleagues in business schools around the world, we leave you with the following advice:

- Do high-quality research that you find interesting, and it will find an appropriate publication outlet. Don't ever apologize for any of your publications – they each fill an important niche in your overall program of research.
- National professional norms should be followed, not local norms (that is, the journal list) – you know what the premiere journals are; the market for our services does not reside in the town in which you are now located; instead it is in the national and international profession within which we operate.
- Find good colleagues with whom you enjoy working and discussing your ideas, and work with them. Good training, scholarly, fecund collegial interactions and hard work are your friends, and will yield success.
- Every successful researcher we know understands the concept of 'chair time' (that is, you have to spend time in your desk chair writing articles), so we suggest you follow their lead.
- Don't let a socially constructed local list be your guide. Make scholarly contributions that incrementally advance what we know about the management discipline.

REFERENCES

Barney, J. (1991), 'Firm resources and sustained competitive advantage', *Journal of Management*, **17** (1), 99–120.

Baron, R.M. and D.A. Kenny (1986), 'The moderator–mediator variable distinction in social psychological research: conceptual, strategic, and statistical considerations', *Journal of Personality and Social Psychology*, **51** (6), 73–82.

Kerr, S. (1975), 'On the folly of rewarding a, while hoping for b', *Academy of Management Journal*, **18** (4), 769–83.

Kerr, S. (2005), 'On the folly of rewarding a, while hoping for b', *Academy of Management Executive*, **9** (1), 7–14.

27. Publishing in special issues
Timothy Clark

INTRODUCTION

This chapter focuses on exploring a range of issues concerned with submitting to special issues. A number of contributors to this volume (see Chapters 5 and 24) have alluded to special issues being associated with a number of dark practices. It is often not clear how a special issue was commissioned, how the editors were chosen, how papers were reviewed, and so on. Many people comment on the closed and opaque nature of special issues. As an author, I have experienced some of these frustrations. Similarly, many colleagues have voiced their annoyance and anger following their perceived mistreatment by special issue editors. While grumbles about rejection from journals are not uncommon, indeed, they are the stuff of everyday corridor conversations, they seem more intense in relation to special issues. I have witnessed colleagues hunt down special issue editors at conferences to vent their ire. Anyone who has edited a journal will know that occasionally hiding you name badge gives you a moment of peace at a conference. On one occasion a very frustrated collaborator dragged me to the publishers' exhibition at a leading international conference. They thrust the latest edition of a journal into my hands and asked if I was aware of this special issue. I was not. It focused on an area of research in which we had a joint interest. To us and others we spoke to it seemed to have emerged via some secretive process.

Special issues, owing to their thematic nature, perhaps intensify the issues that attach to journal publishing more generally because they appeal to a defined subset of the academic community. If your article is not included in a special issue, a rejection may hurt more than normal because your work is being evaluated within a tighter field. Your work is not only being evaluated in relation to similar work but also the operation of cliques and their biases becomes more apparent. This is in turn intensified by the review process. Given their focused nature, special issues draw on a narrower pool of reviewers, some of whom will know your work well. It can be difficult to maintain an anonymous review process in these circumstances. From a journal editor's point of view, the journal invests its reputation with a theme that may not generate the requisite number of quality articles and in editors who may be untested in relation to the management of manuscripts.

In an attempt to partly demystify the process I address a series of questions that relate to different stages in the lifecycle of a special issue. The chapter thus begins by considering how special issues and their editorial teams are chosen, and then proceeds to consider different approaches to reviewing and decision-making.

HOW DO SPECIAL ISSUES BECOME COMMISSIONED?

This question is at the heart of the vignette I recounted above. Many people in the field were unaware of the special issue to which I referred until it was published. It was a closed special issue both in terms of submission and reviewing. The work published was therefore drawn from a pre-selected group and not subject to the normal reviewing conventions, in that people who usually review in the area of interest for the journal in question were not contacted.

As a former journal editor, I have experienced on many occasions approaches at conferences and through emails from people who have a ready-made collection of papers from a conference, seminar or workshop that they believe will make an excellent themed special issue. Indeed, the promise of a special issue may be what brought people to that event in the first place. The people who push these journals are like barrow sellers in markets. They metaphorically wheel their barrows up to editors and tip the contents onto the floor in front of them and say 'will you publish my lovely papers', which more often than not are past their sell-by date and have been previously dropped in front of three other editors prior to their 'fortuitous' meeting with me.

In my experience, special issues derived from such approaches tend to serve the interests of those involved rather than significantly advance the state of knowledge in a particular area. On taking up an editorial role I have inherited a number of special issues that appeared to have been commissioned on this basis. In these cases, the special issue editors proceeded on the assumption that the publication of the issue was guaranteed. Consequently, the standards of reviewing fell below those for a normal issue and they did not result in a sufficient number of quality papers to justify a special issue. On several occasions, in consultation with the other editors of a journal, I have had to inform the special issue editors that there is either insufficient quality in the papers for a themed issue, and so it is cancelled, or a few papers may be publishable and have to be refashioned as a smaller themed section within a normal issue. This has resulted in very problematic correspondence.[1]

To avoid these problems, increasingly journals are adopting open commissioning processes in which they advertise that they are seeking special issue proposals. These are then reviewed by subject specialists or the editorial board and a small number selected. Alternatively the editors of a journal may identify an emergent area to give it a push, or an established area that they think requires detailed critical examination. Again, these ideas may be reviewed by the editorial board and individuals with more specialist knowledge before being approved. Regardless of the manner used to select special issues, calls for papers are commonly advertised in issues of journals, on their websites, distributed at conferences and circulated to relevant email lists in order to ensure that the community of relevant scholars is fully informed about a forthcoming special issue and has an opportunity to submit a paper for possible publication.

IS THE NORMAL REVIEWING PROCESS FOLLOWED?

The extent to which the reviewing process conforms to that used for normal issues varies. In large part, it depends on the degree of discretion afforded to the special issue editors. As a journal editor, I have been very conscious that one has to establish and consistently enforce a clear threshold for acceptance in order to secure a reputation as a leading management journal. This has meant not acting as a 'post box' simply accepting and rejecting papers based on the balance of reviewers' recommendations but rather actively reading papers and coming to a judgement that usually is consistent with that of the reviewers but occasionally is not. Trusting special editors to understand the threshold of publication is therefore critical in determining where control of the reviewing process lies.

This places a critical emphasis on selecting the right team of special issue editors. Experience of the editorial process is a critical issue. Do they understand the manuscript review process? Have they experience of making editorial judgements? Do they understand the threshold for publication? In relation to these issues, prior experience of editing special issues in equivalent journals or other forms of editorial experience are key indicators. Do they have links to the journal (e.g., published in it, acted as reviewer and so forth) that would suggest they understand its ethos and mission? How open are they to submissions from different areas? Do they have sufficient credibility as a team to attract an appropriate number of potentially publishable submissions? What is their strategy to engage the community and publicize the special issues as well as help develop submissions? These are all key questions that are asked to ascertain the competence of the proposed editorial team.

With respect to the review process, I have operated two approaches both as a journal editor and as an editor of special issues for other journals. The first process is simply to put special issue papers through the same reviewing process as papers submitted to normal issues. When the reviews are returned, these papers are sent to the special issue editors for an initial revise and resubmit decision. These preliminary decision letters are then sent to the editors/associate editors of the journal to ensure the quality of decision making and feedback is consistent with normal papers. Under this approach, special issue editors are typically only able to recommend a paper for publication, so authors would receive a conditional acceptance. An action editor from the journal is responsible for making the final decision. Apart from ensuring consistency between normal and special issues of a journal, this also overcomes the difficulties special editors find themselves in when rejecting papers of people known to them (see also endnote one). The second option is to delegate the whole reviewing process to the special issue editors including decision-making on acceptance and rejection of papers. Some journal editors adopt this approach but ask to see the list of reviewers to assure themselves that an appropriate group is being contacted. Apart from heightening the potential inconsistency in reviewing standards and decision-making, this approach can result in poorer feedback to authors and accusations of favouritism.

Understanding which reviewing process is being adopted is important because as an author you need to know who will make the final decision to accept or reject your paper. I have experienced situations both as an author and editor where a special issue editor has written an acceptance letter only for the journal editor (me in some cases) to require further work to get the paper to point of publication. In a very small number of instances, I and my fellow editors have disagreed with the decision of the special issue editors and rejected papers that subsequently were unable to address the issues raised. Unless the decision-making process is clearly communicated, this can lead to confusion and resentment.

Who controls the reviewing process has important consequences of which many contributing authors may be unaware. Although journals increasingly make their content available digitally and many journals are reducing their dependence on paper issues, publishers still establish a page quota for their journals each year. This governs the paper and print costs of a journal and is a key element of a journal's financial budget. Critically, the page quota determines how many papers can be published annually and therefore the number in each issue. The journals with which I have been involved have published an average of six to eight papers per issue.[2]

This means that to be commissioned, a special issue has to be seen to have the potential to publish five to seven papers in addition to an introduction. The special issue editors will therefore feel pressure to generate the requisite number of papers to ensure an issue is filled. Given that top journals have acceptance rates of five percent to ten percent, this would imply that special issues need in the region of fifty or more submissions. That level of submission is very rare. In my experience, special issues rarely receive over thirty submissions and more usually around twenty.[3] Few of these submissions (especially those to a narrowly focused topic) will have the potential to be of sufficient quality to meet the threshold for normal publication. As a consequence, if the incentive to publish the special issue is greater than to ensure quality, a small number of papers that fall below the publication threshold for inclusion in normal issues may be accepted to ensure publication. In these circumstances, the acceptance rate is higher than for a normal issue of a journal.[4] Your odds of acceptance can therefore be many times better in a special issue. The key point here is to ask at the outset where the authority to finally accept your paper lies.

CAN I RESUBMIT MY PAPER TO A NORMAL ISSUE OF THE SAME JOURNAL?

Again, this varies between journals and is a question you should ask at the outset (of course not wanting to undermine the strengths of your paper at the point of submission). It is important to ask in part because you may have written the paper for that journal and remain committed to publication in that outlet regardless of the special issue. It is also important to ask because given my earlier point about the number of papers per issue, there are occasions when there are five slots but six papers of similar quality. In these circumstances one paper has to be rejected for inclusion in the special issue. Usually the decision is made on the degree of fit with the theme. Where this occurs what happens to the sixth paper varies between journals. Also, as I have indicated above, special issues can collapse because not enough papers are deemed publishable. On a few occasions I have seen papers completely rejected by the journal since they do not accept the overflow from a special issue. This can lead to a huge sense of disappointment and resentment with repercussions that may never fully heal. More commonly, journals will publish a paper that did not fit in a regular issue.

CONCLUSION

In this short chapter I have sought to highlight a number of issues that can relate to submitting to special issues. Publishing a paper in a journal is a very gratifying experience. Publishing in a special issue can sometimes be even more pleasing because you are both contributing to a focal area of research and your work is appearing alongside that of a number of peers. In my experience, special issue papers are picked-up more quickly by other researchers. However, I have suggested that you need to clarify who is going to oversee the review process, who will make the final decision on your paper and whether you can resubmit your paper to same journal should it be rejected or a special issue collapse. Doing this will avoid potential future frustration.

NOTES

1. Dealing with 'big names' and the correspondence that can follow a rejection led me to develop a second level of anonymity when I was a general editor of *Journal of Management Studies*. Mike Wright and I did not know the identities of the authors submitting the papers. We were thus not influenced by prior encounters with authors.
2. Publication backlogs in the printed issue of a journal are often caused by acceptance rates exceeding the number of papers that can be published in a year.
3. This might suggest that they are frequently too tightly framed, with the consequence that there is not the volume of potentially publishable work in relevant communities to be submitted. Editors also have to keep a close watch on other journals in their field to ensure that they are not commissioning special issues that potentially overlap with those either being commissioned or published.
4. The reverse is also true. The number of submissions to a special issue can be too low to sustain the publication of the issue.

28. Open access and open conversations: the role of digital technologies in promoting and extending published work

Aija Leiponen and Will Mitchell

INTRODUCTION

Online media and other media innovations are providing increasingly powerful ways to promote our work and to develop and extend our ideas. This chapter addresses ways of stimulating discussion around our scholarly work, including building a base, leveraging institutions and engaging social media. Our core premise is that research will have the strongest conceptual and applied impact if, rather than ending a project after being accepted by a journal or other outlet, we instead engage with a wide range of audiences before and after publication.

The decision to disseminate the research insights using digital media increasingly presents opportunities to exploit open access publishing. As we discuss media strategies for scholars, we also review and assess the existing evidence regarding the evolving role of open access in scholarly publishing.

BUILD YOUR BASE

- *Conferences and seminars.* Research impact begins long before publication. Actively seek opportunities to present and discuss your work in large-scale meetings, smaller conferences, research seminars and informal lunchtime sessions. Highlight the links of your ideas to the work of your colleagues, and encourage, or even help, them to build on and refer to your work when they present their research, even as you refer to their work in your own presentations.

- *Pre-publication and publication links.* Once your article is accepted, post a link to a pre-publication working paper on your own website and/or on professional websites such as the Social Science Research Network (SSRN), ResearchGate, Kudos and Academia.edu, provided this is permitted by your publisher's copyright agreement. In turn, when your article is published, update the sites with links to the formal article, including pre-publication posting that many journals now offer (for example, the 'Early View' links on Wiley's Online Library). You can find the URL for your article by signing on to your publisher's website.
- *Email signature.* Add the publications page on your website to your email signature, and add a direct link to a recent publication as an easy way to tell colleagues about your new work.
- *Your research community.* Send links to your article to scholars who are likely to be interested in your work. At a minimum, send links to people who you have cited in the research, to help them see the connection with their work. 'Table of content' alerts from your core journals offer useful ways to follow the evolving discussion around your topic. Several publishers also have relevant mobile apps that include journal abstracts, book recommendations and conference information that help track the discussion.
- *Wikipedia.* People commonly start their research about a topic by searching Wikipedia. Look for relevant Wikipedia pages about your research topics and add a link to your work.

CONSIDER OPEN ACCESS PUBLISHING

Open access means that an article, or the whole journal, is available to readers free of charge. There are emerging open access management journals such as *Organization Theory*, a new journal associated with the professional society EGOS (European Group for Organizational Studies) launched in 2019, as well as *Health Management, Policy, and Innovation* (*HMPI*), an applied journal for healthcare and life sciences research.[1,2] Some governmental research funding agencies, such as the Research Councils in the United Kingdom, require articles they have funded to be published as OA.[3] In the United States, the National Science Foundation requires that articles based on research it has funded must be openly accessible after an embargo period of 12 months, whereas the National Institutes of Health require funded research to be immediately upon acceptance to a journal available in full-text, pre-publication manuscript format via PubMed Central. Zhang and Watson (2017) reported about 71 known funding agencies requiring openly accessible articles from agency-funded research. As universities are grappling with increasing journal subscription prices, open access publishing is becoming a topical, even urgent, consideration, including active discussions and negotiations with publishers of scholarly journals.[4] In the near future, open access will be part of the mainstream publishing ecosystem.

Types of Open Access

There are several types of open access publishing. Under the heading of 'gold open access' there are three ways to publish: first, journals that are free of charge both to publish and to read. These journals, such as *Organization Theory* and *HMPI*, are usually supported by a professional society or association. Second, there are open access journals that are supported by article processing charges (APCs) paid by authors. Third, there are traditional subscription-based journals that offer authors the opportunity to make their article open access in exchange for APCs. Solomon and Björk (2012) compared APCs across a wide range of journals and found an average charge of US$906 across journals, but usually varying from US$8 to US$900. High impact factor disciplinary journals tend to charge around US$2000 per article. These gold open access articles are immediately available to all readers.

In addition, authors may publish their research in subscription-based journals using the 'green open access' model. In this case, authors deposit their article in a research repository such as ArXiv.org, RepEC or SSRN in pre-print format after the publisher-specified embargo period has elapsed. For example, ArXiv.org is a repository owned and operated by Cornell University and is funded by Cornell and dozens of member institutions, including most top research universities in the world.[5] The Registry of Open Access Repositories (ROAR) promotes open access publishing by maintaining lists of institutional (single-university based) and open research repositories throughout the world.[6]

Potential Benefits of Open Access Publishing

The benefits of, and obstacles to, open access publishing have been studied for some time, with primary focus on its impact on the citation performance of articles. It stands to reason that a more liberal dissemination policy supports greater readership and, subsequently, more citations and research impact. Nevertheless, while most studies suggest a positive, substantial and statistically significant effect of open access on citation rates, 17 out of the 70 studies reviewed in 2015 showed no citation advantage to open access publications (SPARC Europe, 2015). At least two confounding factors complicate the estimation of the citation impact of OA.

The two factors involve time and selection. First, open access publications may be available for a longer time via online repositories such as ArXiv, where articles may be posted as working papers before journal publication. Therefore, they may have accumulated a greater number of citations compared with articles not posted to open repositories. Second, authors may opt to pursue open access to their best articles, especially if this implies a cost to them. Thus there may be a selection bias to open access publishing.

Using a different approach to assess the citation impact, Björk and Solomon (2012) compared the citation performance of open access and subscription journals. When controlling for discipline, journal age and publisher location, the two types of journals exhibit no meaningful differences in citation rates. However, free open access journals performed worse than open access with APC, and the latter performed equally as well as subscription-based journals launched in the same time period. Thus, although, correlationally, subscription-based journals may have higher citation rates, those rates are confounded by other journal characteristics such as age and prestige. However, when journals switched from subscription-based to open access with APC, they experienced a substantial citation increase, especially if they were a top-ranked journal (McCabe and Snyder 2014). Low-ranked journals, by contrast, tended to have a reduced citation rate after switching. Thus, it appears that open access better supports high-quality journals.

Finally, comparing articles within subscription-based journals that are made open access through APCs, Sotudeh et al. (2015) found that APC-supported open access substantially boosted citations, but the effect was the smallest in social sciences and humanities (only 3 percent increase). Thus, it appears that open access benefits research in other disciplines more than in social sciences. However, when the quality differences between open access and regular articles were removed through automatic inclusion in an open access pilot scheme and through controlling for the authors' institutions as a measure of quality, the citation advantage in economics shrunk to 0.4 percent according to Mueller-Langer and Watt (2014), compared with the raw citation impact of over 22 percent before controlling for quality differences.

On Balance

It appears that open access publishing is still in its early stages of large-scale acceptance; according to Zhang and Watson (2017), only 22 percent of their sample of physical science research was published using OA, mostly in open access journals with APC. However, these scholars found that citation rates per article were very similar across gold OA, green OA and non-open access (but not controlling for journal or article quality). Considering the very limited impact found for open access publishing of social science, particularly controlling for selection biases owing to quality differences, and the substantial APCs charged for authors, it is difficult to argue that open access publishing is justified by its citation impact alone.

Nevertheless, open access publishing may make sense because of funding agency requirements or university policies attempting to level the negotiating positions between publishing companies and universities. The cost of academic publishing for publishers has been substantially reduced after switching to largely all-digital formats, and the profits of publishing companies have soared, therefore many universities and scholars feel that publicly funded research should be publicly available and that the fruits of scholarly labor should be more evenly distributed.

Alternatively, the open access evidence suggests that new open access journals supported by APCs can perform equally well as traditional subscription-based journals, controlling for other journal characteristics. Also, switching a high-quality journal from subscription-based to open access can boost impact. Thus, scholarly leaders within the management discipline could begin to collectively start shifting the emphasis of publishing toward open access. This is most feasible through society journals that have an established scholarly community backing, as the example of the European Group for Organizational Studies (EGOS) and *Organization Theory* suggests.

Moreover, independent of the scholarly impact, payers and funders are strongly pushing toward open access models. Hence, very soon the issue for scholars is not whether they will need an open access strategy but, instead, what type of open access strategy is most effective for them. Hence, learning how to position articles in an open access world is a key step in disseminating our work.

LEVERAGE YOUR INSTITUTIONS

- *Media relations.* In addition to posting on your own website, send the URL to your school and/or university's media relations office with a description of your work so they can include the information in their promotional activities. Develop the skill to prepare short, clear descriptions of your work, which will help the media relations staff provide cogent summaries or press releases. Media offices often work with these tip sheets that they then circulate with their relevant external media contacts, such as journalists in related outlets. If your tip sheet offers a timely and intriguing viewpoint, reporters may approach you for an interview. The two-part abstracts that Strategic Management Society (SMS) journals have recently adopted, including both 'academic summaries' and 'managerial summaries', provide a model for concise descriptions. As always, the core issue here is to take the viewpoint of the audience you want to connect with, and use the language that they find compelling.
- *Publisher services.* Several publishers now offer publication support services, such as tracking your accepted articles through production, nominating colleagues for free access, optimizing search engines, and other activities. The links at Wiley Author Services provide an example of these services.
- *Media.* If you know of upcoming news coverage and have a chance to contribute, prepare a tip sheet and make sure that the outlet has the article's website URL. The university media relations office may have contacts with business and economics writers in major media outlets to whom you or the media office can reach out.
- *Your journal.* Your journal has an incentive to promote your work. Let your editor know if your article is mentioned on blogs, websites and listservs in your field or is included in major media outlets. You can track media mentions of your work on services such as Altmetrics.

ENGAGE SOCIAL MEDIA

- *Post.* Share your work with a link on Twitter, Facebook, LinkedIn and other accounts. The SMS groups on Facebook and LinkedIn are active sites for discussing the research, teaching and management implications of your research.

- *Twitter.* Many scholars use Twitter to follow people whose ideas they are interested in and to spread their own ideas. It is useful to build a following on Twitter with an ongoing stream of thoughtful comments about your work and related ideas.
- *Video abstracts.* Several journals and academic societies are now posting video abstracts of published work, typically with links to the published article. Discuss this opportunity to prepare brief video summaries with your editors. You can gain ideas for how to frame your work with a video abstract by watching the videos on the SMS's YouTube channel, which has a range of video models to consider. In addition to postings on your journal's and publisher's sites, the videos are useful for your institution's media relations office and, potentially, for your own video channel on YouTube, Vimeo or elsewhere.
- *Blogs.* Many scholars and scholarly communities are experimenting with research blogs.[7] It is useful to search for discussions that are relevant to your research activities and thoughtfully tie your ideas to the discussions. Consider starting your own blog, ideally with focused discussions of important ideas that are relevant to your research. Blogs work best when they are updated regularly; but take on this activity only if you are prepared to keep the discussions fresh and regular. If you only wish to blog occasionally, you may be able to write for commercial management blogs, such as for *Forbes*.[8]
- *Lead a discussion.* Once you have posted an item, whether on a social media group or your own blog, encourage active discussion of the ideas. You can prompt ideas with questions, responses to comments from members of the group, links to relevant ideas and ongoing summaries of the discussion. One-off threads tend to fall below the radar in social media groups – you can keep the discussion alive with thoughtful refreshment and new relevant ideas.
- *Social media style.* The attention span of scholars and practitioners reading social media tends to be very short. Therefore, your writing style should be clearer and more pointed than in regular scholarly writing. Think about the hook to engage the reader's interest. Positive humor often works well to capture attention, as do thought-provoking questions. However, take care in considering your tone – sarcasm can be difficult to interpret! Although you will want to be perceived as a thoughtful and professional contributor to intellectual debates, social media necessitates a sharper communication style

than many academics are used to, both in terms of the core ideas and their areas of potential application – how the ideas matter.

These are only a few of the many ways that we can use online media to expand the reach of our research. The core point to all these ideas – and for many others – is that our opportunities and responsibilities as scholars do not end with publication. Research impact does not occur by 'counting coup' with an entry on our curriculum vitae. Instead, the impact of our research comes from active, wide-ranging discussion with as many people as possible, much of which ranges far beyond the actual publication in a journal. The power of social media is that it engages scholars and practitioners globally, 24 hours a day, seven days a week. This engagement has risks; misinterpretation and flame wars are too common, even in academic settings. Instead of ignoring or running from the risks, we will have the most impact and take the greatest control of our ideas by finding ways to engage that suit our personal preferences and skills.

NOTES

1. https://uk.sagepub.com/en-gb/eur/organization-theory/journal203655#description (accessed 29 August 2019).
2. https://hmpi.org/ (accessed 29 August 2019).
3. https://www.ukri.org/funding/information-for-award-holders/open-access/open-access-policy/ (accessed 29 August 2019).
4. https://www.sciencemag.org/news/2019/02/university-california-boycotts-publishing-giant-elsevier-over-journal-costs-and-open (accessed 29 August 2019).
5. https://confluence.cornell.edu/pages/viewpage.action?pageId=340900096 (accessed 29 August 2019).
6. http://roar.eprints.org/ (accessed 29 August 2019).
7. For example, https://strategicmanagementsociety.wordpress.com/, https://asqblog.com/ and www.digitopoly.org (all accessed 29 August 2019).
8. www.Forbes.com (accessed 29 August 2019).

REFERENCES

Björk, B.C. and D. Solomon (2012), 'Open access versus subscription journals: a comparison of scientific impact', *BMC Medicine*, **10** (73), accessed 29 August 2019 at http://bmcmedicine.biomedcentral.com/articles/10.1186/1741-7015-10-73.

McCabe, M.J. and C.M. Snyder (2014), 'Identifying the effect of open access on citations using a panel of science journals', *Economic Inquiry*, **52** (4), 1284–300, accessed 29 August 2019 at http://dx.doi.org/10.1111/ecin.12064.

Mueller-Langer, F. and R. Watt (2014), 'The hybrid open access citation advantage: how many more cites is a $3,000 fee buying you?', Max Planck Institute for Innovation & Competition Research Paper No. 14-02, accessed 29 August 2019 at https://papers.ssrn.com/sol3/papers.cfm?abstract_id=2391692.

Solomon, D.J. and B. Björk (2012), 'A study of open access journals using article processing charges', *Journal of the American Society for Information Science and Technology*, **63** (8), 1485–95, accessed 29 August 2019 at https://onlinelibrary.wiley.com/doi/full/10.1002/asi.22673.

Sotudeh, H., Z. Ghasempour and M. Yaghtin (2015), 'The citation advantage of author-pays model: the case of Springer and Elsevier OA journals', *Scientometrics*, **104** (2), 581–608, accessed 29 August 2019 at http://dx.doi.org/10.1007/s11192-015-1607-5.

SPARC Europe (2015), website of the open access citation advantage service, accessed 29 August 2019 at https://sparceurope.org/what-we-do/open-access/sparc-europe-open-access-resources/open-access-citation-advantage-service-oaca/.

Zhang, L. and E.M. Watson (2017), 'Measuring the impact of gold and green open access', *Journal of Academic Librarianship*, **43** (4), 337–45.

29. Should you publish in an open access journal?

Charles C. Snow

Young scholars in the organizational sciences are trained and advised to publish in the top academic journals. Often, a promotion and tenure committee uses a pre-specified list of top journals to encourage if not demand that junior faculty focus their attention on publishing in those journals. Moreover, articles published in the top journals tend to be cited more frequently than articles in lesser-quality journals, so publishing in the top journals is widely viewed as the best way to build your academic reputation and create visibility for your research program.

All of the top journals in the organizational sciences are subscription journals. These journals are owned by publishing companies or professional associations, they have a defined amount of space per issue that is set contractually and they charge readers to gain access to the knowledge contained in their pages. Top journals are also difficult to publish in, with acceptance rates for submitted papers running at 10 percent or less.

In recent years, a new type of academic journal has emerged called open access. Open access journals offer a publishing alternative to subscription journals, but as yet no open access journal in the organizational sciences has been judged to be a top journal. Therefore, it is reasonable to ask, should you try to publish papers in open access journals?

In my role as founding co-editor of the *Journal of Organization Design* (*JOD*), an open access journal established in 2012 (https://jorgdesign.springeropen.com), I want to take this opportunity to build a case for publishing in the *JOD* and other legitimate open access journals. The *JOD* is owned by the Organization Design Community (www.orgdesigncomm.com), an international community of scholars, executives and organizations dedicated to advancing the theory and practice of organization design. The mission of the journal is to publish theoretically sound and practically relevant articles on all aspects of organization design. The *JOD* has a distinguished editorial board and a double-blind review process, ensuring that the journal maintains rigorous scientific standards and publishes high-quality work. The *JOD* is covered by the major abstracting and indexing services, and in 2019 plans to apply for an impact factor from the Web of Science. The editorial team of the *JOD* is committed to conducting a prompt review and editorial process so that authors are able to publish their ideas and findings in a timely fashion. The *JOD* publishes certain types of articles that traditional (subscription) journals do not. Potentially, you can make a contribution to the organizational literature that might not be possible if you submitted your paper to a traditional journal.

OPEN ACCESS PUBLISHING

Open access means unrestricted online access to, and reuse of, peer-reviewed scholarly research (Wikipedia 2014). Building on the early self-archiving practices of computer scientists and physicists, the original concept of open access was primarily intended for scholarly journal articles. The term itself was first formulated in three public statements: the Budapest Open Access Initiative (2002), the Bethesda Statement on Open Access Publishing (2003) and the Berlin Declaration on Open Access to Knowledge in the Sciences and Humanities (2003). The Budapest statement discusses open access as follows:

> By 'open access' to this literature, we mean its free availability on the public internet, permitting any users to read, download, copy, distribute, print, search, or link to the full texts of these articles, crawl them for indexing, pass them as data to software, or use them for any other lawful purpose, without financial, legal, or technical barriers other than those inseparable from gaining access to the internet itself. The only constraint on reproduction and distribution, and the only role for copyright in this domain, should be to give authors control over the integrity of their work and the right to be properly acknowledged and cited. (http://www.budapestopenaccessinitiative.org/read)

The benefits to various audiences of open access publishing include the following:

- Open access journal articles are free to read and reuse (even though each journal must have a sustainable cost-recovery business model). With open access, researchers anywhere can read and build on the findings of others without restriction.

- Much scientific research is paid for with public funds. Open access allows taxpayers and funding agencies to see the results of their investment.
- Researchers, teachers and students around the world have free and quick access to the growing stock of information and knowledge in a scientific discipline. Free access is particularly valuable in emerging economies that cannot afford to pay for the high cost of many subscription journals.
- Open access helps to diffuse knowledge by breaking down some of the barriers associated with academic fields. An open access article is accessible by anyone: a professional in the field, a researcher in another field, a journalist, a politician, a civil servant or an interested layperson.
- Although the evidence is not definitive, all else being equal, open access articles may get cited more frequently than articles published in subscription journals (Craig et al. 2007; Hamad and Brody 2004; Lawrence 2001; Pringle 2004). In any case, combining open access and traditional publishing allows authors to maximize their research impact by reaching wider audiences.

In early 2019, more than 12 300 open access journals were listed in the Directory of Open Access Journals. There are many open access journals that focus on business and management topics. Unfortunately, some of those journals – no one knows for sure how many and which ones – are not legitimate. An illegitimate open access journal can be spotted if it has an undistinguished (or unknown) editorial board, invites authors to be on the editorial board at the same time they submit their papers, publishes irregularly, offers unrealistic time frames for peer reviews and authors' revisions of their papers, and so on. Most academics would agree that journals of this sort are not publishing properly vetted studies, and authors should shy away from such journals when submitting their papers.

There is recent pressure from some quarters that seeks to increase open access publishing. For example, in October 2018 the European University Association (EUA 2018) adopted a statement expressing its concern about the lack of transparency and competition in the scholarly publishing business sector in Europe. The EUA believes that the current state of publishing hinders the development of true open access to scientific publications in Europe, a declared priority of the European Commission and European universities. It may also inhibit the implementation of Plan

S, signed by research funding organizations and the European Commission, to make publicly funded scholarly publications openly available from 2020.

REASONS TO PUBLISH IN OPEN ACCESS JOURNALS

The flexibility provided by the open access format has led the creators of some open access journals to attract submissions that most traditional journals do not embrace. In the case of the *JOD*, it can be distinguished from traditional journals in three main ways. The first is the journal's objectives and audience. Authors are always advised to carefully investigate a target journal, as well as other candidate journals, before deciding where to submit their paper (Day 2007). The *JOD* seeks to publish any paper that has implications for how organizations are or could be designed and managed. The journal is concerned with both theory and practice, unlike traditional journals that tend to focus on one or the other. Moreover, the *JOD* will publish any paper that, in the judgment of its reviewers, contributes to the scientific record. Authors are not required to contribute to theory, present empirical evidence or otherwise conform to criteria set by the journal. They must simply convince the experts on the *JOD*'s editorial board that their ideas, arguments and findings contribute to the scientific literature on organization design.

A second differentiator involves the *JOD*'s focus on the future. The *JOD* seeks papers that focus on the future and determine its impact on the present. It wants papers that examine future states and derive their implications for organizational strategizing, decision-making and behavior. It welcomes papers based on research methodologies such as experiments, computational modeling, thought experiments, scenario development and planning, and simulations and prototyping. Traditional top journals are reluctant to publish articles on what might or could be. As a result, they tend to focus on organizations, situations and data from the past. By contrast, the *JOD* is able to publish articles on new and trending topics.

Finally, the *JOD* offers authors multiple formats in which to submit their papers. The standard format for a theoretical or empirical research article is available, and there are several other formats from which authors can choose. A translational article, for example, is one in which an organizational concept or study is translated for practitioners, with clear implications for organization design. A point of view article allows the author to comment on the design and/or management of organizations from a particular theoretical or practical perspective. A research primer focuses on a particular research stream and derives its implications for organization design theory or practice. A case study article can take a variety of forms; for example, as a detailed example of a concept or practice, a description of a new type of organization or management approach, and a demonstration of the need for a new concept or the modification of an established theory. The underlying evaluation criterion for a paper in any of these formats is that it advances organization design theory or practice.

CONCLUSION

Open access publishing in the organizational sciences appears likely to increase in the future, offering researchers more opportunities to publish their work. Open access publishing reflects the growing trend of open science – a more inclusive, collaborative and transparent way of doing scholarly research. The *JOD* is a pioneer in this domain as it gives both scholars and practitioners a variety of ways to contribute to the literature on organization design, and it makes this knowledge openly available to everyone.

REFERENCES

Berlin Declaration on Open Access to Knowledge in the Sciences and Humanities (2003), accessed 29 September 2014 at openaccess.mpg.de/Berlin-Declaration.

Bethesda Statement on Open Access Publishing (2003), accessed 29 September 2014 at legacy.earlham.edu/-peters/fos/Bethesda.htm.

Budapest Open Access Initiative (2002), accessed 29 September 2014 at www.budapestopenaccessinitiative.org/.

Craig, I.D., A.M. Plume, M.E. McVeigh, J. Pringle and M. Amin (2007), 'Do open access articles have greater citation impact? A critical review of the literature', *Journal of Informetrics*, **1** (3), 239–48.

Day, A. (2007), *How to Get Research Published in Journals*, 2nd edn, Aldershot: Gower.

Directory of Open Access Journals (DOAJ), website, accessed 29 August 2019 at http://www.doaj.org.

European University Association (EUA) (2018), 'Scholarly publishing: EUA asks European Commission to investigate lack of competition', accessed 29 August 2019 at https://eua.eu/news/188:scholarly-publishing-eua-asks-european-commission-to-investigate-lack-of-competition.html.

Hamad, S. and T. Brody (2004), 'Comparing the impact of open access (OA) vs. non-OA articles in the same journals', *D-Lib Magazine*, **10** (6), accessed 29 August 2019 at http://www.dlib.org/dlib/june04/harnad/06harnad.html.

Lawrence, S. (2001), 'Online or invisible?', *Nature*, **411** (6837), 521, accessed 22 September 2014 at http://citeseer.ist.psu.edu/online-nature01/.
Pringle, J. (2004), 'Do open access journals have impact?', *Nature*, Web Focus, accessed 26 September 2014 at http://www.nature.com/nature/focus/access debate/19.html.
Wikipedia (2014), 'Open access', accessed 22 September 2014 at en.wikipedia. org/wiki/Open_access.

PART III

Publishing Across Disciplinary Boundaries

30. Publishing in finance versus entrepreneurship/management journals

Douglas Cumming

INTRODUCTION

I was pleased to be invited by the editors to write a brief chapter on my experiences publishing in finance versus entrepreneurship/management journals. I am sure there are better folks than me for this job (including, but not limited to, the editors of this book), but I do think I have a few things I can share. I do so with the hopes that I do not overly offend someone (to be a nerd and put it in economics terms, I hope that this chapter is Pareto optimal), and if I do, then at least I hope the harm I cause to some will be outweighed by the benefit I will do for others by sharing my experiences (back to being a nerd, if Pareto optimality is not possible, I nevertheless hope that this chapter is Kaldor–Hicks optimal). Also, although I express concerns with some reviewers through anecdotes herein, overall I hope to convey that I have greatly benefited from feedback from colleagues and through the review process. While the experiences I share here reflect my personal biases, I nevertheless hope they are helpful for others in the future. In this chapter I address two questions that I am often asked by other professors. The first is often asked by junior professors: 'How do I publish in different fields?' The second is more often asked by both junior and senior professors: 'Why do I publish in different fields?'

To begin, I briefly explain what my experience has been to date so that you can deem whether or not I am qualified to write anything on this topic. I have experience publishing in leading journals in finance (*Review of Financial Studies* and *Journal of Financial Economics*), management and international business (*Academy of Management Journal* and *Journal of International Business Studies*), entrepreneurship and innovation (*Research Policy* and *Entrepreneurship Theory and Practice*) and economics and law (*Economic Journal* and *Journal of Empirical Legal Studies*). Since 2000, I have published 18 books and over 170 refereed journal papers, including many sole-authored papers. In the last ten years, I published on average more than ten papers per year. I am the founding Editor-in-Chief of *Annals of Corporate Governance*, a current Managing Editor-in-Chief of *Journal of Corporate Finance*, a co-editor of *Corporate Governance: An International Review* and an associate editor of the *British Journal of Management*. I have previously served as a Co-Editor of *Entrepreneurship Theory and Practice*, and *Finance Research Letters*. I have guest edited a number of special issues of different types of leading journals, including the *Journal of Corporate Finance, European Financial Management, European Journal of Finance, Journal of Banking and Finance, Journal of Business Ethics, Journal of International Business Studies* and *Strategic Entrepreneurship Journal*.

DIFFERENCES BETWEEN FINANCE AND ENTREPRENEURSHIP/MANAGEMENT JOURNALS

The differences between orientating a paper towards a management journal or a finance journal are straightforward, if you allow me to overgeneralize. Finance journals typically do not want a verbal theory section, and if there is a section that speculates a few (reverse engineered) hypotheses then it needs to be rather short and to the point. Formal mathematical models are occasionally appropriate in finance journals but rarely used in management journals. Finance papers want the best and most up-to-date data and the most rigorous robustness checks. Management papers prefer to focus on longer verbal theory sections. I am aware that many finance folks view these long verbal theory sections as being superfluous because they do not involve mathematics. In my experience, counter to what I have heard many finance professors claim, not everyone is capable of writing theory sections in management papers, and a tremendous effort is needed to do so. The section needs to be very well reasoned with consideration given to alternative explanations. Empirical tests in management papers are often less concerned about the quality of the data and/or whether there is a complete set of robustness checks as long as the research question is new and interesting, while finance papers, by contrast, are extremely resolute about demonstrating robustness even when (at times, in the view of some folks) the research question is not new or very interesting.

PUBLISHING HOME BIAS IN DIFFERENT DISCIPLINES

Why would someone ever want to publish in a journal that is not in the field of their home department? I begin by explaining that there is home bias among faculty in different departments to prefer their own journals, and this home bias is particularly strong in finance. Finance professors like finance journals, and do not pay much respect to non-finance journals. Finance faculty members are more inclined to think that finance journals are substantially harder to publish in than management journals (despite the acceptance rates at many top journals in both fields tending to be in the region of 5 percent). Management faculty likewise prefer their own journals, but in my experience management faculty are more inclined to acknowledge that it is difficult to publish in top journals in all fields. Cumming and Johan (2017) present evidence from Google Scholar that shows that in the field of entrepreneurial finance (where work on the topic significantly overlaps in management/entrepreneurship and finance journals), finance journals are statistically much less likely to reference managements and entrepreneurship journals, whereas entrepreneurship and management journals are more likely to reference all types of journals.

My home department has been finance in each of the universities where I have worked (previously I was at a university where my home was finance and I was cross-appointed to entrepreneurship; at my current university I am professor of finance and entrepreneurship). For those that are not familiar with finance departments, it may be helpful to share a few stories about the typical very strong and negative sentiment that finance professors have for the research done by non-finance professors. Two of my stories are as follows. First, one day, shortly after joining a new university, a finance colleague walked into my office, uninvited, and proceeded to tell me that I am 'cheating by publishing in crappy management and entrepreneurship journals as a way to artificially inflate my publication numbers'. Second, a finance professor indicated to everyone at a visiting speaker department seminar that 'publishing in *any* finance journal would be better than stooping so low as to publish in a management journal'. The people involved in these stories may not be completely representative, and to be fair, my son's middle name is 'Jedi' and I like to joke that these episodes are 'disturbances in the force', so perhaps I too am not perfectly representative of finance faculty.

Nevertheless, I believe that these stories are quite representative. I have worked either as a regular finance faculty or as an extended visitor at different universities around the world, including universities in Australia, Canada, China, England, France, Germany, the Netherlands and the USA. I have experienced this negative sentiment by finance faculty towards management journals at most of the universities where I have had the opportunity to work and visit. I have spoken with countless others at different universities and have been told about a similar sentiment universally held at other institutions that I am aware of. Most finance faculty I have spoken with even contend that B- and C-level finance journals are substantially superior to A* management journals even though the impact factors of the B- and C-level finance journals are substantially lower. Finance faculty counter that their journals tend to have lower impact factors than management journals because reference lists are longer on average in management journals than finance journals. Possibly, but I have no basis to confirm whether or not this is true and know of no other objective or quantifiable measure by which to compare these journals.

What does this home bias mean for authors contemplating sending their paper to a journal outside their own area? It means that referees and editors will probably be suspicious that your paper was rejected by one or more journals in your own area. Therefore, if you drift to a journal outside your home area, you have to take extra care to ensure that the paper has been written with the journal and target audience in mind. Make sure that the paper has been properly formatted to the target journal requirements and that all relevant literature has been cited. Minimize cites to your home area.

Despite a negative sentiment to publishing outside your own area, sometimes you have a good reason to do so, and this should be made clear to your target journal editors and referees. For example, I have recently become more been interested in the topic of fraud, and have a paper relating gender to fraud. I do not like to tell my finance colleagues that I have worked on such a paper (I mentioned it to one finance colleague and he looked at me like I was crazy, so I stopped telling other finance folks that I have such a paper). I confess that this paper was desk rejected very quickly at a finance journal (the editor merely said the paper was obviously incorrect). However, thankfully, many fields other than finance are interested in the topic of fraud, and the paper was published in the *Academy of Management Journal* (Cumming et al. 2015) and featured in a *New York Times* column. I am aware that the paper has been referenced by those that work on legislative reform, such as the Ontario Securities Commission in the work on minimum standards for the proportion of women on boards. In short, I feel lucky to have had the opportunity to look outside the normal range of finance journals to publish on topics that are industry relevant but not within the normal range of topics considered by finance journals. Moreover, the advice and helpful comments from the three referees and editor at the *Academy of Management Journal* was extremely detailed, helpful and constructive.

CITATION HOME BIAS IN DIFFERENT DISCIPLINES

Finance referees tend to not like cites to management papers, and likewise management referees tend to not like citations to finance papers, unless they are directly on point (typically, management referees are more open to cross-citations to other disciplines than are finance referees). Moreover, the normal practice in the top three finance journals has evolved from only citing papers in other similarly ranked journals in finance, to not even properly citing papers in journals of a similar top-three rank.[1] That is, not only do the top three journals not cite journals outside finance (or economics), they do not cite journals that are not at the same rank. Sometimes this type of practice can be upsetting for some scholars in finance who feel that their work is not referenced. Numerous examples can be found on the well-known blog, EJMR.[2] The end result of the citation practice in finance is clear. Someone's work has no guarantee of being cited, and cited properly, by other finance academics. One of my colleagues relayed a story to me that a top-three finance journal editor told him that citations of finance academics do not count unless those citations are from the top three finance journals (I am not joking, and I have heard this repeated by others many times). This traditional sentiment has been known by finance academics for many years. To academics outside finance, it might seem surprising, but to academics within finance, this is not surprising at all. A more recent trend is that even if a paper has been published in a top-three finance journal, there is no obligation on the part of other academics to reference that work at all or properly.[3]

A possible implication of the citation practice in finance journals is that in recent years, when there is an important topic for which research on an issue could be sent to a finance journal or to an entrepreneurship or management journal, many academics who are worried about the narrow process of getting into a top finance journal will not want to submit their paper to such a journal for risk of being scooped (or worse), and hence will first submit to an entrepreneurship or management journal. The best example I have seen is work on crowdfunding. To date, it is widely acknowledged that most academic work on crowdfunding appears in entrepreneurship and management journals. An example is from one paper in the *Journal of Finance*[4] that I discussed in 2014 at a conference in Honolulu. That paper did not mention crowdfunding in its 2014 version, but in my discussion I had mentioned to the authors that it was similar to work in entrepreneurship and management journals on crowdfunding and showed them that work. Thereafter the authors referred to crowdfunding, but not work in entrepreneurship or management journals. It reinforces the decision of many coauthors I know, who work on the topic of crowdfunding, to not send their work to a finance journal and instead send their work to a management or entrepreneurship journal. This perhaps in part explains why crowdfunding has been a much more popular topic in entrepreneurship and management journals than in finance journals.

PAPERS THAT ARE INCONSISTENT WITH PRIOR WORK

It is very hard to publish a paper that is inconsistent with something that has been written by one of your potential referees. There is a massive probability that your referee will reject you. Moreover, if you write a paper that is inconsistent with the leading professor(s) in your area of research, you may reasonably expect that person to have a long memory about how you dared to challenge his or her authority on the topic. There is an inherent problem in some disciplines where those that are first on a topic and become other folks' referees can distort the evolution of an area in ways that favour their own interests, possibly even after their views have been discredited. Your options to avoid such a referee are to seek a lower-tier journal in your same field, or switch fields. Switches are possible with some topics, albeit not all (for example, corporate governance and corporate finance topics are more often transferable across fields, while asset-pricing topics are scantly transferable across fields).

To shed further light here, at the risk of sounding disgruntled, let me refer to a personal example. One of the original topics from my 1999 JD/PhD thesis at the University of Toronto was venture capital (VC) contracting. There are many papers (over 100) in the literature that all say the same thing: convertible preferred equity is the optimal security in VC contracts (with the only evidence coming from small samples in the USA with up to 213 observations) – and this view is most strongly expressed in finance journals. As a Canadian, I discovered that venture capitalists (VCs) often do not use convertible preferred equity in Canada (I first learned this fact in January 1997 – a 'eureka moment' for me). I subsequently discovered the same thing when visiting Europe in 2001 and 2002, that European VCs use different securities, not just convertible preferred equity. After more travel around the world that decade, I discovered that the only country in the world (of the countries where data have been collected) where convertible preferred equity is the most commonly used form of VC finance is the USA. The narrow set of finance VC referees in the late 1990s and early 2000s – all of whom published papers on the optimality of convertible preferred equity or had working papers on the topic – were apparently not particularly welcoming of the idea that VCs might do something other than what they say they do. So, after receiving rejection letters from a massive number of finance journals saying I am a complete idiot (and/or that Canadians and European VCs are not as sophisticated as US VCs, and that the Canadian VC data collected by the Canadian VC Association involving over 10 000 deals was not as accurate as the proprietary hand-collected data of 213 deals by US academics, and more generally that non-US data are clearly wrong unlike the US data, and so on) I contemplated the idea that I should look to publishing in journals in other disciplines such as entrepreneurship and management, and even law. Fortunately, I had enough success doing so in so far as it helped save my career from oblivion (surprisingly I am now a tenured professor, even with a Chair). Luckily for me at that time, two well-known law professors (Ronald Gilson and David Schizer) wrote a paper (my favourite paper) in the 2003 *Harvard Law Review* that shows the US VC contracting evidence is distorted by tax biases particular to the US, which has helped me to gain credibility that my non-US data were worth looking at, and enabled me finally to get published on this topic. However, I am aware of a couple of finance folks that were not so lucky and were forced out of academia where they could not get around a small set of hostile referees for daring to challenge their work, and I would guess the senior people who are responsible could care less what they did to these folks and were simply content to protect their turf.

Given the time I invested in a topic where the international data showed the opposite of what prior US academic work had shown, without the option of publishing in different fields I would never have obtained a tenured position and would most likely be working somewhere in industry right now. It took seven years to finally find a home for my first international VC contracting paper in 2005. I eventually published papers on this topic in the *Review of Financial Studies*, *Journal of Corporate Finance*, *Entrepreneurship Theory and Practice*, *Journal of Business Venturing* and *European Economic Review*, among others, but it was a long haul after a million rejection letters ... well, maybe not a million, but at least a thousand. Perhaps my earlier work was the rubbish folks said it was. However, the time lag enabled others to publish on the topic before me, without proper referencing of prior work, despite very wide dissemination of the work on the topic on Social Science Research Network (SSRN) and numerous conferences over many years. In one case, the paper was published in a journal where the editor and author were at the same university, and it appears to have been accepted within a year of it being released as a working paper; if you are not familiar with the literature you would think this paper is the original paper on topic, particularly owing to the timing of securing a spot in a journal. I have heard a joke repeated many times that some journals are the working paper series for the faculty within the same university as the journal's editor, particularly when there is competition on a topic.

SHOULD YOU POST YOUR WORK ON SSRN OR OTHER PUBLIC WEBPAGES?

The short answer: for finance, yes (typically); for management, no (typically). In today's world, it is hard to not have working papers or their titles widely disseminated on the Internet or at least searchable on the Internet. It is substantially more prevalent in finance than management to see papers online at finance conference webpages and venues such as SSRN.com, so much so that many finance journals do not keep the author's identity blinded as it would be a fiction to pretend the referee does not know the identity of the author.

Finance is distinct from management and entrepreneurship in that almost all working papers are available online long before the work appears in a journal. In management and entrepreneurship, editors prefer that the paper not be online and that the paper is truly hidden. Management journals may even desk reject you if they see your paper has been widely disseminated on the Internet (or, at a minimum, the editor will ask that you remove the paper from any webpages before they review the submission). Personally, I find the practice of dissemination online to be appropriate because the posting 'time dates' your work. Also, posting online facilitates or enables others to provide feedback on your draft before it appears in print. Further, it enables folks to gain traction with citations as a measure of the paper's quality as a signal to editors.

If you don't post online, be careful. I am aware of a sentiment, often repeated in some academic circles, that senior faculty who control different areas would gladly kill a junior professor's paper, at massive cost to the junior in terms of his or her career, in order to protect their own turf with the trivial benefit to them of securing an additional paper which has no bearing on their own career (or possibly no bearing, as unfortunately there are research awards and folks that engage in this type of behavior too often receive research rewards). Even among senior faculty there have been well-publicized fights (where complaint letters were posted online and sent to their competitor's deans) about who was first on a topic. For example, there was a dispute in 2014 between two chaired professors at two of the leading universities in California, and this dispute was a huge topic of discussion (hundreds of postings and thousands of views) on the online forum 'Finance Job Market Rumours'. Fights such as this may in part be resolved by looking at who posted first on SSRN.

SHOULD YOU GET A BIG-NAME CO-AUTHOR?

In finance, normally the top three journals use only one referee (although recently, the *Journal of Finance* often seeks two reports). Finance departments are particularly prone to a growing trend that rewards faculty, particularly junior faculty, only for publishing in the top four finance journals. Senior professors who control the top four journals reinforce their oligopoly that faculty must send their best work to their journals. The set of referees at these journals will be especially narrow in some fields, which serves to increase the 'rents' earned by those that rise to the top and control specific sub-fields.

There are rents earned by academics that rise to the top in certain fields and control what does and does not end up being published in the leading journals. Many junior finance faculty members invest their time to do anything to gain favour with the folks that control their area of interest. Instead of working on their own papers, many junior faculty members merely strive to become co-authors with senior folks that control an area. Junior faculty members appear to spend enormous time and money attending conferences to meet top authors with the objective of securing a top author as a co-author. I have even seen junior faculty members who secure a big co-author becoming incredibly arrogant about their new academic status and importance, with the expectation that in the future they will be the person that junior folks will kowtow to. In some cases, there are even rumours of junior faculty doing things that are unethical to be affiliated with senior faculty (I am intentionally not elaborating here at the suggestion of some helpful colleagues). The by-association benefits to the junior author are huge (by way of an analogy, think of the weakling in jail and a big bully that acts as the protector). Editors at journals appear to be more likely to pay attention to securing suitable referees for papers where there is an established co-author on the paper.

In summary, it can help to have a big-name co-author. However, if as a junior faculty member you can get into a top journal with a solo-authored paper, there may be long-term benefits in terms of the respect you will have earned among your peers and your ability to get tenure and be promoted.

GETTING PUBLISHED: THINGS TO DO

Regardless of where you publish, it is helpful to be a 'good citizen' in order to get published and cited. Being a good citizen includes offering comments on your colleagues' papers, attending seminars, serving on external review committees, refereeing papers, writing book chapters that may not get as many citations as you would like, making sure you are fair in your own citation practices, being friendly to people that you meet at conferences, acting as a reviewer for other people's conferences even when you know that the conference organizers are likely to reject your own work, and so on. As regards journal review requests, I (almost) never turn down requests (the exception is from journals that ask for reviews within two weeks – sometimes that is just not feasible when you are away from the office). In a typical year I review dozens of papers, and I never tell an editor that I am too busy to help with a referee report (despite often feeling too busy – please see the second paragraph of this chapter) and simply agree to do it and get it done. I likewise don't think it is appropriate to selectively review for some journals and turn down requests from others (academics talk, and people quickly figure out what you do, and the person that you are too important for today may subsequently become the person you are kowtowing to tomorrow). How likely do you think it is that someone cites you or gives you a good referee report if you are likewise not a good citizen and act as a fair and diligent reviewer yourself? More generally, good work is not limited to a small number of journals, counter to the claims I have too often heard from others.

Sometimes, even when you have the best intentions and are a good citizen, someone may try to label you as a bad citizen, especially if they are exposed as having done something inappropriate. As an example related to some of my earlier work when I had merely a few publications, a practitioner colleague asked me to work with him on a topic that came to him from his business interests (and if I did not, he would simply do it himself or find another colleague to do it with him). Around the same time, a senior professor mentioned to me at a conference that he was doing something along this line of research. I thought it would be acceptable to go ahead anyway and work on this topic with my practitioner colleague (who had no knowledge of what other academics were doing), but apparently not. As I failed to appreciate, the senior professor was reputed to be extremely hostile to folks who stepped on his turf, and apparently I did, which appears to have been at a long-term cost to me (in some senses, but a benefit in others). For readers not familiar with these types of 'academic eraser fights', match the famous line 'everything I needed to know in life I learned in elementary school' with the other famous line 'academics fight so hard because the pie is so small'. If you inadvertently get caught up in a conflict, just brush it off, say too bad and 'oh well, don't sweat the small stuff', as life goes on and you cannot please everyone. Keep doing the things that you do and keep being a good citizen, regardless. Keep writing good papers, and if you get a few rejections from folks who you have upset, then just move on and try elsewhere (remember the old adage, 'God grant me the serenity to accept the things I cannot change, the courage to change the things I can, and the wisdom to know the difference'). There is always a home in a good journal for a good paper.

GETTING PUBLISHED: THINGS TO NOT DO

Academic dishonesty can come in a variety of forms, and the presence of different fields can facilitate that dishonesty. If you do things that are dishonest, it can make it difficult to publish later on. Think of a short-term benefit at a long-term expense.

Misconduct is sometimes observed among editors and referees. For example, I have encountered editors and referees who have not kept submissions confidential, and/or borrow ideas from a paper or a conference and use it for their own benefit in their other work. I have also encountered editors who do not fully pass along complete referee reports to authors – including cases of hiding negative comments to support publication, and cases of hiding helpful comments to be unfriendly to authors, and cases of hiding comments to distort what a referee has said to create conflict between a not-so-blind referee (it is easy to guess the identity of a referee in many cases) and the authors. There can be short-term benefits to borrowing ideas, or disclosing such information to help colleagues' competing papers (or other benefits), but at a longer-term cost if other people find out about the misconduct or breach of confidentiality. I have also encountered editors that 'go on the offensive' when you inadvertently get caught up in misconduct by another editor, co-editor, guest editor or referee. The best response is to try to distance yourself from the misconduct. The returns to whistleblowing are more often than not negative.

Misconduct is perhaps more often observed among authors. For example, in working as an associate editor and a co-editor at a number of different journals, I became aware of a junior faculty member multiple-submitting the same paper to at least two journals at the same time. It is possible that this person thought that he would get away with it, because the referees would normally be different in different fields. As another example, I have seen, at first hand, folks borrow ideas from one field and introduce them in another field, claiming to be innovative and not referencing the proper source. This type of activity can occur across management and finance. It can even occur within a field such as finance where I have seen ideas from work on private firms applied to studies of publicly traded firms without acknowledging that the same work was previously carried out on privately held firms. I have also encountered authors who knowingly publish work that is wrong and remove tables from working papers to hide their mistakes.

Misconduct is sometimes observed among co-authors and colleagues. For example, I have heard of co-authors removing names of colleagues from drafts of work. Also, I have heard of colleagues spreading false rumours as a result of perceived need to cover up misconduct and/or for retaliation. Further, I have heard of misconduct among deans and acting deans. For example, I have seen evidence of an acting dean changing the terms of someone's contract after that person gave up a job at another university to protect himself from a complaint; the acting dean initiated a full blown investigation into the character of the person harmed and spread false rumours about that person's character.

As another, funny, example of misconduct (based on hearsay), it is rumoured that a well-known chaired professor was not happy about a working paper that was inconsistent with their own work. They were so unhappy that apparently they called the data provider to stop the distribution of the competing working paper, with the rationale that the data was being used to the detriment of the industry which the data provider represents. The data vendor apparently indicated that the agreement was not being violated, and the working paper was not inconsistent with the use of the data, and that the working paper did not make the industry look bad, but instead only made them look bad. I cannot verify the accuracy of this story, but I can say that I have heard it repeated more than once. To be fair, the apparent source of the story is someone who deleted a reference to one of my own papers on the exact same topic as one of their papers (with a main difference being the unit of observation) at the page-proof stage, despite my working paper having appeared over 12 months before their working paper (first presented at the same annual conference a year later). This person emailed me and my co-author within a day of the journal posting their accepted paper online, showing us their paper was now accepted and asked us to update our reference to their paper as forthcoming. Our paper was accepted a few months after his was accepted. Unfortunately you cannot control the speed of reviews. If you have upset someone in the past, or just happen to be dealing with an unethical person, then that person can hold up your paper to enable a follow-on paper to come out first in a journal, thereby making you lose credit for originating the idea and giving that credit to someone else to whom it is not due.

In summary, there are many rumours of misconduct and many cases of actual misconduct, and neither the rumour nor the actual misconduct is helpful for getting your work published or cited. It is just distracting for everyone, and it makes you and everyone else involved look bad. Avoid at all costs, and try to minimize contact with, unethical folks. There are plenty of highly ethical people in academia, and if you surround yourself with those folks then you can reasonably hope for the best long-term outcomes.

TAKE-AWAYS

To wrap up, many business academic topics can be researched and published in various journals. For example, corporate governance and corporate finance topics can be published in finance journals and management journals. In this short chapter, I have offered some anecdotes and advice about the opportunities and pitfalls that different fields offer to researchers. I hope these stories help scholars in the future decide how to position their work and to manage their careers.

Finally, let me say a warm thank you to Sofia Johan, David Robinson, Armin Schwienbacher and Ralph Winter for helping me to edit this chapter and take out any details that could possibly lead to any person or journal being identified in any of my stories. Also, I owe many thanks to the editors Tim Clark, Mike Wright and Dave Ketchen for their helpful comments and suggestions.

NOTES

1. The top three journals in finance are *Journal of Finance* (*JF*), *Journal of Financial Economics* (*JFE*) and the *Review of Financial Studies* (*RFS*). The *Journal of Financial and Quantitative Analysis* is widely regarded as the fourth best finance journal and is also included in the FT50 list. The top five economics journals are typically considered to include the *American Economic Review*, the *Journal of Political Economy*, *Econometrica*, the *Review of Economic Studies* and the *Quarterly Journal of Economics*. *Management Science* is a top interdisciplinary journal that sometimes publishes finance work.
2. For example, https://www.econjobrumors.com/topic/board-diversity-and-risk-research and https://www.econjobrumors.com/topic/new-family-ruptures-aer-nber-is-rip-off-of-obscure-paper (both accessed 30 August 2019).
3. For example, https://www.econjobrumors.com/topic/hrm-strategy-for-publishing-in-rfs (accessed 30 August 2019); see also Cumming and Johan (2019).
4. https://onlinelibrary.wiley.com/doi/full/10.1111/jofi.12470 (accessed 30 August 2019).

REFERENCES

Cumming, D.J. and S.A. Johan (2017), 'The problems with and promise of entrepreneurial finance', *Strategic Entrepreneurship Journal*, **11** (3), 357–70.

Cumming, D.J. and S.A. Johan (2019), 'Capital-market effects of securities regulation: prior conditions, implementation, and enforcement revisited', *Finance Research Letters*, 29 January, accessed 29 August 2019 at https://ssrn.com/abstract=3317546.

Cumming, D.J., T.Y. Leung and O.M. Rui (2015), 'Gender diversity and securities fraud', *Academy of Management Journal*, **58** (5), 1572–93.

31. Publishing in management journals: how is it different from economics journals?

Saul Estrin and Sumon Kumar Bhaumik

INTRODUCTION

This chapter identifies the key differences between reporting empirical research in journals belonging to the field of economics, and of management. Our focus is restricted to empirical papers; we do not consider purely theoretical research in either field. In the case of theory papers, the differences are equally pronounced, but are somewhat different. We also focus attention on top journals in economics and management respectively, by which we mean either leading general journals or top of their field journals. The differences are similar in less highly ranked journals but are less sharply drawn.

The structure of this chapter is as follows. We first outline the principal differences between the expectations of the two types of journal for submitted papers in terms of structure and content, at a general level. We then illustrate these arguments with reference to several of our own works published in both management and economics journals.

KEY DIFFERENCES: THE STRUCTURE AND CONTENT OF PAPERS

Differences in Structure of Paper

There is considerable latitude in how papers are organized and structured in both economics and management. However, in practice, many papers in each field follow a fairly standard format, and many of the differences in expectations about the papers follow from this difference in structure. In this section, we compare a stylized form of the standard structure in management and economics papers, respectively, and then go into greater detail about the differences in content within each section.

The structure for standard empirical papers in economics and management journals is shown in Table 31.1. The key differences are that management papers will usually contain new theoretical insights, formulate explicit hypotheses and discuss in an independent section (Discussion) whether the findings are consistent with the hypotheses.

Table 31.1 Structures of standard empirical papers in economics and management

	Economics	Management
Introduction	✓	✓
Literature survey/theory	✓	✓
Hypotheses (sometimes merged with theory)		✓
Data and methods	✓	✓
Results/findings	✓	✓
Discussion		✓
Conclusion	✓	✓

The stylized strategy for formulating hypotheses is strikingly different in the two literatures. Consider, for example, the following two papers: Bhaumik and Estrin (2007) which was published in the *Journal of Development Economics*, and Meyer et al. (2009) which was published in *Strategic Management Journal*. As we discuss in more detail subsequently, Bhaumik and Estrin (2007) de facto hypothesize that if market-supporting institutions exist the relationship between a firm's output/performance and inputs would follow a predictable pattern, for example, output change would be positively associated with changes in labour and capital. They use this implicit hypothesis to discuss the wider issue of development of market institutions in China and Russia. The central hypothesis in Meyer et al. (2009) is that the choice of entry mode of multinational enterprises when they enter emerging markets is dependent on the interaction between their resource needs and quality of local institutions. However, they explicitly tease out the implications of this meta-hypothesis for specific combinations of resource needs and institutional quality, so that the paper has a series of explicit hypotheses. We discuss the empirical implications of this difference later in the chapter.

Difference in Contents of Papers

These differences in structure underlie greater substantial differences in content, even within sections in similar titles. In this subsection, we compare the typical content within each section of the two types of journal

Introduction: this section typically would be short in both management and economics journals. The economics journal paper would probably lay out the research question, explaining its importance or significance, and then explain the dataset. There would probably be a summary of the key literature on the topic and of the principal findings of the paper. The content would be similar in a management journal paper, but we expect to find more emphasis on the research contribution, relative to the literature. There is increasing emphasis on highlighting the contribution(s) of the paper at the start, within the first couple of pages of the manuscript text. There could also be more explicit explanation of how this work builds on research that had been carried out recently, with reference to calls in previous papers for research of this type to be undertaken.

Literature survey/theory section (economics journal) compared with theory section (management journal): the economics journal would probably summarize in detail what has been found in the literature to date, as well as the data employed, methods and methodological weaknesses. It is generally good practice to clearly outline a heuristic model (see Bhaumik and Estrin 2007) on which the subsequent empirical analysis is based. However, once the broad strand of the literature – for example, neoclassical or agency theory – has been identified, references are generally made to key theoretical and empirical contributions in the literature. Since economics is based on a single discipline, there is little or no debate about the underlying conceptual lens through which issues are addressed.

In contrast, it would be extremely difficult for a paper to be published in a leading management journal without a well-defined contribution to the theory, in addition to supporting empirical evidence. This even applies to primarily empirical papers. Further, the management field is multidisciplinary and hence theoretical contributions have to be couched within a particular framework, for example, the resource-based view, or transactions-cost theory (see Meyer et al. 2009).[1] For example, this framework could be used to identify a class of outcomes which previously appeared to be only ambiguously related to a set of independent variables, but owing to the theoretical development, a new set of subclasses can be identified. Increasingly the theoretical development would take the form of a new construct whose effect would not be additive (as is the norm in economics) but is multiplicative – a so-called moderating effect which works through other independent variables.

Hypotheses section (usually only in management journals): the theory section would lay out general cases about the relationship between phenomena. However, to move to applications there would be specific hypotheses linking particular dependent variables to independent variables. This section might be combined with the theory section if there are no sharp distinctions between the new concepts being considered and the manner in which they might be tested in practice. The development of explicit hypotheses aligns these hypotheses with specific aspects of the empirical analysis. For example, if regression analysis is used to test the hypotheses, each hypothesis is generally associated with a single coefficient in the regression model (see Bhaumik et al. 2010, p. 443).

In the absence of explicit hypotheses, the nature of discussion of empirical results in economics papers can be significantly different. It would be wrong to surmise, however, that in the absence of explicit hypotheses up front it is acceptable to use *ex post* justification of results in economics papers. Even though economics papers rarely have explicit hypotheses, as in the Bhaumik and Estrin (2007) paper, subsequent analyses of results have to flow from the underlying theories in an *ex ante* consistent manner.

Data and methods section: in economics journals, datasets are often secondary sources and have been used before, often quite frequently. Hence there is little analysis of the quality of data. However, there is considerable emphasis on empirical methodology. Thus we, for example, might expect emphasis on how the paper is going to address issues of stationarity, endogeneity, collinearity and reverse causality. This focus leads naturally to an emphasis on strategies to address instrumentation. A major concern of the economics journal will be to ensure that the results themselves are highly robust in terms of causality and specification.

However, management journals would typically place relatively more emphasis on the data itself and how it was constructed. This is because many management datasets are developed for the research in question, while economists tend to use data which is in the public domain. Hence readers will want to understand the research judgements made in building the dataset. Also there is the issue of whether the data used actually captures the ideas in the hypotheses; the theory will contain constructs which the data is seeking to measure, and how well this has been achieved is an issue. Variables would be categorized into dependent variables, independent variables and control variables (derived from the previous literature), a distinction which is rare in economics papers.

However, there typically might be less importance attached to pure methods in management papers, and the expectations about econometric methodology might be relatively less exacting, although this is changing.

Results: this typically would be a very long section in economics papers, with reports about the key results using a basic equation, and numerous further tests and specifications, for example, addressing questions of collinearity and especially endogeneity. A wide range of cutting-edge econometric methods would be expected and emphasis would be placed on test statistics and implications of differences in results, for example, between regressions which have and have not been instrumented. In management journals, this section would often be rather short, simply enquiring whether hypotheses are confirmed or rejected by the data in the regressions reported. However, there might also be a number of robustness checks of the results to make sure that they hold with different specifications or methods or measures of the hypothesized concept. In contrast, in an empirical economics paper, this section involves long discussions of the results and many tests to establish robustness of the results.

Discussion section (usually in management journals only): the discussion section is typically merged with the results and/or concluding sections in economics journals, and has a less formalistic flavour because the analysis is not usually framed in terms of hypothesis testing. In management journals, this is a long section in which the results of the previous section would be considered in terms of contribution to the literature (from the introduction) and to evaluate the theoretical ideas outlined in the second section and the hypotheses in the third section. This section would also contain a serious discussion of the limitations of the study, for example, that the measured concepts did not quite measure what the theory was trying to capture, or that the dataset was small or weak in some way.

Conclusions: this section would be similar in economics and management journals, considering the implications of the research and the findings for future research. However, in economics journals there might also be a concern to draw out the implications for policy-makers, while in management journals the audience might include practitioners in the business community.

EXAMPLES OF ECONOMICS AND MANAGEMENT PAPERS

Let us first consider papers targeted at economics journals. To recapitulate, good economics journals prefer empirical papers that have a firm theoretical basis, whose results are generalizable (and thereby have implications for the conceptual discussions in the literature), and which demonstrate the robustness of the results using rigorous empirical analysis. However, the relative emphases on these characteristics of empirical papers can vary considerably both across journals and among papers published in the same journal. In this section, we discuss two papers as illustrations of these points.

Consider the Bhaumik and Estrin (2007) paper that has been mentioned above. The paper addressed a question that is rooted in traditional microeconomic theory but which has interesting implications for the conceptual discussion about the evolution of market capitalism in transition (and, by extension, developing) economies. Specifically, the paper proposes that if market capitalism works in an economy, then the relationship between a firm's output and tangible inputs such as capital and labour, and other characteristics such as ownership, should be predictable on the basis of stylized firm and agency theories. There is already a huge literature about the forms of that stylization. If, however, economic reforms fail to develop market institutions, then these predictable relationships may not be observed.

It is easy to see that the paper is rooted in economic theory – its empirical basis is the extended production function that captures the relationship between a firm's output and tangible and intangible inputs – and that its results and conclusions have implications for the discussion about conceptual issues that link development and transition economics to new institutional economics. That is, the conclusions are generalizable and not specific to the Sino-Russian contexts. Specifically, the results have a bearing on whether there are optimal approaches to developing market-based economic systems, and the contrasting experiences of China (which emphasized the development of market institutions over private ownership of resources) and Russia (which emphasized rapid privatization over establishment of market institutions) provided a natural experiment to address the aforementioned question. Further, the paper paves the way for a discussion about the 'deep' institutions and political economy of economic reforms that results in choice of alternative pathways for reforms, some of which may be suboptimal.

This brings us to the robustness of the results which makes them attractive to the referees and journal editors. The Bhaumik and Estrin (2007) paper uses data from separate primary firm-level surveys in China and Russia, which use slightly different, but comparable, survey instruments. This is a little unusual in that most papers in this field use data generated from national surveys such as the census of production. However, information of this type is not in the public domain for either China or Russia; hence the use of surveys. The data are for a comparable period; 1995–2000 for China and 1997–2000 for Russia. The nature of the data (including missing observations) permits simple difference-in-difference estimation, but not panel data estimation and corresponding econometric methods such as the generalized method of moments (GMM) that can address potential problems with endogeneity and other econometric issues. The paper, therefore, addresses the robustness issue in a different way.

First, it starts with a simple specification of the production function, where the change in output depends only on changes in labour and capital, and thereafter incrementally adds other firm characteristics, and controls for industry and location to demonstrate that the key results are unaffected by this expansion of the model specification (Table 31.2). Second, given the incident of the Russian sovereign default and associated crisis in 1998, which has implications for formal institutions but is exogenous to individual firms, it examines the aforementioned relationship between firm output, and inputs and other firm characteristics in the Russian context, for the pre- and post-1998 periods. Third, it unpacks the dummy variables for the regional controls and replaces these dummies with economic and institutional characteristics of regions such as the initial levels of per capita gross regional product and legislative quality. The basic results for Russia, for which the aforementioned relationship did not hold, and hence required careful explanation, were robust to these exercises, thereby highlighting their reliability.

Our second example of an economics paper, published in the *Review of Economics and Statistics*, is by Bruno et al. (2013) and is about a similar topic, namely, the effects of institutions on economic behaviour. Once again a fairly standard economics concept is being investigated, that is, the effects of entry barriers on the rate of entry of new firms into different industries. It would typically be argued that entry rates would be lower when barriers are higher and there is strong evidence to that effect from around the world. However, especially in developing countries, political processes may also play a role in new firm entry. However, the impact is hard to identify in cross-country studies because so many phenomena other than political processes may also be changing. The

Table 31.2 Empirical analysis for economics journals: an example

Determinates of sales growth in China

Explanatory variables	Spec 1	Spec 2	Spec 3	Spec 4	Spec 5	Spec 6	Spec 7	Spec 6a	Spec 7a
Changes in (logarithm of) quantity of labour	0.81*** (0.27)	0.78*** (0.28)	0.78*** (0.28)	0.77*** (0.28)	0.78*** (0.28)	0.75*** (0.27)	0.79*** (0.28)	0.78*** (0.28)	0.83*** (0.29)
Changes in (logarithm of) quantity of capital	0.49*** (0.12)	0.49*** (0.12)	0.49*** (0.13)	0.49*** (0.13)	0.42*** (0.14)	0.44*** (0.13)	0.41*** (0.14)	0.42*** (0.13)	0.39*** (0.14)
Logarithm of sales in 1995				−0.01 (0.04)	−0.02 (0.04)	−0.04 (0.04)	−0.04 (0.05)	−0.02 (0.04)	−0.03 (0.04)
Percentage of capital stock that is less than 5 years old					0.006 (0.004)	0.006 (0.004)	0.006 (0.005)	0.006 (0.004)	0.006 (0.004)
Index of firm-level restructuring						0.008* (0.005)	0.006 (0.005)	−0.001 (0.05)	−0.01 (0.05)
Dummy variable for change from full state ownership to corporatized status							−0.31 (0.21)		0.38* (0.21)
Constant	−0.45*** (0.08)	−0.43*** (0.15)	−0.42** (0.19)	−0.31 (0.43)	−0.32 (0.44)	−0.71 (0.43)	−0.52 (0.44)	−0.32 (0.41)	−0.17 (0.42)
Industry controls	No	Yes	Yes	Yes	Yes	Yes	Yes	Yes	Yes
Regional controls	No	No	Yes	Yes	Yes	Yes	Yes	Yes	Yes
Adjusted R-square	0.22	0.19	0.17	0.17	0.18	0.19	0.19	0.18	0.19
F-statistic (Prob>[F])	18.44 (0.00)	7.91 (0.00)	5.98 (0.00)	5.31 (0.00)	5.03 (0.00)	5.22 (0.00)	4.67 (0.00)	4.71 (0.00)	4.26 (0.00)
N	138	138	138	138	138	138	137	138	138

Notes:
1. The values within parentheses are standard errors.
2. ***, ** and * indicate significance at the 1 per cent, 5 per cent and 10 per cent levels, respectively.
3. Specifications 6 and 7 use the broader measure of index of firm-level restructuring, with a range of 32–160.
4. Specifications 6a and 7a use the more restrictive measure of firm level restructuring, with a range of 0–15 that is comparable with the corresponding index for Russia.

Source: Bhaumik and Estrin (2007, p. 383, table 2).

main contribution of the paper is therefore to move beyond standard cross-country modelling to analyse cross-regional and cross-sector entry rates within a single economy, Russia. This gives the work the character of a quasi-natural experiment, because other sources of heterogeneity in the data are controlled for. The data are derived from different publicly available sources, on entry, institutions and political change, respectively.

However, to address problems of spurious correlation or endogeneity, the paper exploits the concept of natural entry rates in the context of difference in difference methods, using the rate of entry by industry in developed countries as a proxy for a sector's natural entry propensity. These natural entry rates are taken to reflect, for example, technological barriers in the industry caused by economies of scale or organizational efficiencies gained by incumbents. The emphasis in the paper is on econometric method, and the results are clear; that heterogeneity in Russian regional institutions over time does affect entry rates relative to the levels that pertain in developed market economies. In particular, it finds that political change has a negative effect on entry rates in industries in which the barriers to entry are lower. Thus, industries characterized by higher entry rates in Western economies experience comparatively less entry in those Russians regions which suffer from greater political change. Once again, the analysis is set up in such a way that the findings are generalizable from the Russian context.

We now turn to the management literature, where there is more emphasis on theory development and data, and less on the econometric methodology. Recapitulate that theory development in this literature, which unlike in the economics literature does not have widely accepted paradigms, refers to the development of postulates or hypotheses based on critical analyses of the extant literature. While this requires a very different way of approaching research questions relative to economics, it nevertheless allows interesting innovations, in some cases by synthesizing two or more different strands of literature.

Consider, for example, the aforementioned paper by Meyer et al. (2009). It addresses a much-discussed question in the international business literature, namely, the determinants of the choice of entry mode by a multinational enterprise (MNE) that enters a developing country (or emerging market) economy. A great deal of the literature on entry mode choice is based on the logic of transaction costs, and thereby focuses on the institutional context of foreign firm entry. The Meyer et al. (2009) paper facilitates a much more fine-grained analysis by bringing together two frameworks that dominate the international business literature; the transaction-cost and resource-based views. Specifically, it argues that while institutional improvements in developing countries reduce the likelihood of entry by way of joint venture (JV), the intensity of an MNE's needs for tangible and intangible resources is positively correlated with choice of JV and acquisition-based entry modes. The interaction between quality of host country institutions and resource needs of MNEs, which is the key contribution of the paper towards theory development, is summarized in Figure 31.1.[2]

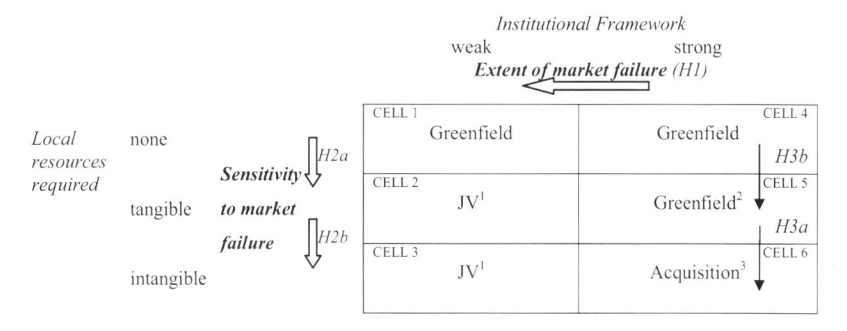

			Institutional Framework weak strong	
			Extent of market failure (H1) ←	
Local resources required	none	*Sensitivity* ↓ H2a	CELL 1 Greenfield	CELL 4 Greenfield ↓ H3b
	tangible	*to market failure* ↓ H2b	CELL 2 JV[1]	CELL 5 Greenfield[2] ↓ H3a
	intangible		CELL 3 JV[1]	CELL 6 Acquisition[3] ↓

Notes:
1. In rare cases acquisition may be feasible (for example, acquiring a subsidiary of another MNE).
2. Except when asset specificity is high, when acquisition or JV may be appropriate.
3. Except when market failure is bilateral and takeover is infeasible (for example, owing to scale issues), when JV may be appropriate.

Source: Meyer et al. (2009, p. 66, fig. 1).

Figure 31.1 Theory of hypotheses development for management journals: an example

This figure is the basis for the following hypotheses:

H1: The stronger the market-supporting institutions in an emerging economy, the less likely foreign entrants are to enter by joint venture (as opposed to greenfield or acquisition).

H2a: The stronger the need to rely on local resources to enhance competiveness, the less likely foreign entrants are to enter an emerging economy by greenfield (as opposed to acquisition or joint venture).

H2b: The effects of hypotheses 2a is stronger when requiring intangible assets compared to tangible assets.

Note that the hypotheses indicate a clear direction for the nature of the expected relationship between the outcome (that is, entry mode) and the relevant explanatory variables. Correspondingly, there is a clear match between each of the hypotheses and an estimated coefficient in the regression model.

Aside from the nature of theory, the characterization of the explicit hypotheses in management papers, which we have discussed previously, is also evident from this example. We should also note that while regression results in economics papers rely on the two-tailed test (against the null hypothesis of non-significance), and thereafter discuss the sign and economic significance of coefficient estimates in the light of theory and the relevant literature, the explicit hypotheses of papers in management journals require one-tailed tests (of positive or negative coefficients).

Thereafter, given the emphasis of management journals on data (including measurement issues), the Meyer et al. (2009) paper explains in a reasonable amount of detail the choice of measure(s) for institutional strength (or quality) and resource needs of firms. While the former is based on the five items of the economic freedom index developed by the Heritage Foundation, the latter is based on data collected specifically for this study in four emerging markets using a survey instrument. Next, the paper addresses the issue of multicollinearity, which is a major concern of referees of management journals. While this paper allays concerns about potential multicollinearity by reporting the correlation matrix for the explanatory variables, other management papers often also do so with reference to the variance inflation factor (VIF).[3] The correlation matrix is usually reported in management journals as a matter of course, as a basis for discussion of multicollinearity, but this is less common in economics journals.

Following the rigorous discussion of the data, however, the empirical strategy of the paper is simple, as with most papers published in management journals, and involves the use of the multinomial logit model. (It is virtually standard in the management literature to report the marginal effects for probit and logit models, rather than the raw regression coefficients.) Given the detailed theory development leading up to the hypotheses and the explicit connection between the hypotheses and corresponding regression coefficients, the discussion of results in the Meyer et al. (2009) paper is less nuanced than in empirical papers published in economics journals. These papers also illustrate that, while not mandatory (for example, Bhaumik et al. 2010), management journals generally require a discussion of the limitations of the paper and future research directions as well as a discussion about the managerial implications of the results. In contrast, while empirical economics papers sometimes have discussions about policy implications of the results, they more rarely include explicit discussions about limitations of the papers themselves.

CONCLUSIONS

We have argued and illustrated that there are significant differences in the way that papers in economics journals compared with those in management journals are constructed and written. For example, in the former there is more emphasis on econometric method and robustness of empirical results; in the latter on theory development (in the management sense) and hypothesis testing. However, that does not mean that with appropriate fine-tuning a given project can be simply written up for either a management or an economics journal. In practice, the differences reach back to the nature of the research question, and to the methodologies developed in order to test that question. Management research is more deeply rooted in the need for theoretical development and explicit hypothesis testing, perhaps using datasets specifically developed for the purpose. Economics journals which rely on a common intellectual paradigm expect less conceptual novelty and data originality but are more demanding in terms of the use of econometric methodology.

An illustration will help to consolidate these differences. If you are writing a paper for a management journal, it is best to start with the research idea, linked to a literature/intellectual framework. For example, if the phenomenon of interest is multinational firms from emerging markets, for a management journal we have to start by choosing the theoretical framework with which the question will be addressed. We then have to identify the ways in which emerging market multinationals might differ from the types of firm that have been analysed already in the literature. This indicates that the differences are likely to relate to home-country effects, as the most obvious thing that is new theoretically about such multinationals is that they are based in less developed economies. However, the reasons why they internationalize their activities, and the impact of their internationalization, have already been studied extensively and it would be hard to publish a replication study of this phenomenon, even if the source economies under consideration were different. From here, we might conceptualize how being based in less sophisticated business environments might affect the capabilities that such firms have developed, giving them advantages, for example, in expanding their operations to other emerging markets but disadvantages in more developed economies. This could form the basis for hypothesis development and testing, using a dataset perhaps gathered for precisely that purpose. The empirical work would represent a counterpart to test the theoretical development, and not necessarily represent a large proportion of the written paper.

In contrast, economics journals might be interested in new empirical findings from a new database which covered a different sample of firms and source countries, without expecting any systematic theoretical originality or the use of a proprietary dataset. Also, it might be hard to develop an original theoretical insight; the concepts in this field are well established in economics but their application to new countries would be original. Thus, the issue would be whether the paper had interesting findings and whether these were econometrically robust. In this sense, 'interesting' would include facts or relationships not hitherto identified, or the converse – relationships which have traditionally held in developed economies but which do not seem to pertain in emerging market multinationals. However, the standards of proof for the robustness of the new relationship identified would be very high.

NOTES

1. For a summary of the frameworks used most frequently in strategic management research, see Kenworthy and Verbeke (2015).
2. Similarly, the theory development in the Bhaumik et al. (2010) paper is based on the reconciliation between the agency-theoretic and resource-based views of family firms with the stylized international business literature about a firm's decision to invest in overseas locations.
3. See, for example, Bhaumik et al. (2010). The rule of thumb is that a VIF test statistic value of 5 or less is acceptable from the multicollinearity perspective.

REFERENCES

Bhaumik, S. and S. Estrin (2007), 'How transition paths differ: enterprise performance in Russia and China', *Journal of Development Economics*, **82** (2), 374–92.

Bhaumik, S., N. Driffield and S. Pal (2010), 'Does ownership structure of emerging market firms affect their outward FDI? The case of Indian automotive and pharmaceutical sectors', *Journal of International Business Studies*, **41** (3), 437–50.

Bruno, R., S. Estrin and M. Bytchkova (2013), 'Institutional determinants of new firm entry in Russia', *Review of Economics and Statistics*, **95** (5), 1740–49.

Kenworthy, T. and A. Verbeke (2015), 'The future of strategic management research: assessing the quality of theory borrowing', *European Management Journal*, **33** (3), 179–90.

Meyer, K., S. Bhaumik, S. Estrin and M. Peng (2009), 'Institutions, resources and entry strategies in emerging economies', *Strategic Management Journal*, **30** (1), 61–80.

32. Publishing in management journals as a social psychologist

Rolf van Dick

INTRODUCTION

One of the main fields of social psychology is the study of stereotypes and prejudice. Prejudice is the unfounded generalization of (mostly negative) characteristics to every member of a certain group and, as a result, unjust discrimination against the individual as a member of that group. I was trained as a social psychologist in my postgraduate education, I completed my PhD at Philipps-University's social psychology department where I taught social psychology courses in the undergraduate psychology program. After a period in a UK business school at Aston University I returned to Germany and for almost ten years I have been a chair of social psychology. Therefore, I think I know what I am talking about when (self-)stereotyping social psychologists as a bunch of 2×2 researchers. I am, of course, exaggerating greatly and there are certainly as many social psychologists who have never conducted a laboratory experiment as there are management scholars with backgrounds in economics, marketing or sociology who run experiments within and outside the laboratory. However, I think the following example is a good way to illustrate the challenges a social psychologist may face when trying to publish in management journals.

THE SOCIAL PSYCHOLOGIST AT WORK

The stereotype of a social psychologist is that they sit in their office all day thinking about a clever way to manipulate some variables (normally two, called a 2×2 experiment) and then running an experiment with first-year psychology students to test whether the manipulation has any effect. To keep the number of participants manageable, each of the two manipulated variables comes in two levels: high and low. So, a typical experiment may want to test the hypothesis that poor academic performance has a negative effect on self-esteem but that this is the case only when the performance dimension is seen as important. The researcher invites participants to the laboratory, asks them to perform a mathematics test which is introduced to half of the (randomly assigned) participants as very established, highly reliable and valid for the prediction of academic performance. The other half is told that this is just some test that needs to be pilot tested for use in future laboratory studies on people's endurance in laboratory experiments. So, this makes the first '2' of the first manipulated factor – in this case importance of the test, high versus low. Then (again randomly assigned) each half of the participants who have taken the important test and half of those who have taken the unimportant one are told that they have performed below average, whereas the other participants are informed that they have performed above average. So, this makes our 2×2 design complete with the second factor being poor versus good performance. Finally, participants are asked to complete a standard self-esteem scale with items such as 'I feel I do not have much to be proud of' and then they are rewarded for participation (usually with course credits) and fully debriefed, that is, told that they have been subject to some manipulation (or deception) that in no way reflects their true abilities and so on. The measure of self-esteem then makes the dependent variable, test performance and importance of the test comprise the independent variables, and the researcher may predict one main effect (when test performance is above average, self-esteem is higher than in the other condition) and an interaction effect (for example, that the main effect is enhanced when the test is seen as more important). An analysis of variance between the four groups of participants with self-esteem as the dependent variable is then performed and means in the four conditions compared against the predictions.

Sounds like a plausible theory of practical relevance and an appropriate way to test it, doesn't it? If the researcher – given that the ANOVA produces significant results – writes up his or her results and sends them to a classic top tier social psychology outlet (*Journal of Personality and Social Psychology*, *Personality and Social Psychology Bulletin*, *European Journal of Social Psychology* or *Journal of Experimental Social Psychology* to name but a few), he or she will probably receive some positive feedback from reviewers and may have a good chance of being invited for a resubmission. The decision letter often asks for an additional experiment ruling out an alternative explanation, but rarely are social psychologists asked to replicate their results in a longitudinal design or with external (or even objective) data sources.

PUBLISHING SOCIAL PSYCHOLOGY RESEARCH IN MANAGEMENT JOURNALS: ISSUES WITH EXPERIMENTAL WORK AND STUDENT SAMPLES

Let us assume that the social psychologist thinks he or she should submit to a management journal because he or she works in a business school. The school may have a relatively narrow list of journals that are considered top outlets; some schools, for instance, use the *Financial Times* list of 50 journals as a basis for promotion or reward pay decisions. Social psychology outlets are not included in this and similar lists, and they would thus not help our colleague much with his or her career. The social psychologist may therefore think, for instance, of the *British Journal of Management* (*BJM*). For over a dozen years, I was involved in several work and organization and management journals, including three years as editor-in-chief of the *BJM*. From my experiences there and with many other journals – as author, reviewer or board member – I estimate the chances of getting such an article published in *BJM* or any other good management journal is very close to zero. The social psychologist may instead receive a desk reject letter without his or her paper even being reviewed. Why? First, because reviewers and editors of management outlets typically do not like purely laboratory research with it's completely artificial settings and relatively artificial manipulations and measured variables. Secondly, because reviewers and editors will certainly ask whether the findings would, in any meaningful way, generalize to a non-student (that is, practitioner) population.

Some of these problems are due to misunderstandings and stereotypes, and may be overcome. The experimental researcher, when conducting experiments such as that described above, for instance, is interested less in generalizability but in cause and effect. That is, he or she is less concerned with external (or ecological) validity and more with internal validity. He or she puts in a lot of effort to develop good manipulations, realistic cover stories and to get the random assignment of participants to experimental conditions right. If this is achieved, the experiment is able to answer the one question it was designed to answer: whether variable A influences variable B. This may sound simple but is, in practice, not always easy to translate into a study design and often goes well beyond a purely correlational study that shows a relationship between the two variables. Moreover, it is highly relevant for any practical application – only when I have proof of a causal relationship, can I start devising interventions that help increase (or reduce) the variable that causes the effect.

Also, the experimental social psychologist does not care whether his or her participants are psychology students or not. Rightly so! Why should students of theology, chemistry or business administration be better or worse as participants? Also, business school students (certainly in MBA and EMBA programs) have working experience. However, even if an experiment could be run with students from many different academic disciplines, it would still not be generalizable to the general public. This is not a big problem because an experiment's main purpose is not to generalize (see above). However, if we look at management research, do we see much difference? Almost every published study has been conducted in either one organization or (often a convenience sample of) several organizations. So can I generalize from a single study conducted, for instance, in a bank to other working populations, for example, in the health industry or in the blue collar sector? Or can I draw serious inferences from a sample of employees in manufacturing organizations to populations of school teachers, nurses or call center agents? Probably not, even if we talk about an excellent study with a good response rate of all employees and a very respectable sample size of several hundred participants. These arguments have been made by prestigious research methods experts such as Highhouse and Gillespie (2009), but they are hardly heard by editors and reviewers. One reason for the ignorance of such arguments may be the extreme scarcity of journal space – when 90 percent (and sometimes more) of all submitted papers are rejected, editors use heuristics that fit their respective journal's mission and scope statements – and these often explicitly reject student-based studies.

One way I got around this problem in my own work is to combine experimental research with laboratory studies. In some of our papers which found their homes in top-tier applied journals, we even used this as a key selling point. For instance, in a paper with Johannes Ullrich and Oliver Christ (Ullrich et al. 2009) published in the *Journal of Applied Psychology*, we combined two studies: first an experimental scenario study with 127 students as participants in which we manipulated leader prototypicality and leader fairness as two independent variables and then tested the manipulations' effects on student reports of how much they would support the leader. As a second study, we added a survey with a heterogeneous sample of the working population, spreading across industries and sectors, in which we measured the above variables. We stated in the general discussion: 'Our findings demonstrate that this moderator effect can be generalized from distributive to procedural fairness and from the lab to applied contexts when personally relevant outcomes are at stake' (Ullrich et al. 2009, p. 243).

Sometimes, student samples are also perfectly acceptable in a single study paper for other types of research such as studies with student project teams in settings where students work together on real projects and the outcomes of their joint work are important to them (for example, for their marks or when they can earn real money). The journal *Academy of Management of Learning and Education*, for instance, frequently publishes research based on student samples. In management journals, however, this is the exception rather than the rule. As an example, in a paper on the moderating role of students' beliefs that team diversity was good or bad for their teams' performance on the relation between ethnic diversity in team composition and their level of identification with their teams (van Dick et al. 2008) we eventually were published in *Human Relations*. During the review process we had a very hard time convincing one reviewer that our work was suitable for this (applied) journal. We could not easily change our sample nor did we want to collect new data in an organization as it was already a rather lengthy paper reporting two studies, but we were successful by adding the following paragraph which included appropriate references to groundbreaking books and research in other top-tier management journals:

> One might also consider the use of student samples a limitation. Note however, that our main aim was to provide a first test of a new theoretical proposition. In accordance with Cook and Campbell (1979; see also Calder et al. 1982) we therefore think that external validity, which pertains to generalization of established findings, is a secondary concern. Nevertheless, it is important to note that the context and setting in which the groups operated closely resemble work environments of project teams in organizations. As in many organizational settings, tasks were often complex. They required a variety of activities such as the identification of problems, decision-making, generation of solutions, generation and implementation of action plans and the generation of presentations and reports. Thus, although these student teams are not the same as teams in organizations, they do rely on the same processes and mechanisms (such as communication, or active management of time and other resources) to succeed on their tasks (see, for similar arguments for the validity of student project teams as research subjects, Taggar 2002). Based on the nature of our sample and setting of the research, we therefore believe that our findings can be generalized to other work and organizational contexts. (Van Dick et al. 2008, p. 1484)

DESIGN ISSUES AND THE RESEARCH GAP

Sometimes it is the nature of the samples used to test your hypotheses but sometimes it is also the study design. Management researchers are in principle also often using a 2 × 2 framework but, instead of manipulating two factors (in the laboratory or in the field), they measure the two variables on continuous scales and use moderated regression analysis instead of ANOVA. Both designs have advantages and disadvantages. As mentioned previously, the manipulation of independent variables helps answer the causal direction of relationships but the measurement of continuous variables allows depicting the relationship in a more complex way. Reality often is more complex than just the all or nothing of a manipulated variable; and measuring them allows, for instance, testing for curvilinear relations.

Finally, a good strategy to start a paper in the management and marketing literature is to identify the research gap early on and to include a statement about why filling the gap is important for the journal's readers. In a paper in the *Journal of Marketing* with Jan Wieseke et al. (2009) we obviously hit the right buttons with editors and reviewers by illustrating the research gap in a figure combining existing research in the three fields of identity, leadership and marketing research and literally presenting the gap as a hole in the center of these three areas. We also clearly stated the research gap in the following paragraph:

> In light of its definition and nomological validity, the construct of OI is undoubtedly relevant to research on internal marketing and should be the ultimate goal of internal marketing. However, the three research streams – leadership, internal marketing, and OI – have yet to be systematically integrated. This discussion reveals important gaps in the internal marketing and OI literature. First, the role of leaders' OI in building followers' OI remains unexplored. Second, previous research has largely ignored the link between OI and important firm outcomes. To the best of our knowledge, no previous research on OI has directly examined financial performance as a consequence of OI, especially at the business unit (BU) level. This void deserves close attention because such a link would not only provide for external validation of the effects of OI but also help managers evaluate the effectiveness of their firms' internal marketing efforts. Methodologically, OI researchers have exclusively focused on a single level, leaving much of the rich phenomenon of how OI can be developed across levels of leader–follower interaction uncharted. (Wieseke et al. 2009, pp. 123–4)

Usually, social psychologists are a little less concerned with making the contribution of their work obvious so early on – as far as it concerns applicability or organizational relevance.

As I have said elsewhere (van Dick 2011), good research will eventually find its home somewhere, but it is important to not only target the specific journal carefully but also to think about the general audience early on when planning your research and when writing the paper. Some of my early work that was ultimately published in an organizational psychology journal (van Dick et al., 2005) comprised two organizational surveys, one with a small experimental manipulation. Because of this manipulation, because of the social psychology theory I used (social identity theory) and certainly because I was working in a social psychology department when writing the paper (and in which social psychology journals were seen as better than management journals), I submitted it to two prestigious social psychology journals first. The editor of the first journal (with 'experimental' and 'social' in its title) came back to me several weeks after submission with the following letter:

> Dear Dr Van Dick, after carefully reading your paper myself, I have decided not to send it out for review. My main reason for rejecting the paper is that I think it is a poor fit with [name of journal] and would be better suited for an organizational psychology journal ...

Foe the above reasons, I did not listen and submitted to a second social psychology journal. This time, I made a step forward and the paper was sent out for review – which in the end was more a curse because it took almost half a year before I received another letter: 'Dear Rolf, ... most of all that the paper is not suited to be of interest to [name of journal]'s readership ... lead me to reject the paper.' So, I lost considerable time and had to learn the hard way that the paper was better submitted to a more applied journal, which in this case was the *Journal of Occupational and Organizational Psychology* (published as van Dick et al. 2005) – not too bad a journal I guess and one to which I submitted many times thereafter, several times with success.

CONCLUSIONS

To find a home for his or her paper faster, the social psychologist who wants to publish in management journals should carefully target the journal even before designing the study and analyzing the data, so that it fits the management literature's readerships' expectations. Targeting the right journal means, for instance, reading the respective outlets' mission and scope statements, screening the past issues for potential papers that the author can refer to, or even sending a brief email to the editor prior to submission inquiring whether he or she thinks that the paper might be of interest (although I would use this approach sparingly and only when having serious doubts about fit with the journal). Social psychologists have interesting theories to offer and they normally have an excellent grasp of the state-of-the-art tools to analyze their data. Getting work published is not only rewarding for the individual but will also enrich management both as an academic discipline and an organizational practice.

REFERENCES

Calder, B.J., W. Phillips and A.M. Tybout (1982), 'The concept of external validity', *Journal of Consumer Research*, **9** (December), 240–44.
Cook, T.D. and D.T. Campbell (1979), *Quasi-experimentation: Design and Analysis Issues for Field Settings*, Boston, MA: Houghton Mifflin.
Highhouse, S. and J.Z. Gillespie (2009), 'Do samples really matter that much?', in C.E. Lance and R.J. Vandenberg (eds), *Statistical and Methodological Myths and Urban Legends: Doctrine, Verity and Fable in the Organizational and Social Sciences*, New York: Routledge, pp. 249–68.
Taggar, S. (2002), 'Individual creativity and group ability to utilize individual creative resources: a multilevel model', *Academy of Management Journal*, **45** (2), 315–30.
Ullrich, J., O. Christ and R. van Dick (2009), 'Substitutes for procedural fairness: prototypical leaders are endorsed whether they are fair or not', *Journal of Applied Psychology*, **94** (1), 235–44.
Van Dick, R. (2011), 'Publishing management research', in C. Cassell and B. Lee (eds), *Challenges and Controversies in Management Research*, London: Routledge, pp. 138–51.
Van Dick, R., U. Wagner, J. Stellmacher and O. Christ (2005), 'Category salience and organisational identification', *Journal of Occupational and Organizational Psychology*, **78** (2), 273–85.
Van Dick, R., D. Van Knippenberg, S. Hägele, Y.R.F. Guillaume and F. Brodbeck (2008), 'Group diversity and group identification: the moderating role of diversity beliefs', *Human Relations*, **61** (10), 1463–92.
Wieseke, J., M. Ahearne, S.K. Lam and R. van Dick (2009), 'The role of leaders in internal marketing', *Journal of Marketing*, **73** (2), 123–45.

33. Publishing historical papers in management journals and in business history journals

Steven Toms

Business history and management research have, until recently, evolved as separate disciplines. At first sight this divergence seems surprising, but has important implications for management researchers publishing in business history journals and for business historians publishing in management journals. Business history emerged originally as a branch of microeconomics and economic history (Supple 1977) and quickly developed methodologies based on the traditional tools of historical research based on the investigation of archives. These methods typically do not feature in social science research methods texts (Gunn and Faire 2012), nor by the same token in business and management research methods texts. Notwithstanding the divergent origins of business history, opportunities for historical research in business and management have widened subsequently. From the 1980s, reflecting increasing involvement in the discipline of business history by business and management school academics (Kipping and Uskiden 2008), new areas of historical investigation have included management strategy themes such as networks, family capitalism, corporate governance, human resource management, marketing and brands, and multinational organizations. To make the most of these new opportunities requires careful consideration of suitable research questions, bearing in mind the still influential differences between publishing in business history and mainstream management journals. The chapter outlines these opportunities, while providing advice on how to accommodate the differences. There are many possible approaches to historical writing that might be considered by management scholars. For convenience, three specific approaches are considered here. A fourth, reflecting the purist business history tradition, is also explained for the purpose of contrast.

The first approach available to management scholars is to use business history to test, or augment, existing management theories. In general, management theories may use static approaches, and the introduction of a time-based dynamic creates the opportunity for historical analysis. The possibilities include building on the work of Nelson and Winter (1982), Chandler (1977) and Teece (2010) to develop a dynamic capabilities view of business history (Edwards 2011). The value of this approach was recognized recently in a special issue of the *Journal of Management Studies* devoted to business history themes. Accordingly, Bucheli et al. (2010) follow a similar approach to examine time-specific circumstances where vertical integration fails in the absence of certain transaction cost considerations. Similarly, Jenkins (2010) enhances the existing view that incumbent firms have difficulty adapting to discontinuities by showing that firms can develop sustainable resource configurations to deal with such discontinuities. In parallel, there have been recent moves in the business history field to develop a 'new business history', which utilizes a range of methodologies with the objective of obtaining generalizable results (De Jong and Higgins 2015).

The second approach is to use historical anomalies to develop new theories. For example, Williamson noticed that forward integration occurred in some industries in the late nineteenth century but not in other industries, and attributed the differential response to transaction costs arising from asset specificity and opportunistic behaviour in the value chain close to the point of sale (Williamson 1981, pp. 561–2). In a recent application of this type of approach, Reveley and Ville (2010) use counterfactual analysis to complement the comparative method of organization studies to suggest new theoretical approaches to the investigation of trade associations.

The third approach is to use management theory to test generalizations using historical data. Chandler's (1977) contention that structure follows strategy would be an important example, which he put to convincing effect in his subsequent work on scale and scope (Chandler 1990). This approach can be used to illustrate contrasting publishing opportunities in the two types of journal. Writing in a management journal, Filatotchev and Toms (2003, 2006) take the strategic management literature as their point of departure, building on the theoretical model developed by Robbins and Pearce (1992) to examine declining industries and opportunities for turnaround contingent on corporate governance factors. More specifically, Filatotchev and Toms identify a gap in the management literature (2006, p. 409) 'to suggest that managerial inaction may not in itself be the product of poor management, particularly where financial constraints operate', while also noting that the finance literature does not address the impact of such constraints on the process of strategic decision-making. To scrutinize the process and dynamic interaction of strategy and finance, their paper uses historical evidence to suggest that governance changes are an important precondition to strategic action and subsequent restructuring. In contrast, writing in a business history journal, Toms and Wright (2002, 2005) use a historical approach to examine the evolution of the British and United States corporate economies since 1950. Their point of departure from the business history literature is the incompleteness of Chandler's explanation, with the need to extend economies of scale and scope to incorporate external economies, and to incorporate variations in corporate governance. By taking a historical approach from the outset, they add a dynamic element to two established theories in the management literature: the resource-based view (Barney 1991) and resource dependency theory (Pffefer and Salancik 2003), which are shown to interact, thereby explaining patterns of corporate growth and restructuring. Their approach (Toms and Wright 2002, pp. 93–5) recognizes knowledge as a common ingredient in both theoretical approaches, as a basis for competitive advantage, on the one hand, and as a monitoring mechanism, on the other. Based on this conceptualization, information cost is utilized as an empirical variable to investigate its role historically as a determinant of corporate change. In summary, both these approaches use history to address conceptual gaps or integrate mainstream management theories. The important difference is how they are rooted in the separate literatures, and underline the importance of reading the literature in both disciplines.

The three approaches outlined thus far are increasingly welcomed in mainstream management journals and in business history journals. A fourth possibility would be the 'history for history's sake' approach, which is an avenue open exclusively for the latter type of journal. Since the typical managerial scholar is not a trained historian, this approach is to be treated with some caution.

The enormous growth of business history over recent decades has established it as a *sui generis* discipline and, crucially, it has its own literature. The impetus for the rapid growth of business history literature has come from the discipline's three core journals, *Business History*, *Business History Review* and *Enterprise and Society* which have published around 120 papers per year between them, in addition to the journals specializing in management (as opposed to business) history, numerous non-English language journals with the same objective, and further specialist journals in fields such as accounting history and marketing history. The literature in the business history journals covers familiar managerial themes, with an agenda that is often empirical, and a focus on filling gaps in historical knowledge or challenging generalizations. For example, business historians (Toms and Wilson 2003) have challenged and adapted the earlier conclusions of Chandler and others on the performance of the British economy. Where the pure historical approach is not intended, it nonetheless performs a useful function for present purposes in terms of specifying the delimitations of management research using historical methods.

In general, management scholars who are not historians first and foremost will be more interested in the three approaches outlined above than this more empirical agenda. Moreover, the history journals increasingly welcome such contributions as the discipline continues to grow and integrate with the mainstream literature. Even so, the methodological traditions of business history remain important, and the traditional scope of these journals is suggestive of mistakes to avoid. One mistake would be to assume that an old dataset would, of necessity, be of interest to the editors of a history journal. Datasets which have become old as a result of previously failed attempts at publication in mainstream journals are particularly inappropriate. If they have failed in their original task of investigating a contemporary problem, there is nothing to suggest that they will become any more useful for testing the same problem as it recedes into the historical record. Datasets, unlike port wine, do not improve with age. Recycling datasets from successful mainstream projects into historical journals is similarly to be guarded against. Understandably, in both these cases, business history journal editors will be determined to ensure the relevance of the research for their core audience, which means, in practice, identifying an appropriate research question based on the *ex ante* business history literature. Generating such a research question on the basis of a dataset that has already been created for another purpose is, in general, not to be recommended as the basis for a successful publishing strategy.

At the opposite end of the spectrum is the purely empirical approach. Business history is highly resistant to antiquarianism (Hannah 1983), and autobiographical musings, which although no doubt of interest to the individual involved, do nothing to engage a wider audience concerned with questions of historical significance. The single-company case study, in some respects the traditional bedrock of the Chandlerian and Harvard approaches to business history, is likewise discouraged. In part, this is because extreme specialization can often easily guarantee some empirical originality in historical research, without necessarily contributing much to knowledge. Where the researcher, for example, notes a previously undiscovered fact about fish processing in the nineteenth century, unless they can also show how the wider literature should be modified in consequence, the research will be unsuitable for publication.

Even so, and of necessity, there is extensive and often extreme specialization in the business history field. Expertise ranges from the role of entrepreneurs in medieval England (Casson and Casson 2014) to systems of innovation in late twentieth and early twenty-first century Japanese pharmaceuticals (Umemura 2014). Perhaps more so than in mainstream journals, it is easier to speculate about whom the likely reviewers will be, as the editor may have only a small group of expert specialists to draw upon. However, a balance is needed. The more specialized your submission, the less likely it is to have a wider impact and, therefore, the more likely it is to be rejected. Drawing out the lessons of the paper for a wider audience is therefore an important requirement, but also increases the likelihood of involvement by non-specialized but highly experienced reviewers. It is these reviewers that it is best to have in mind when preparing your manuscript, while also keeping in mind that a more specialist second reviewer is likely, whose expertise can still lead to the enhancement or rejection of your paper.

Stylistically, the business history tradition reflects important differences. These can best be described by explaining the role of footnotes in business history journals. In the management literature, footnotes provide some embellishment of the main argument, but are treated as otherwise marginal and are actively discouraged by many journals. In business history, on the other hand, footnotes are of methodological significance. They indicate the data sources used, most commonly from the archive, revealing the process of investigation for future researchers. Specification of the scope, location, type of document and so on, with respect to archival evidence, provides the basis for judgement by the reader and reviewer as to its adequacy, and for replication by future researchers.

Although such considerations emphasize that business history may seem to be steeped in empiricism, many of its leading advocates nonetheless place strong emphasis on theory. Organization theorists increasingly agree 'history matters', adding that a theoretical stance is essential (Rowlinson et al. 2014, p. 250). This 'historic turn' in organizational studies (Clark and Rowlinson 2004) was based in part on 'some of the newer and influential research programmes within organization theory' such as neo-institutionalism and population ecology (Üsdiken and Kieser 2004, p. 321). Lamoreaux et al. (2007) meanwhile have argued for a reconsideration of the value of economics for business history. Lazonick (2005), for example, favours using business history to investigate the fundamentally historical characteristics of capitalism, as described by Marx and Schumpeter, rejecting the apparently timeless characteristics of behaviour that feature so strongly in mainstream economics (O'Sullivan and Graham 2010). In the spirit of this approach, a special issue of *Business History* features a series of parallel papers using the evolutionary theory of Nelson and Winter (1982) in step with business history-style approaches to triangulate specific themes of investigation. For example, evolutionary and business history approaches to the history of financial services (respectively, Jacobides 2015 and Toms et al. 2015) are contrasted and evaluated (Nelson 2015).

These examples form part of a wider trend, likely to promote further integration of management research with business history as both disciplines reach maturity. As this develops, the divergent traditions of the disciplines will become less relevant and the opportunities to publish historical papers for a business and management audience will increase, certainly along the lines of the three approaches suggested earlier. They illustrate a tendency to relate history to our understanding of the present and show how management research can move 'forward by looking backward' (O'Sullivan and Graham 2010). Similarly, the discipline of business history aims to learn the lessons of the past to inform current agendas.

To take advantage of the publication opportunities set out in the different approaches sketched above, several general points are worth bearing in mind. Joint authorship between business history and management scholars can be especially productive, as each can provide the relevant expertise for dealing with the literature. Collaboration helps to ensure that for business history publications, the relevant business history literature is engaged with and used to motivate the study and the research questions. Similarly, the management literature should provide the relevant starting point and motivation when publishing historical papers in mainstream management journals. Methodological differences can influence the appropriate writing style, and should also be borne in mind; for example, the requirement to document archival evidence in business history research. Differences in methodological traditions suggest a certain caution for management researchers. In the end though, the objectives of both disciplines overlap, and are likely to increasingly converge, making for productive publication opportunities.

REFERENCES

Barney, J. (1991), 'Firm resources and sustained competitive advantage', *Journal of Management*, **17** (1), 99–120.

Bucheli, M., J. Mahoney and P. Vaaler (2010), 'Chandler's living history: *The Visible Hand* of vertical integration in nineteenth century America viewed under a twenty-first century transaction costs economics lens', *Journal of Management Studies*, **47** (5), 859–83.

Casson, M. and C. Casson (2014), 'The history of entrepreneurship: medieval origins of a modern phenomenon', *Business History*, **56** (8), 1223–42.

Chandler, A.D. (1977), *The Visible Hand*, Cambridge, MA: Harvard University Press.

Chandler, A.D. (1990), *Scale and Scope: The Dynamics of Industrial Competition*, Cambridge, MA: Harvard Business School.

Clark, P. and M. Rowlinson (2004), 'The treatment of history in organisation studies: towards an "historic turn"?', *Business History*, **46** (3), 331–52.

De Jong, A. and D.M. Higgins (2015), 'New business history?', *Business History*, **57** (1), 1–4.

Edwards, R. (2011), 'Divisional train control and the emergence of dynamic capabilities: the experience of the London, Midland and Scottish Railway, c. 1923–c. 1939', *Management and Organizational History*, **6** (4), 391–410.

Filatotchev, I. and S. Toms (2003), 'Corporate governance, strategy and survival in a declining industry: a study of UK cotton textile companies', *Journal of Management Studies*, **40** (4), 895–920.

Filatotchev, I. and S. Toms (2006), 'Corporate governance and financial constraints on strategic turnarounds', *Journal of Management Studies*, **43** (3), 407–33.

Gunn, S. and L. Faire (eds) (2012), *Research Methods for History*, Edinburgh: Edinburgh University Press.

Hannah, L. (1983), 'New issues in British business history', *Business History Review*, **57** (2), 165–74.

Jacobides, M. (2015), 'What drove the financial crisis? Structuring our historical understanding of a predictable evolutionary disaster', *Business History*, **57** (7), 716–35.

Jenkins, M. (2010), 'Technological discontinuities and competitive advantage: a historical perspective on Formula 1 motor racing, 1950–2006', *Journal of Management Studies*, **47** (5), 884–910.

Kipping, M. and B. Usdiken (2007), 'Business history and management studies', in G. Jones and J. Zeitlin (eds), *The Oxford Handbook of Business History*, Oxford: Oxford University Press, pp. 96–119.

Lamoreaux, N.R., D.M.G. Raff and P. Temin (2007), 'Economic theory and business history', in G. Jones and J. Zeitlin (eds), *Oxford Handbook of Business History*, Oxford: Oxford University Press, pp. 37–66.

Lazonick, W. (2005), 'The innovative firm', in J. Fagerberg, D.C. Mowery and R.R. Nelson (eds), *The Oxford Handbook of Innovation*, Oxford: Oxford University Press, pp. 29–55.

Nelson, R. (2015), 'Evolutionary economics and the recounting of business history', *Business History*, **57** (7), 769–72.

Nelson, R. and S. Winter (1982), *An Evolutionary Theory of Economic Growth*, Cambridge, MA: Belknap Press.

O'Sullivan, M. and M.B. Graham (2010), 'Guest editors' introduction. Moving forward by looking backward: business history and management studies', *Journal of Management Studies*, **47** (5), 775–90.

Pfeffer, J. and G.R. Salancik (2003), *The External Control of Organizations: A Resource Dependence Perspective*, Stanford, CA: Stanford University Press.

Reveley, J. and S. Ville (2010), 'Enhancing industry association theory: a comparative business history contribution', *Journal of Management Studies*, **47** (5), 837–58.

Robbins, D.K. and J.A. Pearce (1992), 'Turnaround: retrenchment and recovery', *Strategic Management Journal*, **13** (4), 287–309.

Rowlinson, M., J. Hassard and S. Decker (2014), 'Research strategies for organizational history: a dialogue between historical theory and organization theory', *Academy of Management Review*, **39** (3), 250–74.

Supple, B. (1977), 'Introduction: approaches to business history', in B. Supple (ed.), *Essays in British Business History*, Oxford: Clarendon, pp. 1–8.

Teece, D. (2010), 'Alfred Chandler and "capabilities" theories of strategy and management', *Industrial and Corporate Change*, **19** (2), 297–316.

Toms, S. and M. Wright (2002), 'Corporate governance, strategy and structure in British business history, 1950–2000', *Business History*, **44** (3), 91–124.

Toms, S. and M. Wright (2005), 'Divergence and convergence within Anglo-American corporate governance systems: evidence from the US and UK, 1950–2000', *Business History*, **47** (2), 267–95.

Toms, S. and J.F. Wilson (2003), 'Scale, scope and accountability: towards a new paradigm of British business history', *Business History*, **45** (4), 1–23.

Toms, S., N. Wilson and M. Wright (2015), 'The evolution of private equity: corporate restructuring in the UK, 1945–2010', *Business History*, **57** (5), 736–68.

Umemura, M. (2014), 'Crisis and change in the system of innovation: the Japanese pharmaceutical industry during the Lost Decades, 1990–2010', *Business History*, **56** (5), 816–44.

Üsdiken, B. and A. Kieser (2004), 'Introduction: history in organisation studies', *Business History*, **46** (3), 321–30.

Williamson, O.E. (1981), 'The economics of organization: the transaction cost approach', *American Journal of Sociology*, **87** (3), 548–77.

34. Publishing human resource management research in different kinds of journals

Bill Harley

INTRODUCTION

A number of authors, myself included, have suggested that human resource management (HRM) research – and certainly that published in 'top' journals – appears to be dominated by a particular approach which emphasizes positivist methodology, a managerialist frame of reference and reliance on theory drawn from social psychology (Harley and Hardy 2004; Kaufman 2012; Godard 2014). Nonetheless, academic HRM is a broad church, with scholars from a range of disciplinary backgrounds publishing quantitative and qualitative research informed by a range of theoretical traditions. This diversity may reflect the changing nature of universities, with many scholars who would previously have worked in discipline-based departments finding themselves in business schools as the former shrink and the latter grow. Particularly in the UK, Australia and Europe, there is a strong tradition of critique from scholars who work in business schools but who question much of the theoretical and practical foundation of contemporary HRM.

Reflecting the nature of the field, work on HRM is published in a wide range of journals. First, there are the general management journals such as *Academy of Management Journal*, *Journal of Management* and *Journal of Management Studies*, which publish papers on HRM alongside papers from the other major management areas. Second, there are discipline-based journals in psychology (for example, *Journal of Applied Psychology* and *Personnel Psychology*), sociology (for example, *Work Employment and Society*) and economics (for example, *Labour Economics*) which publish work on HRM. Third, there are subject-based journals, including some dedicated to HRM such as *Human Resource Management* and *Human Resource Management Journal*, and journals such as *Industrial Relations* and *British Journal of Industrial Relations*, which publish a good deal of HRM material as well as more traditional industrial relations papers.

There are other dimensions on which the relevant journals vary, notably the extent to which they emphasize practice versus research, the extent to which they tend to favour either US- or European-style research (see Üsdiken 2014), their openness to overtly critical research and the prestige they hold within different scholarly communities. There are, therefore, many potential outlets for research on HRM and a potentially confusing set of choices, particularly for early-career scholars. My aim in this chapter is to reflect on my own experiences and approach in a way which I hope will be useful to others, while noting that there is no single recipe for success in HRM publishing.

MY BACKGROUND AND PERSPECTIVE

Before turning to specific examples of publications in different kinds of journals, it may be useful to outline my own disciplinary background, career and general approach to publishing. Our backgrounds and career trajectories both shape and reflect our approach to research and publication. Thus, the material I present about publishing in different kinds of journals is likely to make more sense if it is placed in context.

I completed a PhD in 1994 in a political science department, supervised by an academic with a background in economics and sociology. My topic linked macro-level changes in industrial relations policy in Australia to micro-level changes in workplace practices and outcomes. My particular concern was with how national-level policy changes had an impact on employees and their experiences of work. My research drew on theoretical resources from political science, sociology and industrial relations literatures, and was informed by a critical sensibility. It was primarily based on secondary analysis of large-scale national survey data, augmented with qualitative studies of two industry sectors. While my doctoral research was clearly relevant to the field of HRM, it was not framed with reference to mainstream HRM work.

At the time I graduated, there was massive growth of job opportunities in business schools and a corresponding decline in job opportunities in traditional social science departments. My first job as a lecturer was in a business school, teaching some industrial relations, but predominantly HRM, and my appointments since then have all been in business schools. My publishing, however, reflecting my background and interests, has not been primarily in mainstream HRM journals. My approach has always been to target the journals which I find interesting and stimulating, and in which I have judged my work most likely to have an impact. I have not pursued a strategy of choosing journals on the basis of their rankings alone and then framing my work to fit in. Indeed, I feel a certain discomfort with the emphasis that is currently placed on targeting 'big hits' at all costs. My approach has led me to target different journals with different kinds of papers at different times, although I cannot say that the quality of journals as captured by impact factor has not been among my considerations. In the next part of the chapter, I reflect on a few of these publications and what they might tell others about positioning HRM research for different kinds of journals. My reflections are informed not only by my experience as an author, but also as an editor of *Journal of Management Studies* from 2010 to 2015 and a reviewer for numerous general management, discipline-based and subject-based journals.

GENERAL MANAGEMENT JOURNALS

By definition, general management journals publish across a range of different management-related topics and disciplines, and hope to attract a broad readership, although the extent to which they are open to critical work varies considerably. The challenge for authors publishing in these journals is that they must submit papers which seek to meet two possibly competing aims. First, they must have something to say that has implications beyond their own field and that appeals to readers from a range of fields within management. Second, at the same time they must seek to make a serious contribution to their own discipline and retain credibility within it. While this can be a challenge, there is some comfort in that virtually all management scholars work within a sub-discipline of management, so we are all in the same situation when it comes to submitting to general management outlets.

My experience of publishing in general management journals is limited, simply because I have made a choice to focus on discipline- and subject-based journals, but I have published some papers in such outlets. An example which illustrates the points above is Harley and Hardy (2004). Our paper was published in a special issue of *Journal of Management Studies* which celebrated the career of a long-time editor, Karen Legge, who was herself a scholar of HRM. Our aim in the paper was threefold: to reflect on Legge's work, to make a contribution to the field of HRM and to contribute to broader methodological debates within management. In an attempt to balance these aims, we wrote a paper which used discourse analysis in an attempt to make sense of why

Legge's work had been less apparently impactful than that of David Guest, as measured by citations. This allowed us to engage with a methodological debate within HRM, which could be summarized as positivism versus social constructionism and in which Legge was a key participant, at the same time as contributing to broader methodological debates in management studies.

A paragraph from the introduction of this paper summarizes the way in which we sought to achieve our aims:

> This paper makes a number of contributions. First, by using discourse analysis to examine a selection of texts that is indicative of a larger corpus of texts on HRM, we are better placed to understand how academic HRM discourse has developed and how academic knowledge is produced. Second, we provide an understanding of some of the challenges confronting critical researchers as a result of the discursive context in which they work. A third contribution is the identification of some of the ways that critical researchers might engage in discursive work to meet these challenges. Finally, we make a methodological contribution by developing a systematic approach to discourse analysis. (Harley and Hardy 2004, p. 378)

Therefore, while the paper was squarely focused on research on HRM, it also sought to make a contribution to broader debates about methodology and about academic practice within the management field.

DISCIPLINE-BASED JOURNALS

Here there is a similar challenge to that faced by HRM scholars publishing in general management journals, in the sense that authors must say something relevant to those working within the core discipline of the journal – sociology, psychology, economics, and so on – while simultaneously making a contribution to HRM scholarship. The extent to which those twin aims present a challenge depends in part on how broad or narrow the disciplinary focus of the journal is.

Some of the issues can be illustrated by considering my experience with one discipline-based journal. I have published a number of papers in *Work, Employment and Society* (*WES*), which is the British Sociological Association's journal dedicated to the sociology of work and employment. Since the journal focuses on work and employment, it is a more natural home for HRM research than a broad sociology journal would be, and the types of HRM papers published reflect the preferences of the readership (and editors and reviewers). These are typically characterized by a foundation in sociological theory, but also by an orientation which is explicitly critical of mainstream HRM research and which commonly focuses on issues of power, domination and exploitation in the labour market and the labour process. Given my own disciplinary background and interests, *WES* might be seen as a natural home for my research, but positioning papers appropriately nonetheless presents challenges.

This can be illustrated by the example of Harley et al. (2010). The paper addresses a staple of mainstream HRM research – the apparent links between 'high performance work systems' practices (hereafter HPWS) and employee attitudes to work – and seeks to explain why such practices appear to be received positively by employees. The notion that HRM is universally good for employees and that good HRM can generate gains for both employees and organizational performance has been challenged vigorously by critical sociologists. The challenge for this paper was to try to explain how such practices might generate gains for employees, by using critical sociological theory, and simultaneously offer an alternative explanation to mainstream unitarist approaches and some of the more simplistic critical approaches.

How did we do this? The paper started with a review of the empirical research on employee responses to HPWS to establish the lack of consistency in findings and to suggest that the prior debates had reached an impasse because they were couched in terms of HPWS being universally good or bad. This provided the motivation for an alternative approach. The paper then suggested that the failure to bring sociological theory to bear on understanding HPWS and employee responses had limited our understanding.

> This article seeks to develop a research agenda which draws on social and political understandings of the workplace and explicitly considers the role of interests in shaping outcomes. The agenda is informed by labour process theory (LPT), which underlies many of the critical analyses of HPWS (see Ramsay et al., 2000). While there are divergent views within LPT, at its heart is an understanding of workplace relations as shaped by the structure of capitalism and involving relations between capital and labour, rather than simply between human actors. (Harley et al. 2010, pp. 742–3)

The paper then utilized Edwards et al.'s (1998) disciplined worker thesis to propose that HPWS were favourably received by employees when they enhanced order and predictability in work processes. Statistical analysis of survey data was then used to assess the extent to which a scale capturing order and predictability mediated associations between HPWS and positive employee outcomes. This provided an empirical basis to argue for the value of sociological theory for explaining outcomes which had previously been explained almost exclusively by psychological theory.

To summarize how we positioned this paper, we took a well-recognized finding – that HPWS are, in at least some cases, associated with positive employee outcomes – then problematized both the universality of this finding and the dominant explanations, thereby providing a critique of prevailing understandings. We then demonstrated, bolstered by statistical analysis, that positive outcomes could be explained by critical sociological theory, thereby producing knowledge with a strong empirical basis and a critical sociological orientation which fitted with the orientation of the journal.

SUBJECT-BASED JOURNALS

By subject-based journals, I mean those that focus on HRM, but which are cross-disciplinary in the sense that they do not publish papers exclusively within a particular base discipline. For example, the *British Journal of Industrial Relations* (*BJIR*) focuses on industrial relations and HRM, but publishes papers informed by a number of base disciplines, notably sociology and economics. Researchers working on the subject which is the concern of subject-based journals have the luxury of being able to write for an audience that is likely to be familiar with the specialist knowledge and language within that subject area, and prospective authors do not have to write for as broad an audience as they would if they were targeting a general management or a discipline-based journal. Subject-based journals in HRM tend to publish relatively high proportions of quantitative work, reflecting the disciplinary foundations of HRM scholarship in economics and organizational behaviour.

While some subject-based journals are broad and inclusive, others are narrow in their focus, both in terms of the topics covered and the range of perspectives which are welcomed. I have not often targeted mainstream HRM journals, since the orientation of my research is towards critical perspectives. I have, however, published papers in the aforementioned *BJIR*, and consideration of this experience provides some potentially useful insights for HRM scholars targeting subject-based journals. In Harley et al. (2007), my co-authors and I presented research on associations between HPWS and employee experiences of work, which sought to explore the moderating effect of occupation on the outcomes for employees. The aim was to examine the extent to which the structure of labour markets within the service sector appeared to shape the outcomes of HPWS by asking whether lower-skilled workers were denied the apparent benefits of such practices. In this way, we engaged squarely with debates within the HRM literature, while also bringing in concerns likely to be relevant to industrial relations scholars informed by sociology and economics.

Because we were writing for an audience which was familiar with the HPWS literature, we could deal quickly with this and then turn very quickly to debates about working arrangements in the service sector and the role of employee skills – both staples of HRM and industrial relations literature. We thereby positioned the paper around streams of literature current in the subject area. In doing so, we were able to use language specific to the subject area, for example:

> The theoretical arguments made against the general applicability of HPWS in the service sector are based on the segmentation of employment in services. The logic of the argument is that markets for services are very clearly divided into low-value and high-value segments with the result that employment in service organizations is correspondingly segmented ... According to this argument, in the low-value/low-skill segments of the sector, where work can be standardized to deliver a standard product, work will be characterized by Taylorist or neo-Taylorist practices, while in the high-value/high-skill segments, workers may enjoy more humanistic HR practices ... (Harley et al. 2007, p. 610)

We could safely assume that readers were familiar with these debates and this language, in a way which we could not have if we had been targeting a general management or discipline-based journal.

As *BJIR* is read by many scholars with backgrounds in economics and typically publishes a good number of statistical papers, we presented numerous figures and tables summarizing statistical analysis and assumed knowledge about technical terminology. In common with some general management journals but generally not discipline-based journals, the subject-based HRM journals tend to emphasize practical implications. Thus, we concluded the paper, *inter alia*, with some consideration of practice:

> In practical terms, [the findings] suggest that workers can benefit from HPWS in the service sector. This is not to say that workers and unions should rush forth and embrace HPWS. Rather, it is to caution against the assumption that they should necessarily resist such practices. The challenge for researchers who wish to inform practice is to build on existing research and to identify the conditions under which HPWS is beneficial for workers. (Harley et al. 2007, pp. 623–4)

DISCUSSION AND CONCLUSIONS

In the final part of this discussion, I briefly recap what seem to me the important lessons I have learnt from over 20 years as an author, reviewer and more recently as an editor.

Most importantly, while it is crucial in terms of credibility and professional satisfaction to publish in journals which we find interesting and credible, there is a range of such journals available to HRM scholars. This dictates that thought be given to how best to position papers when submitting to different kinds of journals. In general management journals, the key success factors appear to be appealing to a broad audience, while also speaking to HRM scholars, and to make a contribution to broader debates. In discipline-based journals, we need to say something relevant to scholars working in that discipline – notably by framing our work in theory drawn from that discipline – as well as to HRM specialists. When seeking to publish in subject-based journals, we have the luxury of 'preaching to the converted', but there is often an emphasis on practice. I do not pretend that this brief chapter covers everything which might be considered by HRM scholars when developing their publishing careers, but I hope that some of these insights are valuable.

REFERENCES

Edwards, P., M. Collinson and C. Rees (1998), 'The determinants of employee responses to total quality management: six case studies', *Organization Studies*, **19** (3), 449–75.

Godard, J. (2014), 'The psychologisation of employment relations?', *Human Resource Management Journal*, **24** (1), 1–18.

Harley, B. and C. Hardy (2004), 'Firing blanks? An analysis of discursive struggle in HRM', *Journal of Management Studies*, **41** (3), 377–400.

Harley, B., B. Allen and L. Sargent (2007), 'High performance work systems and employee experience of work in the service sector: the case of aged care', *British Journal of Industrial Relations*, **45** (3), 607–33.

Harley, B., L. Sargent and B. Allen (2010), 'Employee responses to "high performance work systems" practices: an empirical test of the "disciplined worker thesis"', *Work, Employment and Society*, **24** (4), 740–60.

Kaufman, B. (2012), 'Strategic human resource management research in the USA: a failing grade after 30 years?', *Academy of Management Perspectives*, **26** (2), 12–36.

Ramsay, H., D. Scholarios and B. Harley (2000), 'Employees and high-performance work systems: testing inside the black box', *British Journal of Industrial Relations*, **38** (4), 501–31.

Üsdiken, B. (2014), 'Centres and peripheries: research styles and publication patterns in "top" US journals and their European alternatives, 1960–2010', *Journal of Management Studies*, **51** (5), 764–89.

35. Publishing in top international business and management journals

Stephen Tallman and Torben Pedersen

INTRODUCTION

Publishing in top international business and international management (IB/IM) journals generally follows the same paths with many of the same expectations and requirements as presented for top general management journals. There is, however, one main exception; that is, the absolute need to follow the journal's guidance in defining what makes the content of an article international in scope. We develop a discussion and provide some examples of this in the next section of this chapter. We also believe that expectations relating to topics, relevant literature, data collection, methods and presentation tend to be a bit different in the IB/IM literature from general management literature. These, though, are matters of degree or focus or preference, while the demand that a paper be 'international', whatever is meant by any particular journal in using that word, is essential.

INTERNATIONALISM: THE DEFINING CHARACTERISTIC

International business and international management (IB/IM) involve the study of cross-border activities of economic agents, or the strategies and governance of firms engaged in this type of activity. International scope is comprised of many parts as we could claim that very few economic activities do not have an international dimension. Increasingly more economic activities are becoming international and global, so the context for studying economic activities will often be international, where the objects of study are different cross-border activities.

However, in IB/IM the key is not just to use the international dimension as the context of study, but to make the international dimension a key part of the study. The basic claim in IB/IM is that the international dimension is not just a matter of degree, but changes the nature of many of the issues we scrutinize. When compared with domestic activities, international activities entail more risks, uncertainty, psychic distance, cultural distance, institutional distance and so on, but also more opportunities that come from diversity in knowledge, resources and user preferences. These fundamental differences in conducting business domestically and internationally are at the core of IB/IM studies.

Therefore, all the key journals in IB and IM stress that the international dimension needs to be the primary focus of attention. Often, this is a make-or-break criterion for publishing in the top IB/IM journals. Box 35.1 offers short abstracts of the editorial policies of three major IB/IM journals (*Journal of International Business Studies*, *JIBS*; *Journal of World Business*, *JWB*; and *Global Strategy Journal*, *GSJ*) as described in their web pages, and these are all very explicit about the key importance of the international dimension. The text that addresses this issue is highlighted in italics.

BOX 35.1 ABSTRACTS FROM WEB PAGES OF EDITORIAL POLICIES FOR *JIBS*, *JWB* AND *GSJ*

Journal of International Business Studies (*JIBS*)

'JIBS seeks to publish manuscripts with cutting-edge research that breaks new ground, rather than merely making an incremental contribution to international business studies. Manuscripts should address real-world phenomena, problems or puzzles; recognize that their contributions stand on the shoulders of prior researchers to highlight what is interesting and different; and include a clear statement of what it is they contribute to international business research. Theories whose *central propositions are distinctively international are encouraged*, as are theories where both dependent and independent variables are international.

The major theme of a JIBS paper should highlight the insights that can be derived for the *international aspects of business activity* as such. Papers in which international business is in the background, or in which international business issues are secondary or peripheral to the main argument being developed, are not suitable for JIBS. Hence, a paper is applicable for JIBS *when the core argument developed and examined is inherently international in character*, which is not judged by the nature of the data used as such in any accompanying empirical investigation.'

Journal of World Business (JWB)

'JWB publishes cutting-edge research that reflects important developments in the global business environment and advances new theoretical directions and ways of thinking about global phenomena. Although JWB's primary readers are scholars and researchers, the journal values contributions that explore and explicate implications for global enterprises and their managers, as well as consequences for public policy and the broader role of business in society.

While manuscripts may focus on a single country or small group of countries, *all submissions should reflect some cross-border or comparative dimensions*, or explore and advance other *issues affecting international business*, consistent with the global scope of the journal.'

Global Strategy Journal (GSJ)

'The domain of GSJ, as implied by the journal name, will be the study of any and all aspects of the environment, organizations, institutions, systems, individuals, actions, and decisions that are a part of or impinge on the practice or study of strategy and strategic management of business and non-business organizations in the global context. By global, we explicitly mean any cross-border activities described as international, global, transnational, multinational, multi-regional or by any other term that substantially implies that the activities take place in multiple countries and/or are integrated across borders.

The journal will be defined clearly by its *focus on international and global organizational strategic management, rather than a universalistic approach to the study of strategy*.'

The next question then is, 'What does it more precisely mean to say that the international aspect is at the centre of the study?' This implies that the theoretical part of the paper includes discussions of the international aspects and their implications for the theories and phenomena under investigation. Typically this should also be reflected in propositions or hypotheses that might well include some contextual variables evolving from the international setting – such as organizational complexity, institutional or cultural distance – that are affecting (for example, main effect, moderating or mediating) or being affected by other variables. As editors of *GSJ* (Tallman and Pedersen 2011, p. 2), we say that the journal is 'primarily concerned with strategy in context or with the moderating effects of geographical, cultural, and institutional differences on strategic management', and that it is not interested in 'universal or context-free approach[es] to the study of strategy'. Thus, the idea that international business or management studies should be explicitly focused on the international context and its effects on the discipline under consideration, strategy in the case of *GSJ*, is vital to IB/IM scholarship.

More especially this implies that a study that uses a multi-country dataset to test whether a theory of some aspect of business already established in a domestic context can be applied globally, while controlling for country effects (sources of international heterogeneity or variation), might not qualify as appropriate. For example, a study of how the use of performance appraisals affects firm performance would not be appropriate, even if the data used to test this was collected in multiple countries and possibly even if the study controlled for country differences. However, if the same data was used to study how the cultural context moderated the relationship between performance appraisal and firm performance, so that the theory and hypotheses focused on this interaction between the local culture and the tool of performance appraisal (that is, how it might be perceived differently in different contexts), then it typically would meet the criteria of being inherently international in character.

A single-country study of a question such as 'Are MNEs [multinational enterprises] more risk-averse than purely domestic firms?' would also qualify as an IB/IM study if the theoretical discussion centres on how the international or multinational dimension might determine behavioural differences between MNEs and purely domestic firms. Likewise, a comparative study of business or management practices and consequences in multiple countries or regions is typically seen as an international study, presuming that the comparison is made both conceptually and empirically. A single-country study in which all observations are domestic, but in which explicit comparison is made to similar studies set in other countries and in which differences in national context are salient, may be considered international in scope in some journals, but perhaps not in others.

The main issue highlighted here is that what makes an IB/IM study is not the multi-country nature of the applied data, but the theoretical and conceptual insights on the implications of conducting cross-national activities that the study puts forward. That this conception of 'What is international?' is both relevant and poorly understood is supported by the well over 50 per cent desk rejection of articles submitted to *JIBS*, according to its editors – the significantly increased rate over the 40–50 per cent typical of top journals is mostly owing to rejection of submissions of single-country, non-US based studies as not being international research, and therefore inappropriate for the journal. *Global Strategy Journal*, as a new journal, has a lower desk rejection rate overall and a less rigorous definition of 'single-country study', but perhaps a third of desk rejections are for a non-international perspective.

WHY SINGLE-COUNTRY STUDIES ARE NOT CONSIDERED INTERNATIONAL

The majority of IB/IM journals, and all of the major journals in these fields, while mostly published in the USA or Europe, take an explicitly global perspective on their research domain. Thus, while *GSJ* is largely edited in the USA and Europe and published by Wiley in the UK, it does not consider itself to be a US-centric or industrial world-centric outlet. Therefore, the idea that anything published about actions or operations of companies, industries or economies taking place in locations outside the USA is automatically international is not an accurate reflection of editorial policy. Instead, these are treated as domestic studies based in countries other than the USA or the UK. Thus, a study of local business responses to corruption in the legal system of a West African nation would be just as single-nation domestic in scope as a study of local business responses to boycotts in an American city based on local police shootings. Neither the firms involved, the activities monitored, the conceptual relationships nor the data offer any insight on doing business across borders, the activities of MNEs in or from the country or comparisons between business actions in multiple countries. However, if the same studies proposed and tested that multinational firms operating in the same local market would respond differently than locally based firms, owing to home-country cultural or institutional distance from the host, we would have a study in which international issues affect theory, models, data and resulting conclusions, and which would indeed be eligible for top IB/IM journals.

COMPARATIVE MANAGEMENT

The majority of papers published in IB/IM journals address the activities of multinational firms or activities such as foreign trade that implicitly involve cross-border transactions. However, for scholars of international business and management, comparative studies of business or management topics as they are pursued in different countries clearly are relevant to these journals. In the past, comparative management studies were relatively popular, as scholars grappled with differences in national settings. Comparative studies are also relatively popular in studies of the effects of cultural differences and national institutions, perhaps less so in the study of international strategies. However, there is much to be learned from comparisons of business or management processes and outcomes, whether at the individual, firm or industry level, as they are manifested in different national contexts.

From the IB/IM perspective, the effects of national context are clarified in such studies. From a business or management studies perspective, such comparative studies are most useful in differentiating the universal aspects of the concepts from the international setting as a significant part of the modelling, not just some international data applied to a generic management framework. In some journals, a comparative study will be expected to directly compare management in two or more countries, using the same instruments and analytical tools. In others, a single-country study that pursues concepts that have been developed previously in other countries and benchmarks results explicitly (taking a theoretical concept well-developed empirically in the US setting and developing comparable data and methods to compare responses in China and to then extend the theory to be more general, for instance) may be accepted as international in scope despite the single-country nature of the original empirical work.

CONCEPTUAL SECTIONS

Literature reviews for IB/IM articles are likely to be more extensive and complex than for non-international research. Particularly in the top journals, the disciplinary literature (economics, strategy, organizational behaviour, consumer behaviour, and so on) will usually be brought into play, but the relevant international literature (trade theory, global strategy, cultural effects, institutional distance, and so on) also must be represented. In strongly empirical papers in a well-developed part of the field, most references may be to other international business research, but more conceptual pieces will generally address the question of how general theories must be adapted to different contexts through the addition of moderating or mediating effects.

General business and management journals often focus on theory testing, using some specific setting as a source of data and to infer specific outcomes that should be able to support or deny the expectations of the theory or theories in question. International business and international management articles may be set up as a test of theory, particularly of moderating and mediating hypotheses that the strong contextual effects of an international setting are likely to highlight. However, with so many differences from place to place, phenomenological studies are very common in IB/IM. In these studies, the primary focus of the paper is to describe the actions of companies or other organizations or their members. Theories are brought into play to build and organize expectations of how the organizations, markets or consumers in one country might respond to particular conditions and stimuli. These papers are also found in top field journals, but the rich environment of international business makes such studies perhaps more common, but also of greater importance to scholarly researchers. Top journals still expect to see business/management theory being used to explain what is happening and why, but offering insights into investment into emerging market countries, for instance, is seen as equally important as whether tests on emerging market data tend to support or not to support current management theory. This is true in all management studies, but is much more apparent in IB/IM studies.

International business (IB) studies typically include some consideration of the setting or context, whether as the main topic, the setting of the study or a source of potential moderating effects. Characteristics of the international business environment, location-specific or 'distance' effects of the specific national/regional setting, the role of non-business actors such as international organizations (for example, the European Union, the World Trade Organization and the United Nations), non-governmental organizations (NGOs) or social networks are all considerations that are important in IB transactions. These contextual or locational considerations should be an explicit and apparent part of the conceptual development of the paper. They should be shown or predicted to affect, through moderating or mediating relationships, the relationships between the actions and outcomes of the business and managerial phenomena in question. They should also be an explicit part of the application of any business or management theories that are brought to bear on the study. Including IB/IM concepts in the conceptual development of the research is the key to making the paper inherently international in scope.

In building a conceptual framework for the research, we find that most business and management theories have some relevance to most locational settings and have been used in international business at one time or another. However, the manifestations of these theories – that is, the exact mechanisms by which they operate and the relative importance of the various organizational and competitive factors that impact their operations – are likely to vary from location to location, driven by differences in cultures, institutions, economic development and infrastructure across borders. Thus, the resource-based view, institutional theory, real options and other macro theories still apply, but the issue of varying contextual settings means that the organizational variables may interact extensively with locational variables; context is hard to avoid. In more micro studies, aspects of human psychology or social interaction may be fundamental to our species, but the exact decisions and actions undertaken by individuals are likely to be heavily influenced by cultural expectations and institutional constraints.

In creating testable frameworks of hypotheses and developing causal diagrams to outline empirical tests in IB/IM research, scholars should include explicitly international variables as explanatory variables, perhaps as the fundamental inputs to a structural equation model; as moderating variables, suggesting perhaps that the effect of company resources on performance may be moderated by their cultural appropriateness; or as control variables, but with explicit effects, so that perhaps state ownership might need to be controlled for in a study of the effect of technology on human resource policies. If an author does not see a role for location-based variables in his or her model, whether purely theoretical or for empirical testing, he or she should expect a high probability of desk rejection by an IB/IM journal.

VARIABLES

Dependent Variables

Dependent variables in IB/IM studies are qualitatively much like those in any business or management research, whether measuring some organizational outcome or performance in the market or another external context. Thus, choice of acquisition or alliance in an expansion, profitability resulting from a strategic decision or retention of employees might all be outcomes in any business or management research. In international business studies, though, contextual aspects may shift the exact terms of the dependent variable. For instance, an expansion may be across borders, so governance decisions focus on specific markets. Profitability might be for the entire corporation, but is often focused on national or regional units, and employee retention considerations might result in a comparison of home and host country nationals' retention rates. Many IB/IM studies do not use explicitly international dependent variables at the firm level, but when international or cross-border considerations are explicitly part of the dependent variable, establishing the study as international in nature is relatively straightforward.

Explanatory Variables

Again, the organizational variables that drive the dependent variable are often quite typical in quality, but may reflect geographical or locational considerations that do not appear in domestic studies. Thus, international diversification is much like product/market diversification in any study in terms of its anticipated mechanisms and effects, but at the same time explicitly incorporates considerations of differences across locations. Other possible independent variables, such as cultural or institutional distance, are often critical to an IB/IM study, but are in effect irrelevant or meaningless in a domestic setting. If variables measure stocks and flows of resources, products, ideas, or capital across borders or differences among national units or specific location-tied characteristics, this is often an indicator of an international study.

Moderating Variables

International or cross-border moderating considerations often are where international context comes into empirical estimations, as organizational variables are predicted to have differential effects under different location-tied contextual conditions. When incorporated into the conceptual framework and modelled explicitly with measured variables, country-specific moderating variables are perhaps the most typical way for international effects to appear explicitly in organization or industry-level studies. As well as establishing a clear international provenance, however, the importance of context to the actual operationalization of many business and management concepts is demonstrated by the moderating effect of national differences. This, then, is often how the benefits of international studies to understanding the nuances of larger theoretical and conceptual models of business management are demonstrated. Where a domestic study may appear to support the expectations of a universalistic theory, an international study using appropriate variables and interactions can go far towards establishing the boundary conditions, limitations, and relevance of such theories.

Control Variables

International management studies typically offer multiple location-based control variables. Place matters, and we often see dummy variables for countries, but specific controls for cultural differences; levels of economic development; legal, political and regulatory standards and requirements; geographical differences and other aspects of location that might affect markets or organizations also are common. In general, IB/IM studies will use all the controls for organizational types typical of equivalent work in the discipline, then add a variety of controls related to international markets and/or the specific home and host markets.

DATA

Firm-level data is often not categorically different from that used in any related discipline-focused research, but may well be much more complex to collect and organize. Even secondary data on financial variables is inconsistent across legal jurisdictions. Cultural and institutional differences might mean that management and organizational measures are very different in scope, even in their meaning. Some of these issues are gradually being resolved by converging accounting standards and generally increasing transparency for publicly traded firms. An item of note, though, is that the relative importance to their local economies of state-owned, family-owned and other firm types whose shares are not traded on public exchanges means that even when data is accessible, the importance of the observed organizations may vary widely across countries.

Data collection is often much more difficult. Gaining access to secondary data may be difficult for foreign-based researchers, so local collaborators are often necessary. The trustworthiness of data collected in emerging markets with less secure legal institutions may well be less than in industrial market economies. In addition, databases are typically expressed in the local language, often requiring translation, and again emphasizing the value of local collaborators. Likewise, collecting firsthand data through surveys or interviews requires more than a little additional effort, and often a multinational research team. Translation and back translation are essential. Careful pre-testing on individuals from the test country is needed. Variables may have different meanings to managers in different places and descriptive phrases may not translate directly and meaningfully. It is necessary to follow procedures precisely and to maintain control of collection efforts when the validity of the data and the collection effort are likely to be queried (Chang et al. 2010). That is, the problems of single-method, single-instrument, single-respondent research when using surveys are always at issue, but, especially in emerging markets, limits on communication and travel may make reliable data collection a real issue with a limited array of solutions. For instance, a poor telephone service may limit the possibilities for telephone surveys, unreliable mail may make mailed surveys uncertain, and cultural responses to intrusive questions in a setting where guarantees of confidentiality are seen as dubious may require person-to-person interviews even to administer closed-ended surveys (and these are difficult to schedule, particularly for foreigners). Also, the lack of reliable secondary data may eliminate complementary sources of some measures. Reviewers are typically hyper-alert to these issues in international research.

Multi-country data is generally expected in international business and management studies to avoid single-country studies, but it is not necessarily the case that multi-country data always makes for an international business study. If the conceptual aspect of a study is completely driven by disciplinary theory and the modelling does not include contextual controls or moderators, simply using non-US or even multi-country data does not necessarily offer the necessary focus on international business to pass the 'desk reject as inappropriate' test. Also, although data from only one country may pass muster in a study with a strong explicit comparison to previous work based in other countries in some journals, the general expectation is that multi-country data will be used to test these explicitly international models.

CONCLUSION

Typically, phenomenon-focused international studies may primarily offer opportunities to develop concepts and ideas about understanding what is happening in international or foreign markets or among foreign suppliers, customers or partners. A challenge for authors focused on top international IB/IM journals is to move beyond this focus on what is happening in the world to understanding how and why it is happening, which generally means applying business and management theoretical concepts to the phenomenon in order to understand how the international context is or is not different from previously studied domestic contexts. Also, to clearly model the impact of the international or multi-country context, the setting must be explicitly included in the specification of the theoretical and empirical frameworks. Early papers addressing an important new phenomenon may survive with little effort to build explicitly international models, but any novelty quickly fades, and theoretical inputs and consequences again take precedence.

Such issues can be seen, for example, in early studies of market entry into China; this was so new that any rigorous paper with seemingly reliable data could be published in virtually any journal. Within a short time, though, studies in top journals were expected to apply, test and extend management theory in the Chinese setting, and IB/IM journals began to require a focus on the character of the multinational partner, the role of contextual distance in explaining differences across markets, and the development of new theoretical constructs for investment in emerging markets. Just having reliable Chinese data was no longer sufficient.

In pushing for a focus on theory-related (applying, testing, proposing and extending) papers in the top journals, we also suggest that while theory-based papers must be able to address conceptual concerns in the IB disciplines (international management, international strategy, and so on), they will be stronger if they also have something to say about theory development in their primary disciplines. Opportunities to propose boundary or moderating conditions for the relevance or application of the primary theory(ies) are common, but frequently overlooked, in IB/IM studies. As the top journals in the international business and management area are constantly concerned with becoming and remaining part of the larger business management conversation, explicit consideration of the potential impact of their published research on the underlying disciplines is very attractive. While the impact of cultural difference on the choice between contractual and equity alliances for market entry may be publishable, a study that considers cultural distance as a way of measuring uncertainty and bounded rationality for corporate decision-makers, who then choose entry modes as much for behavioural as for rational economic reasons, is even more likely to attract interest among the top journals. The higher ranking (or aiming) the journal, the more an explicit effort of theory building in both international and primary disciplines will help in justifying a supportive editing and review process.

As at the start of this chapter, we want to emphasize how much top IB/IM journals are like any top field journals in business and management. They look towards the theoretical impact of articles, whether to explicate the mechanisms of phenomena in their field, to test existing theory, to extend this theory or to build new theory. The main difference is that they are interested in both disciplinary and internationally focused theory, and especially at the intersection of the two. The international context offers excellent opportunities to build understanding of the boundaries and limits of business and management theory, and taking advantage of these opportunities is the focus of the top journals. However, the first and most fundamental characteristic of IB/IM research at all internationally orientated journals is that it is international in its intellectual scope, not just in its data or its setting, but in its conceptual development.

REFERENCES

Chang, S.-J., A. van Witteloostuijn and L. Eden (2010), 'From the editors: common method variance in international business research', *Journal of International Business Studies*, **41** (2), 178–84.

Tallman, S. and T. Pedersen (2011), 'The launch of *Global Strategy Journal*: comments from the co-editors', *Global Strategy Journal*, **1** (1–2), 1–5.

36. Publishing at the interfaces of psychology and strategic management

Gerard P. Hodgkinson

INTRODUCTION

Every leading journal has a clear mission and attendant set of foci. Manuscripts falling across the desks of busy editors and reviewers are evaluated first and foremost in terms of the extent to which they fall within the thematic purview of the target journal. The craft of addressing messages to appropriately targeted audiences is thus an essential skill cultivated by all successful academic writers. Drawing on a range of examples, in this short chapter I offer my personal reflections on how in practice I have implemented this advice in the positioning of my own work and, in so doing, anticipated the likely reactions of potentially critical reviewers.

In a highly insightful book, Huff (1999) introduced the metaphor of 'conversation' as a means of analysing the all-important question of how to position scholarly journal articles to particular audiences. It is a metaphor that I have found to be helpful when reflecting on the relative successes and failures of my own work. Over the course of an academic career now in its fourth decade, for the past 35 years the bulk of my scholarly research activity has centred on three major inter-related themes:

1. The construction and psychometric evaluation of instruments for the assessment of work-related individual differences (see, for example, Gill and Hodgkinson 2007; Hodgkinson, 1986, 1987, 1992, 1993; Hodgkinson and Sadler-Smith, 2003; Hodgkinson et al. 2009b).
2. Cognition in the workplace (see, for example, Healey et al. 2015b; Hodgkinson and Healey 2008a; Hodgkinson and Sadler-Smith 2018), encompassing, *inter alia*, the psychological analysis of strategic

Publishing at the interfaces of psychology and strategic management 335

   management processes (see, for example, Hodgkinson 1997a, 1997b; Hodgkinson and Johnson 1994) and the development and evaluation of tools and wider practices for intervening in such processes (see, for example, Healey and Hodgkinson 2017; Hodgkinson et al. 1999, 2002, 2004; Hodgkinson and Healey 2008b; Healey et al. 2015a).
3. The significance of scholarly management and organizational research for academia and wider publics (see, for example, Anderson et al. 2001; Hodgkinson, 2006; Hodgkinson and Rousseau 2009; Hodgkinson and Starkey 2011; Hodgkinson et al. 2001; Romme et al. 2015).

Given the diversity of my interests, not surprisingly my work has appeared in a wide array of scholarly outlets, spanning both general and subject specific journals, both in the management and organization sciences, and the wider social and behavioural sciences. Without exception, the journals in which my work has appeared have been chosen because the messages I wanted to convey had the potential either to (1) start a conversation of likely significance among a recognized community of scholars within the relevant focal body of literature whose work I was looking to influence in some way; or (2) contribute in significant ways to an ongoing conversation among a recognized community of scholars, again with a view to influencing the future direction of its work and hence the focal body of literature at hand.

Adopting Huff's (1999) conversation metaphor, in order to initiate successfully a fresh conversation, or to contribute meaningfully to an ongoing conversation, it is important that writers first clarify with whom (that is, the audience) and on what subject matter (that is, the content) they wish to converse. The breadth of the target audience and the content of the conversation will vary enormously from one context to another. In this chapter, therefore, I compare and contrast several of the strategies I have adopted variously across a range of disciplinary and interdisciplinary contexts, demonstrating how in each case the respective process adopted resulted in one or more successful publications; that is, publications that were acceptable to editors and/or reviewers and that have attracted subsequently the attention of scholars within the focal body of literature thus targeted, and in some cases extending well beyond it.

The chapter is structured in five sections. Following this introduction, the second, third, and fourth sections offer my reflections on each of three strategies I have adopted over the years in relation to the framing of my work depending on the nature of the target audience and content. The final section offers my reflections more generally on the significance of these strategies as a means of ensuring a more suitably focused and coherent contribution to the body of literature thus targeted.

FOSTERING CONVERSATIONS WITH MORE SPECIALIST AUDIENCES AND A MORE RESTRICTIVE FOCUS

This strategy is perhaps best illustrated by the work I have published that falls within my first stream of work. The audiences to whom I have addressed my various articles on the development and validation of instruments for the assessment of personality and related individual differences (for example, Gill and Hodgkinson 2007; Hodgkinson 1986, 1987, 1992, 1993; Hodgkinson and Sadler-Smith 2003; Hodgkinson et al. 2009b) have been relatively narrow, in comparison with the more generalist audiences I have targeted either directly or indirectly within the second and third streams of my work. Furthermore, the articles I have published within this first stream have set out to achieve relatively modest scientific objectives; these pieces, which report the application of well-established concepts and statistical procedures pertaining to psychometric theory, with a view to ascertaining the reliability and validity of the instruments concerned, are aimed primarily (although by no means exclusively) at a group of researchers with a focus on applied psychological measurement.

Given this comparatively restrictive focus, each of these papers was framed at a level of granularity that would appeal to researchers and practitioners looking to use instruments for the purposes of assessing work-related individual differences. Illustrating this approach, consider the paper reporting the 'development and validation of the five-factor model questionnaire (FFMQ)' (Gill and Hodgkinson 2007). In this article, the primary focus was on persuading a predominantly technical audience why (yet another) personality assessment instrument for the assessment of the 'big five' personality traits (that is, neuroticism, extraversion, agreeableness, openness, and conscientiousness) in the workplace was actually required. The article then set about reporting the development and validation of the new instrument in question, which entailed a total of five methodological studies.

The front-end framing of this paper first establishes the ubiquity of the big five and the related five-factor model of personality underpinning this particular collection of traits. The introductory section then problematizes the wide range of extant big-five instruments, noting that they have been devised primarily for general usage or more particularly clinical usage, as opposed to being work-related assessment tools. It then highlights that the bulk of instruments currently available are targeted predominantly at well-educated, North American respondents. One further issue of note raised as an important motivation for the work reported in this paper is that the individual questions used to assess the big five are typically composed of statement-based items, whereas simpler, adjectival-based items, of the sort adopted in the FFMQ, are often more desirable.

That this paper was published in *Personnel Psychology*, one of the world's leading technical journals devoted to personnel selection and assessment issues, illustrates how through such careful conversational targeting it is possible to 'sell' the importance of establishing the psychometric efficacy of an instrument devised primarily for use outside the US context to an audience composed largely, although by no means exclusively, of US readers: 'The development process for the FFMQ had the clear objective of producing a valid and reliable set of adjective-based measures of the Big Five for use in work-related settings. The resulting instrument is simple to administer, rapidly completed, and easily interpreted' (Gill and Hodgkinson 2007, p. 736). Highlighting the limitations of the dominant US instruments, and demonstrating the broader applicability of the newly constructed alternative, resulted in a publication in one of the world's leading (US-based) field journals. Although this article went through several rounds of revisions, the overall journey from initial submission until final acceptance was relatively smooth. I believe the high degree of careful framing and preparatory work in designing and then reporting the constituent studies, to ensure that they contributed cumulatively, in a logical and coherent fashion to the overall goal of the paper, as encapsulated in the above quotation, was the most crucial factor that led to this relatively pain-free and successful outcome.

FOSTERING CONVERSATIONS WITH BROADER AUDIENCES AND A LESS RESTRICTIVE FOCUS

The relatively narrower approach to framing the various personality and individual differences pieces outlined in the previous section stands in marked contrast to the approaches to framing I have adopted in the framing of the various articles I have published under my second stream of work, falling under the theme of cognition in the workplace. Much of my work within this second stream has sought to initiate, or contribute to, rather broader conversations with a wider range of participants (see, for example, Healey et al. 2015b; Hodgkinson and Healey 2008a; Hodgkinson and Sadler-Smith 2018; Pillai et al. 2017). To illustrate the key features of this approach I highlight two particular publications: 'Intuition: a fundamental bridging construct in the behavioural sciences' (Hodgkinson et al. 2008) and 'Cognition in organizations' (Hodgkinson and Healey 2008a). In both of these cases the targeted readership was broad, with the intention of initiating a series of conversations that would cut across specialist subfields, with a view to fostering more highly innovative theory and research.

The overriding aim of the Hodgkinson et al. (2008) article was to provoke scholars working within the various specialist areas of academic psychology (for example, cognitive psychology, social cognitive neuroscience and personality psychology) and its main applied areas (for example, educational psychology, occupational/industrial–organizational psychology) to recognize the many parallel and complimentary developments occurring across their respective scholarly domains that pointed toward the possibility that intuition (and more precisely dual-processing accounts of cognitive processes) might serve as a scientific foundation for greater cooperation across the psychology field as a whole. The *British Journal of Psychology*, which publishes research on all aspects of the discipline, was thus a natural home for this piece, in which we evaluated critically work published in selected mainstream journals in the various subfields and domains of application encompassed by our review.[1]

The Hodgkinson and Healey (2008a) *Annual Review of Psychology* article was predicated on a similar logic of seeking to initiate a series of conversations among scholars who would not otherwise typically engage with one another. In this case, however, the focus was centred more narrowly on the subfield of occupational and organizational/industrial–organizational psychology. Intentionally wide-ranging in its coverage of topics, this article commences by outlining the history of theory and research on cognition in organizations, from its inception in World War II up to the early 2000s, and then offers an integrative review across ten major areas of industrial–organizational psychology, with a view to identifying points of convergence and divergence in theory advancement, empirical endeavour, and the development of new methods. The article seeks to deepen a conversation between scholarly researchers falling variously in the human factors tradition and the organizations tradition, and highlights opportunities for greater collaboration across those traditions. In so doing, it advances a cross-cutting agenda across the ten substantive domain areas surveyed, covering the period 2000–2007.

Although ambitious and wide-ranging in scope, again I believe the key factor that led to the acceptance of these particular pieces was the careful groundwork undertaken beforehand, thus ensuring that in each case the constituent subfields/topic areas addressed were covered in just sufficient depth to enable my co-authors and I to lay suitable foundations for subsequent engagement on the part of the scholarly communities thus targeted, avoiding the twin pitfalls of superficiality and unnecessary detail. Relative to my other publications, these two particular pieces amassed high citation counts across a wide range of disciplinary subfields and topic areas, over a short space of time, suggesting that our fundamental goal of seeking to attain significant cross-disciplinary and cross-topic reach across our targeted areas was indeed successful, although it remains to be seen to what extent the cross-fertilization of ideas, through interdisciplinary and cross-functional team-working, has occurred on the scale we were ultimately hoping to achieve.

FOSTERING BROADER CONVERSATIONS WITH MORE SPECIALIST AUDIENCES

This third framing strategy is perhaps best illustrated with two papers I have published that fall respectively within the second and third of my research streams. The first example, 'The practitioner–researcher divide in industrial, work and organizational (IWO) psychology: where are we now and where do we go from here?' (Anderson et al. 2001), appeared in a special issue of the *Journal of Occupational and Organizational Psychology* that celebrated 100 years of the field's achievements at the turn of the twenty-first century (Patterson 2001). Unlike the other contributors to this particular volume – whose papers offered state-of-the-art reviews of the literature pertaining to some of the field's central topics such as personnel selection and assessment (Robertson and Smith 2001), performance and appraisal and management (Fletcher 2001), and well-being and occupational health (Sparks et al. 2001) – our own paper was intentionally framed more broadly, in an attempt to stimulate a wider-ranging conversation across the IWO psychology community as a whole, regarding what we argued was a growing divide between research and practice, with a view to encouraging a re-strengthening of the scientist-practitioner model, arguably the bedrock of the field. Deliberately provocative, our goal was to engender feelings of discomfort among our readers, with a view countering what we saw as some unfortunate consequences of the effort-reward mechanisms in play among the academic and practitioner wings of the profession. Contrasting research that is highly rigorous but largely irrelevant to practice (pedantic science) with research that is seemingly highly relevant but of poor scientific quality (popularist science), and research that is both irrelevant to practice and of poor scientific quality (puerile science), we argued that researchers should be encouraged to advance the cause of research that sought to achieve the highest possible standards of scientific excellence, but also with a focus on the more difficult and enduring problems of concern to the practitioner wing of the profession (pragmatic science). As intended, our thesis stimulated a rich and highly diverse debate that has spilled over into many other fields and subfields, well beyond the confines of the specialist IWO psychology audience to which it was initially directed.

Once again, I believe it was the judgement calls we made in respect of the front-end framing of this particular piece for the constituent audience of the target journal that led to its ultimate success. In this case, the call for papers accompanying the special issue reflecting on a century's achievements provided us with a suitable platform on which we were able to build on a series of conversations we had held informally with journal editors, and fellow researchers and practitioners, through attendance at the main professional and academic conferences over many years. I believe that the enduring success of this article is in no small part due to the basic framework and embryonic concepts we articulated, which captured the growing sense throughout the IWO psychology community that all was not well among its academic and practitioner wings, an analysis that seems to have resonated with several other branches of the psychology field and the wider social and behavioural sciences, evidenced by the breadth of citations it has attracted.

Further illustrating the efficacy of this third framing strategy of fostering broader conversations with more specialist audiences, I turn now to consider one of my relatively recent papers on the psychological foundations of strategic management (Hodgkinson and Healey 2011). From the outset of my career, the bulk of my work on this topic (see, for example, Hodgkinson 1997a, 1997b; Hodgkinson and Johnson 1994; Hodgkinson et al. 1999), like much of the behavioural strategy literature in general, has centred on the analysis of cognitive processes in strategy formulation and implementation (for a recent overview, see Powell et al. 2011). Drawing on the insights of state-of-the-art-advances that have taken place in the affective sciences over the past two decades, our goal in the Hodgkinson and Healey (2011) paper, which appeared in a special issue of *Strategic Management Journal* devoted to 'the psychological foundations of strategic management' (Fox et al. 2011), was to move along the conversation on cognition and strategy away from an affect-free conception of strategists as cognitive misers (and sense-makers), toward a 'hot' cognition alternative, which recognizes that strategists are ultimately 'governed by thoughts and feelings: always boundedly rational, but manifestly driven by emotion' (Hodgkinson and Healey 2011, p. 1512). Using the much-cited dynamic capabilities paper of Teece (2007) as an overarching framework, our analysis demonstrated systematically how each of the psychological foundations underpinning Teece's (2007) framework are predicated on psychological conceptions that are outmoded when viewed in the light of more recent advances in social cognitive neuroscience (for example, Lieberman 2007) and neuroeconomics (for example, Loewenstein et al. 2008), in turn rendering his prescriptions for fostering dynamic capabilities (through increased efforts to engage in systematic and disciplined reasoning and analysis) problematic. Our analysis highlights instead the central role of meta-cognitive awareness and emotion regulation as essential psychological foundations of strategic adaptation (see also, Healey and Hodgkinson 2017; Hodgkinson and Healey 2014). Once more, in framing this particular paper, the occasion of a special issue provided a useful enabling context to raise questions that ran against the grain of the mainstream alternatives dominating the literature, in ways that have begun to move the conversation on the role of cognition in strategy formulation and implementation in new and innovative directions: the primary goal of the special issue guest editors.

CONCLUDING REMARKS

Over the course of an academic career now well into its fourth decade, I have been privileged to work with some of the world's brightest and most distinguished scholars in the business and management research community. Their generous friendship and mentoring has nurtured my ability and given me the confidence to submit to, and ultimately publish my work in, some of the best North American (for example, Gill and Hodgkinson 2007; Healey et al. 2015b; Hodgkinson et al. 1999; Hodgkinson and Healey 2008a, 2011) and European (for example, Hodgkinson 1997a, 1997b; Hodgkinson and Healey 2008b; Hodgkinson and Johnson 1994) journals and other distinguished outlets (for example, Hodgkinson and Starbuck 2008). In this chapter I have offered my reflections, all too briefly, on the important question of how, as an interdisciplinary researcher situated primarily at the interfaces of psychology and strategic management, I have variously positioned my journal articles to particular audiences.

Returning to Huff's (1999) conversation metaphor, I have identified three distinctive types of audience–content combinations across a range of disciplinary and interdisciplinary contexts, demonstrating how in each case the essential messages were anchored to current debates in the focal literature I was seeking to influence. My paper reporting the development and validation of the FFMQ (Gill and Hodgkinson 2007), for instance, was positioned within a growing stream of literature that has debated how to enhance the validity of big-five assessment practices in the workplace (see, for example, Salgado 2003). Similarly, the Hodgkinson and Healey (2011) *Strategic Management Journal* piece and related publications that have appeared more recently (Healey and Hodgkinson 2017; Hodgkinson and Healey 2014), arguing the case for re-theorizing strategic adaptation as a 'hot' cognitive process, used Teece's (2007) well-known dynamic capabilities framework as the entry point and key foundation for organizing the contribution as a whole, thus ensuring that our arguments would appeal to a wide-ranging audience of strategy scholars.

Arguably, the single most valuable lesson I have learned, both as an editor and as a writer in my own right, is that, almost invariably, the authors of successful journal articles render abundantly clear their intended contribution within the first three or four sentences. Known as the hook, it is these early passages that explain the significance of an article to its intended audience, thus addressing the 'so what?' question at the outset.

Irrespective of the (inter)disciplinary field or subject matter, the abstract/summary and opening paragraphs of the main body of text and concluding discussion sections of any academic paper are arguably its three most important elements. Confronted by a myriad of manuscripts to consider for potential publication, when new submissions arrive electronically in their inboxes or land on their desks, hard-pressed editors-in-chief and their teams of action editors and reviewers typically first scan the abstract and then read the first few sentences of the main body of text to gain an overall sense of what the authors are claiming to have contributed to the literature pertaining to the focal topic at hand. Next, they typically move to the concluding discussion and similarly read the first few sentences, to ascertain the extent to which the promise of the manuscript's opening claims are revisited systematically as the authors bring their contribution to a close. In an empirical contribution, they then typically jump finally to skim read the methods and results sections to ascertain the extent to which the research design and results are appropriate for the conclusions thus presented.

The actions I have just described constitute the most important features of what is commonly known in scholarly editorial circles as the coherence test. A manuscript is coherent to the extent that the fundamental contribution stated at the outset is supported, consistently, throughout. All seasoned editors and reviewers adopt this test as standard practice. Any manuscript failing the coherence test, which takes only a matter of minutes to complete, is in serious trouble. The majority of such manuscripts are desk rejected routinely by the world's leading journals. If, however, an editor or action editor in receipt of such a manuscript decides to err on the side of generosity, the odds of it surviving the next stage, the first-round of the double-blind peer review process, are at best extremely low.

The three strategies I have enumerated in this chapter illustrate some of the ways in which I have striven to ensure that my own work passes this best test. Devising a hook that is compelling for the target audience and ensuring it is used intelligently to anchor the remainder of the manuscript content is, I believe, the basis of my success, both in stimulating new, and contributing to ongoing, conversations. Although taking the time and trouble to reflect on how best to align the content of an article with the needs of its target audience may seem an obvious piece of advice, surprisingly, based on my many years of experience as a journal editor and reviewer, it is a piece of advice that all too often I have found even the most seasoned of authors neglect to their cost.

NOTE

1. Reflecting the third approach to be discussed in this chapter (fostering broader conversations with more specialist audiences), outlined in the next section, a second piece (Hodgkinson et al. 2009a) sought similarly to bring this body of work to the attention of scholars working within the more specialist field of strategic management. Returning to the current approach of seeking to foster conversations with broader audiences, Hodgkinson and Sadler-Smith (2018) have undertaken a further, more extensive review of fundamental developments in psychology, in order to highlight the varying, incompatible psychological assumptions underpinning the various dual-process formulations now permeating multiple streams of research in the management and organization sciences more generally, spanning strategic management, entrepreneurship, organizational behaviour and human resource management, with a view to fostering a more nuanced conversation, centred on the attendant implications of these alternative conceptions for explicating more comprehensively the behavioural microfoundations and neural substrates of managerial and organizational decision-making.

REFERENCES

Anderson, N., P. Herriot and G.P. Hodgkinson (2001), 'The practitioner–researcher divide in industrial, work and organizational (IWO) psychology: where are we now and where do we go from here?', *Journal of Occupational and Organizational Psychology*, **74** (4), 391–411.

Fletcher, C. (2001), 'Performance appraisal and management: the developing research agenda', *Journal of Occupational and Organizational Psychology*, **74** (4), 473–87.

Fox, C.R., D. Lovallo and T.C. Powell (eds) (2011), 'Psychological foundations of strategic management', *Strategic Management Journal*, **32** (special issue), 1369–524.

Gill, C. and G.P. Hodgkinson (2007), 'Development and validation of the five-factor model questionnaire (FFMQ): an adjectival-based personality inventory for use in occupational settings', *Personnel Psychology*, **60** (3), 731–66.

Healey, M.P. and G.P. Hodgkinson (2017), 'Making strategy hot', *California Management Review*, **59** (3), 109–34.

Healey, M.P., G.P. Hodgkinson, R. Whittington and G. Johnson (2015a), 'Off to plan or out to lunch? Relationships between strategy workshop design characteristics and outcomes', *British Journal of Management*, **26** (3), 507–28.

Healey, M.P., T. Vuori, and G.P. Hodgkinson (2015b), 'When teams agree while disagreeing: reflexion and reflection in shared cognition', *Academy of Management Review*, **40** (3), 399–422.

Hodgkinson, G.P. (1986), 'A note concerning the comparability of standard and automated versions of the Vocational Preference Inventory', *Journal of Occupational Psychology*, **59**, 337–9.

Hodgkinson, G.P. (1987), 'The effect of variations in answer sheet format on performance on the DAT – Clerical Speed and Accuracy Test', *Educational and Psychological Measurement*, **47** (2), 473–75.

Hodgkinson, G.P. (1992), 'Development and validation of the Strategic Locus of Control Scale', *Strategic Management Journal*, **13** (4), 311–17.

Hodgkinson, G.P. (1993), 'Doubts about the conceptual and empirical status of context-free and firm-specific control expectancies: a reply to Boone and De Brabander', *Strategic Management Journal*, **14** (8), 627–31.

Hodgkinson, G.P. (1997a), 'The cognitive analysis of competitive structures: a review and critique', *Human Relations*, **50** (6), 625–54.

Hodgkinson, G.P. (1997b), 'Cognitive inertia in a turbulent market: the case of UK residential estate agents', *Journal of Management Studies*, **34** (6), 921–45.

Hodgkinson, G.P. (2006), 'The role of JOOP (and other scientific journals) in bridging the practitioner–researcher divide in industrial, work and organizational (IWO) psychology', *Journal of Occupational and Organizational Psychology*, **79** (2), 173–8.

Hodgkinson, G.P. and M.P. Healey (2008a), 'Cognition in organizations', *Annual Review of Psychology*, **59**, 387–417.

Hodgkinson G.P. and M. Healey (2008b), 'Toward a (pragmatic) science of strategic intervention: design propositions for scenario planning', *Organization Studies*, **29** (3), 435–57.

Hodgkinson, G.P. and M.P. Healey (2011), 'Psychological foundations of dynamic capabilities: reflexion and reflection in strategic management', *Strategic Management Journal*, **32** (13), 1500–1516.

Hodgkinson, G.P. and M.P. Healey (2014), 'Coming in from the cold: the psychological foundations of radical innovation revisited', *Industrial Marketing Management*, **43** (8), 1306–13.

Hodgkinson, G.P. and G. Johnson (1994), 'Exploring the mental models of competitive strategists: the case for a processual approach', *Journal of Management Studies*, **31** (4), 525–51.

Hodgkinson, G.P. and D.M. Rousseau (2009), 'Bridging the rigour-relevance gap in management research: it's already happening!', *Journal of Management Studies*, **46** (3), 534–46.

Hodgkinson, G.P. and E. Sadler-Smith (2003), 'Complex or unitary? A critique and empirical re-assessment of the Allinson-Hayes Cognitive Style Index', *Journal of Occupational and Organizational Psychology*, **76** (2), 243–68.

Hodgkinson, G.P. and E. Sadler-Smith (2018), 'The dynamics of intuition and analysis in managerial and organizational decision making', *Academy of Management Perspectives*, **32** (4), 473–92.

Hodgkinson, G.P. and W.H. Starbuck (eds) (2008), *The Oxford Handbook of Organizational Decision Making*, Oxford: Oxford University Press.

Hodgkinson, G.P. and K. Starkey (2011), 'Not simply returning to the same answer over and over again: reframing relevance', *British Journal of Management*, **22** (3), 355–69.

Hodgkinson, G.P., P. Herriot and N. Anderson (2001), 'Re-aligning the stakeholders in management research: lessons from industrial, work and organizational psychology', *British Journal of Management*, **12** (special issue), S41–S48.

Hodgkinson G.P., J. Langan-Fox and E. Sadler-Smith (2008), 'Intuition: a fundamental bridging construct in the behavioural sciences', *British Journal of Psychology*, **99** (1), 1–27.

Hodgkinson, G.P., A.J. Maule and N.J. Bown (2004), 'Causal cognitive mapping in the organizational strategy field: a comparison of alternative elicitation procedures', *Organizational Research Methods*, **7** (1), 3–26.

Hodgkinson, G.P., N.J. Bown, A.J. Maule, K.W. Glaister and A.D. Pearman (1999), 'Breaking the frame: an analysis of strategic cognition and decision making under uncertainty', *Strategic Management Journal*, **20** (10), 977–85.

Hodgkinson, G.P., A.J. Maule, N.J. Bown, A.D. Pearman and K.W. Glaister (2002), 'Further reflections on the elimination of framing bias in strategic decision making', *Strategic Management Journal*, **23** (11), 1069–76.

Hodgkinson, G.P., E. Sadler-Smith, L.A. Burke, G. Claxton and P.R. Sparrow (2009a), 'Intuition in organizations: implications for strategic management', *Long Range Planning*, **42** (3), 277–97.

Hodgkinson, G.P., E. Sadler-Smith, M. Sinclair and N.M. Ashkanasy (2009b), 'More than meets the eye? Intuition and analysis revisited', *Personality and Individual Differences*, **47** (4), 342–6.

Huff, A.S. (1999), *Writing for Scholarly Publication*, Thousand Oaks, CA: Sage.

Lieberman, M.D. (2007), 'Social cognitive neuroscience: a review of core processes', *Annual Review of Psychology*, **58**, 259–89.

Loewenstein, G., S. Rick and J.D. Cohen (2008), 'Neuroeconomics', *Annual Review of Psychology*, **59**, 647–72.

Patterson, F. (2001), 'Developments in work psychology: emerging issues and future trends', *Journal of Occupational and Organizational Psychology*, **74** (4), 381–90.

Pillai, K.G., G.P. Hodgkinson, G. Kalyanaram and S.R. Nair (2017), 'The negative effects of social capital in organizations: a review and extension', *International Journal of Management Reviews*, **19** (1), 97–124.

Powell, T.C., D. Lovallo and C.R. Fox (2011), 'Behavioral strategy', *Strategic Management Journal*, **32** (special issue), 1369–86.

Robertson, I.T. and M. Smith (2001), 'Personnel selection', *Journal of Occupational and Organizational Psychology*, **74** (4), 441–72.

Romme, A.G.L., M.J. Avenier, D. Denyer, G.P. Hodgkinson, K. Pandza, K. Starkey et al. (2015), 'Towards common ground and trading zones in management research and practice', *British Journal of Management*, **26** (3), 544–59.

Salgado, J.F. (2003), 'Predicting job performance using FFM and non-FFM personality measures', *Journal of Occupational and Organizational Psychology*, **76** (3), 323–46.

Sparks, K., B. Faragher and C.L. Cooper (2001), 'Well-being and occupational health in the 21st century workplace', *Journal of Occupational and Organizational Psychology*, **74** (4), 489–509.

Teece, D.J. (2007), 'Explicating dynamic capabilities: the nature and microfoundations of (sustainable) enterprise performance', *Strategic Management Journal*, **28** (13), 1319–50.

Index

2 × 2 experiments 296–7, 300–301

'ABS Guide' 2, 225
academic age 134–8
academic impact, *see* citation impact; research impact
'Academic Journal Guide' 2
academic journals 223
academic responsibilities 122–3
Academy of Management 75
  Code of Ethics 42
Academy of Management Journal (AMJ) 66, 271–2, 312
Academy of Management of Learning and Education 300
Academy of Management Review 220–21
acceptance 1
  rates 1, 57, 215, 261
    for special issues 250
  reviewers' recommendations 97, 98–9
acquisition-based entry mode 291
Administrative Science Quarterly (ASQ) 96
administrators 244
age, academic 134–8
agreement between reviewers 6, 97–8, 101, 105
Aguinis, H. 185
aiming at the right level 226
Alakangas, S. 136, 137
alternative measures 181
ambicultural approach 90
analysis
  ensuring quality 192–4
  new analyses suggested by reviewers 198–9
  robustness 181–3

analytical modelling 14–16, 17, 18, 24
Anderson, M.S. 34–5, 48–9
Anderson, N. 339–40
annual performance reviews 63
Antoniou, T. 37
argumentation 158
article processing charges (APCs) 254, 255, 256
ArXiv.org 254
Asia Academy of Management 84
Asia Pacific Journal of Management (APJM) 83, 84, 85–6
Asian management journals 83–93
  development 84–5
  next era of Asian management research 88–91
  regional relevance and global impact 85–7
  rigour/relevance tradeoff 87–8
  vs Western management journals 84–8
attention
  to detail 121
  misallocation of 121–2
audience 335–43
  broader 337–9
  specialist 336–7, 339–41
Australian Business Deans Council Journal Quality List 2
authors
  dealing with unreliability of peer review 106–9
  gift authorship 42
  misconduct by 279–80
  order of 77
  perspective on the publishing process 13–24
    insights 20–23

347

as reviewers 30, 75
reviewers nominated by 28–9, 211–12

Barney, J. 229, 241–2
Baron, R.M. 242
Bassiri, M. 157
Basu, S. 36–7
Bedeian, A.G. 37, 41, 42
Bedi, A. 35
Berlin Declaration on Open Access to Knowledge in the Sciences and Humanities 262
Bethesda Statement on Open Access Publishing 262
Bhaumik, S. 283, 287–8, 289
bias
  citation home bias 272–3
  in data collection 179–81
  first-term 209–10
  in peer review 6, 101–2
  publishing home bias 270–72
big five personality traits 336–7
big-name co-authors 276–7
Björk, B.C. 255
blogs 131–2, 258
Bloomberg Business Week 2
books 67
Boyd, B.K. 216–17
Brass, D. 158
British Journal of Industrial Relations (BJIR) 313, 317–18
British Journal of Management (BJM) 298
British Journal of Psychology 338
broad audiences 337–9
Bruno, R. 288–90
Bruton, G.B. 86
Budapest Open Access Initiative 262
business history 304–11
  approaches to historical writing 305–7
Business History 306, 309
Business History Review 306
business model development under uncertainty 13–24
business press outlets 7

business schools 2–3, 25
  journal lists and recognition of scholarship 240–45
  ratings of 109

capacity to excel 215–19
care 129, 130
career breaks 62–3
career stage 134–8
Carney, M. 85
case study articles 265
Castaneda, C. 159
cause and effect 296–7, 298
Ceci, S. 3–6, 101–2
celebrating small successes 157
Centre for Management Buyout Research (CMBOR) 58, 59–61, 68, 70–73, 78–9
Centre National de la Recherche Scientifique (CNRS) journal list 2, 225
Certo, S.T. 114
challenging a rejection decision 205–8
Chandler, A.D. 305
change agency 158
Chartered Association of Business Schools (CABS) 2, 25–6
Chen, M.J. 90
China 283, 287–8, 289, 331–2
'Chrysalis Effect' 42
citation home bias 272–3
citation impact 127–41
  accessing citation data 132–4
  citation levels, career stage and discipline 134–8
  improving 129–32
  open access publishing 254–5, 256
  reasons for valuing it 128–9
  resources 138–9
citations 64–5, 241–2
  to articles in the journal chosen for submission 46
  coercive 47
  open access publishing and 31
  papers desk-rejected by editors 103–4
Clark, T. 2–3, 75

CNRS journal list 2, 225
Coase, R. 64, 68
co-authors 22, 74–5, 118, 129–30, 172–6
  adding at the revise and resubmit stage 123
  big-name and finance articles 276–7
  drama 174–5
  fixing problems 172–3
  keeping promises 175
  misconduct 279
  sandbagging 173–4
  targeting journals 235–7
  team building 75–8
coercive citations 47
cognition in the workplace 334–5, 337–41, 342
coherence test 343
Colella, A. 114
collaboration 156–7, 158, 169–70
  between business history and management authors 309
  improving citation impact 129–30
  team building 75–8
  see also co-authors
colleagues 245
  feedback from 163, 170, 218
  learning from 169–70
  misconduct by 279
collections of conference/seminar/ workshop papers 247–8
commissioning of special issues 247–8
Committee for Publication Ethics (COPE) 47
communication 110
  improving citation impact 129, 130–32
comparative management studies 324, 325–6
competence 129
competition 33–4
complementarity of expertise 76
conceptual papers 223
conclusion section 283, 286
conference networking 131, 228
conference papers 40–41, 247–8

conferences 252
conflict
  between article authors 277–8
    avoiding by posting online 275–6
  in family firms 237
constructs, defining 217
content 142
  audience breadth and 335–42
  comparison of economics and management journals 284–6
content analysis 188
context
  consideration of in IB/IM studies 327–8
  cultural 85, 89, 91
continuous variables 301
contribution 157
  and fit 225–6
  identifying and developing in the discussion section 164–7
  JOD and 264
  parallel publication 43–5
  targeting journals and assessing 234–5
  writing the introduction 146–7
control function estimators 180
control variables 329–30
convenience samples 216
conversation
  broader conversations with more specialist audiences 339–41
  choosing which conversation to join 143–4
  metaphor 334, 335, 341–2
  summarizing research traditions of 144
  with broader audiences and less restrictive content 337–9
  with specialist audiences and restrictive content 336–7
convertible preferred equity 273–4
corporate governance 305–6
correlation matrix 292
crafting 91
crediting ideas/concepts/methodology 43
CrossRef 133, 134
crowdfunding research 272–3

cultural context 85, 89, 91
Cumming, D. 270

Daft, D. 172
data 27
  accessing citation data 132–4
  comparison of economics and management journals 283, 285–6
  ensuring quality 192–4
  IB/IM studies 324, 330–31
  out-of-date datasets 307
  robust datasets 179–81
data analysis, *see* analysis
data collection
  IB/IM studies 330–31
  robustness 179–81
data fabrication 35–6
data falsification 35–7
data trimming 37
deadlines 169
deans 63, 279
defence contract bid 6–7
defensiveness 198
delaying other authors' articles 279–80
deliberate practice 215–19
dependent variables 328
desk rejection 103, 107
  avoiding 27–8
  choice of journal and 222–3
  rates 3, 324
Dess, G. 234
detail, attention to 121
dialectic trajectories 106
different way of seeing 157–8
digital media 109–10, 252–60
  building a base 252–3
  leveraging institutions 257
  online queue 45–6
  open access publishing, *see* open access publishing
  social media 67, 131–2, 257–9
Dimensions 133, 134
Directory of Open Access Journals 263

disagreement between reviewers 15–20, 97–8, 100–101, 105
discipline, citation levels and 134–8
discipline-based journals 312, 315–17, 319
discourse analysis 314–15
discrepancies between reviewers and editors 206
discussion section 121–2, 342
  comparison of economics and management journals 283, 286
  identifying and developing the contribution 164–7
discussions on social media 258, 259
drama 174–5
Drucker, P. 242
dynamic capabilities 305, 341, 342

early-stage projects 116–18, 119, 125
econometric methodology 287–90, 293
economics, and business history 308–9
economics journals 282–95
  content of papers 284–6
  examples of papers 287–90
  structure of papers 282–3
editorials 26, 45
editors 197
  acting as reviewers 197–8
  approaches to managing reviewers 4–5
  authors as 75
  case study of the publishing process 13–24
    insights 20–23
  challenging rejection decisions of 205–8
  consulting before submission 224
  dealing with novice expert editors 209–13
  desk rejection, *see* desk rejection
  discrepancies between reviewers and 206
  misconduct by 278–9
  peer review 95–6

dealing with unreliability of 106–9
improving 110
statistical evidence of unreliability of evaluations 99, 102–4, 106
personal connections 104, 228
personal contacts as reviewers 28–9
requirements of a submission 28
special issues 246, 248–9
unscrupulous 45–7
Einstein, A. 241
email signature 253
emailing 132
emerging economies 73, 74
MNE entry modes 283, 290–92
emotional response to review 105, 107, 198
'emperor editors' 5
empirical motivations 166
empirical research
business history 307–8
papers and fit 223
unresolved empirical issues 145, 148–9
employee responses to HPWS 316–17
employee skills 318
endogeneity 179–81
engineering 136–8
Enterprise and Society 306
entrepreneurship 86
and risk propensity 192–4
strategic entrepreneurial approach 68–73
Entrepreneurship Theory and Practice 236
entry barriers 288–90
entry mode choice 283, 290–92
ERIH Plus 2
errors
factual 206
measurement error 217
mistakes in responding to reviewers 196–200
type I and type II 120, 217
Estrin, S. 283, 287–8, 289
ethics 33–56

inappropriate and questionable research conduct 35, 38–45, 48, 50
research misconduct 33, 35–8, 47–8, 51
unscrupulous editors, JIF-boosting and coercive citations 45–7
European Group for Organizational Studies (EGOS) 256
European Parliament 7
European Reference Index for Humanities (ERIH) 2
European University Association (EUA) 263
executive summary 202
experts' predictions 102
explanation of revisions 108, 202–3
explanatory variables 329

fabrication 35–6
Facebook 257
factual errors 206
falsification 35–7
familiness 237
family business research 233–9
Family Business Review 236
Fan, S. 131–2
favouritism by editors 104
favours 86
feedback 225
from colleagues 163, 170, 218
field-corrected citation data 135
Filatotchev, I. 305–6
'Finance Job Market Rumours' 276
finance journals 268–81
being a 'good citizen' 277–8
big-name co-authors 276–7
citation home bias 272–3
differences between finance and entrepreneurship/management journals 269
misconduct 278–80
papers inconsistent with prior work 273–5
posting online 275–6
publishing home bias 270–72
Financial Times 7

journal list 2, 225, 298
first paragraph 143–4
  literature reviews in 148
first sentences
  the hook 342
  of paragraphs 120–21, 143–4, 145, 146
first-term bias 209–10
fit of paper to journal 26, 221, 222, 223–6, 230
five-factor model questionnaire (FFMQ) 336–7, 342
flexibility 14, 15–16, 22, 24
focus 122–3, 157
focused commitment 13, 14, 24
footnotes 308
formats 264–5
formatting responses to reviewers 201–2
framework, theoretical 216, 284, 327–8
Franklin, B. 185
fraud 271–2
Freeman, R. 33
Frey, B. 40
friendly review 120, 170
future, focus on the 264

gaps in the literature 145
gender bias 174
general management journals
  HRM research in 312, 314–15, 319
  see also under individual names
generalizability 186, 187, 298–9, 300
generalizations, testing using historical data 305–6
getting papers out 168–71
gift authorship 42
Gill, C. 336–7, 342
Gilson, R. 274
Ginsberg, R.B. 158
global impact 85–7
Global Strategy Journal (*GSJ*) 322, 323, 324, 325
gold open access 31, 254, 256
Gomez-Mejia, L. 157, 166
Gonzalez-Benito, J. 186

'good citizen' approach 277–8
Google Scholar 133, 136–8
Google Scholar Citation (GSC) profile 131
Google Scholar Profiles 133, 134
Gottfredson, S.D. 97, 100
Gottinger, H.W. 37
Gray, B. 156–7
green open access 254, 256
greenfield entry mode 291
Gretzky, W. 168
Guest, D. 315
guest editing special issues 66

h-index 33, 49, 128, 134, 136–8
Hardy, C. 314–15
HARKing 41–2
Harley, B. 314–15, 316–17, 317–18
harsh judgements 4
Harvard Business Review 67, 220
Harzing, A.W. 135–8
Healey, M.P. 338, 340–41, 342
Health Management, Policy and Innovation (*HMPI*) 253, 254
Heckman selection correction 179
heterogeneous portfolio 64–5
hIa-index 135–8
high performance work systems (HPWS) 316–17, 317–18
historical anomalies 305
historical papers 304–11
Hodge, B. 156
Hodgkinson, G.P. 336–7, 338, 340–41, 342
Hofstede, G. 85
holdout samples 189
Hollenbeck, J. 122
home bias
  citation home bias in different disciplines 272–3
  publishing home bias in different disciplines 270–72
Honig, B. 35
hook, the 342, 343
'hot' cognition 340–41, 342
Huff, A.S. 334, 335
Human Relations 300

human resource management (HRM)
    research 312–20
  discipline-based journals 312,
      315–17, 319
  general management journals 312,
      314–15, 319
  subject-based journals 312–13,
      317–18, 319
humanities 136–8, 255
hypotheses 101
  comparison of economics and
      management journals 283, 285,
      293–4
  development in management
      journals 291–2
  retrofitting to empirical results
      (HARKing) 41–2
  unsupported tests of 187

ideas
  crediting other people's 43
  in the research pipeline 116–18
identity 301
illegitimate open access journals 263
impact 220–21
  global 85–7
  research impact, *see* citation
      impact; research impact
inappropriate research conduct 35,
    38–45, 48
inconsistency with prior work 273–5
individual differences, assessing
    work-related 334, 336–7, 342
industrial relations policy 313
industrial, work and organizational
    (IWO) psychology 339–40
Institute for Scientific Information
    (ISI) 2, 132, 134, 136–8, 225
instrumental variable estimation
    179–80
instruments for assessment of
    personality and individual
    differences 334, 336–7, 342
integrity 33–56, 199
  inappropriate and questionable
      research conduct 35, 38–45,
      48, 50

research misconduct 33, 35–8,
    47–8, 51
unscrupulous editors, JIF-boosting
    and coercive citations 45–7
interesting phenomena 162
internal marketing 301
internal validity 298
international business and
    management (IB/IM) journals
    321–33
  comparative management 324,
      325–6
  conceptual sections 326–8
  data 324, 330–31
  defining characteristic of
      internationalism 321–4
  single-country studies not
      considered international 324,
      325
  variables 328–30
*International Journal of Management
    Reviews* 222
inter-reviewer reliability 94–113
  dealing with 106–9
  implications 104–6
  statistical evidence 97–104
introduction 142–52, 342
  common mistakes in writing it
      148–51
  comparison of economics and
      management journals 283, 284
  length 147, 150–51
  simple framework to position
      papers for publication 143–8
    first paragraph 143–4
    first sentences of paragraphs
        143–4, 145, 146
    second paragraph 145
    third paragraph 146–7
intuition 338
ISI (Web of Science) 2, 132, 134,
    136–8, 225

Johan, S.A. 270
joint ventures 291
Journal of Business Research 236
Journal of Business Venturing 236

Journal of Family Business Strategy 236
Journal of Finance 273
journal impact factor (JIF) 45–7
Journal of International Business Studies (*JIBS*) 322, 324
journal lists (journal rankings) 1–3, 225, 261, 298
  journal selection and 25–8
  and recognition of scholarship 240–45
Journal of Management 236, 241–2, 312
Journal of Management Inquiry 155
Journal of Management Studies (*JMS*) 2–3, 66, 75, 236, 305, 312, 314–15
  Point-CounterPoint Section (PCP) 65–6
Journal of Occupational and Organizational Psychology 302, 339–40
Journal of Organization Design (*JOD*) 261–2, 264–5
Journal of Personality and Social Psychology 242
journal rankings, *see* journal lists
journal selection 25–8, 109, 264
  positioning papers for different types of journals 220–32
Journal of Small Business Management 236
Journal of World Business (*JWB*) 322, 323
'judge editors' 5
junior faculty 237–8
  big-name co-authors 276–7
  conflict with senior faculty 275–6

Kenny, D.A. 242
keynote articles 65
King, S. 143–4
knowledge 99
knowledge disseminators 158
knowledge generators 158

Laband, D.N. 103, 104

labour process theory (LPT) 316
Larcker, D. 180
late-stage projects 116, 118–20, 125
leadership 301
  prototypicality and fairness 299
learned societies 75
Legge, K. 314–15
Leung, K. 88
level of work 25–6
Lewin, K. 216
life sciences 134–5, 136–8
lifted text
  crediting 42–3
  plagiarism 35, 37–8
limitations of a paper, discussion of 292–3
LinkedIn 257
literature reviews 27
  articles based on 66
  comparison of economics and management journals 283, 284
  IB/IM articles 326
  mistakenly put in first paragraph 148
lobbying for journal quality 242–3
Locke, E. 157
Lubatkin, M. 171, 233

Mahoney, M.J. 102
management buyout research 58, 59–61, 68, 70–73, 74
managerial roles 62
manipulation of independent variables 296–7, 301
Manz, C. 157
Mao Zedong 90
market-supporting institutions
  development in China and Russia 283, 287–8
  MNE choice of entry mode 283, 290–92
Martin, B.R. 38, 39
maternity leave 62
maturity 165
McNamarian approach 117–18
Mead, M. 158
measurement error 217

media outlets 257
media relations office 257
Medoff, M.H. 104
meta-analyses 192–4
methodology 102
  econometric 287–90, 293
  explication of 217–18
  and fit 223
  rigour 216
methods section 283, 285–6
Meyer, A. 157
Meyer, K. 283, 290–92
Microsoft Academic 133, 134
Miller, D. 90
Miner, J.B. 192, 193–4
misallocation of attention 121–2
misconduct 278–80
  research misconduct 33, 35–8, 47–8, 51
mission, aligning with 162, 211
mistakes, in responding to reviewers 196–200
moderating variables 329
monographs 67
motivation 164, 166
multicollinearity 292
multi-country data 324, 331
multinational enterprises (MNEs)' entry mode choice 283, 290–92
multiple top-tier publications 114–15
multi-stage estimators 180
Mumford, M.D. 34

National Institutes of Health 253
national research assessment exercises 62, 63–4
  UK REF 7, 25, 68
National Science Foundation 218, 253
natural entry rates 290
natural sciences 134–5, 136–8
nature of the paper 221, 223–4
Necker, S. 34
negative information 206
negative thoughts 171
new firm entry 288–90
new/unrelated research areas 65
Newton, I. 155

nominated reviewers 28–9, 211–12
'Non-Stop' (Lin-Manuel Miranda) 122–3
norms
  national professional 243, 245
  sampling 185, 186
novice expert editors 209–13
  tips for getting published by 210–12

objective 164–5
O'Boyle, E.H. 41–2
omitted variable bias 179
online queue 45–6
online repositories 130–31, 254, 255
open access publishing 31, 109–10, 253–6, 261–6
  benefits 254–5, 262–3
  reasons to publish in open access journals 264–5
  types of 254
Organization Design Community 261
Organization Science 236
organization theory 308
Organization Theory 253, 254, 256
organizational identification (OI) 301
organizational learning theory 19–20, 24
out-of-date datasets 307
out-of-date journal lists 243

p-hacking 34, 36, 49
page quota 31, 109, 250
paradigms 105–6
paragraphs
  first 143–4, 148
  first sentences of 120–21, 143–4, 145, 146
  second 145, 148–9
  structuring 121
  third 146–7, 149
parallel publication 43–5
Park, H.-U. 36–7
path with a heart, finding a 159
patience 161–3
peer review 3–6, 205

'no reviewer is ever wrong' golden rule 94–6
recommendations for improving 109–10
reliability of evaluations 94–113
   dealing with 106–9
   implications of 104–6
   statistical evidence 97–104
   see also review process; reviewers
perfectionism 159
perseverance 157
persistence 157, 229
personal connections 104, 228
personal websites 130
personality, assessment of 334, 336–7, 342
Personnel Psychology 337
Peters, D. 3–6, 101–2
PhD research 58, 69
PhD theses 43–4, 51
phenomenological studies 326–7
Picasso, P. 155
Piette, M.J. 104
plagiarism 35, 37–8
   self-plagiarism 38–41
Plan S 263–4
point of view articles 264
policy-making 67–8
polishing a paper 210–11
politics 196
position/think pieces 65–8
positioning papers
   for different types of journals 220–32
   family business research and targeting journals 233–9
   for publication 142–52
      common mistakes in writing an introduction 148–51
      simple framework 143–7
post-doctorate publication career 58
post-tenure publication career 62
'postie editors' 4–5
posting online 257
   finance research 275–6
poverty 86
practicalities 221, 226, 230
practice, interaction with 67–8

practitioner journals 67, 223
practitioner–researcher divide 339–40
prejudice 296
pre-prints 40
pre-publication posting 253
presentation 142
prior publication (in self-plagiarism) 39–41
prior work
   disconnecting radical new theories from 149–50
   inconsistency with 273–5
private equity research 7, 59–61, 68, 71, 72, 78–9
problem identification and fixing 172–3
procrastination 159
professional development 78
prolific, being 157
promises, keeping 175
promotion after tenure 62
promotional services 257
propensity-score matching 180–81
properties of scholarly papers 100–101
psychological foundations of strategic management 340–41, 342
psychology 334–46
   audience breadth, content and conversation 335–43
   social psychology 296–303
public commitment to submission 169
publications career, sustaining a, *see* sustaining a publications career
'publish or perish' rule 34, 156, 220
publisher services 257
publishing home bias 270–72
publishing process case study 13–24
   abstract of initial submission 24
   abstract of published paper 24
   first round of reviews 15–16
   fourth and fifth rounds of reviews 20
   initial submission 14–15
   insights from the review process 20–23
   second round of reviews 16–18
   third round of reviews 18–20

Puffer, S.M. 86
purist business history tradition 306–7
purpose 164–5

quality
  and fit 221, 224–6
  of writing 27
quality shots on goal 119–20
questionable research conduct 35, 38–45, 48, 50

radical new theories 149–50
Raju, N.S. 192, 193–4
random samples 216
Reagan, R. 240
real-world impact 6–8, 127
redundant publication 38–41
refusing to review 30
regional relevance 85–7, 88
Registry of Open Access Repositories (ROAR) 254
rejection 1, 196, 229, 238
  accepting 159
  circumstances justifying challenging 205–8
  desk rejection, *see* desk rejection
  rates 3
  resubmission to same journal 108
  reviewers' recommendations 97, 98–9, 101–2
  social psychology article 301–2
  from special issues 246
  submission to another journal without alteration 46
relevance
  regional 85–7, 88
  and rigour 6–8, 87–8
reports 67–8
repositories, online 130–31, 254, 255
reputation 47, 221, 224–6
research
  approach to get published in top journals 215–19
  developing quality research 217–18
  including fundamentals in papers 27
  patience and 161–3
  purpose of 100

responsible 218
research community 253
research conduct 33–45, 47–9, 216–18
  inappropriate and questionable 35, 38–45, 48, 50
  research misconduct 33, 35–8, 47–8, 51
  responsibility of researchers 48–9
Research Excellence Framework (REF) 7, 25, 68
research gap 300–302
research grants 78–9
research impact 68, 127–41
  accessing citation data 132–4
  citation levels, career stage and discipline 134–8
  h-index 33, 49, 128, 134, 136–8
  improving citation impact 129–32
  real-world 6–8, 127
  reasons for valuing 128–9
  resources 138–9
  on society 218
research integrity 33–5, 199; *see also* research conduct
research pipeline 114–26
  early-stage projects 116–18, 119, 125
  late-stage projects 116, 118–20, 125
  moving projects along the stages 124–5
  revise and resubmit 116, 122–3, 125
  second revise and resubmit 116, 123–4, 125
  under review 116, 120–22, 125
  visualizing 115–16
research primer articles 264–5
research programs 69–73
research question 146, 151, 162, 216
research teams 76–7
resource acquisition 14, 15–16, 22, 24
resource-based view 229, 241, 306
resource dependency theory 306
resource optimization 227
responding to reviewers 30, 123–4
  mistakes authors make 196–200
  reviewer's perspective 201–4
response bias 185, 186, 187

response rate 185, 186, 225
responsible research 218
resubmission 30, 101–2, 108–9
  to normal issue of same journal after rejection by a special issue 250–51
  revise and resubmit, *see* revise and resubmit
  without revision or reorientation 46
results/findings
  comparison of economics and management journals 283, 286
  robustness 178–83
retractions 35
retrofitting hypotheses to empirical results (HARKing) 41–2
review process
  case study 13–24
    first round 15–16
    fourth and fifth rounds 20
    insights of author and editor 20–23
    second round 16–18
    third round 18–20
  flaws in 4–6
  special issues 248–50
  see also peer review; reviewers
reviewers 3–6, 28–31, 169
  agreement between 6, 97–8, 101, 105
  assuming the mindset of 162–3
  authors as 30, 75
  business history papers 308
  dealing with 28–30
  disagreement between 15–20, 97–8, 100–101, 105
  discrepancies between editors and 206
  'good citizen' approach 277
  learning from experience of others 228
  misconduct 278–9
  'no reviewer is ever wrong' golden rule 94–6
  novice editors' reliance on 210
  perspective of a reviewer on author's response to review 201–4
  responding to, *see* responding to reviewers
  role in improving papers 22
  selection of 28–9
  similarity to co-authors 169
  suggested 28–9, 211–12
  targeting journals 235–7
  unreliability of evaluations 94–113
    dealing with 106–9
    statistical evidence 97–106
  see also peer review; review process
revise and resubmit (R&R) 206–7, 227
  grades of 29
  managing a research pipeline
    first round 116, 122–3, 125
    second round 116, 123–4, 125
  under novice expert editors 212
revisions 107–8, 165, 196–8
  case study 16–20
  explaining 108, 202–3
  getting advice on 170–71
  integrity and 199
  reviewers' recommendations 97, 98–9
rhetoric 158
rigour 6–8
  tradeoff with relevance in Asian management journals 87–8
risk propensity 192–4
robustness 178–83, 269
  analyses 181–3
  dataset 179–81
  economics and management journals compared 286, 287, 288, 293, 294
Rogelberg, S.G. 187
Roosevelt, E. 157
rules for getting published 155–60
Russia 283, 287–8, 290
Rusticus, T. 180

salami publishing 38–9
sample 184–91, 216, 217–18
  checklist for sample design preparation 185

preventative tactics 184, 185–7
reactive tactics 184, 187–9
second sample 189
size 186
student samples, *see* student samples
sample selection bias 179, 180–81
sampling norms 185, 186
sandbagging 173–4
Schizer, D. 274
Schulze, W.S. 233, 235
sciences (natural sciences) 134–5, 136–8
scientific progress 90
Scopus 133, 134, 136–8
second paragraph 145
summaries of theoretical and empirical arguments 148–9
second revise and resubmit 116, 123–4, 125
second sample 189
selection bias 179, 180–81
self-belief 229
self-management 107
self-plagiarism 38–41
seminars 252
senior faculty 237–8
conflict with junior faculty 275–6
sensitivity analysis 180
service sector 317–18
Shookarian approach 117
shotgun approach 234
Silera, K. 103–4
Sims, H. 157
'Simultaneous experimentation as a learning strategy; business model development under uncertainty' (Andries et al.) 13–24
single-country studies 324, 325
skills, employee 318
Small Business Economics 236
social capital 73–5
social construction 105
social media 67, 131–2, 257–9
social psychology 296–303
design issues and the research gap 300–302
experiments 296–7

issues with experimental work and student samples 298–300
Social Science Research Network (SSRN) 275
social sciences 136–8, 255
Solomon, D. 255
Sotudeh, H. 255
special issues 228, 246–51, 339–41
APJM 85–6
commissioning of 247–8
guest editing 66
resubmission to normal issue of same journal 250–51
review process 248–50
specialist audiences 336–7, 339–41
specialization 307–8
SSRN 275
Stanton, J.M. 187
Stapel, D. 36
Starbuck, W.H. 4, 6, 97, 99
statistical models 149
statistical power 185, 187, 216–17
statistical significance inflation 36–7
statistical tests 28
strategic entrepreneurial approach 68–73
Strategic Entrepreneurship Journal (SEJ) 13–24
strategic management 334–46
Strategic Management Journal 340
stray citations 133, 140
structure
discussion section 166
economics and management journals compared 282–3
student samples 296–7
issues with 298–300
study design 300–302
style
of journal 27, 226
social media 258–9
subject-based journals 312–13, 317–18, 319
submission
case study 14–15
abstract of initial submission 24
getting papers out 168–71
rates 3, 57

research pipeline management and readiness for 120–22
suggested reviewers 28–9, 211–12
summarizing reviewer comments 198
Susman, G. 156
sustaining a publications career 57–82
  pressure points 58–63
  reasons for 63–4
  routes for 68–79
  strategies for 64–8

targeting 157, 167, 233–9, 264, 301–2
  assessing contribution 234–5
  co-authors and reviewers 235–7
  positioning papers and 233–9
    for different types of journals 220–32
  publishing for tenure 234
team building 75–8
teamworking 300
Teece, D.J. 341, 342
tenure 62
  publishing for 234
Tenzer, H. 132
Teresa, Mother 156
testable propositions 17–18, 18–19, 20
theoretical motivations 166
theorizing 91
theory
  developing quality research 217
  disconnecting radical new theories from prior work 149–50
  emphasis in business history 308–9
  new advance for 167
  sections
    comparison of economics and management journals 283, 284–5
    differences between finance and entrepreneurship/ management journals 269
  testing or augmenting management theory using business history 305
  testing generalizations using historical data 305–6
  testing in IB/IM articles 326–7
  theoretical contributions in Asian management journals 87–8, 91
  theoretical framework 216, 284, 327–8
  universal 89
  unresolved theoretical issues 145, 148–9
theory development 216
  Asian management journals and 87–8
  comparison of economic and management journals 290–92, 293–4
  IB/IM studies 332
  using historical anomalies 305
think/position pieces 65–8
third paragraph 146–7
  summaries of theoretical and empirical arguments 149
Thomas, J. 173
Toms, S. 305–6
topic
  and fit 221, 224
  new advance for 167
translational articles 264
triangulation to previous studies 188
Tsui, A.S. 88–9, 90
Twitter 131, 257, 258
two publications per year rule 156
type I and type II errors 120, 217

Ullrich, J. 299
uncertainty, business model development under 13–24
under review stage 116, 120–22, 125
universal theory 89
unrelated research areas 65
unresolved theoretical/empirical issues 145, 148–9
unscrupulous editors 45–7
unsupported hypothesis tests 187
unsupported rejection decisions 206, 207

Van Dick, R. 300
Vandenberg, R.J. 185
variables

continuous 301
in IB/IM studies 328–30
instrumental variable estimation 179–80
manipulation of in social psychology experiments 296–7, 301
omitted variable bias 179
varieties of capitalism (VoC) 85–6
venture capital (VC) contracting 273–5
video abstracts 258
Vienna List 225

Wall Street Journal 7
Wansink, B. 36
Watson, E.M. 253–4, 256
Web of Science (ISI) 2, 132, 134, 136–8, 225
websites, personal 130
Weick, K. 158
Westernization 88

white papers 67–8
Wieseke, J. 301
Wikipedia 253
Williamson, O.E. 305
Winsorization 37
Work, Employment and Society (*WES*) 312, 315–17
working papers 40–41
workplace divas 174–5
work-related individual differences, assessing 334, 336–7, 342
Wright, M. 2–3, 306
writing
  developing quality research 217–18
  quality 27
  routinized approach 170
  skills and Asian management journals 91
  skills development 158–9, 163

Zhang, L. 253–4, 256
zombie papers 27